What We Did Instead Of Holidays
*A History Of Fairport Convention
And Its Extended Folk-Rock Family*

Clinton Heylin

route

Published by Route
PO Box 167, Pontefract, WF8 4WW
info@route-online.com
www.route-online.com

ISBN : 978-1901927-78-8

First published in hardback in 2018
This paperback edition 2019

Clinton Heylin asserts his moral
right to be identified as the author of this book

© Clinton Heylin

The photos in the three photo sections were kindly provided by the following:
Richard Lewis (p1), Phil Smee (p2), Scott Curran (p3, 5),
Philippa Clare (p6, 8,10-12,14, 16), Ashley Hutchings (p9, 15).
Every attempt has been made to contact copyright holders, where possible.

Cover design:
Baker

Printed in EU by Pulsio SARL

To Bill Allison, Richard Lewis and Steve Bragger,
for their prediluvian prescience.

PRELUDE:

A Coat Of Many Colours   7

PART I: ONE LONG HOLIDAY [1965–70]

1. Emil Does The Ethnic Shuffle   13
2. East Meets West   29
3. She Moved Through The Fairgrounds   51
4. M1 Breakdown   71
5. Open The Door, Chamberlayne   89
6. Now We Are Five   111

PART II: FLEE AS A BIRD [1970–74]

7. The Folk-Rock Family Flies The Coop   137
8. Solo Singer, Needs Band   167
9. Albion Sunrise   181
10. The Splinter Group In Action   197
11. Time Out   223
12. Rise Up With The Moon   237

PART III: NIGHT COMES IN [1974–82]

13. Why Don't You Love Me Like You Used To Do?   261
14. Adrift In Rocky Seas   281
15. Without Prospects   301
16. A New Day?   321
17. Life After Death   343
18. Shoot Out The Bright Lights   357

CODA:

One Last Bow   376

Notes   379

Prelude:
A Coat Of Many Colours

As every self-respecting folk-rock fan knows, each and every Fairport Convention incarnation has burned bright but ne'er long. Between June 1968 and June 1974, England's premier folk-rock band would release no less than ten albums, while passing through just as many line-up changes. Only one line-up – 1971's – would manage two consecutive albums, *Angel Delight* and *Babbacombe Lee*, before it was also rent apart by inevitable divisions.

Their most acclaimed configuration – the line-up responsible for the groundbreaking *Liege & Lief* (1969) – lasted barely four months, playing only a handful of gigs before losing singer Sandy Denny and founding father-figure, bassist Ashley 'Tyger' Hutchings, to aftershocks from a twice-fatal motorway crash. No wonder the band at times preferred to call itself Fotheringport Confusion (a reference to the number of members from Sandy's post-Fairport combo who later joined her parent band).

But it would be the alumni from the era of the four consecutive classic Fairport albums, *What We Did On Our Holidays, Unhalfbricking, Liege & Lief* and *Full House* – recorded between June 1968 and April 1970 – who would challenge even their parent band's prodigious output.

Ian Matthews, who would leave Fairport halfway through *Unhalfbricking*, went on to record an astonishing ten albums between 1969 and 1973, three of them with the chart-topping Matthews Southern Comfort. Ashley Hutchings, who quit less than a year later, would be responsible for eight projects between 1970 and 1973, three with Steeleye Span, his first reconfiguration of the English folk-rock sound and ultimately its most successful exponent.

As for Richard Thompson, after his own January 1971 departure he would record three era-defining albums over three-and-a-half years: *Henry The Human Fly, I Want To See The Bright Lights Tonight* and *Hokey Pokey* – the latter two with new singing partner, Linda.

Such an outpouring of product was possible because of a unique confluence of Circumstance: a commercial climate which abounded in the British MusicBiz for the first and last time, collectively brought about by a handful of young ambitious producer-managers, astute independent label-owners who catered entirely to the new 'prog' audience (and ceding artistic control to the bands themselves), complementing a family of musicians constantly pushing each other to define their place in the ever-changing panoply of popular song.

'Twas a time when Fairport were spoken of in the same breath as Led Zeppelin, with whom they famously jammed at LA's Troubadour in September 1970, and Pink Floyd, with whom they shared a legendary show at the UFO the night Syd lost his mind and Richard Thompson blew a fair few minds – George Harrison's included – with a thirty-minute reinterpretation of Paul Butterfield's 'East/West'. 'Twas also a time when Hutchings's Steeleye Span not only toured with the *Aqualung*-era Jethro Tull, but enjoyed a Top Ten album in the wake of that nationwide jaunt.

Sympathetic to this synergy of style and English content, the producers and label-heads behind the proscenium gave the various Fairporters enough rope to play the jolly hangman. Which is why manager-producers Joe Boyd and Sandy Roberton and Island boss Chris Blackwell loom almost as large in this history of English folk-rock as many a fairweather Fairporter. This trio oversaw and/or rubber-stamped most of the albums that spouted from the folk-rock faucet during this six-year window of opportunity.

And what artifacts poured forth. If Fairport would never again scale the heights achieved between June 1968 and December 1970 – a period which didn't just produce four classic LPs, but also a series of endlessly inventive BBC sessions and landmark gigs no one who witnessed them ever forgot – the members they shed more than took up the slack.

For Ashley Hutchings, the band's founder and erstwhile leader, there would be ever-varying calibrations of English folk-rock, each more challenging than the last. Steeleye's debut, *Hark! The Village Wait*, the Albion Country Band's *No Roses* and the dance-rock experiment *Morris On*, were just three of the works he conceptualised in the two years after *Liege & Lief*'s December 1969 release.

Not content with that blistering burst, over the next eighteen months he threatened to make the Albion Country Band a more authentic version of Fairport folk-rock than Fairport itself, before the psychological scars of a 1969 road crash caught up, driving him to the wiles of Sussex where the healing could begin.

When it came to the star-crossed Sandy Denny, there would be the brave new world of Fotheringay, whose eponymous debut caused almost as many ripples in 1970's rocky estuary as her Fairport parting glass, *Liege & Lief*. That band, though, foundered on the rocks of band-finances and irresolvable arguments about who should be the sea captain. Three promising solo albums followed before Fairport again clutched her to their bosoms for one more sea voyage in 1974-75.

Richard Thompson, the guitar wizard who co-founded Fairport with Ashley Hutchings and Simon Nicol back in July 1966, when barely out of school, came to the realisation no single band could house him or hold him down late. The second of that triumvirate to fly the coop, Thompson would carve his name into the very fabric of folk-rock with his first solo effort, *Henry The Human Fly (1972)*, perhaps English folk-rock's finest moment.

When that album crashed and burned, critically and commercially, he simply rebooted the brand and bounced back with *I Want To See The Bright Lights Tonight*, the first of six albums with the angel-voiced Linda Thompson (aka Peters). This duo would carry the folk-rock brand into the eighties, making music as vital and enduring as any British singer-songwriters in those halcyon days.

But having failed to dent the charts with any of the cult classics which made them critical darlings, the couple parted not as friends. Their bitter musical divorce came in May 1982, documented nightly on a fateful American tour promoting their swansong, *Shoot Out The Lights*, shows which have become steeped in rocklore for reasons only partially rooted in the musical cliff edge they skirted.

Ian Matthews' once promising post-Fairport career hit the buffers Stateside after he took Jac Holzman's Elektra shilling at the end of 1972. Thankfully, the albums he made in 1971-72 – *If You Saw Thro' My Eyes, Tigers Will Survive, Journeys From Gospel Oak* and the two Plainsong albums – continue to reward repeated listens.

Unfortunately, the deal he made with the devilish Holzman required him to disband Plainsong, rather than release their second attempt at a post-Fairport sound worthy of the original. Like Ashley, the singer would never again find the drive and determination to make five quality albums in two years. Like his fellow Fairporters, Matthews would plough on regardless, trading on the faint name-recognition his early output still accords him.

When it came to Fairport itself – left rudderless by the departures of Denny and Hutchings in November 1969 and cut creatively adrift when Thompson quit in January 1971 – Island Records continued picking up the tab as it toyed with projects suggested in turn by Simon Nicol (*Angel Delight*), and furious folk fiddler, Dave Swarbrick (the folk-rock opera *Babbacombe Lee* and *Rosie*).

After finally they chanced on a quasi-folk, quasi-soft-rock niche – part-Fotheringay, part-Fairport – in time to produce the eclectic *Nine* (1973) and a patchy reunion album with Sandy Denny, *Rising For The Moon* (1975), put the original English folk-rock vehicle in reverse for good.

Though the band, in name only, would bounce from pillar to post for another four years, lasting till August 1979, the brand name had been irredeemably tainted by too many mediocre albums since their late sixties heyday.

By then, the cold wind of social and political change had blown in a new business-first spirit, at odds with the creative free-for-all that had afforded so many talented musicians the opportunity to put the Great back in British pop music; for a while, a fair few innovators had snuck under the radar and into the shops and hearts of its many music fans. The land where Henry the Human Fly, Poor Will and the Jolly Hangman, the Poor Ditching Boy, Matty Groves and the Blackleg Miner could roam free was no more.

Thankfully, a whole lot of folk-rock is their enduring legacy. The substantial soundtrack to their own wacky story is an impressive body of music this single band of brothers and sisters produced over a decade and a half; each and every note inspired by that folk-rock codex first formulated in a house in Muswell Hill that the Nicol family rented out to pay the bills. Which is where our story begins, on a day in 1965, when a certain potential tenant, a working stiff his friends called 'Tyger', descends on a house called Fairport, hoping to rent a room above a converted doctor's surgery...

Rolling Stone

'All the N
News

OCTOBER 1

© 1969 by Trans Oceanic Comic Comp

PART I
ONE LONG HOLIDAY
1965–1970

ERIC HAYES

AIRPORT CONVENTION: BEGINNING TO CONTINU

BY RICK SANDERS

According to the readers of Melody Maker, the airport Convention are the eighth best group in Britain. A rowing number would rate them considerably higher than at, but it's still gratifying to see such a spectacular group in so many votes when Tom Jones is still number one alo singer, hips and all. They've had a lot of enforced anges thrust upon them, culminating in the road cident a couple of months ago in which Martin Lamble, e drummer, and Genie the Tailor (of Jack Bruce fame) ere killed. They've brought in two new members: Dave warbrick, reputed to be the best violinist on the folk ene, has joined, having played on several tracks on the oup's last album, *Unhalfbricking*, and Dave Mattacks is e new drummer. The line-up now reads: Sandy Denny, cals, guitar, violin; Tyger Hutchings on bass; and chief sciplinarian, Simon Nicol, vocals, guitar, violin; Richard

recently-departed member of the group, Ian Matthews, who has just finished making his own album with occasional collaboration from the group.

For a group such as the Fairport to come so high in the list, other factors than simply their musical quality, which has been taken as read by a minority for ages, would seem to have played a part. Firstly, there was the accident, which with tragic irony splashed their name all over the papers. Secondly, there was the success of *Si Tu Dois Partir*, their recent Bob Dylan-in-French single. There's irony in that too. Richard Thompson explains how the quirky semi-knockout song appeared: "It was a big joke. We were sitting around backstage at Middle Earth and someone was playing the song. We thought yes, that's got a nice rhythm, won't it be interesting to tackle it in the vein of Louisiana cajun music — it's right for the accordion, fiddle and triangle scene. This was all conjecture, no

recorded it and somehow it got on to the album, but we didn't really want it on. We certainly didn't have it released as a single and we actually tried to have it stopped. It helped us in one way, that we can sell more albums to people, but on the other hand it's very unrepresentative of us. I dunno, people probably think we're a frog jug band. On a French kick, man."

In fact, the group have been through a fairly serious bout of cajun music. Typically, they searched out a form that hadn't been done to death by pop bands looking for a new wellspring of rootsy music. Thompson's record collection, an incredibly varied one, includes much Louisiana stuff, from which he played me a Doug Kershaw thing — "The next superstar, man", he declared — and one concludes that the jokey self-depreciation is not without its irony. Also in the collection are some South African

1. Emil Does The Ethnic Shuffle

The sixties was the British beginning of the real expression of teenage culture. The fifties was very drab, post-war drab, rationing and all that kind of stuff. It didn't really happen in the fifties, the way it did in the States ... [but] in the sixties suddenly you had Carnaby Street and swinging London and The Who and The Kinks and The Beatles. There was this great explosion of youth culture. If you look at suburban London, you had all these bands from art schools, like The Rolling Stones ... and The Yardbirds.

—RICHARD THOMPSON TO PAM WINTERS

Born into a world of unparallelled musical opportunity – at just the right juncture – were three North London boys, baby boomers to a man: Ashley Hutchings, born January 26th, 1945; Richard Thompson (April 3rd, 1949) and Simon Nicol (October 13th, 1950). Between them, they would form the backbone of England's pre-eminent folk-rock band, Fairport Convention, from 1966 through 1971 – the very best of times to be in a folk-rock band – before continuing to lead the charge for the remainder of the seventies, even as the musical tide turned.

Said trio would share a collective vision from their very first 'band meeting', on July 6th, 1966, at their local bar, JB's, when the elder Ashley 'suggested forming a "folk-rock" group' with the fresh-faced Nicol and Thompson – an event his diary deemed auspicious enough to record in the week 'Sunny Afternoon' replaced 'Paperback Writer' at the top of the UK charts.

Even after they went their separate ways – and save for the occasional annual Cropredy reunion and a 2009 one-off at the Barbican, the last time all three played together was in the prototype Albion Country Band at the end of 1972 – those teenage bonds have continued to bind them spiritually.

The man who forged each initial link in the chain was 'Tyger' Hutchings, who turned eighteen the week 'Please Please Me' crashed into the singles charts. While Nicol and Thompson were still seeing off false knights on the road to school, he was already an errant knight adrift in the adult world of jobs and responsibility, ever burning bright with new ideas and discoveries.

In a pop world where George Harrison – a whole year younger than his fellow Silver Beatles – was the kid of the band, the four years Ashley had on his future comrades-in-alms would always make him something of a father-figure in Fairport. He would also be the ultimate arbiter of the band's musical direction for as long as he remained the Convention head. Even Thompson, the most musically gifted of the original Fairporters, is unequivocal: 'It was Ashley's band, he was always the moving force behind the direction and the policy all the way into folk-rock and the traditional revival.'

It wasn't just the age difference which set Ashley apart from Richard and Simon. He had a confidence and sureness about his and their musical choices that reflected a life spent obsessing about it:

Ashley Hutchings: My father had his own band ... He had a dance band called Leonard Hutchings and His Embassy Five ... [But] he didn't coax me to learn music at all. I found music by myself ... It was really [quite] exhaustive my [personal] quest for knowledge in music. I went to all manner of jazz clubs, folk clubs, classical concerts, rock clubs ... The Manor, the Flamingo, the Marquee. The folk thing then was [also] part of the whole tapestry of musical interest. My week very often might be taken up with six nights out, and each night possibly a different musical form.

Even as he strolled up to the Fairport house that fateful day in 1965, Ashley was a veteran of the kind of ad hoc bands with which every post-skiffle British wannabe did their musical apprenticeship. At the age of sixteen, Ashley was playing guitar in a school band. Even then, he was finding it hard to concentrate on his school work, such was the hold popular music had on him:

Ashley Hutchings: I wasn't into being academic ... That all came later. I was more interested in how I looked and whether my quiff was in place. It might go some way to explain [why], when I got the folk-bug I poured myself into libraries and books, which I hadn't done at school.

Leaving school at sixteen was the norm in those days, as was undertaking some kind of formal apprenticeship. Ashley, determined not to start 'as a tea boy' and work his way up, became a trainee journalist, firstly at *Furnishing World* before graduating to the dizzy heights of *Advertisers Weekly*. What mattered most was that the nights were his own, spent hoovering up music, music, music.

By 1964 he was immersing himself in the r&b boom that had already spawned The Rolling Stones, The Pretty Things and Downliners Sect, forming a band of his own that he described thus: 'Dr K's Blues Band were quite a good blues band, playing pubs and small clubs, outside of Muswell Hill, but not out of London.' For now, he was playing the blues, not living them.

Perhaps Hutchings's heart was not in Chicago. As soon as he bonded with his new landlady's teenage son, Simon, he took a rootsier route. An equally short-lived band Hutchings and Nicol formed at the end of 1965 displayed a more downhome brand of blues. The Ethnic Shuffle Orchestra were an all-acoustic combo whose one known recording, 'Washington At Valley Forge' – included on *The Guv'nor Vol. 1* – hinted at the shape of things to come:

Simon Nicol: The Ethnic Shuffle Orchestra … owed more to Jim Kweskin and Lovin' Spoonful than anything else. We did rural blues – Mississippi John Hurt, Rev. Gary Davis. Dr K's [Blues Band] was much more [a] Muddy Waters/south side of Chicago thing. That didn't involve me much. I was the spotty kid with the twelve-string, [which] was my point of value for Ashley at that point.

If Simon had barely turned fifteen when he began making music with his mother's new tenant, Ashley's musical magnet was already pulling him in. It was a feeling for music he shared with other like-minded friends, some of whom would prove central to the early Fairport sound, though none would contribute a single note:

Simon Nicol: Growing up in North London there were hundreds of places to go. Some nights Richard Lewis, John Penhallow [and

I] might go to the blues club or a trad jazz club or avant garde jazz or the Liverpool poets. Anything. All big pubs had upstairs rooms. Manfred Mann, John Mayall, Chris Barber, the musical panoply was amazing. I remember seeing Ravi Shankar in a pub down near The [Islington] Angel. [The] place was rammed.

Entirely independent of Hutchings, Simon and his like-minded sidekicks began going 'to the Saturday night folk evenings at Cecil Sharp House and see[ing] people like Alex Campbell, Shirley Collins, Ewan MacColl, real stalwarts'. Already, Britain's homegrown musical tradition was starting to encode the Fairport DNA, even as the four national music weeklies continued depicting popular musical styles as exclusively American.

Unlike his friends, though, Simon allowed music to take him over so completely that he turned his back on what his teachers vainly tried to teach him in readiness for life. His father had died a slow, lingering death from cancer when the growing boy was just fourteen, after which the young Nicol quickly developed a mind of his own. He concluded he could not see the point of a formal education when the most exciting pop culture revolution in 350 years was happening a bus ride away:

Simon Nicol: I had been a very good student through my early years of secondary school, but I'd become disenchanted with education, and I dare say the death of my father derailed [me]. I found schoolwork easy, but it stopped being easy when other things raised their heads and music had a lot to do with it. If you play music as a youngster, you don't play it on your own, you play it in concert with other people – it becomes a communal activity. Music fulfilled that side of my life and it became more and more important to me. I kinda dropped out of school during my O-levels. I didn't go to most of the exams. Mum bit her lip about it. I tried not to disappoint her by going off the rails but Ashley led me astray. He was four, five years older ... We still have a bit of that senior partner/junior partner relationship.

Simon was keen to introduce Tyger to his equally music-obsessed friends, for whom he also became a mentor of sorts. Not that such an all-inclusive approach to live music was confined to Tyger's immediate circle. It was either a sign of the times, or something they were putting in the water at North London secondary schools because a short bus ride away up the A1 was Highgate, where another questing soul, attending William Ellis School, was soaking up the sounds of the city with a similar sponge-like avidity:

Richard Thompson: [I] took in everything from jazz to traditional folk and blues. I saw the Indo Jazz Fusions, High Level Ranters, Jesse Fuller at The Starting Gate in Bounds Green. The Watersons at the Black Bull, Whetstone. All kinds of stuff. The Marquee Club with The Who on Tuesdays and The Yardbirds on Fridays. Gary Farr and The T-Bones, Spencer Davis Group, Davy Jones and the Lower Third.

Even before his path crossed with the like-minded pair, the young Thompson shared one important common bond with the Muswell Hill gang, at one degree of separation. It was a sneaking suspicion that English r&b – for all its immediacy of impact – offered little more than a watered-down version of American roots music.

In conversation with an American biographer in 1999, Richard suggested the early English beat bands 'just played bad r&b – which [only] later developed into great rock music. The Rolling Stones made some great records, but at first they were dreadful, a perfectly dreadful band.' A decade earlier, in a *Guitar World* profile, he was no less dismissive of other English r&b contemporaries:

Richard Thompson: There were very few talented people on that [British blues] scene. I think Peter Green was a talent, but not many others ... It was the usual story: two or three talented people who could imitate black music very well. The Downliners Sect [et al]. But glorifying The Yardbirds? They were a pretty tacky band, really. Clapton was okay, but he didn't sound great in the Yardbird days. I thought John Mayall was pretty bad ... I was familiar with the original American blues guys, so I didn't care for the locals. [1989]

At the time he kept such concerns to himself. Approaching school-leaving age in summer 1965 – having already seized several opportunities to see The Who's 'very, very exciting' residency at the

Marquee – he was galvanized into forming (or joining, according to the drummer) a covers band whose repertoire was almost exclusively Anglo-beat music.

The self-taught Thompson even tutored schoolmate Hugh Cornwell to play bass in order to fill the band's vacant slot, setting him on a course to punk-rock fame in The Stranglers. On drums was the precocious Nick Jones, later a rock journalist in his own right and already with his own direct conduit to the pop wellspring:

Richard Thompson: Nick [was the] son of Max Jones, a very fine jazz writer on the *Melody Maker*. Because of that we found some obscure material, some great B-sides, and so developed a very interesting repertoire for a school band ... Max used to get all the stuff on pre-release demos in those days. That's where we found 'Jack O' Diamonds' by Ben Carruthers and The Deep. [1988]

'Jack O' Diamonds' was a Bob Dylan poem the American singer had allowed his friend, actor Ben Carruthers, to put to music, only to then baulk at the credits on the resultant 45, which was hastily withdrawn.[1] It was the one song which would transfer from Thompson's school band – named Emil and The Detectives, after the popular children's novel – to the early Fairport set.

Though Nick Jones seems to think The Detectives lasted only a few months, both Cornwell and Thompson insist the band (if not the name) existed for at least eighteen months. To them, at least, it was a lot more than some mere hobby-horse – as evidenced by the fact that both are still making music half a century later.

Cornwell also remembers Richard's father, by now a senior policeman at Scotland Yard, allowing them access to some confiscated musical equipment, and even driving them to some gigs. Thompson's elder sister, Perri, also suggested father John went as far as getting them a paying gig, only to despair when his number one son would not play to the crowd:

---

[1] In the 2016 Blu-ray edition of D.A. Pennebaker's *Dont Look Back*, Dylan is seen typing out the lyrics for Carruthers in his Savoy Hotel suite in May 1965.

Perri Thompson: Father got him booked at some funny pub in North London ... Father was always furious because Richard would never play what everyone wanted to hear. Father thought he should change his style and he should play good old dance numbers – in other words, he should be more commercial.

According to the precocious heir to the Thompson fortune, Emil and friends had little choice but to tow the popular line – the times demanded it: 'We used to play whatever was the common currency of the time – Who numbers [&c.].' He had yet to develop an aversion to electric r&b or spurning a helping hand from other family members:

Hugh Cornwell: Richard was [already] a marvellous guitar player, and we'd play blues from his collection. We were doing 'Smokestack Lightning', Chuck Berry songs, old rhythm and blues really ... We used to play at all the Hornsey College of Art dances because Richard's sister was the Social Sec.

At the same time, Thompson was keeping his options open, playing the odd folk club gig solo or, more 'usually, with somebody else for a bit of moral support – 'cause it's pretty unnerving playing acoustic. [It was] the usual stuff, Leadbelly, Tom Paxton ... the Black Bull at Whetstone, The Starting Gate in Bounds Green.'

Also playing the clubs at around the same time was a fifteen-year-old wilomina o' the wisp, Judy Dyble. She had already enjoyed a brief stint in a folk group called Judy and The Folkmen, who as early as December 1964 had recorded what Dyble describes as 'a reasonably respectable version of "Come All Ye Fair & Tender Ladies".'

When Dyble and Thompson were finally introduced to each other by Simon and Ashley, Judy provided that occasional 'bit of moral support' on joint forays into the folk clubs. They even once or twice performed as an acoustic proto-Fairport quartet. In fact, Dyble remained part of Ashley's expanding musical circle throughout this period, insisting in 1970, 'I had known Simon and Tyger since ... I was fifteen ... and I had worked with them in various groups, jug bands and things that they formed from time to time.'

Dyble even made 'a recording ... in the before-Fairport days of

Richard and myself playing free-form recorders, piano, guitar and autoharp, with my brother Stephen blowing into a brass watering can'. And yet, when Thompson, Hutchings and Nicol joined forces for good in July 1966, the lovely lady was not even considered. The band they had in mind was an Anglicized take on American folk-rock – no girls allowed:

Judy Dyble: Initially, the shape of the band was from Ashley. He related very much to what The Byrds were doing with electrified folk music and electrified country music ... and [wanted] to stick Richard on top of that.

Although Thompson was only seventeen, with 'a lot to learn', when he first encountered this disparate group of music-lovers, he was also something of an electric guitar prodigy. He could already play circles around the others. But he was no frontman, Emil and The Detectives notwithstanding. Still painfully shy, he spoke with a noticeable stutter, acquired, according to his mother Joan, 'when he was five. He started school, which unfortunately was a bit rough, and he got dysentery straightaway ... He almost died. And that's when he started to stutter.'

The younger, quieter sibling in the Thompson household, Richard realised life would be easier staying in the shadow of older sister Perri, who according to her brother was 'a seriously independently minded, headstrong, very good-looking teenaged girl who wanted to do what she wanted to do'. He would hide his inner light for a good while.

Yet there was no mistaking how quickly he took to the guitar; another gift bequeathed by his wilful sibling, or more accurately her boyfriends, who invariably found themselves with time on their hands when they came to call on her, only to find she was 'just getting ready' – for two hours:

Richard Thompson: All her boyfriends knew how to play like Buddy Holly, and I picked it up from them. I didn't really think much about it – it was just an alternative to making things out of wood. [1970]

Perri seems to have had excellent musical taste, introducing her younger brother to records beyond the pale to their ultra-conservative parents. As Thompson recalls, 'She had the first Dylan album and a Lightnin' Hopkins record very early on, and Sonny [Terry] and Brownie [McGhee] stuff ... I [also] remember having my ear to my sister's bedroom [wall], hearing "Great Balls Of Fire" – wonderful.'

The next semester's coursework in Thompson's extra-curricular degree came when he 'started getting *Melody Maker* religiously every week. It was a great education. People like Max Jones ... had a three-page jazz spread, [and it had] a folk page [&c.].'

The one music weekly where the adjective carried more weight than the noun, *Melody Maker* had the best gig listings in the land. Scouring its pages, Thompson discovered The Who were playing the Marquee every week. And in early 1966, he saw the first London appearances of the Paul Butterfield Blues Band which still featured 'Dylan's guitarist' Michael Bloomfield, then taking the r&b format into realms as yet unimagined by callow English rockers with the title-track to their second album, *East/West*:

Richard Thompson: I used to listen to Otis Rush, Hubert Sumlin, and some of the white guys. I thought Bloomfield was great, the most exciting player. When the Butterfield Band came over in '66, that really knocked me out ... [But] after listening to someone like Otis Rush, John Mayall's Bluesbreakers just weren't as good. If you'd heard Albert King, you already knew the solo [to] 'Strange Brew'. [1985]

The experienced Bloomfield gave the young Richard a new guitar-hero, and an idea of where he wanted to go. All he needed now was some like-minded musicians prepared to follow his lead, and a mentor willing to take the weight of band leadership from those permanently-hunched shoulders.

Fortunately, a fast-developing reputation was sufficient for him to come to Hutchings's attention, thanks to fellow William Ellis pupil Brian Wyvill, who actually lived in Muswell Hill, two houses down from Ashley and Simon. According to the latter, Wyvill 'used to go on about his wizard friend, who was just as good a guitarist as Hank Marvin'.

At some point, a sceptical Ashley asked the boy wonder to show him what The Shadows had to fear. As it happens, a lot. Thompson was promptly co-opted into the Ethnic Shuffle Orchestra. When that outlet proved unable to contain such instrumental prowess, a vehicle more suited to his gifts was conceived. Meanwhile, Ashley, Simon and Richard indulged in the musical equivalent of sticking a pin in the donkey. As Thompson later said, 'The pre-Fairports were [sometimes] a jug band, a blues band or a folk band – with a Pentangle-type sound – before we got a definite structure.'

It would be July 1966 before these failed models went to the breakers yard and a suitably souped-up sound found. That evening at JB's culminated in Tyger persuading Thompson to throw his Strat into the ring; his diary recording the moment: 'I suggested forming a "folk-rock" group with [Simon] and Rich Thompson. We agreed to give it a go. Went back to [Simon]'s place after and we thought up numbers to do.'

They had all agreed on one thing at JB's, as Thompson recalled in 1982: 'We were very interested in songs. We used to like The Byrds because they did interesting material with strong lyrics.' In fact, their idea for a Byrd-brained band was more radical than any of them initially realised:

Richard Thompson: We were doing very eclectic things for the time, jug band music and such. I think it was a revulsion at the day's standards really ... There were lots of these really bad bands imitating the Tamla/Stax stuff. So we looked around for other music ... Phil Ochs, Dylan, Joni Mitchell, Jim and Jean, The Left Banke. There was a real boom over [in the US] in songwriting: the lyrics were becoming artful, and nothing like that existed in Britain ... We wanted all the songs [we did] to be strong ... These days they love country and western in Britain, but back then you really had to do some serious research to get hold of the records; you just didn't hear it [on the radio] ... Ashley Hutchings loaned me my first Hank Williams record, and it amazed me. Fairport went ahead that way. To us, it was very adventurous and groundbreaking, because nobody else was doing anything close. [1989]

Throughout the next nine months, while the rest of London was immersed in psychedelia, they would remain firmly out of the loop, formulating a sound and direction before making their official live debut. It allowed the musical climate to change from what Thompson rightly depicted as 'bad music à la Geno Washington, and blues bands' to something as English as opium-eaters: 'By the time we turned professional we had what might be called a "psychedelic" audience.'

The collective brain-power of Ashley, Richard and Simon, however, was unable to supply a good name for the new-fangled outfit. Their first chosen name seemed to be pitched at the 'psychedelic audience':

Richard Thompson: Fairport's early name was Tim Turner's Narration. Tim Turner used to be the narrator on this 20-minute documentary slot they showed before the main film at the cinema, a thing called *Look At Life*. It would look at hairdressing or Eskimos, anything. It just seemed to be the time for obscure names. Hapshash And The Coloured Coat were rearing their ugly heads, so it seemed necessary to get a name with at least eight syllables. [1988]

Nor was it just the name which was intentionally obscure. Ashley's penchant for the less explored byways of music also held sway. As Simon says, 'Even then, he was prone to come up with more obscure material than that which was in circulation.' It is a charge he willingly accepts:

Ashley Hutchings: We would [certainly] have done something from Paul Butterfield's first album and Joan Baez was a source, Dylan was a source, The Byrds were a source ... [as were] Phil Ochs, some of the singer-songwriters on Elektra ... We were quite derivative, but our sources were pretty obscure ... Richard Fariña ... was a great influence. We did two or three of his songs ... 'Reno Nevada' was there from early on. [And] something from *Blonde On Blonde*.

The 'something from *Blonde On Blonde*' was 'Absolutely Sweet Marie', sung by Simon, at a time when the band rotated vocals like three musical Musketeers. 'Jack O' Diamonds', transplanted from Richard's school band, provided another early Dylan connection, initially sung by Richard. Even at this stage when Thompson took flight, the others seemed to intuitively know how to ride the slipstream:

Simon Nicol: There were eighteen months [sic] when we were tiddling about with other names – Tim Turner's Narration [&c.]. Which is [when] I [really] learnt to play guitar, by looking over Richard's shoulder. But I never wanted to ape him, and I hope I gave him space to go off on one. I was content to do that, rather than make the duelling twin-guitar sound [then in vogue].

In those days, the Fairport collective was as much of a Musical Appreciation Society as an actual band. The quest for obscure material required the input of fellow obsessives, and Fairport had three willing stooges who fed them a regular diet of American imports and obscure B-sides, replacing the Max Jones connection with their own one-stop shop of vinyl rarities:

Simon Nicol: The key figures [of those] who do not appear on the albums were Kingsley Abbott, Richard Lewis and John Penhallow. Richard was ahead of the game with singer-songwriters, more [interested in] the words – Dylan, Cohen, Ochs, Buckley, that was his area. Kingsley [was] more about the rarities.

Richard Lewis recalls a pattern soon developing in which 'Ashley and Simon would come to my house in Leaside Avenue and listen to my records, [or] I'd take my records round there and play them at Fairport'. The same duo would also go round to the Abbott household and raid Kingsley's collection. On one such occasion, they picked out a song called 'Time Will Show The Wiser', the B-side to The Merry-Go-Round's 'Live', the kind of import single Abbott lived to uncover.

The song would end up opening the Fairport's eponymous debut LP, providing the perfect opportunity to announce this new kid on the block who carried his axe like a mannish boy. Indeed, that performance was such a perfect introduction to the early Fairport sound it became the opening cut on the definitive Island-era Richard Thompson anthology, *(guitar, vocal)* (1976).

Whether they played it at Tim Turner's Narration's one and only gig, the Golders Green Bowling Alley in March 1967, has gone unrecorded, but before they could take Tim Turner's Narration for a spin around Muswell Hill, they decided they needed a better drummer and a stronger name, in that order.

Finding a drummer was proving an intractable problem, threatening to stop the band in its tracks. Thompson finally suggested they audition Emil and The Detectives' ex-drummer, Nick Jones. But Jones had not kept up his chops and when they asked him to play along to 'Eight Miles High' and 'For What It's Worth', he struggled to keep up.

It was Simon's turn to suggest a candidate. The one he came up with was Shaun Frater, 'who was in my class at school; not a close friend at all, but he had a drum kit. He must have had an indulgent parent.' With Frater in, it was time to unveil the happening new band who had been making such a racket nightly at the house on the hill they called Fairport. It was Richard Lewis who came up with the name, mainly because Fairport 'was where they used to convene for rehearsals'. It was just in time for the band to make its unofficial debut at a party at the Lewises' own Leaside Avenue residence in April.

They had meantime acquired a manager of sorts in John Penhallow, another member of the Muswell Hill Musical Appreciation Society. Simon confirms that Penhallow 'had a lot to do with marshalling the forces. Ashley was too busy thinking about songs and [song] lists and getting certain musicians together. John was a good foil for us in the very early days and he got us the gigs which eventually got us noticed.'

Penhallow's first idea was a simple one – place a series of adverts in the *Melody Maker* gig listings announcing not an actual gig, but rather lines like 'Fairport Convention stays home again patiently awaiting bookings', and a phone number. After this three week media blitz, a larger advert instructed readers, 'Become Converted!!! Fairport Convention Happen at St Michael's Hall, Golders Green.'

The date was May 27th, 1967; the set-list would include Love's '7 And 7 Is', a Byrdsian reinterpretation of Dylan's 'My Back Pages' and Chuck Berry's 'Johnny B. Goode', perhaps a concession to Richard's retro tastes or just a way for him to let rip. For Penhallow, it was a momentous occasion, which he later recalled in his brief history of the period, *Fairport Folio*:

I helped organise the gig – Simon and I were good mates through our school years and beyond, although we were not at the same school ... So when Simon announced that he was joining a new band with Ashley, aka Tyger Hutchings and they wanted to play at a bigger venue than the Northbank Youth Club, I couldn't help getting involved as I had been running the dances up at Northbank from time to time since the tender age of 15 and knew what had to be done.

I booked the hall and got the tickets printed ... I asked my girlfriend's brother-in-law, Keith Roberts to get involved. Keith was older (25 or more) than all of us, had a car and his own printing company so he donated the posters. Together, under the cover of darkness, we travelled the major roads between Muswell Hill and Golders Green fixing these black on dayglo orange posters to prominent trees and lamposts. I pre-sold as many 5/- tickets as I could. It was my home phone number on the poster, not that it was ringing off the hook! The big day arrived, Keith and I set up the hall, helped the band in with the PA, and then manned the door ... Kingsley Abbot wrote in his book[let] that there was only 20 people there – I'm sure it was more than that, as there would have been at least 20+ friends of the band on the guest list. At the end of the night Keith and I had the money to get our five quid hall hire fee back and then buy the band and friends a late meal at the local Chinese restaurant. It cost all of ten quid so, by my reckoning, at least 50 punters must have paid! Tyger and Richard shared the vocals on their mix of Byrds, Love and Chuck Berry covers ... Shaun Frater was on drums for his first and only gig.

It would turn out to be Shaun Frater's last Fairport gig thanks to another confluence of fortuitous circumstance. Kingsley Abbott had brought along Martin Lamble and at the end of the night, as the lights came on, Lamble turned to Kingsley and told him that he 'wanted to play drums for *that* band'.

He was quietly convinced he could do a whole lot better than the guy currently occupying the drum stool, a view he promptly shared with Fairport's band leader, who decided to call the upstart's bluff.

A couple of days later, Lamble slotted effortlessly behind the others and Fairport were converted. With a fully committed drummer on board, this Convention were officially open for business and ready to reveal what they had been cooking up at the Fairport house in the months spent rehearsing an American-centric repertoire.

Meanwhile, The Beatles had been recording the grandiloquent *Sgt Pepper's Lonely Hearts Club Band* at EMI's Abbey Road studios. By June 1967 the deleterious influence of that deeply flawed fall from creative grace for the once-Fab Four was already being felt in London circles, putting Fairport on a collision course with the newly adopted psychedelic sounds reverberating around 'town' that heady summer.

Their desire to set themselves apart was not a secret for long. Indeed, the small ads for their debut album, released the following June, was almost a manifesto for the band without portfolio:

> *Fairport Convention* does not turn you on. That's something you'll have to organize for yourself. Won't blow your mind. Try Vietnam for best brain blowing results. *Fairport Convention* is a Polydor LP put together by unusual personalities for that insignificant minority of seekers to whom real music, oddly enough, seems to matter.

MIDDLE ○ EARTH

43 King Street, Covent Garden, W. 1.   240 1327

Friday 27 October   10.30 p.m. - Dawn

THE NICE
EYES OF BLUE
THE LIMOUSINE
WEST INDIAN STEEL BAND
JOHN PEEL

Feature Films ... Short Films ... Poetry

MEMBERS: 10/-   GUESTS: £1

Saturday 28 October   10.30 p.m. - Dawn

THE INCREDIBLE STRING BAND
with MIMI and MOUSE
FAIRPORT CONVENTION
THE BLUES COMMUNION
JEFF DEXTER

Feature Films/Short Films/Poetry/Guest Musicians

MEMBERS: 10/-   GUESTS: £1

FANTASTIC SCENE AT THE ELBOW ROOM LAST SUNDAY!!

EVEN BETTER THIS WEEK SO DON'T MISS IT!!

AT THE ELBOW ROOM SUNDAY, DECEMBER 10th

THE FAIRPORT CONVENTION - GREAT WEST COAST SOUND GROUP.

SHADES OF JEFFERSON AIRPLANE. DIRECT FROM JOHN PEEL'S
TOP GEAR SHOW ON SUNDAY AFTERNOON, TO THE RAINBOW REALM
AT THE ELBOW ROOM. BRINGING WITH THEM THEIR OWN LIGHT SHOW

*FAIRPORT CONVENTION + LIGHT SHOW

*PLASTIC JEWELS FROM THE REALM OF RAINBOW STUDIES FEATURING

    *NEW STONES L.P.
    *NEW DOORS L.P.
    *NEW CLEAR LIGHT L.P.
    *MAGICAL MYSTERY TOUR
    *AND MANY OTHER INTERSTELLAR HAPPENINGS

*LATE NIGHT SOUL DISCOTHEQUE.

AT THE ELBOW ROOM
HIGH STREET, ASTON.
SUNDAY, DECEMBER 10th
8.00-12.00
7/6

Anyone who dares compare us with the Jefferson Airplane will be pelted with bad herrings!

—JUDY DYBLE, *DISC*, 23 FEBRUARY 1967

[Yes,] there are similarities [with West Coast bands] ... but there's one big and basic difference. They all seem to be doing a cross between rock and soul ... It's not all that far from the sock-it-to-me thing – and very American.

—RICHARD THOMPSON, *BEAT INSTRUMENTAL*, NOVEMBER 1968

From gig one, Fairport would cut a swathe through the London scene, reliant neither on extended blues jams or studio trickery to cultivate an audience of their own. And yet, almost immediately they found themselves being compared to those bands who continued to believe the west is the best.

Though the three co-founders of Fairport had gone out of their way to make sure they sounded nothing like any other band on London's nascent psychedelic scene, this did not remain free of comparisons for very long. Right from that first performance, their West Coast reference points were unmistakeable: Love, The Byrds, even The Leaves, whose December 1965 45 provided Fairport's template for 'Hey Joe' – as opposed to the Hendrix version just leaving the UK charts.

Also in that early repertoire was a song first recorded by Dino Valenti, 'Let's Get Together', a song known to them more from its appearance on the debut album of San Franciscan electric folk forerunners, Jefferson Airplane.

Airplane's debut, called simply *Takes Off*, did nothing of the sort, partly because the band lacked a natural frontperson to provide a visual focus. It was the recruitment of vocalist Grace Slick from The Great Society which would propel them into the charts both sides of the pond with the radio-friendly, ultra-trippy 'White Rabbit', planting the seed for a similar reinvention in Muswell Hill.

Confirmation that the Fairports continued paying close attention to events out west came the very first time they garnered a review in the national music press, in early August 1967. That *NME* review of a show at the UFO Club (pronounced U-Fo) noted the inclusion of 'Plastic Fantastic Lover', the closing track on the sophomore Airplane album, *Surrealistic Pillow*.

By then, the Muswell Hill boys had come to the same realisation Balin and co. reached after *Takes Off*: they might be a confederation of equals but they lacked a focal point on stage. Indeed, one of the great dichotomies thrown up by Fairport from the off was that decisions were generally made by its three founders, not one of whom wished to stand centrestage. Thompson, in particular, described 'coming forward to do a vocal' as 'like walking through flames'.

Simon Nicol: I sang one song in that early formulation of the band … It was Richard [who usually sang] – reluctantly. He didn't enjoy the eye contact with the audience. He was intensely shy – when he went off on his solo, he would sometimes have his back to the audience, but at the very most it would be eyes closed, head down, mop of hair. The privacy blinds were there. But that suited the mystique of the times as well, [thinking,] 'That's quite trippy – oh, he's away with it.'

By his own admission Thompson preferred to 'be the J.J. Cale figure hiding behind the Marshall stack'. Perhaps what they really needed was a girl singer. The trio didn't have to think too long before they remembered they already knew someone suitable:

Richard Thompson: Judy used to sing in folk clubs and she played the autoharp … [which] were extremely lingua franca at the time, so we were happy to have her. Plus she had [that] Mary Travers-ironed hair – which was very important.

Judy Dyble: I didn't actually know many other musicians at that stage … and had never known 'electric' musicians before. All I knew was that they could all play anything they wanted to, sound like anything they wanted to, and seemed to know what the others were going to play before it was played. I added a female voice, an autoharp, and the ability to play the piano and recorder a bit.

The band Dyble formally joined in July 1967 were still sitting on the rickety fence separating pop from folk, wondering which side they should be on. As she recalled in 1970, 'When I joined them they were doing things like Richard and Mimi Fariña songs, early Dylan, really hackneyed folk songs like "The Water Is Wide". We were always influenced by the music we had heard most recently. For a while, it was Clarence Ashley and Tex Isley.' The addition of Dyble gave them options. The formerly all-male four-piece just seemed delighted to have a feminine presence, and a photogenic one at that:

Simon Nicol: She looked great, and she was quirky … and she brought her knitting when Richard was off on one. People loved that … Jude was a very welcome addition because she was a focal point. It's just a real shame [that] when she learnt to sing, it was in a very folk-club environment: in a small room and everyone was very hushed.

However, if Dyble thought that she had joined an electric-folk combo, she was quickly disabused of the notion. For all his hiding behind amps, Thompson was still Fairport's primary focal point, invariably providing the tipping points in Convention sets. To Dyble's delight, she found the young Richard had blossomed into one helluva guitarist since last they played together:

Judy Dyble: Quite a lot of the songs that we did were a basis for Richard to fly away, [leaving] me to listen with amazement and pride. There would be maybe a phrase that he picked up on that would start him off, but however his solos started, they would definitely be his own after the first couple of bars … Sometimes Richard's solos would last a long time and sometimes they would be short and very sweet, but the rest of the band were always there as a powerhouse of an engine to anchor Richard. And they always knew to the nanosecond when the solos were about to end and would bring the song back to the part where Ian and I would come in.

Simon Nicol: That was Richard's trump card – his ability to free-express music. I didn't know anyone else like him. I didn't know anyone else at the time who played the guitar with such an open mind. Clapton with Mayall was extremely focused and very exciting, but Richard was far less circumscribed by regular musical forms. He was much more influenced by free-jazz and the free-thinking classical composers who were atonal. You still hear that in his solos to this day – those jarring assonances which make perfect sense in their context. I don't know how much he studied it, but it worked and we didn't feel, 'Oh, he's been doing it long enough, let's go back to the final verse.' We were [perfectly] happy – Martin, Ashley and I – standing there keeping the pulse going. And people loved it.

By the time Judy joined Fairport, Thompson had already attained a musical plane few guitarists in their prime reach, let alone someone in his teens. And it was fast attracting comment, as Kingsley Abbott notes, 'Richard's playing [generated] a lot of interest ... especially the way that he would interweave other themes into various songs. My favourite of these often happened during "East/West", the Paul Butterfield Blues Band number, when Richard used to insert a piece of Coronation Scot towards the end.'

It was on such songs where Thompson's Fender tended to catch fire. But the fledgling Fairport were not always able to incorporate their wilder workouts into their sets, which sometimes barely ran to twenty minutes, let alone half an hour. Such was the case the night American manager-producer Joe Boyd caught an embryonic (Judy-less) Fairport Convention doing 'A Public Audition' at Soho's Happening 44 club in late June.

Yet even without Richard's six-string pyrotechnics or Judy's 'Mary Travers-ironed hair', the band sounded unusual enough for Boyd to book them to play his UFO club at the end of July:

Joe Boyd: I was looking out for bands to play UFO because every time a band played UFO their price went up. So I was looking for new groups who were cheap, and somebody said, 'Go see this group, they're doing a kind of audition type performance at this club in Gerrard Street.' So I went down and I was impressed.

It was just the break Fairport needed – it may even have prompted them to recruit Dyble, for she would make her live debut that night at UFO. If they were looking for a leg-up professionally, Boyd was equally desperate to find a band he could mould – and hang onto. He had endured a highly frustrating time working for almost a year as Jac Holzman's English Elektra A&R man, having tried and failed to convince Holzman he was hip to the West End jive:

Joe Boyd: I tried to sign The Move and the Pink Floyd to Elektra before I left [the label]. They wouldn't sign either group, or Eric Clapton who was expressing an interest in [us] signing his new group, [Cream]. Jac Holzman expressed [no] interest in the idea. And [then] Elektra gave me the sack, because I wouldn't do what they wanted me to do.

By July 1967, Boyd was growing increasingly worried that England's psychedelic revolution was passing him by. After producing 'Arnold Layne', the groundbreaking debut 45 of Syd Barrett's Pink Floyd, he had seen the band snatched from under him; The Move had signed with Tony Secunda; while Cream had clasped themselves to the bosom of a rapacious Robert Stigwood.

When Boyd witnessed the five-piece Fairport for the first time at his beloved club on July 28th, 1967, he tried to convince himself his favourable judgement was 'purely objective, based upon the music and hearing Richard Thompson play the guitar'. Only later did he come to accept that, 'to a certain degree, it was [seizing an] opportunity. They were completely unknown and unsigned, whereas a lot of the other people [I was interested in] were already attached to various things.'

According to Kingsley Abbott – there at UFO to provide moral support – Boyd latched onto the band even as they warmed up a sell-out crowd for the increasingly influential Pink Floyd, riding high in the charts for a second time in six months with the visionary 'See Emily Play':

Kingsley Abbott: They played their usual good first set, which had been well received by an audience who were all sitting or lying on the floor of the old ballroom. I doubt that many of them could have stood for too long, but they gave the band a laidback ovation as they waited for Floyd. During the interval Joe Boyd arrived backstage to talk to Fairport and to offer them management that included the likelihood of a record deal. As I talked to Tyger, it was obvious that he was ... impressed with Joe's credentials.

Ashley Hutchings: In classic Tin Pan Alley style, this American breezed into the dressing room and said, 'Hey, you guys are great and [how] would you like to make a record?' ... He spoke with such authority. I don't think that we knew a lot about him or his pedigree until later. We just ... knew that he and Hoppy Hopkins ran the UFO club.

Boyd had yet to see just how far Fairport could stretch – further even than the Barrett-era Floyd – when he had barrelled his way backstage after their 'warm up' set. By the time Fairport returned for their second set, a couple of pivotal events had changed the dynamic at U-Fo.

Firstly, Syd Barrett arrived belatedly at the club more than a little worse for wear, to perform with *his* band. He was greeted at the club entrance by Boyd himself, who was shocked to see 'black holes' where Syd's dancing pupils had once been. According to Floyd's drummer, Nick Mason, Syd spent most of the ensuing set with 'his arms hung by his side ... occasionally strumming' his guitar. The boy prodigy would never be the same again.[2]

Perhaps this mystifying (non-)performance by Floyd's frontman persuaded Fairport that they should carry the baton of improvisation themselves. Or perhaps, as Ashley suggests, 'Because of Pink Floyd's reputation for improvisation, we included a couple of things to show off our instrumental skill – or Richard, as he was known.'

Whatever the case, the following week's *NME* ran an account of their second set which described them 'ironing out of first set difficulties [as] they played with growing confidence. Included were "Flower Lady" and "Plastic Fantastic Lover" before they closed with thirty minutes of "East/West".' Boyd, still slightly sceptical about some of their cover choices, was left stunned by their finale:

[2] The full story of Syd's struggle with his demons is told in my *All The Madmen* (Constable-Robinson, 2011).

Joe Boyd: [Initially] I was dubious about their direction and choice of material, because I'd fled America to escape that kind of stuff … but the group in general were impressive. It was [mainly] Richard. My approach was [always] to lock in to really extraordinary talent and worry about what to do with it later. I never … focused on the guitar. In fact that was part of what interested me about Richard. I was so bored of white, lead guitar players. That, for me, was not the most interesting part of the current scene. [So] to hear Richard play with all the rhythmic intensity and all the structure of blues-based rock, but to be so original within it and not sound like anybody else … [was] really interesting. The track that really knocked me over was 'East/West'. When they announced it, I thought, 'That's nuts. Why would you want to do that?' And then he took Mike Bloomfield to the cleaners … It followed the structure of the Butterfield thing but he just improvised much more convincingly in this kinda cod-Indian raga way.

He was not the only member of a thinning audience to feel this way. Also there that night, indeed most UFO nights, was George Harrison, who had gone there 'to see Floyd … when they launched their [first] album. Fairport Convention were playing and I was amazed by how well Richard Thompson played.' Such an endorsement from a Beatle was quite a feather in Fairport's cap and a validation of their general direction:

Ashley Hutchings: We couldn't quite believe in the abilities of each other perhaps, until it was pointed out to us – until Joe Boyd raved over Richard and [the band] in general.

They had certainly risen to the occasion. They had also definitively shown that they belonged on the same stage as the band whose original sound Boyd first captured in the studio. As Boyd says, it was 'a lucky break for both' of them:

Richard Thompson: We were very lucky to fall in with Joe because he had a very good musical pedigree; he grew up listening to jazz records and an outstanding collection of boogie-woogie 78s, and had been the stage manager at Newport when Dylan went electric, and had recorded Paul Butterfield ... He put in a lot of very sound input and turned us on to a lot of very good music that we later covered. He actually knew Joni Mitchell and Phil Ochs, and that connection was important to us. We saw ourselves as a song-playing band. [1988]

Dyble, who had joined at just the right time, felt similarly uplifted by the experience: 'Right from day one it was something special. Other bands that we would go and see then were r&b bands or soul bands; finesse and musicality weren't usually high up on the list.' If the choice of covers was usually daring, the arrangements also had an inventiveness and intelligence which set Fairport apart:

Ashley Hutchings: We didn't just lift a song, we arranged it. For example, our arrangement of 'Chelsea Morning' is incredibly complicated. There's an ascending run that the bass and the two guitars play ... Our arrangements were very carefully worked on. I think we put our own character into them. 'Suzanne' is a case in point. It doesn't sound anything like Leonard Cohen, or indeed Judy Collins, doing it. It has this very strong rhythmic staccato thing which is all based around the drum kit.

Arranging and selecting the songs had become almost a full-time job for Ashley. Now he could afford to make it so. For some time he had thought, 'I'm going to give up my job and ... try and make a go of the band.' Now they had a proper manager, Ashley could devote himself 24/7 to making 'his' band take off, leaving the management of the band to Boyd.

Some of the others were more cautious, biding their time before quitting regular gigs. In Dyble's case, it meant giving up on her ambition to be 'a world-class librarian'; Richard had been apprenticed to Hans Unger, a graphic designer who had a studio at Muswell Hill Road and had designed windows for Coventry Cathedral. The young Thompson had the tricky job of 'making stained-glass windows' when hungover and dog-tired. Yet even this odd job contributed to his musical education:

Richard Thompson: Before this I was a funky sort of Clapton follower, but in the studio they'd have the Third Programme on all the time. I really became interested in classical music and much of my guitar style comes from people like Debussy. [1968]

Once the whole band was put on a weekly stipend by Boyd's management company, Witchseason, Thompson and Dyble were convinced to give up the unequal struggle. In an era when bands were often expected to play all-nighters, Fairport spent the summer doing an awful lot of bills at The Electric Garden – later to become Middle Earth – leaving a deep impression on Kingsley Abbott:

> The Electric Garden ... did not usually attract more than fifty/ seventy-five [people] in the very early days. However, they did provide Fairport with a valuable platform for them to hone their skills, and to provide testing grounds for new material. They usually played two sets and the intervening periods were spent chatting to audience and other band members. We would often encounter the same batch of bands on the London circuit: Eclection, Blossom Toes, The Action.

Eclection and The Action, fellow regulars on the London club scene, would criss-cross the Convention again and again, as would the likes of Family and Soft Machine, whom Ashley came to consider *sympatico*, 'They did their spot, you watched them, you did your spot and they watched you.'

Never before had rock bands of such diversity slotted so easily into the same grid reference. It truly was a special time. As Thompson recalled, 'It was a perfect atmosphere for playing in ... [Which is] one of the reasons why, when the Fairports started, it was so enjoyable.' The all-night, two-set format allowed the band to expand the parameters of their sound while the audience came and went, literally and metaphorically:

Ashley Hutchings: We tended to play to the people who were coming in, and to the people who had nowhere to go [until] the milkman arrived ... Because the audience was very often not listening, chemically enhanced and under the influence, you learned to perform. You learned that it wasn't good enough to just put your head down and ignore them.

Nor did Fairport confine their all-night extemporisations to The Electric Garden. By the end of that summer they had also become regulars at the Speakeasy, a well-known haunt for movers and shakers, and a place more celebrated musicians would often go to wind down after performing elsewhere.

As it happens, in the summer of 1967 there were more great guitarists playing a square mile either side of the Speakeasy than the rest of the planet put together. And undisputed king of the hill was a young black bluesman from Washington state. Jimi Hendrix had been brought to London less than a year earlier by ex-Animal Chas Chandler and almost immediately lit a blue flame which scorched a trail right through British Pop.

Hendrix just loved to jam, day and night. As Ashley says, 'If there was music going on, Jimi wanted to play.' Playing with others was how the American axeman kept one eye on the competition, and one eye on the prize. Which is why, as Kingsley Abbott wrote, 'Jimi was often [at the Speakeasy] late at night. And he was very friendly to everyone … On one night he came and sat at our table and chatted extensively. It was obvious that he was impressed with the band, and that he enjoyed [its] sense of humour.'

He was also probably gauging the likelihood of sharing a mutual appreciation for Dylan and/or joining Thompson in uncharted territories around 'East/West', something he did on at least two occasions that summer:

Kingsley Abbott: Fairport usually played two sets at the Speak: one at about 10.30 and another later, some while after midnight … When Jimi played with them it was well after the second sets each time, at about 3.30 or four in the morning, when there were only perhaps twenty people left in the club. Each time they played for about forty minutes or so, and the song that really sticks in my mind was an extended version of 'Like A Rolling Stone' during which Richard and Jimi took turns at exploratory solos with both obviously enjoying each other's talents.

Simon Nicol: Jimi Hendrix would often call by, especially after he'd done a gig himself – he was still part of the pop scene then – and he'd stand by the bar … smoking interesting cigarettes. It was very obvious that he was a great admirer of Richard Thompson's playing … He also loved to get up on stage. He clearly didn't want to play Richard's guitar next to me, so whenever he got up, I handed my guitar to him and they'd play together. He and Richard would find some common ground – some blues, a bit of Chuck Berry, something by Dylan.

If such jam sessions – one of which, Simon recalls, was conducted while Cilla Black was 'frugging wildly' – were the stuff of dreams, they were not enough to sustain a career. The band's new manager was already thinking along more practical lines.

Kingsley Abbott: Joe Boyd … had a pretty good idea about the directions that he wanted to take the band, as he introduced them quickly to new material and encouraged them to strengthen vocally … The recorded songs would eventually drive the stage material rather than the other way round.

Boyd realised that this was the way it had to be if Fairport were not to go the way of so many bands from this era who failed to make the transition from club sensation to pop phenomenon. Within a fortnight of formalising their set-up, he began to voice concerns regarding Judy's ability to hold centrestage on her own sweet lonesome. He needed to tread carefully, though, as the group dynamic had shifted somewhat:

Joe Boyd: In conversation with Simon and possibly Ashley, I made it clear that I thought Judy wasn't at the level that I thought the band was … My [real] thought was, 'Let's dump Judy and get somebody else.' But she was Richard's girlfriend, and so I wasn't even going to suggest that, 'cause that was clearly a non-starter. So we collectively came up with the idea of adding a male singer.

Simon Nicol: It was definitely [Joe]'s idea that we should do something about [a singer]. We were content to let things bumble along. But Joe thought we needed someone with more professional experience, [who] had a voice that was meaningful.

The singer they collectively agreed to audition was currently fronting a band called Pyramid, who had just released a single on

Deram. Fortunately for Fairport, Pyramid were about to go the way of the pharaohs. Joe, Ashley and Simon dutifully trundled down to The Cromwellian to see the last dynasty.

As Boyd recalls, 'The whole gimmick of Pyramid was that there was a curtain and these three guys in front and the band behind the curtain. Simon and Ashley came with me. And [then] we had a drink with Ian [Matthews].' It did not take clairvoyance on Matthews's part to realise Fairport were likely to be a more commercial proposition than Pyramid:

Ian Matthews: Joe, Ashley and Richard [sic] … had been tipped off by Tony Hall at [Deram] that Pyramid was about to break up and had a singer that they might want to look at … I suppose I passed the audition [because] the next thing I know, we're rehearsing their stage songs. It was at that point that I discovered what they were doing. I liked anything from Tim Hardin to The Kinks at that point in time. I liked The Byrds. And I liked Joni. I'm not sure if Joni actually had a record out, but I used to spend a lot of time at Essex Music hearing Joni things and Randy Newman songs … I thought I [had been] brought in to the band because they wanted more of a male lead vocal presence. I know they were having trouble with Judy [and] her pitch, but I didn't think the reason for bringing me in was to give it a stronger vocal presence, just to give it a more flexible vocal presence. I think they really liked the idea of having the male/female vocal thing going on; and up until that point I think Richard was singing harmonies to Judy. In those days, Richard was not the singer. Richard really developed his vocal technique through singing harmonies. Once I was in the band, we really had that three-part thing in place [and] he could very easily slot in.

Ian abandoned his excavations just in time. Thanks to Boyd, Fairport were in the process of securing a one-single, one-album licensing deal with Polydor. In fact, they were booked to record their debut 45 at Sound Techniques, Boyd's go-to studio, on August 10th, 1967, with in-house engineer John Wood twiddling the knobs.

Although Fairport and Wood was a musical marriage which would outlive a dozen incarnations, it did not start propitiously. Simon Nicol recollects that they 'recorded [the single] in four sections, then poor

John Wood had to snip it all together on an Ampex four-track vertical machine. [He] was less than enthusiastic about our prospects.'

It would also prove quite an introduction for the band's new vocalist, who had been invited to join them in the studio: 'I had no idea what they sounded like. They were working on "If I Had A Ribbon Bow". Very untypical. But I liked the people. I liked the vibe. We didn't really talk much about direction or repertoire. They were working on that song and I just jumped right in.'

Also there that day was Kingsley Abbott, no longer co-managing the band, but still taking a keen interest. He approached the new vocalist, who 'seemed most surprised that I had a copy of his previous band's single, "Summer Of Last Year" … Ian quietly watched and took everything in that day, and was soon in the band adding a new vocal direction and thus increasing the range of material possible.'

That 'range of material' would continue to be prescribed largely by Ashley, who struck Ian straightaway as 'very obviously a guiding light. Even on that first day it was apparent that Ashley and Joe Boyd, and Richard to a lesser extent, were the ones that were pushing the band's direction.'

Judy Dyble's account of the way new songs entered the Fairport set explicates the then-group dynamic: 'Ashley would find the songs, play them to the others and me, and if everyone liked them we would transform them to suit us. I just really sang the songs while the band played around me and over me.' At this stage, they were still relying on a little help from their friends:

Kingsley Abbott: The band almost always rehearsed without visitors in the evenings, but during the day Tyger and I would sometimes walk round Muswell Hill and talk about the future of the band. Even at this early stage he was well aware that Fairport could not exist for long as a covers band, no matter how good or interesting.

In an era when vocalists largely dominated the English pop groups (The Who excepted), Fairport remained the odd band out. When Matthews joined this close-knit clan, he found out no one thought to involve the singer/s in the decision-making. Years later, Dyble was still complaining, 'I don't think I was consulted about [Ian joining]. But that was how a lot of things happened in the band. I'd just be told do this, be there, sing that.' Adding Ian to the mix did little to change the dynamic:

Ian Matthews: The material was just presented to Judy and I … In that early band, the songs were presented to us singers in the keys that were best for the guitar player. A lot of the time it was too low, [but] unless it was painfully low there was no real room for negotiation. Mostly, Ashley was the one who decided what the songs were going to sound like … I was never one of the leaders of the band. I went along, for the most part, with what was suggested. It was Ashley, Richard and Simon who led the band [and] chose the material.

This meant some songs remained as mere tools to help build a burgeoning reputation rooted in Richard's instrumental prowess. It meant Ian's most pressing task on joining Fairport was to figure out what to do (and what not) when Fairport's founders played follow the leader from east to west:

Ian Matthews: Judy and I talked about [the improvisations] beforehand and I just took a lead from her. She would wander off to one side of the stage and sit. [So] I did the same. I sat and listened. I think I was just trying to get a handle on what the band was all about, and moments like that were great opportunities to actually be able to take it all in without having an active part in it; moving to the side of the stage and listening to them go through their instrumental changes, especially with 'East/West'. It just became a completely different beast eventually. [If] it started out as 'East/West', I don't know what it ended up as … I remember once Graham Nash asking Richard what it was called, and I swear Richard said it was called 'King Midas In Reverse'.

If Dyble usually sat such instrumental sections out – sedately knitting away at the side of the stage – she was more of a musician than Matthews, and would on occasion join in on autoharp, not necessarily audibly. As an early university show review stated, 'The autoharp and girl's voice were often hard to hear [because] the balance of their sound was a little top heavy at times.' Rendering the musical mix even more of a challenge, Simon Nicol would sometimes lay down his guitar and take up the fiddle, drawing from one *Disc* reviewer a comparison with 'nothing as much as John Handy's "Blues For A High-Strung Guitar".'

Simon Nicol: At the end of 'Jack O' Diamonds' onstage I'd pull faces and play 'avant garde' fiddle – as in avant garde a clue how to play it – and we'd play out that song with something called 'Spanish Lady', which we'd nicked from an old John Handy album.

The experience left enough of an impression for American guitarist Jerry Donahue to recall, some years later, seeing an early Fairport set which 'was real psychedelia. At one point Simon Nicol put his guitar down and picked up a fiddle. He started making some really screechy, far out sound effects.'

Those onstage were unfazed by the challenge of making it up as they were going along. As their first female singer suggested to Richie Unterberger, 'We did what we did when the moment seemed right, even if this meant buying an old violin from someone and sticking a pick-up on it because Martin said he'd had violin lessons once, and it might come in useful.' When it came time to go in the studio, though, they faced the same problem as Pink Floyd:

Joe Boyd: There was a feeling in the industry in general, and in Britain in particular … that long, extended tracks were kind of an indulgence [which] disqualified you from getting played on the radio. The Pink Floyd used to do a version of 'Arnold Layne' that went on for ten minutes. But when we recorded it, we did a three-minute version.

When the six-piece Fairport reassembled at Sound Techniques in November 1967 to record their debut long-player, less than six months after their official live debut, the process of selecting tracks forced the band to decide who they were – for now – and what they were not. This meant self-consciously jetissoning songs like 'Plastic Fantastic Lover' and 'Let's Get Together'.

Thankfully, the latter remained in their set long enough to feature on their first BBC radio session, recorded the same month they began vinyl quotation number one. That session, broadcast on December 10th, 1967, was the beginning of a long and rewarding association with 'Auntie', even if Tommy Vance insisted on introducing them as, youguessedit, 'England's answer to Jefferson Airplane'.

As if to prove this was transparently not the case, Thompson ripped off a lead break during 'One Sure Thing' more akin to Creedence Clearwater Revival. It was an impassioned assertion of independence from any and all acid-rock. The studio version, probably recorded a week or so earlier, pales alongside this BBC performance. In fact, the whole BBC experience proved altogether more enjoyable and representative of the band's intuitive brand than an album they were struggling to conceptualize:

Ashley Hutchings: We were more at ease [at the BBC] because we were playing live. We would simply go into a studio, sit around, all play live and then overdub. You would overdub vocals and a guitar solo perhaps. But certainly you started by all playing live. Unlike the first album, which was pieced together.

At that first Beeb session, the band refrained from playing any of their own songs, perhaps reflecting a lack of faith in their own embryonic efforts. Thompson, talking in 1970, was almost apologetic about his own juvenilia: 'I didn't start [writing] until we got a recording contract. It was a question of having to. It doesn't come naturally.' Ashley confirms Richard's assertion, 'We had to come up with our own material. It forced Richard and me to write.'

It was the guitarist who first expressed dissatisfaction with the status quo, by 'saying to Ashley after a gig that I was kind of embarrassed about the material we were doing, because we should have outgrown doing covers … It somehow wasn't good enough.'

Fairport were hardly in a position to discard the songs which had garnered them an audience at this point. Yet, as Simon says, 'A lot of stuff we were doing on stage wasn't worth recording, because [the original] was too well known.' Fortunately, not every live favourite bit the dust and what *was* captured at these sessions was a yearning to try things and a willingness to fail, rare even in those wacky-backy days:

Simon Nicol: [That first album] is madly chaotic – it's like the early life of the universe: all the elements are in there colliding madly, but nothing of significance has coalesced. Can you imagine if it [had been] Mickie Most and not Joe Boyd? We'd have been squeezed into some pre-formed mould and given an identity and a musical direction and you wouldn't have [had] that variety.

Richard Thompson calls the album 'extremely experimental', and as such rather hit and miss – 'a lot of it misfired. [Yet] being in the studio for the first time [was also] really exciting and a challenge.'

Not surprisingly, the two songs which worked best were already firm favourites with West End fans. In particular, 'Time Will Show The Wiser' – which, as Thompson later noted, 'we'd been playing since our early days [so it] sounds more played-in than a lot of the other tracks' – announced the album with a Fenderbender burst of guitar hinting at more potential than the rest of the collection could maintain.

Another highlight was 'Jack O' Diamonds'. Even circumscribed by an erroneous belief that 'long, extended tracks were kind of an indulgence', it was still a sprightly handling of Fairport's first Dylan cover on record. ('Lay Down Your Weary Tune', another firm favourite with the fans and already broadcast on *Top Gear*, was foolishly overlooked.)

If Thompson himself had no problem truncating 'Jack O' Diamonds', when it came time to decide who should take the lead vocal he baulked at the suggestion it should be him. A stubborn streak now emerged, taking band, producer and engineer by surprise. As with a more famous row at the 1970 *Full House* sessions, it was sparked by a profound dislike for his own vocals:

Kingsley Abbott: On stage leads were taken either by Judy, Judy and Ian combined, or by a vocally embryonic Richard. Whilst they all had their strengths, the blends were sometimes [diffuse]. Judy's voice was sweet, but lacking in strength. Ian had a great voice, but it did not always sit that well on some of the more forceful songs. Richard was still [not] confident at singing, yet to my taste produced the most effective rendition of 'Jack O' Diamonds'. This song and … who should sing the lead on the Sound Techniques version led to the only … row that I can ever recall … as to whether Ian or Richard should take it … Richard usually sung it on stage really well, but Ian's voice ended up as the one that was used [on the album].

If Thompson was the only person present who thought his vocals on 'Jack O' Diamonds' would not work, the singer who bore the brunt of vocal duties on their debut did not feel so appreciated. Richard's erstwhile girlfriend was equally wracked with doubt about the quality of her vocal performances, but no one sought to persuade her otherwise:

Judy Dyble: I felt I could have done better. My relationship with Richard had faded away, and I was a bit tangled emotionally. The whole studio thing was really overwhelming to me. I couldn't get the hang of the electronic side of it.

According to Ashley, the process proved daunting for every member of the collective, 'We were a bit in awe. It took blooming ages – we'd have fifteen takes [to get] one backing track down.' It would be some months before the album was completed to Boyd's satisfaction. But when it was finally mixed and mastered, it only served to affirm a growing suspicion that now needed to be addressed:

Simon Nicol: Fairport's sound was getting heavier. [So,] while Judy's voice was great for the early, more folky stuff, the sound of the band was starting to overwhelm her vocals. As the band's approach got more rocky, Judy no longer fitted in. She knew there were times when she was struggling … [and] her presence was beginning to dictate how we played.

Fortunately for Fairport, Ian seemed to be taking the new material in his stride, something a French TV appearance on *Bouton Rouge* in April 1968, confirmed. Sailing through Tim Buckley's 'Morning Glory' and Richard Fariña's 'Reno Nevada', he sounds primed to take on the majority of vocal duties.

In fact, that continental trip would prove Dyble's undoing. In a TV studio, or even a recording studio, one could balance the sound well enough for Judy to be heard. But in a Swiss casino, not a chance – as *Melody Maker*'s Chris Welch discovered when dispatched to report on Fairport's April 1968 debut at the Montreux Festival:

Fairport had to play to a largely unconcerned crowd of socialites in the Casino. They chattered noisily while the group tried to make piping recorders and pretty songs heard above the din. Later we sat in the lounge at Geneva Airport, drinking coffee and wondering what it was all about.

One obstacle to Dyble's removal might once have been persuading Richard – because as Boyd likes to observe, 'Richard's role in Fairport was similar to Syd's in Pink Floyd. He didn't say a great deal but everybody knew that what they were doing there was backing up Richard. So therefore what he thought really counted.'

When Thompson agreed that they could get along without Judy, her fate was sealed. Not that her ex-boyfriend was about to be the one who would break the bad news or let her down gently. It was Ashley, of course, who went to meet her at a nearby bus stop, well away from Fairport, to give her the chop:

Judy Dyble: It was really horrible. I felt like I was being thrown out by my bunch of friends, who didn't like me anymore. I did try to go and see them, but it was very strained, and so I stopped. That's primarily why I didn't want to stay in any bands after that – I didn't want them to throw me out again!

If it was a considerable shock to someone they had previously treated like a little sister, it was a jolt for the singer now charged with fronting the band alone. Ian admits, 'I was just trying to get a clear picture of where this band was going. I don't think I ever really did. I thought I knew the direction we were going in: a singer-songwriter band based on American West Coast influences – that's [certainly] the direction I was heading in – and then bang! Judy was gone.'

For one brief moment, the committee considered carrying on as the all-male band Ashley, Richard and Simon had originally conceived. But this foolhardy notion lasted barely a fortnight, during which time they began to encounter the kind of feedback which made them fear they had dropped a clanger:

Simon Nicol: We were going to be a boy band and then the penny dropped. [Judy] had made more of an impression [than we thought]

... People would go, 'Is the girl sick? What's happened to the girl?' ... We realised we'd established ourselves as a band with a female lead vocalist, and bowed to the inevitable.

With their manager-producer on one of his perennial jaunts to America attending to business, the Fairporters had to decide whether to carry on regardless, recall a shattered Judy or find a suitable replacement who could look the part, had the voice of an angel and could hold her own in the back of a van with a gang of middle-class Muswell hillbillies.

What they hadn't expected to find was a wee Wimbledon lass who not only brought all these qualities to bear, but also had the potty mouth of a Cockney labourer and a capacity to drink liquor by the jeroboam. Her name was not Adele, it was Sandy.

3. She Moved Through The Fairgrounds

New singer for the Fairport

FOR the past month local group the Fairport Convention have had a new girl singer after 19-year-old Judy Dyble, of Wood Green, left to start a group of her own.

Her name is Sandy Denny. She comes from Earls Court and, according to the group's manager, John Penhallow, has been on the folk song scene as a solo singer for about two years now.

It was Judy who sung on Fairport's last record, "If I had a ribbon bow," but Sandy has already been recording some tracks with the group, and will almost certainly be singing on their next single and probably the LP as well.

Local group, The Fairport Convention, with their new girl singer, Sandy Derry (centre).

Pete Brown leaps up, screams words down the mike, and they really begin.

Without stock arrangements, relying on their intuition to guide them, they never really know what they're going to play, Pete leaps about, screaming and cursing and cajoling the audience while the band plays beautifully.

The music is always wild and heavy even if it's quiet. Obviously, the Battered Ornaments must be one of the big names of '69.

Probably the most appreciated band—and the most musically adventurous—is Fairport Convention, who can play quiet folky songs like Leonard Cohen's "Suzanne" and out-and-out rock numbers like guitarist Richard Thompson's "Meet On the Ledge" with equal excitement and authority.

Their most surprising, and successful, number is the closing one—their version of the late Richard Farina's "Jack Of Diamonds" (once a hit for Lonnie Donegan), which starts as hard rock and ends with amplified violin sounding like nothing as much as jazzman John Handy's "Blues For A High-strung Guitar"—which is a complete, utter gas.

The college's apparently huge

There was a definite shift in energy in the band. I mean, [Sandy] was very different to Judy. Judy was very retiring and, as far as I remember, a teetotaller [whereas] Sandy was smoking, drinking, cussing. It became a different kind of band. She was very outgoing and loud, but very sensitive at the same time and caring about [other] people.

.—IAN MATTHEWS TO AUTHOR

Sandy was not shy. Her presence on the scene was unmistakeable as she immediately provided a contrast in manner and appearance to the others. She was confident and had a forceful personality, [though she] could exhibit uncertainties at times. She also liked to drink various spirits, which was not the norm in Fairport ranks.

—KINGLSEY ABBOTT, *FAIRPORT FOLIO*, 1997

The two qualities Sandy had that are most difficult to glean from listening to her music was her extraordinary clumsiness and her foul mouth ... She certainly wasn't somebody who got up there on stage and had her long hair hanging over her face and didn't look at the audience. That just wasn't Sandy at all.

—JOE BOYD TO AUTHOR

[Sandy was] this ungainly, uncomfortable, overweight, clumsy person who would be tripping over guitar leads, dropping her plectrum, getting introductions on stage mixed up, getting tongue-tied – laughing, joking, drinking. And then she would sing and ... she became a different person – she became an angel. It was like all the pounds dropped away off her body.

—ASHLEY HUTCHINGS TO PAM WINTERS

Fairport Convention in 1968 was a repository of shy, retiring North London intellectuals. Teaming up with Sandy was like a Mini colliding with a lorry-load of bricks. She taught us to express our musical passions, gave us a real voice at the sharp end of our creativity ... We played our hearts out with little thought of anything else.

—RICHARD THOMPSON

Alexandra Elene MacLean Denny, plain Sandy to her friends, was a twenty-nothing veteran of the folk scene – with two albums and an unreleased LP made with The Strawbs under her belt, and dotingly judgemental parents in Wimbledon to keep at arm's length – when asked to audition for the vacant female singer slot in Fairport Convention.

By the time she quit the same band, eighteen months later, they had collectively produced three genre-defining albums. Destined to spend the rest of her shudderingly short life trying to recapture that propitious spark in and out of bands, she would remain a restless soul, singing sad refrains all her days.

Throughout both her two stints in Fairport she would remain a handful, to use the idiom; and even more of a handful when she drank; something which her husband reminisced, happened quite often:

Trevor Lucas: Sandy drank, yes. She liked to drink. She liked the effect of alcohol, the feeling of being drunk – which is always dangerous ... But to understand her, you have to consider she'd had a very restrictive childhood, until that time when she actually broke away from home. And when she did get out, and saw there was a good time to be had out there, she was determined to have it ... And like most people who've been confined in that way, she was only more eager to live life to the full. [1989]

That determination 'to live life to the full', aligned to a voice steeped in the centuries, had already ensured she cut a swathe through the still-active British folk scene for the two years she spent playing the folk clubs, preceding her Fairport 'audition'. It was a heady time. For the first time in her life she felt part of a musical family which welcomed her into its non-judgemental bosom:

Sandy Denny: There was a folk club on virtually every corner. There was the Scots Hoose, the John Snow, there was Cousins ... You could go up there any night and you'd be sure of finding the little crowd like John Renbourn and Bert and Jackson Frank and Annie Briggs. It used to be a really fantastic little community. [1977]

But membership of this 'fantastic little community' also had its downside, especially for a diminutive lass touring the country all on her lonesome. Booked to play an incestuous club circuit by manager Sandy Glennon, she would often find the gig organizer was some local enthusiast, who would take an instant shine to the bonny lass. As Sandy herself recalled, 'Afterwards, you [could] always find a floor to crash on or someone will offer you a bed for the night – occasionally, of course, it was their bed, so you had to be careful.'

Sandy soon learnt how to handle herself. She also learnt to let some older Lotharios – like the libidinous *Melody Maker* folk correspondent, Karl Dallas, a man of considerable influence – down gently. Not that she was adverse to an offer of casual sex if the mood (and man) was right. After all, this *was* the high water of the Swinging Sixties.

When it came to something more enduring, she had already displayed a worrying penchant for tortured souls. Her first serious boyfriend was as troubled as they came. Jackson Frank was an American singer-songwriter who had arrived on these shores with a large insurance settlement in his pocket, early signs of mental illness, and a musical bond with another aspiring songwriter, Paul Simon. In 1965, Simon used his contacts at CBS to secure Frank a single-album deal for a set of original songs.

And what original songs! 'Blues Run The Game', 'You Never Wanted Me', 'My Name Is Carnival' were just three such gems Frank dredged from the deep recesses of his imploding psyche. With Simon its ostensible producer for the two days it took to complete, *Jackson C. Frank* gave its namesake a free pass to the entire London folk scene and struck the heart of young trainee nurse, Sandy.

Denny would prove one of Frank's most persistent cheerleaders on the scene, playing songs from that overpowering debut on a regular basis.[3] In fact, her adherence to Frank songs turned at least one powerful figure off when first he caught her act:

Joe Boyd: I think I'd seen her at Cousins, and had rather grudgingly acknowledged that she was pretty good, even though I didn't really approve [of the fact] she was singing something like 'Blues Run The Game'.

It wasn't until he got to know her better that Boyd discovered Sandy wrote songs. Nor was he alone in his ignorance. While Frank

---

[3] Her favourite songs were 'Blues Run The Game', 'Milk And Honey' and 'You Never Wanted Me', all of which she recorded in some form. Paul Simon, though he remembers Sandy fondly, does not recollect her attending the album sessions.

later claimed he 'saw right away that she had tremendous potential ... [and] got her to quit the nursing profession and stick to music full time', others insist she was cowed by Frank's talent, rarely performing her own songs in his presence:

Al Stewart: One day I met Sandy, who was a night nurse somewhere. I remember asking, 'Who are you?' 'I'm Jackson's girlfriend.' The first thing I ever heard her play was 'Ballad Of Hollis Brown'. I didn't know she could sing or play ... It transpired that Jackson wasn't that keen on his girlfriend playing ... He basically thought that was his job.

The tangled relationship with Frank – and the baby of his she chose to terminate – would haunt the lady for much of her life. But what scared her most was his visible mental disintegration, which sometimes manifested itself in lashing out, verbally *and* physically. It was a side of him few saw, but one Sandy did share with at least one female confidant, and fellow folkie, Linda Peters.

When an all-consuming writer's block drove Jackson to abandon England, Sandy swore to herself, Never again. Next time around, she would steer well clear of self-determining singer-songwriters. Instead, in summer 1967 she attached herself to someone who might actually further her career, another Faustian pact:

Joe Boyd: During that summer ... I got to know Sandy ... and we discussed at some length ... what she was gonna do with herself. She felt that she'd gotten as far as she could doing the circuit of folk clubs and she liked the idea of being in a group, but wasn't sure that The Strawbs were the right outfit for her.

Sandy had recently returned from a stint in Copenhagen, where she had recorded a demo/album with Dave Cousins and The Strawbs (previously the Strawberry Hill Boys), which Cousins considered good enough to tout around as a possible official debut. She later insisted, 'I wasn't really looking to join a group. But they asked me, and I thought, "Well, it's something to do." I mean, I wasn't looking forward or backwards.'

For all her protestations, Sandy was ambitious enough to look beyond the basement clubs and pubs of the folk scene. The more worldy Boyd sensed someone who 'was pretty pig-headed about what she wanted to do. There was definitely a frustration in her against the folk scene as such, and [she] had a certain contempt for a lot of the prejudices and schisms that pertained within it.'

After a few weeks becoming more than just good friends, Boyd finally got to hear the unexpected. One evening Sandy arrived at his place carrying an acetate of the 'album' she had cut with The Strawbs. Amid a great deal of innocuous folk-pop was a (solo version of a) song she wrote herself, 'Who Knows Where The Time Goes'.

Originally called 'Ballad Of Time', this remarkably mature meditation on the passage of time seemed to distill something she also intimated to Karl Dallas that September, 'I want songs that mean something to me. If they are folk songs, well, okay ... but there are other songs that have something to say in them.'

Yet Boyd is adamant that he played no part in the recruitment, a few months later, of this former girlfriend into Fairport. Indeed, by the time he heard about it, he was in America:

Joe Boyd: When I left to go to America with Incredible String Band, Judy and Ian were the lead singers ... I got a call. They had been having some talks with Sandy Denny about joining. I was a little alarmed, because I felt she was temperamentally very, very different from them, and I didn't know how it would work out ... I was afraid she might dominate the band. But I underestimated the stubbornness of Richard and Ashley.

Simon Nicol remembers things differently. He is convinced their decision to ask Sandy to audition was down to 'Joe's intervention ... He was brought into the discussion. [So] he certainly knew we were looking and [had] said, "Well, what about Sandy?" He knew her of old. But he had doubts. She did come from a different world.'

Perhaps the concerns Boyd expressed at the time served to convince him he played no part in her recruitment, unlikely as that seems. Others would prove positively eager to take credit. The over-friendly Karl Dallas always claimed to be 'partly responsible for Sandy quitting the solo folk circuit and joining the group', steering Sandy in the direction of Muswell Hill, after receiving a call saying, 'Hi, this is Fairport Convention ... We're looking for a girl singer.'

To which he replied, 'Only one name comes immediately to mind – Sandy Denny.'

Sandy herself, though, never accorded him the slightest credit, suggesting instead it was 'Heather Wood [who] said to me, there's this great group and they're looking for a girl singer. It was just something to do at the time. I phoned up the bloke who was in charge of them, and he said … come along and do an audition.' As a singer in The Young Tradition, Wood certainly straddled enough of the divide to know such people. She was also close enough to Sandy to have known she was already reaching for the folk escape hatch. Less than two months after joining Fairport, Sandy admitted:

> I always had it in my mind to join a group. I joined The Strawbs last year, but I wasn't really ready for it. But now I feel free to sing how I want to … Once you know what can be done with six people … the simplicity and naiveness of one voice and a guitar is rather insipid.

The audition, such as it was, was a 'show me yours first' affair, Sandy insisting that they play her a song before she played one of hers. Richard thinks, 'We played a Tim Buckley song, "The Hobo", Ian sang that, and Sandy sang something for us – I think it was "You Never Wanted Me".' Only question remained, which Simon articulated, 'Was she too shy or nervous to settle in?' As it turned out, that would be the least of their concerns.

If Sandy felt she 'wasn't looking forward or backwards', it was perhaps because, as she suggested in 1970, 'I didn't think anything particularly fascinating was going to happen in the group.' But Fairport's lead guitarist knew right away that they had found a rough diamond: 'That night or the next, she [had] a gig at the Fiesta, Fulham Road. I went down to hear her. She still sounded great.'

Belying the band's concerns, Sandy took to the rock-chick lifestyle like a duck unto water, and would not play 'the Cousins' again until Fairport were in enforced limbo during the summer of '69. Even being told to learn the songs Judy had sung on Fairport's first fab waxing – about to be released the first week in June – failed to faze her.

Nor did it take long for her to realise just how much more 'can be done with six people'. If her first duty was to record the A-side to a second single, 'Some Sweet Day', it was immediately apparent her and Matthews's vocals blended well together. Even on that unreleased 45, the sound they made seemed sprinkled with fairy dust.

The intended B-side had no need of their new singer, and may indeed have already been recorded. A version of 'Suzanne' – inappropriately included on the 2003 remaster of the eponymous debut album – was recorded with Ian taking the solo lead vocal, though Boyd seems to remember 'Sandy was sitting there in the control room'. One of Fairport's most popular performance pieces, it was recorded at this juncture in response to 'popular demand':[4]

Ashley Hutchings: 'Suzanne' was a stage favourite, and audiences would cheer the moment we announced it … The arrangement was all based on rhythm. Martin was going round the kit with beaters, and the two guitars, drums and bass were all doing different patterns. It was a masterpiece of rhythmic interplay.

For some mysterious reason the 'Some Sweet Day b/w Suzanne' single – reported as 'imminent' in the press at the time – was scrapped. Perhaps everyone felt it might muddy the waters, given that the band were still ostensibly promoting an album-length representation of a dead Fairport.

In fact, Sandy had already driven a nail firmly into that particular coffin the minute Fairport turned up at the BBC studios on May 28th, 1968, their new singer in tow. She promptly demolished Dyble's version of 'I Don't Know Where I Stand', one of Judy's finer vocals on her memorial album.

Nor was Sandy content with that demonstration of her peerless vocal control. After reprising 'Some Sweet Day', she put heart and soul into the song that got her the gig in the first place, Frank's 'You Never Wanted Me'. Concluding the *Top Gear* session – and announcing a new force in English rock – Sandy and Ian traded riddles and rhymes on one of tradition's murkiest mummer songs, 'Nottamun Town'. The core of the band left BBC studios that afternoon convinced they had found their keyholder:

---

[4] The tape-box for the single has two mix-downs of the A-side and one of 'Suzanne' but no actual recording information.

Richard Thompson: I remember Ashley saying after the first BBC session we did with Sandy – which was the first thing we recorded with her – 'At last that's something we can be proud of.' … We had actually waxed something that was worthwhile. Even though it was only BBC mono.

It also confirmed that they were still essentially a covers band, one that had yet to make the shift towards country, even though Ian, Ashley and probably Richard had recently experienced an epiphany of sorts as The Byrds – the band on whom the original Fairport had closely modelled their initial conceit – reinvented themselves as country-rock pioneers:

Ashley Hutchings: When I was a youngster, [I was] listening to bluegrass … [I'd already] seen Doc Watson and Clarence Ashley. And then The Byrds, by far and away my favourite group, went country music. I was witness to the unveiling of this at the Piper Club [in Rome]. I was sat in the packed audience in this club and heard this fantastic mixture of country and rock coming from the stage. Gram Parsons was there.

A further induction was needed. And so, on May 6th the trembling trio ran all the way to The Roundhouse to see The Byrds double the fare they'd delivered in Rome. This time Kingsley Abbott tagged along, and remembers, 'Ashley was gobsmacked [at] how they were presenting both the full-on electric folk-rock and this wonderful roots stuff that was stripped bare of the electrics.'

Fairport's captain left Chalk Farm a country-rock convert. He soon set about convincing the others to follow his lead, with Ian and Richard invoked as cheerleaders. Over the next few months the band would invoke the spirit of Nashville with shit-kickin' arrangements of the Everlys' 'Gone Gone Gone', Johnny Cash's 'I Still Miss Someone' and Ricky Nelson's 'Things You Gave Me':

Ashley Hutchings: The turnover of material at that period, 1968, was incredible. I mean, we would learn songs and [then] perform them on stage almost weekly. I have never been in a band since that has done that … There was a certain feeling with that band of experimentation and energy – [a sense of,] 'Why don't we do this song, why don't we do it now?' – and that's what we did … The songs that were being drawn in – the arrangements, everything – it was all happening very, very quickly.

For now, Sandy was content to just keep upright amid the ever-shifting sands in Fairport's sound. But it didn't take her long to find her feet and dig in. By July, she was telling a national music journalist, 'There's not much conflict inside the group. They're all easygoing. I'm the one who tends to get uptight. They watch me as an element on my own. They let me blow up, then cool down.'

Any probationary period was gone, gone, gone. From hereon, her mood swings would have to be endured for the collective good. On those occasions when she did blow up, the rest of the band stayed calm and carried on. As Ashley says, 'She had a temper. We didn't have tempers … We didn't know how to handle it, [so] we just had to let this hurricane blow out.' It proved just the right thing to do.

There was another factor which worked to calm Sandy and keep her onside: the impact on her of working with Thompson. If Richard was – or pretended to be – unaware of the effect he had on her, one insider spotted it straightaway:

Kingsley Abbott: She obviously was very keen on Richard initially. And [that] was crucial in that interlocking with the band. Boyd also remembers a tremendous release of energy in both Sandy and Richard. It was musical love at first sight. I think they had an incredibly stimulating effect on each other, and the group was … caught up in that process.

Still in awe of Richard's talent, Sandy gushed to a reporter seven months after joining, 'The group is based on the ideas of Richard. He's got so many ideas in his head and he's an incredible guitarist as well … To have the sympathy he has for music is quite amazing. I know he's influenced me an awful lot … I'm [even] singing ten times better now than I did a year ago, when I first joined the group, and it's all down to listening to Richard while I'm singing.' It was a mutually beneficial exchange, as he started reaching for sounds more commonly found on a folk record:

Richard Thompson: By about '68, I was definitely trying to do something different from other people. I didn't want to sound like other guitar players; I started listening to other instruments more than the guitar ... At that point in Fairport ... I had to start voicing it to sound more like a fiddle or a bagpipe, so I had to start going towards the sound of those instruments. [1985]

Sandy was hardly the only person on London's close-knit music scene to champion Thompson's playing. Underground journalists, to a man, were already caught in his musical thrall. An article in issue one of England's premier underground monthly, *ZigZag*, called him, 'the pilot of their conglomerate genius ... who steers the group with a film director's vision.' And when Fairport received an extended write-up in the UK's one mainstream musical monthly, *Beat Instrumental*, it focused primarily on Richard's contribution:

> The songs are generally ... jumping-off points for highly progressive journeys into driving improvisation ... On lead guitar is Richard Thompson, reckoned by many to be the best in the country ... With little apparent effort he will switch in a flash from rhythm chords to a searing, wholly integrated solo supported by ... Simon, [who] tends to keep in the background until he lets loose with his wild, eccentric, electric violin.

Those long instrumental interludes which still intersected 'Reno Nevada' and 'Jack O' Diamonds' gave Sandy the opportunity to grab another drink and talk with friends in the audience. When Ashley's mother caught a show, she remembers, 'Every time she finished a song, Sandy came over and sat with her mother and put her head on her shoulder', an early sign of the insecurities which would ultimately consume her. Thankfully, for now she retained an endearing gift for laughing at herself and life in general:

Ashley Hutchings: When Sandy came along, here was someone who not only was happy to introduce, but would crack jokes as well, or collapse laughing in the middle of an introduction. When everybody saw that this was okay ... everybody became more relaxed.

Sandy was particularly keen to impress Ashley and Richard, and so if country music was all right by them, it was all right by her. She had evidently been briefed as to the band's current direction before offering a July 1968 description of Fairport's music: 'The group does a mixture of country and western, folk adaptations, blues – but not like John Mayall.'

This was the very pick'n'mix the six-piece concocted for Sandy's second-ever Fairport gig, supporting John Mayall's Bluesbreakers at the Whittlesey Barn Dance on June 2nd, 1968, a tape of which survives. It includes a Thompson-led 'It Takes A Lot To Laugh, It Takes A Train To Cry', which does not sound at all 'like John Mayall', even though the very first time Dylan tried to record said song he had been backed by the Bluesbreakers.

'It Takes A Lot' was a particular favourite of Ian Matthews – who usually took the lead vocal, something he would do on a solo 1971 BBC version which captures Thompson burrowing deeper than even Bloomfield dared go.[5] Yet it was Sandy who was usually assigned the lead whenever Fairport made a foray into the blues. Even her oldest friend was surprised the first time she turned into a white Etta James:

Winnie Whittaker: I can remember seeing her performing with [Fairport] quite soon after she'd joined. She did a blues number and really belted it out and somebody within my hearing said to his mate, 'Blimey, I thought she was supposed to be a folksinger.'

Another friend from the folk clubs, Linda Peters, already knew Sandy 'had a singing voice like I'd never heard ... [but] I watched it grow. After she joined Fairport, her voice got very powerful [from] singing over the electric instruments.'

Unfortunately, the environment in these dinky clubs were sometimes a tad challenging. Simon Nicol recalls that it was sometimes 'a struggle [to be heard], particularly for the two of them [out front]. It was quite often crashing feedback, and splashy cymbals, [the] resonating bottom end of the bass and too much volume. But people loved it.'

---

[5] The track appears on the first volume of Matthews own archival series of CDs, *Orphans & Outcasts*.

An unfazed Sandy revelled in a collective camaraderie that was daily growing. For now, no one was thinking beyond the present: a gig, a BBC session, the next record. Something was happening, and no one was quite sure what it was:

Ashley Hutchings: There was a very special atmosphere in early Fairport that I have never recreated. I don't think you can ... We had this devil-may-care recklessness – money is the last thing on the agenda. That's why, sadly, in later life people fell out with Joe Boyd ... But at the time money didn't come into it ... With early Fairport, an audience were almost eavesdropping on what we were doing. There were absolutely no concessions to what an audience might like.

There *was* one occasion early on when money did come into it, which was when Boyd explained to Sandy that everyone in the band got by on twelve pound a week, a figure they had arrived at – Thompson explained – after Boyd asked, 'what was the absolute minimum we could live on. And so we thought £12 a week. [But] when Sandy joined the band it was too embarrassing for everybody to be on that little. Sandy couldn't possibly live on under £20 a week, so it went up to £20, because Sandy used to take cabs and drank champagne.'

Anyone lucky enough to witness the reinvigorated Fairport live knew that the lady was worth every penny. As Kingsley Abbott writes, 'There's no doubt that she took them to a higher level ... With Sandy, it was like somebody putting a super V8 engine in a Ford Anglia. Although it was on similar numbers [to previously], there was now that assuredness that a really strong lead singer gives a band.'

She was also bringing her own set of strong songs, starting with Frank's 'You Never Wanted Me'. Even as Sandy continued surfing the sounds of country, she was pushing the others towards a folkier repertoire – and they were pushing back. It was an all-too-brief era of gloriously inspirational give and take:

Simon Nicol: There was an instant melding of the two core repertoires. We had to create middle ground, but our repertoire was changing weekly anyway. We were all familiar with the language of folk music idiomatically, which is what she was bringing to the table.

At the same time, she was taking that same step towards what we were doing. She particularly loved standing in front of a rhythm section and having that force behind her. But above all, she worshipped Richard.

The feeling was mutual – platonic, but mutual. In the November 1968 issue of *Beat Instrumental*, Richard was already talking about what direction he saw the band moving in – and it was towards a folkier sound:

> We think of ourselves as a folk-based band. This is even more pronounced now that Sandy Denny is with us … She really knows what the folk tradition is all about, and the group as a whole are drawing from the English roots. The fact that we're electric doesn't make any difference.

Save for the BBC 'Nottamun Town', nothing to date backed up Richard's assertion, but Sandy's mere presence was providing the triple-tiered band hierarchy the excuse it needed to become more 'folk-based'. And they already knew some of this stuff. 'Nottamun Town', as Ashley said, was 'a song that we had known for some time, since before Fairport, both through Jean Ritchie and Shirley Collins'.

It was a direction their producer welcomed with open reels. As Boyd wrote in 1987 sleeve-notes, 'I [had] felt that Fairport should use their considerable talents in developing their own material and becoming as, well, English as possible.'

As such, there was little collective resistance backstage when one night Sandy began playing a song from her folk-club repertoire: that quasi-traditional Irish perennial, 'She Moved Through The Fair'. Soon enough, Fairport – its male singer excepted – began to busk along:

Ian Matthews: It was a rude awakening for me. We got to a show shortly after Sandy joined, and they were rehearsing in the dressing room … It was a trad song… and I was in shock because I couldn't see a place for myself in it. It wasn't a song that needed harmony and I wasn't playing anything. I think that was the moment I realised that I was going to have rethink this thing, and try and figure out where

I fitted into it … I realised that there was a shift going on, [even though] it was never talked about.

Their version of the folk-club standard was, as Ashley notes, 'basically Sandy's working [arrangement]. She had sung that in clubs by herself and when she sang it for us … we slotted in around her.' Sounds simple enough, but it actually required the band to mute its proclivity to rock out. Fortunately for Fairport, it devolved to Richard to set an example:

Ian Matthews: Richard's a unique kind of person. He could tie all that stuff [together], the traditional side of it and the contemporary side, and make it all sound like one thing, like it all belongs in the same place.

But where this era of Fairport really announced itself during the second half of 1968 was in the original song department. If the formative efforts at songwriting on their debut album had been hastily sidelined – with the exception of 'It's Alright Ma (It's Only Witchcraft)'[6] – Ashley continued to push for more original material from all parties.

At this stage, everyone was expected to pitch in because no one in Fairport could yet be considered prolific – certainly not Sandy, who later admitted she 'never found it easy to write. [But] Ashley made it clear he expected members of "his" band to write songs.' If her songs were still usually tailored to her 'folk' voice, Tyger now came up with one of Fairport's rockiest work-outs, the compelling 'Mr Lacey', all his own work:

Ian Matthews: Tyger wrote this song about this crazy professor who had three robots … Then Tyger said 'I'm bringing him down to play the solo'. And it turned out that the solo was the three robots walking about, making that noise.

It was the one real opportunity on Fairport's Island debut for Richard to cut loose, though once again he reserved the real McCoy

[6] Slade also recorded this song at an early BBC session, released on the 2-CD *Slade Live At The BBC*.

for a BBC version, broadcast on the Stuart Henry Show (and later released on *(guitar, vocal))*.

Perhaps surprisingly, Ian was allowed to deliver the main vocal, although by his own admission, 'On the more ballsy stuff I would never dream of presuming the lead – I would always let Sandy have it.' An alternate take, with Sandy on lead, emerged recently on another bloated Universal boxed-set, suggesting that Sandy was starting to want a crack at everything. This time she was voted down.

In concert, Sandy did get to do her 'Empress Of White Blues' thing on Muddy Waters's 'You're Gonna Need My Help Someday'. But although it was recorded twice for the BBC, it was probably too bluesy for Boyd to green light it for the album. He had his own prejudices to overcome on this front, having previously worked with the legendary bluesman.

Fortunately, at every turn, Richard Thompson – the one Fairport figure to whom Sandy readily deferred – was determined to steer the band in ever more productive directions. When Fairport's frontman penned a set of lyrics for an unexpected entry in the band's internal songwriting competition, it was to Richard he turned to make a song of it – a 'Book Song':

Ian Matthews: I saw myself being pushed a little into the background, because Sandy was a songwriter … [and] *What We Did On Our Holidays* is when Richard blossomed as a songwriter. It was like the race had started and Richard came out of the blocks. He came out with all these songs, and they weren't simple songs. They weren't straightforward songs. And I think that probably jolted me into action, realising the future lay in being a songwriter as much as a singer. There was no more 'just being a singer in a band'. At that point I started trying to write lyrics and came up with 'Book Song'. I took the lyric to Richard, 'cause we all lived in the house in Brent at that point, and he liked them enough to put the music to them. I realised that being lyricist was not going to be enough. I needed to learn to play an instrument. [So] I went to Richard and said, 'Will you show me some stuff?' He went with me and helped me choose a guitar … and that was the beginning of me becoming a songwriter.

For all her bluster, Sandy remained reluctant to show her own wares in the song department – and she certainly had some – preferring to keep all she'd stockpiled over the past two years under the nearest bushel. It meant there would be as many Ian Matthews and Ashley Hutchings compositions as Denny originals on Fairport's sophomoric album.

Yet it was Sandy's 'Fotheringay', a song penned pre-Fairport (to a tune from an even earlier original) that drew the most comment, perhaps because it was quite a statement. Inhabiting the same quasi-traditional domain Padraic Colum consciously emulated on 'She Moves Through The Fair', 'Fotheringay' is told from the vantage point of an imprisoned Mary, Queen of Scots, awaiting execution at the behest of her cousin, Elizabeth I. The song's sheer originality convinced Fairport to make it side one, track one. But it would be Sandy's last songwriting contribution, for now.

Perhaps she was still not sure her other originals suited the group sound. Even this self-penned song was essentially a solo performance, over which the band spun a pretty web of sound. Nor did 'Fotheringay' easily slot into the regular live set to vie with 'I'll Keep It With Mine', her other vocal tour de force on the resultant album.

For all its eclecticism, the second album was almost as unrepresentative of Fairport live as their Polydor debut. The likes of 'Morning Glory' (chosen for their BBC-TV debut in August 1968), 'Jack O' Diamonds', 'Suzanne' and 'Reno Nevada' all survived the switch in singers and remained popular in performance. While of the eight songs performed live on Dutch TV and the Royal Festival Hall's 'Festival of Contemporary Song' in September 1968, just two – Dylan's 'I'll Keep It With Mine' and Ashley's 'Mr Lacey' – feature on the album they were recording.

'Suzanne', the set-closer at the Festival Hall, would not be so memorialised. As for another outstanding Fairport reinterpretation of a Leonard Cohen song, 'Bird On A Wire', performed in Holland and at two BBC sessions that autumn, it did not even warrant a Sound Techniques runthrough. Someone was consciously steering the recorded band in a diametrically different direction to the one its audience delighted in live. That person was their producer-manager, delighted by the shape-shifting Sandy spawned:

Joe Boyd: When the band is recording a record that is basically Judy Dyble singing a Joni Mitchell, you may end up making a pleasant record but you're not actually going anywhere. But then when you have Sandy writing new songs, Richard writing new songs … stimulated and challenged by Sandy, the first steps in various directions became real interesting steps, rather than just [a] lack of direction.

Boyd had always felt there was more to come from the diffident Thompson. Second time around, he was proven right. The guitarist, rising to the challenge, raised the stakes on his fellow Fairporters – and put some songwriting distance between him and them – with three originals ('No Man's Land', 'Tale In Hard Time' and 'Meet On The Ledge') that collectively delineated a unique brand of doom and gloom.

Of these, just 'Meet On The Ledge' was transferred to the live set – a concession Thompson soon came to regret. He had unwittingly provided Fairport with its first anthem. Simon thinks the song was 'recorded at Morgan Studios, [because] there was some piece of equipment [that] John Wood wanted to get his hands on'. The result, Nicol recalls, didn't 'impress me mightily'. Nor did Richard 'think much of it'. And yet much to the songwriter's growing annoyance, 'It was asked for at every gig, along with Leonard Cohen's "Suzanne".'

Which is perhaps why 'Meet On The Ledge' was denied its obvious spot: the album-closer. The honour went instead to an odd piece of whimsy from Simon, the instrumental 'End Of A Holiday', his one song-credit on a collection where everyone pitched in. On 'Nottamun Town', another classic Fairport arrangement, he contributed, as he says, 'this little patch of double-stopping on the fiddle, [which] came out of nowhere and was never seen again'.

From now on, there would be a surfeit of quality material for the band to draw on. At a November 1968 BBC session, Sandy came up with another compositional curve-ball, 'Autopsy', too late for consideration but evidence that Ashley's insistence on a contribution – and Richard's shining example – encouraged her to raise her own game, 'We gave her Richard, not only as a guitarist but also as a benchmark to write against. It pushed her on.'

If the band continued to treat Sandy with kid gloves, her WASPish producer seemed determined to accord her star billing on an album the band had made collectively. Excluding many of the vehicles on which Ian's was the primary vocal – of which, Richard Fariña's 'Reno Nevada' was the most unforgivable omission – Boyd gave Sandy the only three solo vocals on *What We Did On Our Holidays*: 'Fotheringay', 'She Moved Through The Fair' and her sublime reinterpretation of 'I'll Keep It With Mine', a nightly showstopper.

Sandy's faultless renditions of this unreleased (by) Dylan song and the wholly unreleased Joni song 'Eastern Rain' retained the last tenuous link to the band's original conceit. From this point forward a finer balance between high-quality originals and cleverly arranged covers would become the norm. With that shift, Ian's chances of redressing any growing vocal imbalance was fatally curtailed.

The real memorial for his time in Fairport – and especially those unerring interpretations of American singer-songwriters – would be a collection of 1968 Fairport radio sessions Ashley compiled on cassette in 1975 for mail-order-only. The *Heyday* cassette consciously 'featured songs recorded by the *What We Did On Our Holidays* line-up only'. And, just like the live sets, it was three-quarters covers.

In the same six months Fairport spent making *What We Did...*, they effectively recorded an entirely different album in a handful of afternoons at the BBC. And it may well be more representative of this heyday. In fact, as a mea culpa, Boyd wrote in his notes to its (first) official release, 'I am now forced to admit it is hard to find an American band who can do these songs equal justice.'

Many would mourn the loss of this Fairport down the years. Yet theirs was a natural development – the same one which had changed the Stones, The Who and The Kinks from interpreters to creators. The key difference – aside from sales – was that those bands saw themselves as pop artists, whose hit singles charted their progress.

For Fairport, singles were an afterthought at best. The idea 'that you could have rock'n'roll with very strong lyrics' still served as the main spur on Thompson's creativity, while the 'Byrds numbers, Dylan numbers, and Joni Mitchell numbers' were increasingly viewed as a means to an end. That end, as far as RT was concerned, was to achieve 'a style of our own'.

All they had to do was make sure the six-piece presented a united front for long enough to get *What We Did...* into the shops and 'Meet

On The Ledge' into the charts – a seeming inevitability on the back of almost constant radioplay from ex-pirate radio DJs who had recently taken the licence payers' shilling.[7]

The optimism surrounding Fairport was such that even its most pessimistic contributor, and lead guitarist, sensed the surge of collective hope, which he shared with the nation's leading music monthly as a momentous year for English music drew to a close:

> We all know what we have to do, so there aren't any power struggles. The ideal situation is six separate individuals who evolve their own ideas which can be put back into the group and push it in the same direction. I think we're getting near that state now.

[7] Though 'Meet On The Ledge' would never chart, its inclusion on the budget Island sampler, *You Can All Join In*, ensured it reached every serious music fan in the country.

Fairport Convention, part of the English tradition

have known each other since their schooldays. They did have trouble finding a drummer; before Martin joined there was a succession, none of which fitted. Judy Dyble was once the singer alongside MacDonald, but she left the group over differences of musical outlook.

But now the band are in fine fettle. They have a contract with one of the best production companies, Witchseason—"We were playing at UFO one night when Joe Boyd saw us and decided to sign us up. I can't think why—we played amazingly badly! At that time there used to be a lot of peaks and depths. Sometimes we thought we were great, other times we were really terrible. We've evened out a lot now.

"As we're developing now, we're trying to be simple. It's easy to be very original and complex, but what people like Dylan are doing is to find a new way of saying everything in the simplest possible way. That's the most difficult thing, and that's what you have to aim for." This involves finding a new approach to the subject, and Richard seems to have found a very original field of guitar inspiration.

"I had a job making stained-glass windows. Before this I was a funky sort of Clapton follower, but in the studio they'd have the Third Programme on all the time. I became really interested in classical music, and much of my guitar style comes from people like Debussy—which is by no means as outlandish as it sounds. There are so many ideas which can be taken from classical music."

This attitude is typical of Fairport Convention. They are rapidly becoming known as true innovators, and most certainly not in any dry or academic way. Whatever the theories behind a style of music, it's the end product that gets through to the public. And that's exactly what the group are doing, on an ever-increasing scale.

R.S.

We play so many different kinds of music not because we want to cater for everybody, but because all of us in the group want to play their own kind of music.
—SANDY DENNY, *DISC AND MUSIC ECHO*, 8TH FEBRUARY 1969

The sheer eclecticism *What We Did On Our Holidays* displayed was not lost on reviewers. They were almost universally delighted by what they heard, *Disc*'s review going as far as to claim, 'The album is ... about the sort of holiday we all enjoyed when very young, those feelings of bittersweet nostalgia – and the songs themselves are near perfect.'

If *Beat Instrumental*'s John Ford had 'yet to recover from the superb "Meet On The Ledge"' he found 'all the other numbers are well chosen and flow in unity'. Meanwhile, a belated *Rolling Stone* review informed its ever-expanding readership, 'If you haven't heard this album, you're in for an incredible treat.' And a pithy four-line review in *Melody Maker* simply noted, 'Lots of contrast. The music ranges from hard rock to gentle folk music. Sandy Denny's vocals are outstanding.'

Yet a pattern was already in motion, one the band would not break until just two individuals who helped make this defining statement were left holding the fort. By the time *What We Did...* crossed most reviewers' desks, Fairport were a five-piece again – as they had been in the weeks leading up to their debut release. Already, Fairport line-ups never seemed to last long enough to promote product.

Their original impasse had been resolved by recruiting a more suitable vocal partner for Ian. But if that foil was supposed to pour oil on troubled waters, the lady was ill-equipped to do so. Having quickly handbagged her way into the band's heart and soul, Sandy made it clear from the very off that she was part of a decision-making process which previously devolved to Fairport's founders alone. Although he had been in the band twice as long, the other singer remained on the outside looking in:

Ian Matthews: I never had a close relationship with any of them. I always felt more like a hired hand than a member of the band – because they went so far back, those guys. I was always the 'new boy'. And [yet] when Sandy joined, she seemed to meld right in very quickly and was offering a lot of stuff … Before Sandy joined, most songs were learnt in a suitable key for soloing on. After she became part of it, keys on her songs were determined by her.

The symbolism of such a gesture was unmistakeable. By now, the others knew Sandy was not gifted with the skills of a diplomat. She was the daughter of a blunt Presbyterian mother, inclined to speak her mind and call it straight talking; as evidenced by her ill-advised comment to *Disc,* suggesting 'all of us in the group want to play their own kind of music'. She had laid bare internal tensions which had been brewing for some time, which only recently spilled over backstage as Sandy once again began interpreting an old folk song:

Ashley Hutchings: We were in a dressing room at Southampton University waiting to go on stage and Sandy was playing around in the dressing room and picked up the guitar and … sang 'A Sailor's Life' … We picked up our instruments and joined in. We had a little tuner amplifier in the dressing room and we busked along.

'A Sailor's Life' was another song Sandy 'had been singing … in the clubs for years. It was one of the first real folk songs I learned.' When the others immediately slotted in behind her like they had been playing together for years, a collective decision was made to play it that very night. One band member without a casting vote was less than enthralled:

Ian Matthews: I had no part in it. At that point I was playing congas on stage, [but] they said you can't play congas on a song like that … I really sensed that my time in the band was [becoming] limited. More of Sandy's material was coming in, and more of Richard's new material was coming in, too. Slowly the covers were being booted out. 'Reno [Nevada]' was one of the few that remained.

The very idea that six such different personalities could all 'play their own kind of music' and stay in sweet harmony was always a sixties pipedream. Add to the mix a producer-manager who knew how to get his way, and it was clear to even the most blinkered band member something, or someone, would have to give.

Ian Matthews: I never enjoyed going into that traditional stuff. I didn't have any traditional roots, unlike Sandy, and I didn't have any traditional sense, unlike Richard or Ashley ... There was really no place for me in a band playing that type of music.

Even Thompson – who shared a flat with Matthews – recalled a growing 'feeling that Ian was in the wrong band. There was already a divergence of style.' Also, a divergence of interests. Between gigs and sessions, Ian kept himself to himself. Even Muswell Hill resident Kingsley Abbott saw more of the others, 'Ian was from a different strata with different reference points and he didn't mix socially with the others. At their communal Brent flat, he'd barely come into the other rooms.'

Richard also generally kept himself to himself, but when he did get involved everyone listened. He was indispensable. Ian was not. If Richard was never likely to pull the trigger on his flatmate, Ashley, no longer sharing the communal home, could afford to be more detached. Once the bassist was committed to the new direction, it was curtains for his fellow country-rock fan:

Ashley Hutchings: We were starting to get more folky ... and it was quite obvious to me – if it wasn't to the others – that in order to move in the direction that we were favouring ... Ian would have to leave.

However, this time around everyone knew something was at stake and so the band rumbled on, bathing in the good vibes surrounding their latest album. They even began work on its successor, initially intending to produce more of the same. Two albums a year remained their plan and the industry norm.

Arriving for a January 16th, 1969 session, Ian found he had been allocated lead on a song from a most unexpected quarter – Simon's pen. 'Shattering Live Experience' would not be most folks' idea of an apposite title for this unexpectedly tender love ballad, with its wistful lazy-sunday-afternoon feel. It was an odd choice all round, given that even its author 'never cared for it'. But if he expected the producer to exercise his own veto, he should have known better:

Simon Nicol: Joe would very often sit through an eight-hour session, his size twelve feet on the console, absolutely engrossed in the baseball section of the *New York Herald Tribune* … Joe was there as a kind of monitor. If we were barking up the wrong tree, he'd say, 'Well, I think if you maybe, uh…' – [and] then he'd go back to the baseball.

For now, 'Shattering Live Experience' would remain 'under consideration'. At least it reflected the gradual shift toward original material, and Boyd generally let the band be its own song-sifter, rarely questioning the material they recorded unless something overtly American was in danger of inclusion. He had faith in the Fairport collective process: 'Simon and Richard had very clear ideas about things … We were all in it together, and everybody had their say. [It was] a very egalitarian atmosphere.'

Nonetheless, for some months Boyd had been subtly steering the band away from the singer-songwriter material which for two and a half years had been their very *raison d'être*. Boyd's music biz contacts had already afforded him access to Joni Mitchell's publishing demos, resulting in Fairport recording no less than five of her early efforts – including 'Both Sides Now' – but even her work was jettisoned.

Only Dylan remained immune to this shift in direction-home. Indeed, three of his songs would be recorded for the third Fairport album, two of them as yet unreleased by the man himself, one of which came from Dylan's so-called Witmark demos, songs copyrighted between 1962 and 1964 by the publisher that Dylan's manager, Albert Grossman, had found for him (for a substantial kickback on every single song from both Dylan *and* Witmark).

This particular gem was 'Percy's Song', a moving nine-minute panegyric to a (probably apocryphal) friend unjustly sentenced to ninety-nine years for being 'at the wheel' when a car crashed and four people died. Though Fairport had not yet experienced such a cataclysm, the song was perfectly suited to Sandy, being based as it was on a traditional tune she surely knew, 'The Wind And The Rain'.

For now, the band agreed to use Ian's natural gift for harmonising on this faux traditional ballad. But the session did nothing to allay the ex-Pyramid singer's conviction that the clock on his and Sandy's joint reign was ticking down; nor his suspicion that their producer-manager had a particular place in mind for which no map was forthcoming:

Ian Matthews: I think Joe really engineered a lot of the direction… up until *Liege & Lief*, which [is] when Ashley had a clear picture of where the band was going. I think Joe was making suggestions about what was possible and what his vision of the band was, and Ashley and Richard liked what they heard… [They] liked the thought of being an electric folk-based band … The next thing I remember is them having been in the studio without telling me – to do '[A] Sailor's Life'.

Being excluded from such a momentous recording was bad enough. But to make matters worse, they had drafted in traditional fiddle player Dave Swarbrick to play on the track, adding another notch of electric folk to the equation.

A famously animated fiddler, Swarbrick had begun playing with the Ian Campbell Folk Group in 1960 at the tender age of nineteen, going on to form a highly successful folk duo with Martin Carthy in 1965.

Although already an old friend and drinking buddy of Sandy, it was Boyd who made the call to 'Swarb', having already worked together. In the early months of 1967, before he stumbled on the unconventional Fairport, Boyd produced *Rags, Reels & Airs*, a largely instrumental album designed to show off the more instrumental side of Swarb, Martin Carthy and Diz Disley.

Boyd therefore knew Swarb could be a fast worker. What he did not know was that Carthy and Swarb were in the midst of producing *Prince Heathen*, one of folk's first concept-albums, which would give Fairport the fillip to produce a more electrified take on modern folk later in the year. By then, Swarb would have renounced acoustic folk and plugged in, leaving Carthy to return to the folk clubs of Britain.

But in February 1969, when Boyd's call came through, it was Carthy who knew all about Fairport and Swarb who was in the dark. In fact, it was Carthy who encouraged the curmudgeon to do the session, from which Swarb returned a folk-rock convert, informing a bemused Carthy, 'No reflection on you, but I finished the session and felt that I wanted to play with that guitarist for the rest of my life.'

Although Carthy kept his feelings to himself at the time, the way that Swarbrick treated performing music as a battle of wills had begun to wear on him, obliging him to note that 'Dave had this thing about speed, which I found very difficult when we were working together, not because I couldn't keep up, but because those jigs weren't really meant to be played so fast'.

But Fairport had yet to see that side of Swarb. His playing on 'A Sailor's Life' is both restrained and compelling; just what the producer had ordered. He probably arrived expecting to overdub his part to a pre-recorded track. Instead, he found they had booked a more spacious studio specifically to cut this track live. According to Simon, they went to Olympic Studios, home of many a Stones session, because it 'was eight-track ... [and] we needed space to play. There wasn't a really viable isolation booth at Sound Techniques and we wanted to do a live vocal for "A Sailor's Life". There wasn't any other way.'

The 'flexibility of eight-track' (as opposed to the usual four) gave the producer a couple of spare tracks, should he still wish to overdub. Indeed, the unexpected emergence of an alternate version of 'A Sailor's Life' – *sans* Swarb – on the 1993 Thompson boxed-set *Watching The Dark*, suggests Boyd initially covered his bases by getting Fairport to run down a version akin to the one they had been playing live.[8]

Although no one there that day seems to remember recording this 'other' take, Simon suspects it was probably 'done within hours of the other one. [Yet] it's got so many differences and they're not just points of detail. The whole atmosphere, the whole pace of it, is just different.' It also provides – along with the *Bouton Rouge* 'Reno Nevada' – an insight into what that early Fairport sounded like when taking off on such flights of fancy:

Joe Boyd: There was definitely a feeling at the time that recordings were supposed to be compact; that if you'd heard a track with Richard

[8] A lo-fi audience recording of such a version, from Southampton Univ. in February, does exist.

playing five choruses as a solo, you would then go into the studio
and record him compressing the best ideas from those five choruses
into one ... [But] the artistic success of *Unhalfbricking* is [because] it
did start to occupy the space on record that the group occupied live.

Ashley is keen to connect the dots, 'If you logically trace it, ["A
Sailor's Life"] can be traced to those [earlier improvisations]. It was
surprisingly easy for us to fall into'; even if the very existence of this
Swarb-less 'Sailor's Life' rather explodes the version of events he gave
to Patrick Humphries:

Ashley Hutchings: We said to Joe and John Wood, 'We've got
something for you ... We'd like to do it live and just go for it.' [Joe]
said okay. We played a little bit of it for sound, and [to let] Swarbrick
busk along, 'cause he'd not heard it, and then we set the tape going
and we did it. [1980]

Perhaps what Ashley recalled as them playing 'a little bit of [the
song] for sound' was a fully-fledged, fiddle-less 'Sailor's Life'. If so,
Swarb wisely refrained from busking along until he had a handle on
the band dynamic. But once he *was* added to the mix, the results were
distinctly different from everything the band had done to date, in
the studio or live, confirming to Boyd that there was no longer any
room for Matthews. Having worked with both Carthy and Shirley
Collins, he also knew there was a chasm between earlier folkier
explorations and *this*!:

Joe Boyd: 'Nottamun Town' is a lovely track, but it accepts certain
clichés – it's not fundamentally different in approach from the Ian
Campbell Folk Group and The Spinners ... It smacks of the early
sixties. Whereas 'A Sailor's Life' is completely new.

Ashley was even more enthused, 'The energy and the adrenalin
were incredible. And when we had finished we knew what we had
done, and went into the booth to hear it. Joe and John were almost
speechless ... We *knew* that we had done something different. We
knew that here was a path open to us which hadn't previously been
clear.' Once again, Ashley was looking forward by looking back. In

fact, Richard has a clear recollection of the bandleader 'talking about a whole album of trad[itional] material as early as *Unhalfbricking*. Once Swarb came in ... he [immediately] saw the possibilities.'

Richard was less certain, wondering if this road might be 'thick beset wi' thorns and briars'. As he later stated, 'When we started playing "A Sailor's Life" we really didn't know where the end was.' But at least their nominal guide was a singer thoroughly versed in traditional vérités.

Even before Ian's pre-ordained departure, Sandy was assuming the helm. On February 4th, 1969, Sandy sang two of her own songs solo and took lead on 'You're Gonna Need My Help' (harmonising with Ian on the choruses), hardly counter-balanced by Ian rendering 'Shattering Live Experience'.[9] Less than a fortnight later, the axe finally fell, wielded by Witchseason's wunderkind:

Joe Boyd: They knew that I had expressed misgivings. But one of the things I realised very early on was ... for young kids who had no experience, they had a really good gyroscope. I didn't really have to bully them, or push them ... [Ian had] some good moments, but I never felt his style of singing was the right thing for Fairport. One of his best performances was probably 'Percy's Song', [but] even that just sounds not quite right to me... Whereas Sandy just was so convincing from the beginning. It just worked.

Ian Matthews: Joe Boyd told me they wanted me to leave the band ... We all used to meet up at Witchseason [before a gig] ... I got there at the given time, to find I was the only one there. And Joe took me into his office and said, ... 'The band wants you to leave.' ... [Then] they all slowly arrived, we got in the van to go to the gig and Ashley, who was sitting in front, turned around and said, 'Where are you going?'

At the time, Ian was hurt more than he let on. In a couple of interviews given the following January, he tried to imply it was a mutual decision, 'They wanted me to leave, and I wanted to leave,' and a largely inevitable one, once 'Fairport were doing two or three country numbers ... really only to please me.'

[9] A five-song BBC session a month earlier had included 'Bird On A Wire', 'Jack O' Diamonds', 'I Still Miss Someone' and 'Meet On The Ledge', all songs that relied on Ian.

His own description of his last few shows with the band – 'It ended up with Fairport at one end of the stage and [me] at the other' – suggests he should have seen it coming. It would take a tragic turn of events to mend the fence separating Matthews from the Muswell Hill gang. By this time he would have his own album to make and could claim, slightly disingenuously, he had a clear idea of what sound he wanted to make, and the Fairport sound was not it:

For some time I had been wanting to leave [Fairport] because I really like country music and wanted to form a biggish band with a steel guitarist. – *Melody Maker,* January 31st, 1970.

Basically I left because I was tired of doing things that other people wanted me to do musically, and I just wanted to do what I wanted to do, instead of following other people's ideas. – *Music Now,* February 14th, 1970.

Boyd fully admits he never expected Matthews to carve out a solo career which on a commercial level, at least, would reach higher than any other Fairporter. In fact, he was convinced 'he'd end back in Scunthorpe ... So I take my hat off to him and I acknowledge there was something [there] I didn't see or hear. But the truth of the matter is that his time with Fairport for me was treading water for the group.'

Precious few psychedelic scenesters would have described the preternatural blend of instruments and voices on *Heyday* and *What We Did On Our Holidays* as the sound of 'treading water'.

Thankfully, Ian was smart enough not to ask Joe to help him find another berth. Instead, he ended up 'talking to John Peel about what he thought I should do; whether he thought there was any value in me carrying on'. The influential DJ made Ian realise just how much of an impression he had made in the year and a half he had been a Fairporter and how much goodwill he had left in the bank.

Meanwhile, Boyd continued pushing Fairport gently down the stream of tradition while the Fairporters continued to place their trust in ol' Joe, never once querying how the revenue from constant gigging and extensive radioplay was being 'divvied' up:

Ashley Hutchings: I don't think we asked [Joe] a single question about money in the first year or two we worked together, which later in life was a cause of great disruption and bad feeling. We didn't care. We were young and we were making the music we wanted, and as long as we got our ten pounds a week [sic] we were quite happy … [As far as we were concerned,] he looked after us … and let us get on with the music.

Even as their music was becoming ever more Anglicized, though, Fairport's predominant influence remained the music of The Band and their erstwhile frontman, Bob Dylan, whose post-accident work was infused with the aroma of Americana. Their seeming-authenticity and anti-psychedelic agenda inspired Fairport to emulate them in spirit, just not in sound.

The almost simultaneous experience of hearing – on import – The Band's debut album and the fourteen 'acetate' songs the same outfit had recorded with Dylan in their Big Pink basement in the months preceding *Music From Big Pink*, had a profound and enduring effect:

Richard Thompson: [*Music From*] *Big Pink* came as a bit of a shock back in 1968 … The psychedelic bands were playing bits of blues and country, but The Band seemed to have real authority … It was the perfect antidote to hippie excess, and … those boys certainly knew how to play on the back of the beat.

'Million Dollar Bash' was one Big Pink song Fairport now requisitioned, leaving the other thirteen basement-tape tracks well alone – for now. Instead, they tackled Dylan's 'Dear Landlord', perhaps hoping to have a success similar to the one their old friend Jimi had enjoyed with another *John Wesley Harding* track in need of amplification, 'All Along The Watchtower'. But the vocal was never completed to Sandy's satisfaction and the track went unreleased until 2003 – when it merely served to confirm that Sandy's guide vocals were a match for most singers' finished vocals.

As to why it was never finished, perhaps she feared it might result in the removal of one of her own songs. Now Fairport's sole empress of the stage, Sandy had become emboldened to offer more of her own songs. Previously, as Ashley suggests, 'It was a matter of persuading her to show us things she'd written. I suspect a lot of wonderful Sandy songs remain[ed] unplayed and unheard because she was just too nervous to let them out into the world.'

Now she demoed two songs for the band to consider, 'Autopsy' and 'Now And Then', the latter being sidelined when the Fairporter who could do no wrong in her eyes got to hear a song she had given to Judy Collins, 'She said something about it being a song I wouldn't have heard. Then she picked up her guitar.' 'Who Knows Where The Time Goes' gorgeously filled another gap Ian's departure had left in the live set.

But she still needed to be handled with great care. After February, there was no longer any fallback if this walking, talking, cussing mass of contradictions didn't feel like performing. Richard Lewis, who saw numerous shows in this period, witnessed both Sandys, 'Sometimes she was sure that she could do everything, [and] sometimes she didn't believe in herself [at all].' Even close friends were baffled by the overt neediness of someone so obviously gifted:

Joe Boyd: She was this incredibly bright, incredibly talented person who was very insecure as a female about how she looked and … she responded to this insecurity through drink, through promiscuity, through aggressiveness.

Thankfully, glimpses of Sandy's darker side remained few and far between in these months. Throughout a productive spring of communal songmaking, she fully played her part as the five-piece continued evolving at a bewildering pace. Their efforts were now concentrated on completing that difficult third album and reinforcing their growing reputation as a rock act to catch:

Ashley Hutchings: The accident … tends to overshadow the fact that lots of organic changes were happening anyway – American songs disappearing from the repertoire; Richard emerging as a songwriter; Sandy bringing in her own thing. Then you had … the first experiments with full-blown folk-rock, in the shape of 'A Sailor's Life'.

It wasn't only Fairport's music that was growing up. Two of its key members had both immersed themselves in serious relationships, with demonstrable consequences for their creativity. One would lead to marriage, the other to the terrible beauty of irredeemable loss.

Richard had become smitten by an American clothes designer, Jeannie Franklyn. To the older, more worldly Boyd, she seemed a type which suited Richard down to the ground, being 'a rather assertive, American West Coast girl. In some way, there's a part of Richard that's always been more comfortable with that sort of person, somebody who leaves him alone to do music while she deals with the rest of the world.'

Jeannie's willingness to travel with Richard might once have made her a perceptible threat to Sandy, who had previously enjoyed the status of single rock chick in the Fairport van. However, Sandy was too loved up to notice, having recently become attached by the metaphorical hip to a strapping Aussie folksinger called Trevor Lucas.

Lucas had emigrated to London in the early sixties, where he quickly developed a well-deserved reputation as a ladies man and somewhat less of a reputation as a singer and frontman. Fortunately for Sandy, Trevor's own band Eclection – which had the ever-versatile Gerry Conway keeping the beat – shared many a bill with Fairport. It allowed the couple to spend a great deal of time together. Her own band weren't the only ones to suspect she might well end up collaborating with Trevor musically.

Gerry Conway: Trevor adored Sandy. He did place her on a special pedestal; he regarded her talent as enormous ... They loved each other greatly and certainly at the beginning that would be a natural thing, to want to be together.

The bond tightened irrevocably after Eclection provided support for Fairport at Birmingham's fabled Mothers Club (where Floyd later recorded the live part of *Ummagumma*), on May 12th, 1969. Sandy decided to travel back to London with Trevor and co., rather than the band she now fronted, a decision that may well have saved her life. As it is, the events that night claimed both Fairport drummer Martin Lamble and Richard's girlfriend, Jeannie. Those who survived would be permanently scarred:

Simon Nicol: [It was] just another gig. Mothers. Harvey [Bramham] had been unwell all day and I got a migraine so the gig was do-able, but I was completely wiped out afterwards. I lay down at the back of the van and went to sleep. I would've taken over the wheel from [our roadie] Harvey part way, which was what I did in those days, but I was out cold and only woke up as the vehicle was crashing about. I was the only thing left in the van – all the equipment had gone out the back doors. It was a fifteen-seat, six-wheel transit and we'd taken two rows of seats out to put in the equipment. All the windows were smashed out, doors were hanging off. Everyone else exited the vehicle, I just rattled around inside it. So I was unscathed except for bruises and some glass [cuts]. We ended up at the foot of an embankment, which I scrambled up. Got to the top and started waving [for help]. It was the early hours of the morning. I remember it growing light while we were waiting [for the ambulance]. We were taken to Stanmore. I remember seeing Martin on a trolley, and him being very pale, and them giving up hope of ever bringing him back. Hutch looked absolutely terrible – his cheekbone was smashed. Harvey was the worst injured – he'd gone out through a window and was up against a tree. He was charged afterwards, because in the detritus there was a small 35mm film canister with some dope in it. So they made a big hoo-hah about that. I didn't know [Jeannie] very well at the time, even though Richard, Ian and I were flat-sharing ... I was kept in overnight, they only had to pick one piece of windscreen out of my arm. Richard was just looking at the wall ... We deliberately decided, in casualty, when we knew Martin was dead, that we weren't going to decide what to do [now].

The M1 crash, near Scratchwood Services, had been the result of a dog-tired and possibly doped-up Bramham falling asleep at the wheel and a panicked Thompson attempting, in mid-swerve, to correct the van. Whether he over-corrected, and it was this action which sent the van careering off the motorway, no one will ever know. But it may explain the lingering guilt Richard carried for many years.

Yet it was Bramham – having broken a number of limbs in the smash – who was charged with driving without due care and attention, which would result in a six month jail sentence, later reduced on appeal. The drug charge quietly went away, even though it was a proclivity which had worried others previously:

Ashley Hutchings: Harvey was right for the job, a modern road manager. Hardened, wizened, a character who you'd want on your side if there was trouble. But I never really bonded with him. He indulged in drugs and he and Sandy used to slope off together.

Of the surviving band members, Ashley came off worst. In fact, he looked so bad that when a concerned Ian Matthews came to see his friends, he fainted at the sight – not that the patient was in any state to notice:

Ashley Hutchings: I was out of it … I was in hospital some time. I was the last member of the band to come out of hospital … My face has got over it. I don't know if the rest of me has … I didn't fly for another ten years. I hated getting into cars for years. To this day, I get in the back of a car by choice.

The man who had brought Martin Lamble to Fairport Convention's debut gig was another concerned visitor. He was understandably distraught at the loss of his friend, who had already been pronounced dead by the time he reached the hospital:

Kingsley Abbott: Everyone was in the same small ward, with Richard and Tyger near the door on the right, and Harvey over in the far left hand corner. Tyger's face was bad, but he was making the best of things to some degree. Richard was very quiet. Harvey spoke a little, but appeared mentally detached.

If the crash hit everyone hard, those who had invested body and soul in the band from the outset were hit hardest. For Ashley, Simon and Richard, the death of Martin was deeply personal and never wholly forgotten. For Richard that sense of grief was compounded by the brutal curtailing of a relationship which had barely begun to bloom, the outcome of which could never be known. As he told Brian Hinton thirty years later, 'I lost something and I don't think I'll ever get it back.'

Even when he finally found love (and marriage) with a singer sympathetic to all he had gone through, this was one experience he never talked about – not even five years later, when he resurrected the first song he wrote that summer that addressed feelings of loss and remorse, 'Never Again':

Richard Thompson: I hadn't known [Jeannie] that long, just a few weeks. But it was devastating for me. I felt in a state of shock for a couple of years – it was very hard to put stuff into perspective … I couldn't get an overall picture … It was like being on a drug – seeing the world piecemeal.

Simon Nicol: We did not know … whether we would play music together again. Everyone had their own decision to make, and most were not in a state to do so … It's probably true to say that no one who was in that crash has ever fully recovered from it.

When Sandy – consumed with classic survivor's guilt for not being in the van that night – Richard and Simon were offered the opportunity to visit the West Coast of America and meet the people from the label who had just signed them to an exclusive American contract, they hoped the trip might help the healing begin, or at the very least distract them from the all-consuming grief they were feeling. But it was too much, too soon. When they found themselves in the Bay Area for a few days, hanging out with Richard Fariña's widow, it all bubbled to the surface:

Mimi Fariña: They were definitely in shock and needing to mourn. There was, as I recall, a tremendous amount of silence in our driving around, and it may have been that [which] made me want to sing and communicate some other way. We sang Irish ballads, because it [was] something that I knew from my history … [they] could connect with.

The irony of the situation cannot have been lost on Mimi, who three years earlier had lost the love of her life the very evening of the launch-party for his debut novel, *Been Down So Long It Looks Like Up To Me*. Richard Fariña was killed while riding pillion on a motorcycle, just twenty-nine years old and on the verge of great things. Her loss was so great she never found anyone who could replace her one true love. In that sense, those tragic Irish ballads contained even more resonance for her than they did for a ghost-ridden Richard.

The difference was that Thompson was already processing his grief into art, knowing he would have an audience in America he could now reach. Fairport's new US label, A&M, were delighted to welcome the band into the fold, and seemed genuinely excited at the prospect of releasing their albums, old and new. For Simon, the most business-like of the trio, it all seemed most encouraging:

Simon Nicol: I remember the people we met seemed a lot like [the people at Island]. By the standards of Californian businessmen they were remarkably laidback. And [they] loved the music – really, really loved the music.

Not only were plans afoot to rush-release *What We Did On Our Holidays* – confusingly called simply *Fairport Convention* – but A&M were equally keen to put out the album which had become something of an epitaph for Martin Lamble.

That album was *Unhalfbricking*. Even as the band itself recuperated from the tragedy, and the future of Fairport itself hung in the balance, Joe Boyd – who was once again in America when his charges had needed him most – set about mixing and sequencing an album from the sessions to date. The ever-pragmatic Boyd surmises, 'If they had decided not to [carry on], Island would ... still have released the album, and that would have been the end of things.' Whether this was really the intended successor to *What We Did On Our Holidays* was no longer here nor there:

Ashley Hutchings: We had recorded these tracks – not for a specific album. We were just recording tracks at that stage. Then we had the crash ... and while we were in hospital Joe said the tracks are great, I'm going to put them out on a record ... So things were happening. But we didn't really have a working band.

And yet they now faced the prospect of a hit record, an unexpected by-product of positive publicity and multiple benefit concerts. Island had released the least interesting track from *Unhalfbricking* as the latest Fairport 45, 'Si Tu Dois Partir' – a record Thompson duly informed *Rolling Stone*, 'we certainly didn't want ... released as a single ... We actually tried to have it stopped.'

Instead, they found themselves in the charts, marketed as a novelty act. It meant an appearance on *Top of the Pops*, having assiduously avoided all the ways in which an underground band could be rebranded as a pop act for two years. That appearance did not require an actual band performance, being wholly mimed, but it made at least one Fairporter profoundly queasy. Fortunately, he was never asked back:

Richard Thompson: Narrow brushes with popular music we didn't really like, to tell you the truth. When we went on *Top of the Pops*, it was very uncomfortable. We didn't feel particularly glamorous. We didn't enjoy the machinations and the photography and the way the music was presented. It was all very shallow.

With Ashley still out of commission, it fell to an embarrassed Simon Nicol to inform the vibrant UK weekly music press that the world of Pop was not for them, telling the indefatigable Keith Altham: 'It is true to say that we have not deliberately sought publicity – especially in the early days. We saw the very thin veneer and manner in which other groups were being pre-fabricated and felt it was more worthwhile to create interest in our group by performance and word of mouth.'

After much soul-searching, they had at least agreed to continue the band, but only after wiping the slate clean. In other words, they would start again. The next album would sound nothing like the music Fairport – or its psychedelic peers – had made in the two years since *Sgt Pepper*. Fairport Convention were now officially a heritage rock band:

Simon Nicol: At present we are working on our next album which is concerned with English traditional songs ... Most of those ballads are far better than the songs being written now, and it is a field which has been largely neglected and one in which we can experiment as a group. We are also preparing for our return to live appearances ... [but] we will perform very few of the numbers that we have done previously. [1969]

5. Open The Door, Chamberlayne

"It's music such as we've sung in the islands since before Chaucer, to tell our histories, to preserve our tongue, to reveal our hearts. This is our liege and leif."

SANDY DENNY
vocals
SIMON NICOL
guitar
RICHARD THOMPSON
guitar

TYGER HUTCHINGS
bass
DAVE SWARBRICK
electric fiddle
DAVE MATTICKS
drums

Presented in this seventieth year of the twentieth century by A&M Records and Tapes.

We feel as if we have a commitment to English music, that we have to follow the direction we're taking, to carry it over to people. Practically no one here who listens to music is aware of the British heritage ... In America, their folk music is a straight line ... White music went over and became bluegrass and so on, then it got electrified and it's in Nashville now. Over here, ... folk music is still a guy with a finger in his ear and a pint in his hand at a folk club.

—RICHARD THOMPSON, *ROLLING STONE*, 8TH NOVEMBER 1969

In truth, English folk music was in the rudest health it had enjoyed since the days of Cecil Sharp, Percy Grainger and Ralph Vaughan-Williams. The sixties had been good to the folk-club circuit, which had flourished in tandem with a groundswell of talented young folk artists like Anne Briggs, Martin Carthy, Bert Jansch and Davey Graham plus bands like The Young Tradition and Pentangle.

Dylan's fabled folk-rock apostasy in 1966 had provided a further spur both to the perceptive and the penitent, creating a climate where a full-blown folk/rock fusion could contain a commercial component. At the height of prog, with English whimsy and bludgeoning blues-rock the strangest of bedfellows, independent label-makers encouraged even greater experimentation. In short, Anything Went.

So when Fairport's four survivors convened at Trevor Lucas's SW6 flat in early July 1969, three of them sporting a California tan, there was general agreement that if the band was to continue, it should make distinctly English music. At the back of all three founders' minds was a single thought, 'What would Martin have wanted us to do?' Thompson even remembers asking himself, 'If this is the price for Martin dying, is this what we really want to do for a living?'

Joe Boyd: After the crash, the thought that they could ... become a truly British rock band gave them purpose in keeping the band together ... It dignified the decision to carry on.

Ashley Hutchings: We made a decision that we were going to reform … [but] instead of going back to the old material and teaching it to new people, we [decided to] take the opportunity of maybe exploring this new path that 'A Sailor's Life' had opened up for us.

It was duly agreed that the band would follow its leader's preferred path. And as Simon says, 'Ashley['s] idea [was] for a project album to give the band an impetus – to rebuild the band with a purpose so there'd be an energy for the new line-up.'

Although there were no dissenting voices, there *was* one dissenting mind, someone not known for keeping her feelings in check. But this was a new Sandy, scarred by the experience, plagued by self-doubt and terrified at the thought of being separated from the man whose flat they were now using for band meetings. Even her friend, designer Bambi Ballard, had begun to notice, 'There was [a] neediness in Sandy which was far greater than any she ever had before. She had avoided being in the crash thanks to Trevor, and … it created a dependency on him.'

For Sandy, the decision to carry on was inextricably bound up with residual guilt, fear of abandonment and, just as importantly, a burgeoning creativity she feared could be stifled by the band's collective decision-making process. If her own songs had started to flow, she kept her feelings to herself that night in Parsons Green. But she confided in her coterie of female friends, one of whom – the subject of her latest song – argued against jumping ship:

Sandy Denny: I was actually very slow coming to a final decision. I don't think to this day anyone in Fairport realises how late in the day I made my final decision … I think it was Anne Briggs who finally said I ought to carry on. She said, 'You have to. Those boys need you. They'd be lost without you.'

The transition from *Unhalfbricking* – released in July – to the folk-rock project *Liege & Lief* was so seemingly seamless, few realise the see-saw of emotions the whole band rode before the slate was finally wiped clean. In the process, they acquired a new drummer, a new fiddle player steeped in the stuff they were looking to do, and a newly needy singer torn in several conflicting directions.

At the point when they auditioned drummers, they were still playing some of their previous songs. As Ashley recalls, 'What got [Dave] Mattacks the gig was "Autopsy" because we said that we are going to play this tune that's got three different time signatures ... 4/4, 3/4 and 5/4 ... He seamlessly played the thing with us.'

If 'DM' – Mattacks's moniker now – had known what he was signing up for, he may well have said no thanks. As it turned out, he would not only be obliged to change time signature in mid-song, but would have to learn to keep up with a furious fiddler playing 90mph, sometimes down a dead-end street:

Simon Nicol: Mattacks invent[ed] an entirely new way of drumming – all that cross-beat stuff. Folk-rock drumming – he made it [happen]! And at the same time, Richard is learning to play single-note runs using techniques he had yet to develop on the electric guitar ... [But] it was drummer first ... [At] the point where we said, 'Well, if it's going to be a folk album, why don't we get a folk instrument,' the obvious person was Swarb.

Initially, Swarbrick seems to have persuaded Fairport that his current playing partner, Martin Carthy, should join too, thus restoring the band's male/female vocal duopoly. According to Boyd, 'Carthy agreed for a minute and then backed out.' Perhaps it was the thought of playing electric folk with Swarbrick that convinced the folk stalwart to pass:

Martin Carthy: When we stopped playing together it took me about three months to get my songs slowed down to their proper speed, which may have been one reason I didn't respond too enthusiastically when he asked if I'd like to do some things with Fairport. [1971]

Even Swarbrick's inclusion was possibly temporary, 'They had the idea of doing a concept album of English traditional stuff, and they got me in to do [that].' But the fulminating fiddler later admitted he 'was enthralled by the sound, by Richard, by drums, by the whole electric thing', and he soon set about making himself indispensable to the others, drawing on his vast knowledge of traditional music. Unexpectedly, he also showed an aptitude for adapting traditional-sounding tunes to the original songs the Fairport collective initially continued writing.

Swarbrick welcomed the opportunity to broaden his musical boundaries, telling the music papers at the time, 'A lot of the music we'll be doing will be [only] very loosely folk. It will be based on traditional music, [but] not just an electric copy.' He was of a mind that the fourth Fairport album should not merely amplify the folk music he had been playing for a decade, but reinvent it.

In fact, two press pronouncements regarding the Fairport project which appeared in August issues of *Melody Maker* and *NME* suggested no shortage of ambition in Fairport's ranks, even if the album they described bears only a passing resemblance to the one they would end up recording a couple of months later:

> Tyger is writing some interesting stuff in the style of the English ballads, but without the … archaic imagery which makes them unsingable in an electric context. And Sandy's still writing, better than ever, and so is Richard. – *Simon Nicol.*

> The next album is going to be completely different. It will be based around traditional British folk music to which we may put new words if necessary. And we've got a great violin player in Dave Swarbrick to help us … We're not making it pop, though. In fact, it will be almost straight: only electric. What does it sound like? Heavy traditional music. – *Sandy Denny.*

Actually, the only song on *Liege & Lief* based 'around traditional British folk music, to which [they] put new words', would be Thompson's 'Farewell, Farewell', which he put to 'Willie o Winsbury' (Child Ballad 100) – not, on the face of it, a natural fit but a remarkably effective one.

He was biding a fatalistic farewell to the carefree days of innocent youth by appropriating one of the most romantic ballads in the English language, mainly because, as he later admitted, back 'then I found it very hard to say I love you'.

'Farewell, Farewell' was one of just two Thompson 'originals' on the finished album, both side-closers. In each instance, Thompson provided only the words. His other original, 'Crazy Man Michael', was also originally set to a traditional tune, one which would have fit its aura of despair perfectly – 'The Bonnie House Of Airlie'. But then, Thompson recalls, 'Swarb came up with a really good tune. So we tried to shoehorn it into Swarb's tune, and that's the one we used on the record.'

There would be a fair bit of 'shoehorning' when it came to Swarb's melodic ideas, something Thompson later came to resent. For now, though, he seemed grateful for the collaboration, having never written anything so painfully biographical before.

'Crazy Man Michael' was Thompson's most cogent attempt-in-song to make sense of the shattering near-death experience. He began it while recuperating, 'I was in hospital and I just began writing a story, just enjoying the process of putting down a story. It emerged that it was about stuff close to home.' When he played it to the others, Swarbrick 'thought the words were great, but that the tune weakened it', and offered one of his own.

Unfortunately for the band's unsteady equilibrium, having eased themselves into becoming a band who contributed their own songs, elements of Fairport began to revert to type, a change reflected in the acquisition of multiple copies of the recent Dover edition of Francis J. Child's five-volume *The English And Scottish Popular Ballads* (1882-98):

Simon Nicol: [There were] three sets of Child books in the house at any time … Hutch had planned it all out … [while] Richard found it great fun to play in unison with Swarb.

As the album became more and more about mining unalloyed tradition, it increasingly fell to Swarb to take the musical reins. Each one of the five traditional songs on *Liege & Lief* contains some significant musical contribution from Swarbrick, a process which the others embraced, at least in the short-term:

Dave Swarbrick: The bending was being done the other way – [though] Sandy knew a lot of it, and had a big input on it. [For] 'Matty Groves', Sandy and I put the words together from Child.[10] We put it to an American tune, and I supplied the instrumental tune at the

[10] An almost exact lyrical cross-over with Jeannie Robertson's recorded version, well-known in British folk circles, casts doubt on this statement.

end. 'Tam Lin' I wrote the tune for, based on a slip jig. I just took out all the beats till I got sevenths. 'Reynardine' I'd done with Bert [Lloyd]. 'The Deserter' I'd done with Luke Kelly.

Simon Nicol: It all worked out really well as a project. The way it came together, I don't really remember a single hiccup – not even with the difficult songs like 'Tam Lin', [which was] really elaborate; but Swarb didn't just provide the jigs and reels. His input into 'Tam Lin' and the other traditional arrangements on that record was hugely significant, though a lot of it was parallelled by his contemporary work on the *Prince Heathen* record ... He was directly importing ideas, but it didn't matter. He was at the heart of those arrangements.

Even Ashley acknowledges the key role the new recruit played in song selection once the album became overloaded with direct tradition: 'Swarbrick very often would suggest [the] songs – more than [the] other people [in the band].'

When it came time to pick a tune for 'Matty Groves' – the central ballast on *Liege & Lief* side one – Swarb already knew one, having 'heard Hedy West play a banjo thing to [it]'. 'Twas ever the folk process. And it was also Swarb who provided the audio cue for when Thompson goes off into the Strat-o-sphere at the end of 'Matty Groves'. This Fairportesque free-form extemporisation was to the tune of another Child ballad, 'The Famous Flower Of Serving Men' (Child 106), one Swarbrick had learnt from Carthy (who would not record it until 1972).

At the extensive rehearsals, though, it was not all weal and woe, Child and Sharp. As Ashley fondly recalls, 'We didn't just play traditional songs ... I remember doing "We Need A Whole Lot More Of Jesus (And A Lot Less Rock'n'Roll)" – which Swarb and Richard [really] liked. We did some *Basement Tapes* stuff, too. I think we were attuned to the spirit of Big Pink.'

In fact, the very songs which had served as personal therapy for Dylan in the months after he came off his motorcycle (or not) in July 1966 served as a constant backdrop to Fairport's own healing process, with 'Down In The Flood' and 'Open The Door Homer' both worked up. The influence of The Band remained doubly embedded, even though a direct link to West Saugerties now seems counter-intuitive:

Ashley Hutchings: We loved The Band. We loved The Byrds. But we thought we've got to stop copying what they've done – use them as a model, but use our own tradition – our roots, not their roots … It was like a religious experience.

Joe Boyd: There were many reasons they turned to British traditional music for this new project, but … [one] decisive factor was *Music From Big Pink* … They couldn't stop playing the LP. They loved it, but they were shocked. It was so deeply American, so fully immersed in the roots of that culture that Fairport felt the goalposts may have been moved too far away … But perhaps they could accomplish something parallel to *Big Pink* if they set their minds to it.

Once again, Fairport Convention found itself with too many ideas for one album to contain. When the current 'project' record began to spiral inwards, and a decision to concentrate on 'heavy traditional music' was forced on the collective, it meant *atque vale* to three Dylan songs, the saddest of which was 'Ballad Of Easy Rider', a song he co-wrote with Roger McGuinn. A Richard Fariña song they'd set to the tune of traditional Irish tearjerker 'My Lagan Love', and the famous Scottish Child ballad 'Sir Patrick Spens' also got lost in the shuffle.[11]

When Thompson later painted a picture of Fairport, 'around the time of *Liege & Lief*, [having] a pan-British Isles repertoire – playing Celtic music, English music, Scottish, Irish, Northumbrian, South of England … all mixed in,' he was talking about the live 'repertoire'. Just as *What We Did On Our Holidays* hid part of what made said era their heyday, so the album that came out at year's end was more rigidly defined.

Something happened when the band drew up baroque folk-rock arrangements of the two eight-minute epics which bestride *Liege*

---

[11] 'Bonny Black Hare', to which they returned the following year, had already been recorded twice by Swarbrick. Indeed, the residue from such a rich vein of material was still being mined in 1977, when the band returned to one song worked up that heady summer but never recorded ('Adieu Adieu'). They would also record 'Open The Door Homer' in 1970 and 'Down In The Flood' in 1974, all songs first fired in the furnace at Farley Chamberlayne.

& Lief, 'Tam Lin' and 'Matty Groves'.[12] As the focus intensified, the artifact became ever more Scottish in its remit and ever more traditional in spirit – reflecting a perhaps-unconscious bias from a key creative component:

Richard Thompson: I grew up with a lot of Scottish dance music because my family is Scottish. But you don't connect it as being hip when you're a kid … It was only later on, when I was seventeen or eighteen, that I really wanted to hear the sounds of Scottish … music and incorporate those … drones. [1985]

Richard Thompson: The best songs for me are the Scottish ballads. They're very distilled. They've very terse and [use] powerful language. In one verse you get tremendous economy and tremendous imagery. That's the finest form of songwriting … My father was Scottish and loved music. I grew up … reading border ballads or the songs of Rabbie Burns, hearing Scottish folk songs.

The folk tradition was also deeply ingrained in Sandy's family's DNA. Her grandmother had been a fiercely patriotic MacLean and a traditional singer, whose family name and singing gift her namesake had inherited. But unlike her ancestor, Sandy was an anti-purist at heart. The idea that she had a personal responsibility to 'authenticate' what she sang in folk clubs had always left a bad taste:

Gina Glazer: We'd sometimes go up to … Cecil Sharp House to look up songs … I don't think she was too thrilled at the research … She couldn't understand how I'd get so excited about that oral tradition [thing].

Karl Dallas: She'd stand up [in the early days] and she'd say, 'I'm gonna sing so and so and I don't know what it's about and I can't remember who wrote it.' … I said, 'Look you can't do that. You must research your material.' … Well, I never even saw her try and do that. It just wasn't Sandy.

---

[12] Though the English might like to claim the latter, the earliest text from oral tradition dates from circa 1630 and is Scottish in origin, from the Panmure manuscript.

As soon as the whiff of scholarly rigour began to permeate the new 'project', Sandy began to champ at the bit. All too soon the worry that this band she had met halfway might adopt electrifying tradition as a long-term musical direction began to eat away at her.

Initially, though, she was more than happy to lend her 'expertise' to the communal process, helping to shape and prune the two Scottish ballads – as she had 'A Sailor's Life'.

In the case of 'Tam Lin', what was left rather reflected Sandy's laissez-faire approach to source-material. Rather than using the three copies in Child to paste together a patchwork quilt direct from tradition, she took as her source Sir Arthur Quiller-Couch's *The Oxford Book of English Verse*, trimming down his 'original' 52 verses to a mere twenty-one. But the discredited Quiller-Couch had 'frankensteined' his text from the already bastardized versions Robert Burns and Walter Scott concocted for their 'drawing room' collections.

Sandy cared not a jot for such niceties. She just wanted to tell a dramatic story the way she knew best. Unfortunately, collapsing a song that began life as a metrical romance into an eight-minute folk-rock work-out was never going to bring out the drama of this ancient midsummer dream. The fantastical story of how Tam Lin (aka True Thomas) was kidnapped by fairies and rescued by a maiden he had previously raped was all but lost in the Chamberlayne blender.

The 'Tam Lin' on *Liege & Lief* exemplifies everything good *and* bad about the liberties the survivors from *Unhalfbricking* perpetrated on tradition. Even the tune, another one of Swarb's, began life as a 'slip jig'. The results bore little resemblance to the a cappella versions Anne Briggs and Marion Stewart had recorded a couple of years earlier.

Indeed, 'Tam Lin', with its swooping bass and instrumental flourishes, seemed almost *designed* to rub Fairport's rock'n'reel approach in the faces of staunch folkies. Swarb and Sandy, survivors of the folk wars, were revelling in the rumpus they were intent on causing. Swarb's tune and arrangement was also in accord with the vision spokesman Simon laid out in a September *Disc and Music Echo*, shortly before the entire six-piece decamped to Hampshire:

> Folk is still a form of music that's very alive, but has always been restricted. The songs exist in libraries and in folk clubs, but the people who .... listen, never advance. It's always been the same

people singing the same songs to the same audience. A kind of innate snobbery, if you like. I'm sure the kids are completely unaware of their heritage. I count myself among the kids, because I was reared on music that was always a distillation of American influences. We feel the time is right to bring this music out – getting away from the blues scale and introducing something completely new … You can call it an English electric sound, but the emphasis can switch around a lot, now that we can use Dave to the full.

Unfortunately for Fairport's long-term equilibrium, the longer the band recuperated at Farley Chamberlayne, the more it began to split into camps. As far as Sandy was concerned, *Liege & Lief* was never intended to define her *or* the band with whom she had become synonymous. But the more the others bonded with this music they were collectively discovering, the more she began to withdraw from the debate:

Ashley Hutchings: I thought [*Liege & Lief*] was going to be the future. And it was, for a while. But Sandy, understandably, wanted to do her own songs and baulked at the idea.

The original idea of a retreat – where the band could rest, rehearse and recuperate, in that order – was a practical one. As Simon had explained to *Disc*, 'It's almost impossible for us to work things out in London … We all live so far apart that by the time we've got together, we're too exhausted to think.'

That music flowed was a welcome bonus. The most immediate benefit was internal, certainly as far as Simon is concerned, 'The music we made there was very therapeutic. It's amazing that it produced an album that today everyone regards as a classic; at the time, what it did for our well-being as individuals was beyond measure.' The most damaged individual, physically and psychologically, was the one who seems to have gained the most:

Ashley Hutchings: That was a very happy period for me … There's a whole sequence of photos [which] tell the story. There's the room, big room, us sitting around playing, working on this material, Sandy holding a mike. Everything was set up, and in the morning we'd go down, ... played a bit, ... then we went out in the garden [and played football] and we came back refreshed, and did it again ... I went to London once or twice to find some songs, but generally speaking we just enjoyed being here, away from all the hurly burly – literally recuperating. We were ... getting our equilibrium back ... It was all exciting ... It wasn't just taking English country songs and rocking them up full stop. We're taking medieval ballads and tackling them [head on], trying to make a fifteen-verse ballad interesting ... It was hard work to actually put those things into the rock format, but it was [also] exhilarating and magical.

Once again, though, the pace of change proved a little bewildering to elements within the band and its fan base, especially when Witchseason proceeded pell-mell with a grand unveiling of this new, 'improved' Fairport at the Royal Festival Hall on September 24th, 1969 – just four months after the crash that threatened to end the band for good.

The crowning moment for Boyd's family of artists, sharing the Festival Hall bill would be John and Beverley Martyn and a shy, retiring Cambridge undergraduate by the name of Nick Drake. But all the focus was on Fairport, who had decided the repertoire they had been rehearsing at Farley was *all* they were going to play, making a *tabula rasa* of a band with three albums to their name.

Hindsight does now prompt Simon to admit, 'We were missing a trick or two ... [But] we did make a statement: That was then. This is now.' If they'd been looking to lose friends and alienate people, they could hardly have planned it better:

Ashley Hutchings: Absolutely nothing carried over ... Not the traditional songs we were already playing. Not the songs we had played live, but not recorded. Not even the original songs people in the band had written.

Richard Thompson: Spare a thought for the chap who'd bought a ticket because he'd seen us on *Top of the Pops* ... There we were, with songs about shape-shifting Scotsmen and numerous cuckolds, ... playing the medieval equivalent of 'Flying Saucers Rock'n'Roll'.

And yet, such was the residual goodwill towards Fairport, the entrancing nature of the new material and the spirit of musical bonhomie onstage that the show was both a triumph and a gauntlet thrown down to the already teetering folk revival. Indeed, Tony Wilson, dispatched to write the all-important *Melody Maker* review, wondered aloud, 'It will be interesting to see if there is any reflection of their approach to traditional music from the folk scene in the near future.'

The immediate reaction from one of the doyens of that establishment, A.L. Lloyd, was unreservedly enthusiastic. He walked up to Sandy Denny, an old friend, after the show to say, 'That's the most exciting thing I've heard in years.' For Sandy, who had turned her back on the folk circuit, such praise was music to her ears.

Nerves had been jangling throughout the hour-long set. She duly admitted, 'We didn't know how everyone was going to take it … We were really holding our breath when we went on.' Deprecating introductions like the one to 'Farewell, Farewell' – 'The next song is a traditional tune, but we've put modern words to it, [i.e.] we've ruined it!' – was one way she found of coping with the challenge.

The live unveiling of yet another new Fairport had been a great success. A more national preview of the new sound – a five-song *Top Gear* session recorded the day before the Festival Hall – was broadcast just three days later, allowing fans from all over Albion to hear their take on 'Tam Lin', 'Reynardine' and 'Sir Patrick Spens' for the first time, as well as an impromptu send-up of 'The Lady Is A Tramp'.

As per previous BBC outings, the (rest of the) session was very much a dry run for the next album. Sadly, they included none of the songs they were about to sideline yet featured at the Festival Hall and/or the 'dress' rehearsal at Plymouth's Van Dike club four nights earlier, to which Richard Lewis (and his notebook) travelled with the band. Not their interpretation of 'Have You Had A Talk With Jesus', with Swarb on vocals and Sandy on violin; nor an uproarious 'We Need A Whole Lot More Of Jesus'; nor their folk-rock revampings of two Big Pink demos: 'Down In The Flood' and 'Open The Door Homer'.

When they finally reconvened at Sound Techniques on October 16th, to begin work on the fourth album, Fairport had pruned the set of such vestiges of humour and levity. This was serious stuff.

And there was barely a break in the sombre mood as they set about capturing the eleven songs they chose to memorialise across six sessions during a fortnight without gigs.

Such was the band's determination to capture the project in all its ambient glory they forsook the road entirely. They would only resume spreading the word the night after they finished 'Sir Patrick Spens' – the one Child ballad which would go unused – on November 1st.

The following night they made an emotional return to a venue they had last played when Martin Lamble was the drummer, Eclection were a support act and Fairport were an English rock band with a largely American repertoire – Mothers, Birmingham. This time Sandy travelled back with the band from the gig. For her, it could not have been more traumatic if she had been in the van six months earlier:

Sandy Denny: The emotion of the [Mothers] gig, the long cold journey back, wanting to be with Trevor. I told them I didn't want to do the American tour we had planned. I didn't even want to go to Denmark, where we were booked to play on the radio.

The band were not quite sure what to make of Sandy's after-gig outburst: whether to take it at face-value or as the late-night concerns of a troubled traveller that would vanish with the dawn. But Simon can remember her spending 'most of the journey in tears, about how she loved the band and how she loved Trevor so much; how she didn't want to go to America. She didn't even want to go to Denmark for a week.'

A day after completing an album that threatened to put the band in its anointed place, the top rung of English rock, Sandy was reaching for the parachute cord. She no longer wished to pay heed to Anne Briggs's fateful warning, 'Those boys need you. They'd be lost without you.' She *needed* to be with Trevor:

Sandy Denny: I left Fairport for personal reasons really. My personal life was involved. I didn't like going away for long tours and in January we were due to go to the States for two months. I knew I just couldn't cope with that. [1970]

Simon Nicol: Everyone was really happy about [*Liege & Lief*]. But Sandy's private life was going in a conflicting direction. It was looking like the diary was filling up ... At the same time, she and Trevor had got partnered up and she was very dependent on him for a large part of what she wanted from life ... Sandy was a person who needed a lot of affection and attention. She could see the band getting bigger, and we were talking about going to the States for the first time. She got the horrors about being separated from Trevor for a long period.

Joe Boyd: They had been dealing with an hysterical female a lot or an 'in love' female who didn't want to hang. [It] was not the same Sandy from a year earlier who'd been much more 'one of the lads', who was ready to go out drinking, was ready to just hang in the back of the van.

The time Sandy had spent apart from Trevor visiting the States with Simon and Richard in July had proven excruciating for everyone in Fairport and at Witchseason. Boyd, for one, 'started noticing her becoming more depressed, and more down, and more worried, and more concerned, in a somewhat self-destructive way. She became *very* afraid of flying and travelling.'

At some point, Sandy agreed to sit down with Boyd and talk about her future, but by then it was too late. She was not about to change her mind. In his opinion, she had become just as terrified of the prospect of success as she was of losing the love of her life:

Joe Boyd: I clearly remember discussions with Sandy about the [probable] success of the record ... [Sandy leaving] was a combination of two things: the group being pushed now in this direction of 'folk music', rather than composed songs by Sandy and Richard; and the international nature of the success, which would require airplane flights and long absences from London ... [These] combined to push her out.

To jump or not to jump, that was the question. And it was not entirely personal. Both manager and boyfriend now began to realise how unhappy she had become at the prospect of continuing the great folk-rock experiment:

Joe Boyd: She had been involved with the traditional [scene] for a long time, but always rather ambivalently … [So there] was a [certain] kind of amusement at Ashley's fanaticism, which he came to very late in life. He was discovering things with the zeal of a new convert that she had been familiar with … for years … He would come back from Cecil Sharp House and say, 'I have just discovered this magnificent song.' And she would say, 'Well, I was singing that when I was 17!' … Having gotten into the rock'n'roll business, to suddenly discover that she was now in the same band as someone who was fast becoming almost as doctrinaire about British traditional music as all those people she had fled folk from … was a little traumatic for her.

Trevor Lucas: She didn't want to sing Farmer Jones songs for the rest of her life. She had a huge amount of her own material, was writing very prolifically, and she could see that the band had less and less place for that … It was far cooler, in those days, to say you'd 'found' a song from a traditional source than to actually write something. History lent virtually anything some kind of credibility. And Sandy, from the time she'd worked the clubs, had always copped a lot of flak for writing her own songs. [1989]

When the taxi-cab arrived at Trevor's flat the day after Mothers, to pick Sandy up for the flight to Copenhagen, she was nowhere to be found. Fairport left without her. As the car made its way to the airport, the rest of the band began to openly discuss reverting to the all-boy band they'd originally conceived. If Simon remembers right, 'It was … between Fulham and the airport that Ashley suggested Bert Lloyd join,' a non-starter as far as the others were concerned:

Ashley Hutchings: During the trip over to Denmark, we talked about the future … which way the band might go, about whether this behaviour [from Sandy] could be tolerated. I think I had made up my mind that it was going to go a certain way; that Sandy … maybe wouldn't be in the band in future; and that we would get a traditional singer in and push it further that way … [But] when we arrived in Copenhagen, we had a telephone call to say that Sandy would be on the next plane.

The news of Sandy's return only served to compound the fractures in Fairport. In a pique of fit, Ashley now 'decided, within a day or two, I was going to leave the band ... It was just a feeling of wanting desperately to pursue that can of beans that we had opened and [now knowing] Sandy was particularly against that.'

The discussion with the others – including once reliable allies Simon and Richard – had not gone as Ashley had hoped, 'When I heard from [others in the band] that they imagined it to be a one-off, it came as a shock to me. I personally assumed that we were getting into something for good.'

For the first time, Ashley did not have Richard and Simon on his side when looking to dictate the direction of Fairport. Richard, in particular, was determined to get back to a more equitable balance of originals and covers, allowing room for something as traditional-flavoured as 'Quiet Joys Of Brotherhood':

Richard Thompson: There was a running argument between Ashley in one camp and Sandy and myself in the other – Ashley [was] wanting to do more traditional material. Sandy and I wanting to do more 'trad'-based contemporary songs ... Ashley [also] wanted to bring more people into the band ... Gay and Terry Woods and Martin Carthy and Bert Lloyd. So Fairport [would become] this huge nine-piece collective ... I thought that it was important that we do more writing; [because] we were a contemporary band [founded] upon the traditional principle.

Simon had never thought he was signing up for a lifetime of *Liege & Liefs*. Even in the first flush of enthusiasm, back in July, he had called the album 'a conscious project. We'll just explore it for a while ... [And] we'll be making another LP of the sort of things we've done in the past, but it will be impressed by the other and probably come out more English.' As far as he was concerned, he viewed 'it as a project. It was not supposed to be the doorway to a new world.'

For Ashley, the impasse came as a shock. Misled into believing 'it was Sandy who led the vanguard of the people who felt it should just be a one-off project', he assumed her departure would restore the band's ever-precarious equilibrium and he could again dictate its direction. As such, 'part of what led me to leave was the surprise of learning some people in the band ... now wanted to do something else.'

Ashley Hutchings: Very shortly after flying back [from Denmark], I just said, I'm gonna leave, guys. I didn't know what I was doing. I hadn't planned anything: I just had a vague idea that I wanted to play traditional music.

These things could and should have been thrashed out in a band conference, but that was not the Fairport way, and by now neither Ashley nor Sandy were thinking straight:

Ashley Hutchings: What was at work at that time was the after-effects of the crash – a delayed reaction ... We were still coming to grips with the tragedy. We bounced back so quickly we didn't have time to grieve ... I think I would have stayed, and Sandy would have stayed, had we not been wrestling with something else which made us behave a bit irrationally ... The penny still hasn't dropped with [some] people – we were getting over the crash. Me leaving, Sandy leaving, before *Liege & Lief* was [even] out, what Richard wrote [in his lyrics] at the time, it's all related to that. 'Cause we didn't talk about it.

Sandy Denny: I still don't recall that time very clearly because it was just after the accident ... Everybody was still in shock, and we didn't really know what we were doing. [1977]

When Sandy returned from Denmark, after a superb five-song performance for Danish television and a live gig, she informed the others she was leaving. She wanted to get back to doing her own songs. Boyd recalls, 'Everybody was trying to reassure Sandy, "No we're not going to just do traditional material. You're going to write songs. Richard's going to write songs..."' But it was no good. She was convinced she would be voted down when she tried to do her new songs. Boyd rightly recalls, 'It was classic Sandy; everything she had worked for, everything she wanted, was within reach, but suddenly she wasn't sure it was what she really wanted.'

Ashley had realised he wasn't going to get his way, either. So he turned his back on old friends and returned home to his parents to think about what to do in the future and to hopefully put the pieces of his shattered psyche back together again. The others still did not know how much he was suffering from the after-effects of the crash. His mother knew:

Kay Hutchings: I remember him when he came home, sitting there saying, 'For the first time in my life, I don't know where I'm going.' He had a breakdown. We had to put a bed downstairs for him after the accident. That was when his American girlfriend, Ann, turned up on the doorstep [and announced she was] married.

Ashley now suffered a full-blown breakdown, one he kept from the others. Only in 1971, when asked about his motives for leaving Fairport, did he finally admit, 'There were a lot of conflicting thoughts ... I had a bit of a breakdown around that time.'

What seems to have now set him on course for the next sea-change in a career built on constant movement was the experience of listening repeatedly to an album of traditional songs by Shirley and Dolly Collins issued earlier the same year. He was prompted by a desolation of the soul, the like of which he had never previously experienced:

Ashley Hutchings: In December 1969 I wake up one morning at my parents' house, and I have ... some kind of ... breakdown. I wake up in this desperate mood, feeling awful as I haven't slept for days. I put on *Anthems In Eden* and upon hearing ... that music, suddenly all the tears begin to come ... The doctor's called and he gives me sedation ... to settle me. And very slowly I start to come back to a level ... That's the lowest that I've ever got in terms of health and spirit. I hadn't really got Steeleye started and I couldn't sleep or eat. I simply didn't know where I was going.

With one whole side devoted to a song-suite of eight traditional songs that professed to tell the story of a beginning, a meeting, a courting, a denying, a forsaking, a dream, a leaving-taking, an awakening and, finally, a new beginning, *Anthems In Eden* offered Tyger a way of producing music with a certain thematic unity, that was profound and lasting.

His departure hit Fairport hard. It was he more than anyone who had kept them moving forward through a cavalcade of changes and a scattershot of setbacks. Whatever the future held for Fairport, it could never again be what it had been under Ashley's steadfast stewardship:

Richard Thompson: Ashley, as long as he was in the band, had his hand on the tiller – steering the band. It was a reasonably democratic band but probably the stronger personalities were myself and Sandy, and then Swarb came into the band and he was a strong force. So you had a lot of fairly upfront people with ideas and creativity. I think by the time Swarb joined, there were probably too many and the band started to pull apart just in terms of egos. But as long as Ashley was in the band, I think he was really controlling the direction.

Joe Boyd: They had always relied on Ashley to make decisions and negotiate on behalf of the band. He was very much their leader.

For Boyd, it was a headache he could have done without. He had an album he believed in passionately. It was still not yet released – *Liege & Lief* finally appeared on December 20th – as once again the outfit that had assumed the name gave it back just in time to scupper any promotional tour.

Boyd himself never doubted who should assume the leadership mantle: 'My instinct was always to trust Richard.' But he was not a natural leader, and Swarb was. His continued presence ensured an ongoing clash of personalities – even with Ashley and Sandy gone.

As Sandy herself observed, after another stint locking horns with the maddening fiddler, 'Richard is very strong to have in a band. He will always manage to get across what he wants and get it, you know … [But] I think Richard and Swarb had a fair amount of friction going between them … and what with Tyger as well…'

Put like that, it seems rather remarkable that the band held together as long as it did – a mere four months. And at least the many-layered *Liege & Lief* was the result. But not everyone was so besotted with the end-product that they were prepared to overlook the many-layered multiplicity the band had sacrificed to the folk process.

John Mendelsohn, in his *Liege & Lief* review in *Rolling Stone*, lamented, 'Where is the group's folk-flavoured rock & roll, where are the exhilarating many-voiced harmonies, the sense of fun and feeling of harnessed electricity that made their first two [US] albums together such treats?' And *Disc and Music Echo* roundly concurred:

> As a group they seem to have come a long way backwards since their first album. The exciting electric sound of those days has been replaced by the most traditional of traditional folk, which doesn't make for too much animation.

Even Thompson felt that the end product fell short of the ambition and energy evident throughout those weeks at Farley Chamberlayne: '*Liege & Lief* sounds slightly artificial, too claustrophobic, over-arranged. There was a dimension missing.'

If he was going to find that dimension, he was going to have to find it without Ashley's unswerving helmsmanship or the sublime tonalities of Sandy. Instead, he had the acerbic Swarbrick ever looking over his shoulder, chiselling away to follow his lead. For the other Fairport founder, it was yet another ruction in the time-space continuum:

Simon Nicol: Sandy fails to turn up for a flight to Copenhagen and Ashley has a delayed reaction and goes [off] to hold his head somewhere. And suddenly a significant portion of the band is no longer there.

Whither now?

6. Now We Are Five

Are Fairports now too heavy-handed?

I WISH I could agree with Chris Welch's acceptance of the current Fairports (M.M. 11.7.70). Once the most tasteful of British bands, Fairport Convention have abandoned sensitivity in favour of technique and become, perversely, a sort of folk-rock Ten Years After.

Fairport now revolves entirely around the high-speed violin playing of Dave Swarbrick, which, although skilful, is as meaningless as Alvin Lee's endless soloing.

Compare "Full House" to that beautiful first Fairport album of two-and-a-half years ago. What has happened to the magical subtlety apparent in songs like "Decameron" and "Sunshade"?

Paradoxically, Fairport's off shoots appear to be continuing the work of the original group far more logically. Trader Horne, Fotheringay, Steeleye Span and particularly Matthews' Southern Comfort, all exhibit that type of exquisite, restrained understatement found hitherto only in the music of American bands like Love, Buffalo Springfield and the Youngbloods. — **STEVE LAKE, 27 Galleydene Avenue, Galleywood, Chelmsford.**

NEXT TIME you're listening to Luxembourg on your radio turn the needle one-eighth of an inch further along the dial and you'll be in tune with the first ever adult pop music station.

Radio Geronimo plays tracks from all of the great LPS of today—all the time. Fantastic. — **JOHN BEST, 12 Westhill Road, Torquay.**

IT IS sad that Mailbag has become a shouting ground for knockers and counter-knockers.

As long as freedom of choice exists between artists, and as long as they appeal to someone, somewhere, then their right to entertain is valid, be they Frank Zappa or Moira Anderson. Their relative merits, musically, are really no more important to others than my preference for brown bread. — **JOHN PRATER, 114 Hambledon Road, Waterlooville, Hants. —LP winner.**

ON BEHALF of the many jazz fans who enjoyed the successful Louis Armstrong Tribute Concert I should like to say a big thank you to the Melody Maker, and in particular Mr. Michael Webber, the organiser.

Such a wealth of talent on one programme yet never viewed on Jazz Scene BBC2 (Alex Welsh once).

Why, Oh Why!! — **A. SMITH, 82 Parkside Avenue, Romford, Essex.**

THANKS, Christopher Bird for defending Nucleus and Jazz-Rock. This fusion has brought to front musicians like Chris Spedding, Dick Heckstall-Smith, Dave Arbus and Ron Caines, all very skilful.

Colosseum, East of Eden, and the Keef Hartley Band

There was a Fairport reunion at the Barbican [in 2009]. It was a good night, but one of the things that really struck me – that hadn't really struck me before, and doesn't necessarily strike me listening to individual tracks – is the huge difference in texture between the Full House *material and the* Liege & Lief *material. It's not only the bass playing … it's the songs. It's the type of writing. It was Swarbrick getting much more of a hold on it – [it was] what Richard and Swarb locked into.*

—JOE BOYD TO AUTHOR

The 2009 Fairport reunion Boyd is referring to was intended as a celebration of the band's classic era, 1967-70. The evening began with Judy Dyble singing 'A Satisfied Mind' in front of a four-piece Fairport, included interjections from Boyd (with occasional factual corrections from Simon Nicol), and ended with the (almost full-blown) *Full House* line-up performing most of their fifth album, the last to feature Richard Thompson as a full-time band member.

Without Martin Lamble and Sandy Denny, the only 'classic' Fairport line-up that could be reformed in its entirety in 2009 was the *Full House* era – and until a few days before the Barbican concert, such was the intention. However, at the last minute Swarbrick took umbrage at some (possibly imagined) sleight – or simply baulked at the very idea of celebrating Joe Boyd's contribution to British music – and refused to join in the communal backslapping.

It was a supremely ironic gesture on Swarb's part – an absence at the heart of the last classic Fairport line-up by the very man who would lead the band, resolutely and with unyielding determination, for the next decade as they tried every which way to rework the Fairport formula until they had tarnished the Fairport brand to the point where it lost its shine.

Notoriously quick tempered, here was a man who could hold a grudge in a death grip to the bitter end. And the bad blood with Boyd went all the way back to the time of Witchseason, with Swarbrick convinced that the band were being robbed blind. Whenever Boyd tried to explain the real-world economics for a band who gigged endlessly but never sold serious units, he was met with a stony stare and muttered expletives from Swarb:

Joe Boyd: The fundamental problem was that the records didn't sell ... Everybody got a weekly salary, and all the money came into a pot, and when the pot had more money in it, we'd increase the weekly salary; and when windfalls came in, there would be bonuses. The system worked fine ... as long as the group was full of nice, well brought up middle-class people.

The departure of Ashley and Sandy, and de facto assumption of the band's leadership by Swarbrick, a full-time member for less than six months, put the whole band on collision course with management – especially when Swarbrick co-opted an old friend into the band to replace the absent Ashley. However notable their musical contribution, Swarb and his Brummie friend, Dave Pegg, simply did not share the same communal origins as Simon and Richard:

Simon Nicol: Swarb and Joe – that was never gonna get patched up. And to an extent, Peggy's been a little bit infected by that. But they were never taken under his wing as kids. [To us, Joe] was more than a manager, he was a mentor. That's certainly how Fairport ... learned to survive.

And survive, Fairport did. For which some of the credit should go to the manager. When their sublime singer and bandleader jumped ship just as the band was about to dock in its new folk-rock berth, it was Boyd who initially steadied that ship – as Ashley the outsider affirms: '[Fairport] could have broken up but it had, among other things, Joe Boyd. He was there to lean on. He believed in the band. He believed in *Liege & Lief*. He thought it was a great idea, a great project.' The producer-manager now pushed them to embrace the new sound:

Joe Boyd: Although they were shocked and slightly alarmed at losing this wonderful singer – and Richard certainly [was]... there was another [factor]. Soon after [Sandy] left, one of them (I can't remember who) said, 'It's really good to be just on the road with the lads.' ... There was an element in the group psyche which [took the view], 'Well, it's a shame to lose her, but it's a lot more relaxed without her.'

He needed to put aside the reservations he had regarding Swarb's suitability for the role of bandleader, concerns he had first raised 'during those [*Liege & Lief*] sessions. People would turn to him because he was the one most experienced in that type of music.' Keeping the band together so that they could take the Fairport sound to America was paramount to his mind. Having secured a deal with A&M Records, which placed a foot in the door, it was time to kick it in, not rock a boat only Swarb was prepared to captain. As Simon asserts, 'Swarb was really the one who kept the ball rolling – he'd got the bit between his teeth [and] wasn't going to let the band fold.'

They now needed Thompson more than ever. Without the unflashiest of whizz-kids, in an era that overflowed with show-offs, Fairport had very little save the name. Thankfully, as the guitarist told *NME* in 1974, 'I was very enthusiastic about carrying on. We were all backs-to-the-wall.' Richard also had a direction in mind which required a band in tow:

Richard Thompson: Sometimes people think that if you have anything to do with traditional music, then you're being old worldly or something. A lot of the reviews of Fairport used to take that stance – that we were reviving this rich English history of music. Which wasn't true ... What we [were] try[ing] to do [was make it] contemporary. I think, if you listen to a lot of traditional music and it influences you, then inevitably, what you do will have a timelessness. [1982]

Much of the stimulus that drove Thompson on throughout 1970 – and the hardest he ever worked – came from strip-mining Swarb's immense knowledge of traditional music. As he told Humphries, 'We were discovering stuff all the time. Like, let's make a new tune; let's take one line of this reel and slow it down and move it up a minor third and see what that does to it; let's take one line of this ballad and make a whole song out of it, chopping up the tradition to find new things.'

For now, he was content to work in tandem with Swarb, who continued contributing melodic ideas and arrangements. Almost immediately, the odd couple came up with an epic anti-war anthem, 'Sloth', a song which would define Fairport throughout the seventies. Even at this stage, though, it was not a collaboration of kindred spirits bouncing ideas back and forth across the breakfast table:

Dave Swarbrick: We used to have little meetings about what was going to be written and then we'd each go off and do it ... He would go off and write the words and I'd write the music. On one occasion I gave him the tune first and then he wrote the words – that was 'Sloth'. I'd written the tune in 3/4 and played it to Richard. But he didn't like it in 3/4 and suggested we did it in 4/4.

This slightly impersonal method of collaborations somehow worked, as songs came together in rehearsal and even recording. To quote an awestruck Simon, 'Swarb and Richard ... could produce spontaneous music in the studio, which is jolly difficult. [But] to do the sort of thing they refined on "Sloth" is not really something you can work at.'

Yet work at it, they did, developing a largely new repertoire less than six months on from Farley Chamberlayne. New songs, which actually approximated to Simon's description of the band's direction the previous summer, came quickly. Soon they had a set which was almost exclusively new songs in a traditional vein and folk-rock arrangements of folk fare, incorporating the traditional material released on *Liege & Lief*, reconfigured to take the emphasis away from the singer/s, and in most cases rocked to the core.

Without Sandy, that album's three originals were left well alone, because, as Simon suggests, 'The subject-matter of some of the songs ... was too close to home for anyone to feel comfortable singing them.' 'Tam Lin' and 'Matty Groves', though, were recast in a way that pushed Fairport to the very brink of hard rock; as Dylan's original folk-rock sound had once pushed it to the edge of r&b.

Despite the loss of arch zealot Ashley, the new Fairport combined the evangelical fervour of new converts with the righteous indignation of those for whom all musical boundaries were artificial. As Fairport's supporting guitarist told folkie Bob Pegg, fresh from his own brief encounter with Hutchings's new electric folk band:

I don't care where the music comes from ... There are people who are going into [folk music] more deeply than I am – for instance, Tyger's band ... [But] we're not going to start getting guilt feelings about doing English words to our Irish tune, because that's a lot of cock. If the group likes the end of what they produce, then that's it ... There are people who now take us far too seriously. We spend more of our time now on stage trying to shock people. You can't go on stage now without people saying 'This is profound'.

In a wide-ranging conversation, the opinionated Pegg got both Fairport guitarists to share, Thompson even taking potshots at 'a band like Led Zeppelin that gets up there and really isn't selling any music, they're selling themselves ... There's this great hole ... between what's traditional and what's actually going on ... I really think that if I fully understood English traditional music, I wouldn't be playing electric music ... but I'm as happy as can be. For the first time now I don't have to sing about Louisiana, which is quite a breakthrough.'

Coming from the usually taciturn Thompson, this was an extraordinary outburst – and it would not be the last. Throughout 1970, he was a man on a mission: to adapt traditional vérités and reinvigorate tradition, by force if necessary, a stance he took in every contemporary interview:

Sometimes we might take the tune from one song and use the words from another, or write a new melody to fit some old words ... It's very flexible ... We have no ethnic code to firmly stand by ... [Some people] say the old tunes shouldn't be changed, but [that is] just taking an intellectual approach that isn't worth a thing ... We're not aiming to bring folk music to the masses. We just do it because we like it.

When it came to making music, it was all for one and one for all. Even the hard-of-hearing Swarb was an unapologetic convert to the joys of folk-rock at full volume, informing *Melody Maker* that October, 'We are not a folk group and we don't play folk music ... I mean, the music we play isn't traditional, [though] some, I suppose, is revived traditional.'

This sense of togetherness would once again last just long enough for Fairport to record their fourth masterful album in two years – and within four months of recruiting new bassist Dave Pegg. It was another remarkable regeneration from an outfit who made Doctor Who seem like a stable persona.

Replacing Ashley had always been a more pressing concern than finding another Sandy. His was the void they needed to replace to resume their live explorations. Swarb had the perfect player in mind – and a power base in the band to establish. His friend 'Peggy' could be the perfect foil. He just needed to keep his heavy-rock affiliations under wraps and emphasize his stint in the Ian Campbell Folk Group at a time when Birmingham's pop scene had more sides than a decahedron:

Dave Pegg: The whole of Brum [in the mid-sixties] was very much a family affair – similar to how the London bands must have been when Fairport started up ... I joined this group called The Uglies who were a pop band ... They did a lot of their own songs. The singer was Steve Gibbons ... We did a lot of Byrds stuff, a lot of Dylan songs. And the Lovin' Spoonful ... They were probably very similar to Fairport ... In Brum, every big pub would have a dance ... I played in a group with [Led Zeppelin drummer] John Bonham called The Way of Life. But everybody played with everybody else's group in Brum ... After The Uglies, I joined The Campbells, which was a folk band ... The Campbells ran ... a very successful folk club every Thursday night at Digbeth Civic Hall and they would get three, four hundred people ... [But] I felt restricted, because I couldn't play the [electric] bass and I wanted to get back into another band. Times had changed ... You could have a band and you could play stuff that you just wanted to play.

Pegg himself had thought nothing of the news that his old friend Swarb had joined a folk-rock combo. When informed they were playing Mothers, he called a friend and went along to hear what all the fuss was about, ever open to new sounds. It was November 2nd, 1969, and Pegg thinks, 'It was my twenty-first birthday ... It was [the] line-up with Sandy and Tyger, and we went up there with Harvey Andrews, who is a folksinger I'd done some recording with … He hated it and I loved it.'

The possibility of joining such a cutting-edge band was not even on the horizon when he bid adieu to his old friend after the show. So imagine his surprise when, a matter of weeks later, he got a call from his Brummie buddy informing him that Tyger had left the building and, if he was interested, the gig was his. Swarb didn't feel the need to inform the others of his arbitrary decision, preferring to tell Pegg it was a rehearsal, and Simon, Richard and DM it was an audition:

Simon Nicol: I'd never met [Peggy] before this audition, which immediately became a rehearsal. Swarb was determined to get him into the band – I see that now. It wasn't really an audition, [more like] come and meet the band that you're joining … [But Peggy was] very liberating to play with. It was enough [for Tyger] and myself to play in time and not fuck up, but Peggy is a completely driven musician. So he brought all this unexpected experience. And we already had the world's tightest drummer. [Watch] that Maidstone performance and see how tight they are.

From that first 'rehearsal', there was never any question Pegg would slot in. On a technical level, he could play circles around his predecessor. When Fairport's producer-manager was invited to an early rehearsal – possibly Peggy's so-called audition – he became an immediate convert, rubber-stamping the welcome addition:

Joe Boyd: [I] walked into this little basement room in Kennington, and they were playing 'Tam Lin' or 'Matty Groves', and Pegg was playing all those incredibly difficult bass lines Ashley had invented … [Ashley] never could play them that well … [being] a very inventive, melodic bass player, but not a very powerful one technically. But having had the part explained to him once, Pegg was playing it better than Ashley ever played it.

It wasn't just as a bass player that Peggy fit snugly into the Fairport mould. Any time the spirit of experimentation that once inhabited songs like 'Jack O' Diamonds' and 'Reno Nevada' again infected the body politic, Pegg was as game as the rest. Thus, after endless attempts at reaching a working arrangement of 'Bonny Black Hare' – another hoary folk standard from the Swarb memory bank – Pegg metamorphosed into a folk-rock John Cale:

Simon Nicol: We ... just seemed to be getting nowhere until Dave Pegg started playing the viola, Richard played the mandolin [and] I, the dulcimer – instruments none of us knew as well as our own. [1970]

A band that had always managed to be more than the sum of its instrumental parts no longer needed to fudge the Fairport sound. For most of 1970, Fairport would be one of the most exciting – and loudest – live bands on a British gig scene that still got to pay witness to the likes of The Who, Deep Purple, Led Zeppelin and Jethro Tull at their gut-bustin' best.[13]

The new line-up was like a super-charged version of the *Liege & Lief* band, much to Boyd's evident delight and relief, '[It was] such a smooth transition. Without Sandy to hold them back, it was like they had been let off the leash.' For the first time since Judy left and Sandy joined, they were a single-minded unit. A new-found musical muscle was also immediately apparent to anyone with ears, a gleeful guitarist included:

Richard Thompson: We are more of a group now than we have been. Everyone relates to each other very closely. It seems a lot easier for five people to communicate than for six. It's also an advantage not having a separate singer, and the rest of the band playing instruments. That seemed to cause a rift. Everyone is less inhibited musically than even in the past. Generally, on stage, everyone is enjoying playing more. [1970]

A 'dress rehearsal' at the Country Club in Hampstead was quickly booked for January 29th, 1970. It was not quite the Royal Festival Hall, but this line-up just couldn't wait to get out and play.

There was only one itsy-bitsy problem. The new Fairport had gone

[13] All of those A-list bands played theatre tours of the UK in 1970-71, perhaps the last era when ordinary fans could see such stars without breaking the bank.

from being a band with a surfeit of great singers a year earlier to a band
with no real singers. When 'DM' was interviewed by 'The Crawling
Eye' a week before, he seemed to think a solution was imminent:

> Richard will take most of the lead singing, with Swarb close behind
> in second. Of course he can't sing too well with a violin stuck under
> his chin, so there will have to be a happy medium between his
> singing and his playing. We never even knew the guy could hold a
> note until he started singing along and we found him to have quite
> a good voice. Everyone else is working on voices as well, for we
> have decided to remain a five-piece group and not take anyone on
> to replace Sandy as lead singer.

Once again, Swarb saw this situation as a way to bump up his own
contribution, knowing that Richard was not about to do 'most of
the lead singing', something he continued to equate with 'walking
through flames'. In fact, the lack of a genuine frontperson would
make the transition into a band that played almost as many guitar/
fiddle duels as songs nigh on inevitable. Cue the sight of a beady-eyed
busker, fiddle akimbo, daring Richard to match his musical mania
at every gig.

According to the new bassist, the final division of vocal duties was
only agreed twenty-four hours before their live debut. Perhaps they
should have asked for help from the audience. Because there at the
Country Club, providing moral support to her dear friends, as she
would throughout the years she ploughed a solitary furrow, was senior
cheerleader Sandy, determined to make the occasion a joyous one:

Sandy Denny: Lots of people were shouting out requests – old songs
they didn't do anymore. Somebody kept shouting for 'Meet On The
Ledge' – it could have been Karl [Dallas] … So I started shouting
out silly requests: Dylan songs, old rock'n'roll songs, anything. One
of the wackiest was the Harry Belafonte song ['Yellow Bird'] – and,
bloody hell, they played it.

'Yellow Bird' fitted perfectly into a set which also featured The
Surfaris' 'Wipe Out', Chuck Berry's 'Sweet Little Rock'n'Roller' and
their ironic treatment of 'We Need A Whole Lot More Of Jesus',

but not a single pre-crash sop to former fans. And this was the way it was gonna stay. That Fairport had been buried alongside Martin and Jeannie.

Their third gig marked a return to Mothers, local hero Pegg now in situ. Their sixth revisited the Royal Festival Hall. Quite what the London concert-goers made of a twenty-minute improvisation at the start of the show, involving Pegg, Nicol, Thompson, Dudu Pukwana and ten other musicians, one cannot help but wonder. But the band was starting to find its feet, discerning which songs from the *Liege & Lief* repertoire might suit the new set-up:

Simon Nicol: The first few gigs in particular lacked a great deal of confidence ... It was a matter of believing that we could sing on stage ... and making it sound acceptable to the people who were coming along to make a deliberate comparison with the previous line-up. [1970]

Their Valentine's Day return to the Festival Hall confirmed another unlikely resurrection.[14] Once again, an entirely new Convention had shaken off the formalism of *Liege & Lief* – which had been in the shops for the two months they had been rehearsing a new set – and returned to its roots, its *rock* roots:

Simon Nicol: [Listening to] those *Full House* performances now, they're so manic. You think, those kids have been at the Dexedrine. But it was not the case – it was the energy and excitement of youth.

Richard Thompson: I think people have got an opinion of [Fairport], without having actually seen them. To many, Fairport are considered ... similar to, say, Pentangle. But that wasn't [ever] the case. Fairport were a loud, raucous rock band that played traditional songs – which I don't regard as the same thing as folk songs. I've never played as loud since leaving Fairport, and I left the band thirteen years ago. [1983]

---

[14] A tape of this performance does exist and comprises: Walk Awhile, The Deserter, Lark In The Morning, Sloth, Matty Groves, Flowers Of The Forest, Flatback Caper, Doctor Of Physick, Sir Patrick Spens, Jenny's Chickens/Mason's Apron, the core of this line-up's repertoire.

The folk/rock fans seemed to love it. As a reviewer in *Oz* wrote, after Fairport triumphantly returned to The Roundhouse in April – sharing the bill with the bands Sandy and Ian Matthews had formed – 'Their set was mainly traditional – or so it seemed that way. But it was as exciting and loud as any rock band you care to name, including The Who.'

If there was audible dissent – and there *was* some – it came not from the folk quarter, but rather from old Fairport fans, who disliked the overbearing way Swarb was sometimes dominating proceedings. After a show at the Palladium in late July, one *Melody Maker* reader felt prompted to write, 'Listening to Fairport Convention [that night] … it became more apparent to me that my highly esteemed superlative musicians Thompson and Nicol have been taken over, body and soul, by a gritty-voiced over-electrified fiddler.' Said complaint would be vouchsafed by Steve Lake, soon to be a staff writer at the paper:

> Once the most tasteful of British bands, Fairport Convention have abandoned sensitivity in favour of technique, and become, perversely, a sort of folk-rock Ten Years After. Fairport now revolves entirely around the high-speed violin playing of Dave Swarbrick, which, although skilful, is as meaningless as Alvin Lee's endless soloing. Compare *Full House* to that beautiful first Fairport album of two-and-a-half years ago …. Paradoxically, Fairport's offshoots appear to be continuing the work of the original group far more logically. Trader Horne, Fotheringay, Steeleye Span and particularly Matthews Southern Comfort all exhibit that type of exquisite, restrained understatement.

The calls for Swarb to rein himself in, or be reined in, would serve as a constant backdrop throughout the year, concluding in December with another blistering retort in the letters page of *Melody Maker* by one David Johnstone, who lamented how 'there used to be a maestro of the guitar called Richard Thompson, who played with the Fairport Convention – a shy, unobtrusive man, born to be heard. No one can hear him anymore! Dave Swarbrick is the slickest fiddle around but he seems to drown [out] every other member of the group.' One founding Fairporter accepts the charge on the late fiddler's behalf, suggesting Swarb's choice of medicinal smokes lay at the root of the problem:

Simon Nicol: [The *Full House* line-up could be] self-indulgent. When Swarb had had a little bit too much to smoke he would go off on his own in a quite self-indulgent way. Richard would go off free-forming prior to that, but it was never in that lost-in-time-and-space way that Swarb did when he was under the influence. You could tell he was in a different time zone. I've never been one who wanted to get that far removed from reality – particularly on stage.

There was at least one notable, nay legendary, exception to Nicol's moratorium on escaping reality: the Krumlin Festival, a one-off open-air festival held on the Yorkshire Pennines in August. When the event proved a complete wash-out, Simon by his own admission, 'drank most of Elton John's backstage rider … It [had been] a disaster. Lives were lost. Mountain rescue was deployed … Richard had turned my amp off and I didn't notice.' For most of the infamous set, Simon lay prostrate on the stage.

As has been well documented, every member of this line-up had moments of over-indulgence, Thompson included. As Pegg confirms, Richard was 'one of the chaps. He would never get out of it, like some of the rest of us would, but he did partake of the odd glass of whisky.' In fact, even Thompson found the open bar tab at the famous LA Troubadour in May too much of a good thing. When American singer-songwriter Loudon Wainwright III called in to catch their act, he found Richard 'with his head down on the table at the bar'.

Usually the guitar/vocalist – and indeed the entire band – showed an astonishing capacity for alcohol consumption, one that would prompt his next serious girlfriend to observe, '[Richard] could drink anyone under the table. He had hollow legs.'

Not surprisingly, *Full House*-era performances could be somewhat erratic. Yet recordings of this line-up, both official and unofficial – of which there are no shortage – serve to demonstrate how this was probably Fairport's most musically adept, certainly its most rehearsed, line-up ever. As Pegg recalls, 'We used to rehearse every day – [even if] we may have been half soaked.'

It was the restoration of a communal home – for the first time since Fairport – that made them a 24/7 working unit again. This joint residence was The Angel, Little Hadham, a disused pub in one of the leafier parts of Hertfordshire. When Nicol and roadie Robin

Banks first stumbled on the place it had been, in Simon's words, 'out of commission for six months; it was stark, bare, uncared for, and utterly uninviting. It was unpleasant, dirty, cold. The windows rattled; some of them were broken. It was, in short, a totally unsuitable prospect for a shared habitation. So we jumped straight back in the van and drove back to London.' Swarb, though, had other ideas:

Simon Nicol: Robin got a call from [Swarb] to say ... he'd spoken to the owner of The Angel and would be arriving tomorrow, with fiddles, family, bags ... So that was it ... Against our better judgement, The Angel was to be our new home ... I would certainly never do it again. But, against the odds, at the time it was the right thing to do ... When we were living at The Angel, gigging was ... easier: we all clattered back to the yard and we were home. All you then had to do was stumble back into your own living space in the house. The next morning we piled into the van and headed off to wherever the [next] gig was.

The previously peripatetic Swarb again overrode any objections and one by one the others joined the commune. As Thompson recalls, it was 'a shell of a building ... [with] a shared kitchen [and] one really uncomfortable bathroom'. At least, Pegg confirms, 'everybody had their own hi-fis, [though] the only music that we had in common was *Music From Big Pink* and The Band's second album.' If The Angel would be Fairport's home for a single line-up and album, appropriately called *Full House*, the spirit of the place – and its listening parties – soon made itself felt:

Dave Mattacks: On *Liege & Lief* I'm all over the fucking place, the tempo goes up and down, but on *Full House* I started to think about it a bit more ... The light began to shine a bit then and I started to appreciate Richard ... [Listening to] The Band had an influence as well. [1975]

Full House – released in July 1970 – contained a single leftover from the *Liege & Lief* era, recast in an altogether more muscular guise: the sixteenth-century Child ballad, 'Sir Patrick Spens'.[15] Of the two traditional instrumentals, the arrangement of 'Dirty Linen'

---

[15] Many absurd claims for a greater antiquity have been imposed on this ballad, but the voyage of Sir Patrick Vans circa 1590 seems its most likely historical source.

was credited solely to Swarbrick; the other, 'Flatback Caper', to the entire band; while the three Swarbrick-Thompson originals included the album's 9 min 19 sec centrepiece, 'Sloth'. Meanwhile, the semi-trad 'Flowers Of The Forest' served as another elegiac album closer.

Released just seven months after *Liege & Lief*, the album was another left turn that garnered critical raves and new converts. *Rolling Stone*'s Ed Ward forgave them their traditional trespasses with but one reservation – the liner notes – which read to his mind 'like a pukka sahib on acid' (not the last time Richard Thompson's English humour would sail past our American cousins).

Such minor reservations aside, Ward felt 'the music shows that England has finally gotten herself her very own equivalent to The Band', a compliment the band liked greatly. Ashley Hutchings – who had just delivered his own telling tangent to *Liege & Lief*, *Hark! The Village Wait* – was delighted and a little jealous:

Ashley Hutchings: I thought *Full House* was a great album … I mean, Peggy's a great musician so half of me was listening to the bass playing and thinking, wow, that's fantastic. The other half of me was saying what great songs Richard [and Swarb] wrote.

If the album had one significant flaw, it was the fact that it clocked in at a mere thirty-five minutes. One might have concluded they were short of material had two BBC radio sessions that April, broadcast in the lead-up to the album's release, not belied any such assumption.

On these broadcasts were Richard's sardonic reinterpretation of Dylan's 'Open The Door Homer', a fully realised 'The Bonny Black Hare' and one of Thompson's most compelling attempts to write in the traditional idiom while he rocked the casbah to its roots, 'Poor Will And The Jolly Hangman' (tellingly copyrighted to Thompson-Swarbrick, not the usual Swarbrick-Thompson).

A five-and-a-half minute mystery-play set to music, 'Poor Will' featured a guitar-break blistering enough to be on *Are You Experienced?* And it was not as if they had been unable to capture the song in the studio. They did so twice; once at the BBC, once at Sound Techniques, both in April – only for the perverse guitarist to inform the producer he wanted it removed from the final sequence:

Joe Boyd: Richard didn't really articulate [the problem with 'Poor Will'. Perhaps] it was his vocals – maybe that was part of it – [but] he just said, I don't want it on the record. He wasn't really very articulate in those days. He didn't go into long explanations. He would just put his foot down … [The first pressing of the album] has 'Poor Will' listed on the sleeve. He said, 'No, I told you I didn't want it on. I mean it.'

It was too late to find a substitute, so the track was simply removed from side two, just not in time to stop sleeves listing the song appearing in the shops. According to Boyd, it was one of a number of disagreements he had with the guitarist during the sessions, 'Richard was seemingly becoming more and more perverse in the studio. We had a lot of arguments over *Full House* … Whenever I would say, "I like that solo, let's keep it," … he would say, "No, I don't like that. Let's do another one."'

Boyd had found out Richard could be as immovable as a mountain. Boyd's then-girlfriend Linda Peters would come to know the guitarist biblically, and confirms, 'You couldn't make Richard do anything he didn't want – ever! Joe could make Sandy do things. Joe is a strong, patriarchal WASP, six-foot-five – you did what Joe told you – but you can't make Richard do [anything]!'

As soon as the album hit the shops, the whole debate about where Fairport fit into the vibrant post-prog universe was reawakened. Once again Fairport were required to dispatch spokesman Simon to the music papers to reiterate another folk-rock manifesto:

> We want to write our own music, using English music as a base, rather than American. We are using English themes, but it is in no sense a crusade to promote these old English songs … Swarb and Richard Thompson, our writers, have created a distinctive line between them – neither definitively traditional, nor poppy.

After completing the album, the ultra-English outfit finally dipped their toes in the Atlantic and the Pacific, touring the States during the merry month of May. They even stopped off in la-la-land long enough to play a week of shows at the Troubadour and start work on their next album.

A day session at the legendary Gold Star studio came about because historically-inclined members asked Boyd if they could visit the studio. The ever-pragmatic Joe suggested, '"Why don't we do a session there?" And so I phoned them up. [But] those tapes sat at A&M and we never got them .. The one track that was absolutely brilliant at Gold Star, which ... had one of the greatest sounds I *ever* got out of *any* group in any studio, was "The Banks Of The Sweet Primroses".' This time, the guitarist shared Boyd's enthusiasm for the results:

Richard Thompson: I don't know if we were so hyped up because it was Gold Star, which was where Phil Spector used to record, but we imagined it would sound great before we went in. It was just one of those great sounding rooms, stuff was coming off the tape and just jumping at you ... But when it was time to make the next record, we probably felt that we'd gone past that material.

As it happens, Thompson did not stick around long enough 'to make the next record', so was in no position to decide whether Fairport had 'gone past that material'.[16]

Though no new originals were recorded at Gold Star – only a lively reworking of 'Walk Awhile' which later appeared on the *Bumpers* Island sampler – the Swarbrick/Thompson songwriting partnership continued producing the goods. 'Now Be Thankful' – one of the few Fairport-era compositions Thompson was still performing in 1975 – began with Swarb trying to convey doom and gloom:

Dave Swarbrick: I was very depressed in Boston. It was the end of quite an exhausting few weeks. I wrote a tune to capture the mood, which was called something like 'Sad Little Boston Tune'.

Uncharacteristically, Richard's lyrics saw light at the end of a long, dark tunnel. Released as a single that September, the song sank without trace, not greatly helped by Swarb informing *Music Now*, 'I

---

[16] Certainly, 1971's *Angel Delight* would have benefited from the inclusion of their twelve-minute arrangement of 'The Bonny Bunch Of Roses' – an English ballad from the Napoleonic wars also recorded that July for the BBC – albeit at the expense of their 1977 'comeback' album of the same name.

think "Now Be Thankful" is a nice song, but I don't care if it makes the charts or not, really … The only good things would be getting the music over to a lot more people, [though] I'm not sure I even care about that much.'

The band were hardly in a position to rush into the *Top of the Pops* studio, even if the song had been an immediate hit. August found them back in America, promoting *Full House*, the first Fairport album A&M had an opportunity to promote with the line-up intact.

Although already thinking about the next album, Fairport wisely stuck to the *Full House* repertoire, especially at those shows which provided a mismatch of musical styles. As Swarb complained, on the band's return to Blighty, 'The main problem was that we had to play a lot with heavy blues bands and that didn't give us the chance to find our own audience.'

The tour still had its moments, notably early on when they played the prestigious Philadelphia Folk Festival, to the best reaction they would ever receive Stateside:

Richard Thompson: An [absolute] highspot … We were the first people ever to get an encore, which was very flattering for us: there were just 10,000 people, all dancing. [1974]

Dave Swarbrick: The one time we did get the right sort of crowd was at the Philadelphia Folk Festival. That was incredible. I think it was the best gig we have done anywhere. It was certainly the most appreciated … There were twenty-five thousand people there [sic] and about ten thousand of them were just dancing around. It was an incredible sight. [1970]

That performance was recorded from the desk. It is an exhilarating listen, even though theirs was a necessarily truncated festival set. An excellent ninety-minute audience tape of their final show at the Fillmore West at the end of August is even better, proof positive that when it came to stretching out songs live these folk-rock refugees were no slouches. 'Sloth', in particular, stood comparison with any extemporisation that hallowed hall had heard in the years Ken Kesey and like-minded Kool-Aiders dropped acid in the restrooms.

Fairport continued scaling musical heights the week after the

Fillmore, as a three-night return to the Troubadour in LA became an opportunity for John Wood to record the *Full House* Fairport in eight-track flight. The only problem was that the open bar tab could mean the moments when the band hit their marks and Thompson was firing on all cylinders did not necessarily coincide.

The version of 'Sloth' selected for the original 1977 Island release of these tapes (*Live At The Troubadour*) was a band tour de force with Thompson taking a backseat until a coruscating coda. The version on the 1986 'reissue' (*House Full*) is sloppier, but features a Thompson repeatedly surrendering to the women of Calvary. A case of take your pick, Hobson.

In fact, neither of these attempts at a representative cross-section of the *Full House* era does the deed definitively. Wholly absent are dazzling live versions of 'Poor Will And The Jolly Hangman' and 'Now Be Thankful' (both recorded, both still unreleased), as well as choice examples of country-rock and good time rock'n'roll with which the band nightly interspersed their folk-rock originals and electrified Anglo-trad.

'Silver Threads & Golden Needles', a song which Pegg recalls prompted Linda Ronstadt to 'get up and just busk along … virtually every night', remains unreleased, as does a jam session with elements of the biggest band in the world, Led Zeppelin.

Pegg suggests 'the [exact] details of the night with Zeppelin are lost in an alcoholic haze … we all [just] played things we knew – "Hey Joe", some rock'n'roll, simple blues'. Yet the tapes were certainly rolling as Thompson and Page traded licks; the former having refrained from mentioning how he really hated 'a band like Led Zeppelin that gets up there and really isn't selling any music, they're selling themselves'. There was just never any question of permission being Granted to make this folk/rock collision public. It might have highlighted Page's earnest attempts to keep up with a man who showed no interest in little games:

Dave Pegg: [Richard] could play all the country licks, the rock'n'roll thing … It's something that's just inside of him. It's not what he does, but he has great command of all these various guitar styles. It didn't go unnoticed by the Californian Mafia.

And yet, after covering all bases east to west, Swarb informed the English music papers that, although 'we have some live things recorded, the trouble is a lot of them were on our last two albums'. In the end, the live album that could have shown just how great the *Full House* band was in concert got shelved. Swarb wanted to release something grander, and began talking up a more ambitious project, 'a double album … perhaps one live album and a studio album of new stuff.' It was left to The Who to release the greatest live English rock album of the era, recorded at a Yorkshire pitstop.

One can't help but wonder what happened to all this 'new stuff'. All of the 'new' songs introduced Stateside were traditional songs put through the Fairport wringer: 'Staines Morris', 'Banks Of The Sweet Primroses' and 'Bonny Bunch Of Roses'. And on opening night of a six-week British tour at the Royal Albert Hall on October 7th, 1970, the only new Swarbrick/Thompson original was 'The Journeyman's Grace'. Indeed, much of the set was given over to the instrumentals which allowed Swarb to show off and Thompson to only intermittently shine.

The jig was up. As every other song became an instrumental workout, audiences out for an evening began to grow tired of all this virtuosity at the expense of emotion. Meanwhile, the guitarist at the epicentre of this onstage maelstrom was beginning to doubt his own sanity:

Richard Thompson: All our numbers would start slowly, but after a minute or so everyone was hammering away as fast as they could. We were entertaining but it wasn't for me … You're [also] going to bed at five in the morning, getting up in the afternoon, with nothing in-between … playing the gig. I never actually had a breakdown, but I've been close to it.

A BBC session on the band's return to London in early November suggested some forward motion, with a reprise of 'The Journeyman's Grace' and the BBC debut of new original, 'Sickness & Diseases'. But by now Richard was keeping many of the songs he was writing from the others:

Richard Thompson: One of the main reasons I left Fairport was that the songs I wanted to write refused to come out. I was thinking in terms of other people all the time, instead of satisfying myself ... I really enjoyed the *Full House* band a lot, until about six months before I left. Then I started to get very fed up. [1972]

Blithe bandleader Swarb seemed wholly unaware of Thompson's growing dissatisfaction, or the fact that he lay at the centre of it, as Richard confirmed in a 1988 interview, 'I found [Swarb] quite hard to work with ... He wants something in music that I can't give him.'

In a *Melody Maker* interview in October 1970, the fiddler claimed, 'We get on so much better together than most bands,' while suggesting that if anyone would be moving out of The Angel, it would be him: 'I suppose it's okay living together, but there are many times when I just want to be on my own.'

Even when Thompson finally dropped his bombshell on January 24th, 1971, he made it clear he was staying put, and had no intention of leaving The Angel. And go where? As he put it some years later, he actually said something like, 'I'm really sorry lads but I've got to leave the band. I know it's a shock but I'll go and make some tea and perhaps you'd like to have a chat about it.'

At the time, Richard's oldest friend in the band admitted to feeling 'quite angry. It seemed we had wasted a lot of time; that he should have told us earlier. Later, I realised he'd been working it all out, what he wanted to do.' The bond between the two guitarists was tested as never before, but Simon slowly came to understand what lay at the heart of his friend's defection:

Simon Nicol: He'd written some impressive songs in harness with Swarb, and we were all living together at The Angel, but there were other things in his life. He was into astrology and he'd spend hours in the pursuit of archery – which is very Zen. The inner stillness. The band was denying him the time to do these things by getting in a van and going trundling round the country. So he just stopped coming to gigs. He wanted to stay home. He was still in the house ... I think Richard had [simply] outgrown the band ... He really did want to write songs. And you can't do that when you're in a band with all the gigs we're doing.

On the verge of starting work in earnest on a new album – having just recorded the traditional 'Lord Marlborough' – the Fairport rump found itself left high and dry. Richard had realised he couldn't go on. In the next few years, while carving a career in music for himself and his wife that would strip-mine the rich vein of songwriting he had struck first in Fairport, Thompson would make a number of comments which indicated just how deep his dissatisfaction had become:

Richard Thompson: When I was with the Fairport my songs were really custom-built; designed to be performed by certain singers and players. The ideas behind the songs were ideas that other members of the group could hang on to. [But] I think I made a mistake trying to write that way. [1972]

Richard Thompson: The music I was playing was stunted, I wasn't thinking for myself. I was too aware of what the others were doing, and about that time I forgot how to write songs as well. I was only writing songs that other people could sing or like – there wasn't anything real there. [1974]

Richard Thompson: I was writing stuff that just wasn't right for the band, stuff which ended up on *Henry* [*The Human Fly*] … and [*I Want To See The*] *Bright Lights*. In a sense, it broke my heart, but it was a gut instinct. Fairport's approach was limited … I was trying to do English rock'n'roll, and play traditional music with electric instruments, which I felt could be developed further. [1979]

It may have been the prospect of starting work on a Fairport album without the steadying hand of Joe Boyd which finally convinced Richard to come clean. Though their relationship had become slightly fractious, the guitarist still yearned for an outside voice he trusted, and that was largely agenda-free:

Richard Thompson: I think I was very disheartened when [Joe] left to go to Warner Brothers in America … He'd always been a symbol of a 'good guy'. I don't know if he was, but … he appeared to be more interested in music than anything else, which I've never seen anyone else again show on the 'business' side. He's the only person who I really think was more interested in music than in making money ... The only drawback [was that] Joe's approach wasn't very lucrative – especially for him. [1974]

Having fled English folk-rock at the end of 1970 after selling Witchseason to Chris Blackwell, Boyd was sunning himself in California when he read these comments and 'was absolutely gob-smacked, because I felt like [Richard] was happy to get rid of me ... [But] it was [all] very British. We didn't talk these things through.' It seems Richard hadn't even talked things through with his family, telling *Disc* five months earlier, 'I only see [my parents] once every six months. They are my own parents but I really enjoy being a stranger to my relations.'

As their own Homer went to the kitchen to read the tea leaves, leaving the others to their first band conference as a four-piece, the future of Fairport assuredly hung in the balance. Its newest recruit was sure they had reached journey's end:

Dave Pegg: When Richard left ... I thought, It's all over now ... He was never a pushy character, [but] everyone in the band respected him so much because of his musical ability ... He would come up with great ideas and lyrics, and he was always the leader of that bunch of people .... I thought the group would probably finish then ... I didn't think there would be enough of that energy left in the other[s].

But if the prospect of a return to the Brummie music scene with his guitar-lead between his legs filled Peggy with concern, it was as nothing to how Swarb felt. The bit remained firmly between his teeth, and he was not about to let go. After Ashley, Richard and Sandy had taken to the lifeboats in the eighteen months since he came on board, Fairport was finally ready to be cast largely in *his* image.

QUEEN ELIZABETH HALL

General Manager: John Denison, CBE

Saturday, January 30th at 7.45 p.m.

ROY GUEST presents

PART II
FLEE AS A BIRD
1970-1974

An Evening with

'FOTHERINGAY'

(SANDY DENNY, TREVOR LUCAS, JERRY DONAHUE, GERRY CONWAY,
and PAT DONALDSON)

Tickets: 25/- 20/- 15/- from Royal Festival Hall and usual agents
When applying for tickets by mail, please enclose a stamped addressed
envelope! Thank you.

Our tastes began to develop together, [but] also in different channels, if you know what I mean, which is why people have always been branching out from Fairport.

—SANDY DENNY, *NME*, 15TH JANUARY 1972

We thought [Liege & Lief] would get some rock fans interested in traditional music. But it didn't work that way. The big influence was on the folk scene ... Electric bands are springing up everywhere.

—RICHARD THOMPSON, *NME*, 22ND JUNE 1972

By January 1970, being an ex-member of the most unstable band in Christendom was almost a badge of honour. It just wasn't a career. That was something its survivors would now need to carve from the rock-hard face of the music industry – and in the early months of 1970, the three Fairport recidivists who left in 1969 made their big play for Fairport fans dismayed by the group's current direction.

While debut albums from Steeleye Span (*Hark! The Village Wait*) and Fotheringay would justify much of the expectation, Matthews Southern Comfort would comfortably outsell the combined outputs of both outfits. But whatever their respective sales, Matthews Southern Comfort continued sharing the same column inches and concert halls with Fairport and Fotheringay.

For Ashley, things would remain in the air a while longer. Though a version of Steeleye Span would be resurrected at year's end, with Martin Carthy in tow, it would be a very different outfit from the one that assembled in the wiles of Wiltshire to rehearse an album of traditional songs in the winter of 1970, as Tyger turned his back on both Fairport and all forms of American(ized) music.

That original Span broke up the day of their final session, without playing a single show and with barely a civil word exchanged. Yet the resultant album has come to be viewed as something of an electric folk classic, a high-water mark for electric folk. It would be some time before a band by the name of Steeleye went on to far greater commercial success than Fairport.

Those June 1970 releases by Steeleye Span and Fotheringay ended up sharing the record racks that summer with a 'second' Matthews Southern Comfort album (*Second Spring*), as well as Fairport's fulsome fifth. It seemed to suggest a collective folk-rock crusade prog audiences and the weekly music press could embrace.

Indeed, for the next six months it seemed as if all things were possible – especially after Matthews Southern Comfort secured that number one single the others secretly craved. But the Fairport curse of instability had been transmitted to all these bands, none of whom would remain viable entities for longer than the time it took Richard Thompson to despair of Fairport's current direction. By year's end, the folk-rock revolution would be once again on hold, much to the disappointment of its acolytes in the music press.

The most persistent of these was Karl Dallas, who in an April 1970 Saturday *Times* article had gleefully observed, 'There are, in fact, now five bands in existence which owe something of their origins to Fairport.' But even before the quintet's swathe of summer albums appeared, two of them had already been swept away by tides of internal dissension.

The first of the former Fairporters to release an album that year was also the first to call it a day. Surprisingly, it was Judy Dyble, who in January 1970 released the delightfully quirky *Morning Way* with her new singing partner, the Coleraine-born Jackie McAuley, under the nom de plume, Trader Horne.

The curious couple worked tirelessly on a record that seemed like a perfect English summer record – which is presumably why Dawn, Pye Records' prog subsidiary, released it in bleak mid-winter. But the experience of promoting an album for the first time only served to remind Judy of why she 'went to work at the Revolution [gallery] for a couple of years' after being fired by Fairport. Ian Matthews suggests, 'Judy didn't really process it that quickly. She just [felt] that she'd been sacked because she couldn't sing.' Indeed, the scars were still there to be seen, if not heard.

The one important lesson she *had* learnt in the interim was not to join bands with boyfriends. A brief spell in the proto-King Crimson outfit, Giles, Giles and Fripp, came about because her then-boyfriend,

Ian McDonald – destined for the real King Crimson – had brought her into the fold, only for that association to end when the pair broke up and Fripp and co. went schizo.

Wisely, Dybble made sure her relationship with Irish multi-instrumentalist McAuley was a platonic one, and a fleetingly fruitful one at that, with the latter proving a surprisingly sensitive songwriter and foil for Judy's will o' the wisp vocals and faux-folk sensibility. *Morning Way* and its equally quirky non-album single, 'Here Comes The Rain', have even come to epitomise a pseudo-category given a series of post-psychedelic albums which betray only the most nominal after-effects of acid or folk influence, but suggest much time spent reading Tolkien and having a toke: acid-folk.

By May 1970, though, Judy had remembered that even in 1968 'living in a van really got me down'. She promptly 'quit after a flaming row. The real problem [was] that I really don't like leaping about in vans and waking up with a head full of cotton wool and trying to go somewhere to sing.' It was to be the end of her involvement in music for three long decades:

Judy Dyble: The agency and management were fairly typical of the time and sent us careering all over the country with barely a moment to breathe. Both Jack and I were totally exhausted and there never seemed to be any money at the end of the day. I think I must have had a sort of breakdown that manifested itself as a tantrum. My personal life was going badly and I was all of a heap really. I just wanted to go and hide somewhere.

———

Having cut herself off from the Fairport family, Judy was not about to share her feelings of wanting 'to go and hide somewhere' with teenage friend Tyger, which was a mistake. He knew just how she felt. His own grieving process had barely begun in November 1969, when he began plotting his own escape route from the clan he had played the central part in formulating.

The formation of Steeleye Span was both more fraught and greatly accelerated. Bob Pegg, writing in *Club Folk* the following March, suggested, 'Tyger Hutchings, quit [Fairport] to join with Tim Hart and Maddy Prior, Gay and Terry Woods, in the process screwing a large amount of money out of RCA, and all in the middle of a nervous breakdown,' a scenario Pegg knew to be largely untrue.

The first short-lived line-up of Steeleye actually featured not only Gay and Terry Woods but also Bob and Carole Pegg. It lasted barely a fortnight. Before that, there had already been an ill-fated attempt on Ashley's part to form an alliance with Irish folk combo, Sweeney's Men. Indeed, Ashley stated at the time that he 'left Fairport Convention to join up with the three members of Sweeney's Men – Terry Woods, Andy Irvine and John Moynihan. That was going to be a group.'

The scheme got as far as a meeting at Ashley's home on November 10th, 1969 – just three days after Tyger and his fellow Fairporters played a set for Danish TV. Ashley really had just got off the plane. But with Terry Woods and John Moynihan already at loggerheads, Moynihan wanted nothing to do with any new band that involved the Woods.

As for Pegg's bald assertion that Ashley had succeeded in 'screwing a large amount of money out of RCA', the truth was far from that. While the Sweeney's Men project was still on the table, Tyger chanced to hear of a keen, independent producer-manager called Sandy Roberton who had a production deal with RCA that allowed him the kind of creative freedom enjoyed by only one other producer-manager in post-psychedelic London.

After enjoying a brief career as half of sixties pop duo Rick & Sandy, Roberton had worked his way into this position via the music publishing arm of Chess, Arc Music, and Blue Horizon, home of Fleetwood Mac. When Ashley and Terry Woods came to call, they immediately realised they had found a kindred spirit:

Sandy Roberton: It was while I was setting up the publishing arm for Blue Horizon, Goodie Two Shoes, that's when I got the call from Terry Woods. I suppose it's because I had this deal at RCA, [where] they gave me carte blanche to sign people. I'd signed Keith Christmas, Liverpool Scene, a bunch of others, quite a few of them folkies … I was [just] trying to get things going. It was Terry and Ashley [I met]. I think they had been to Harvest, and they said you should go see Sandy … Ashley had [already] made the contact with Sweeney's Men and brewed this idea up [of] doing a more traditional record. He saw Fairport was going to head in a different direction and wanted away from the whole of [the] Fairport [set-up]. There might have been some bad feeling. I think we agreed a deal there and then, I'd produce it and manage them.

Evidently, this meeting took place during the brief window when Tyger hoped the Sweeney trio would come on board. When he hit that reef, he turned round about and recruited Bob and Carole Pegg in lieu. But according to Bob, 'Carole and I wanted to be a band in our own right' – presumably along the lines of the soon-formed Mr Fox.

It was back to square one, do not pass Go, do not collect £200. Only after Ashley failed to persuade young traditionalists Robin and Barry Dransfield to embrace his grand experiment did he remember an animated conversation with folk duo Maddy Prior and Tim Hart, at the Keele folk festival, while on holiday from Fairport's folk-rock project. An attendant Karl Dallas recalled:

Those were in the days when electric folk was not established as a genre in its own right and they had long and involved conversations with him and with Bob Pegg, who was also there, on the merits of electrifying folk music.

Whatever ideological bond was formed that night, it brought the couple to mind just as Ashley and Terry Woods despaired of finding the right combination. The couple agreed to see how it went, and by mid-December 1969, Ashley was ready to talk to the papers about what he planned to do next:

I want to develop along the same lines as Fairport did. They scratched the surface, now we want to take traditional British songs and adapt them to an electric setting, creating an unmistakeable British sound. With Fairports, we found that this was far more successful than when we played our own material. But Fairports are still basically a rock group, and we would be folk musicians going electric.

A conceit more cogent than taking 'traditional British songs and adapt[ing] them to an electric setting' was quickly subsumed by the sheer necessity of getting such a disparate set of music-makers – and personalities – to gel. All too soon a dynamic was established which made Ashley piggy-in-the-middle of two warring couples. The clash of personalities would make for a very different dynamic from Fairport, even as its founding-father wanted to focus on the future:

> We're certainly not a carbon copy of Fairport Convention. Seven or eight years ago I used to go to folk clubs a lot but then I started playing with an electric band, so I suppose you could say this is a second wave of interest. It was purely an impulsive move forming the group, and we want to continue in the same vein – not necessarily all traditional music but producing a good English sound in the traditional idiom.

When he made such a claim, in April 1970, Ashley already knew this line-up would certainly not 'continue in the same vein'. A decision to rent a property in Winterbourne Stoke, near Salisbury, to work up the material for an album spectacularly failed to revive the bucolic spirit of Farley Chamberlayne, though that was presumably the idea.

In fact, as Maddy Prior later opined, 'This [really] is not the way to get to know people. Living cheek by jowl with complete strangers in the middle of nowhere is no guarantee of continued friendship. [But] despite the inevitable strains of two couples and a referee, the music was surprisingly satisfying.'

It was more than that, it was electrifying. As Ashley recalled the following year, when a more stable Steeleye were treading the boards, 'It just evolved. It sounds very haphazard ... I am continually astounded by what we ... achieved by complete chance.' The songs they worked on in Wiltshire came from the three core collectors, all male. And just as Ashley insisted at the very outset, all twelve were traditional – save for 'Twa Corbies', which he fancifully attributed to William Motherwell's *Minstrelsy* (it was actually one of Walter Scott's literatized reworkings).

Despite Tyger's doctrinaire approach, the material was as broad as it was long, spanning everything from two fine romantic ballads, 'Dark-Eyed Sailor' and 'Lowlands Of Holland', to the social commentary of 'Blackleg Miner' and the hybrid night-visit/press-gang lament, 'All Things Are Quite Silent'.

But for the man who put Steeleye together, the joyfulness of the music-making was constantly offset by a battleground he daily surveyed: 'It was a freezing winter – the wind and the snow was coming over Salisbury Plain. I remember two things about it – one was standing between these two couples trying to keep them apart; and [the other was] the cold.'

Terry Woods later suggested that Tim Hart was to some extent preying on a vunerable Tyger, who 'was not very mentally strong at that point ... He was still getting over that crash ... It [was] not really the "bands of friends" ethic that Ashley and I had started out with.' And yet, when Ashley resurrected the band later in 1970, it would be the Woods not the Harts who drew the short straw.

At least the girls seemed to get along, Gay Wood coaching Maddy in Irish step dancing and working on their vocal harmonies while their partners blew off steam. But by the time Steeleye went into the studio to record the results of their wintry sojourn, it was all but certain the sessions would end this association.

Everyone agreed to keep their mutual animosities in check for the week it took to record the album Ashley had been wanting to make ever since Sandy missed the flight to Denmark. Indeed, the producer completed his part in the project without an inkling that there was no great future for this electric folk collective:

Sandy Roberton: I didn't know even at rehearsals there had been tensions between Gay and Terry, and Maddy and Tim. It was almost a foregone conclusion that they would make [the] record, [but] not perform live. I'd got RCA to commit to the record – they had put up the money and covered the costs for them to rehearse. [Then] they hit me with a bombshell – they're gonna split up ... [which] they told me right towards the end, at mixing, 'cause they wanted to make [the] record – it was a badge of honour.

Ashley Hutchings: It was scrappy in a few places. But ... [*Hark!*] is a leap forward. One thing it introduced was harmony singing, which we didn't have on *Liege & Lief*. Also the squeeze boxes as well – and banjos. It was a move. It wasn't just copying. It was made in a week. We weren't thinking in commercial terms, [but rather] how exciting this was. We did the last session on *Hark!* and broke up – in the studio. It was that instant ... By the time the album was finished, we just wanted to sink back and say, 'Phew, let's not go through that again.' And that was the end of the band ... So we just made the album. We just about made the album, to put it more correctly.

The results delighted all concerned, Ashley in particular, who notified *Sounds'* Jerry Gilbert the following April he considered *Hark! The Village Wait*, 'the most enjoyable to listen to of all the albums I've played on, and that includes the Fairport albums ... The general feeling of the album, technical [deficiencies] aside, is what I enjoy listening to most of all.' It was indeed a badge of honour, if a non-starter commercially in an era when albums were promoted in performance. Remarkably, neither producer nor bandleader seemed greatly fazed:

Sandy Roberton: There was never enough money and ... B&C's royalty department was a joke but, perhaps naively, I didn't mind. I was just delighted to [be] making albums without interference. The great virtue of the arrangement was that my word was enough ... They just left me to get on with it.

Ashley now had a new distraction in his life – the very voice that had rescued him in his darkest hour, the previous December – in the buxom shape of Shirley Collins. Collins was a traditional singer of the old school who, with her sister Dolly, had made some of the purest, most unadulterated records of the whole sixties folk revival. If he had not realised he was besotted with that ideal before, he knew he was by the time he left the home of the English Folk Song & Dance Society one spring afternoon:

Ashley Hutchings: Shirley enters the picture in 1970. We'd formed Steeleye, we'd broken up Steeleye and I met her at Cecil Sharp House. I'd met her once before with Fairport. We did a gig in Liverpool in early '69, where she and Dolly were playing. We treated her like [folk] royalty. We helped carry her portable pipe organ in and out of the venue. Then I went to Cecil Sharp to see something or other and she was there. I walked across the room and gave her a kiss. I was drawn to her, for sure. Then within six months we were a couple. We moved to Sussex. Suddenly I was a stepdad to two children.

Without a thought for how he might make ends meet or continue his musical career, Ashley prepared to hitch his wagon to a way of life he knew not. As he says, 'It was now time to roll up my sleeves, to get dirty and to dig deep, both musically and spiritually ... This was my move from the city to the country.'

But before he headed for the musical wilderness, he had a number of prior commitments, including an impromptu appearance at a 'benefit' gig the Fairport boys were playing for the folk of Little Hadham, Herts. It was August 22nd, 1970, and the *Full House* Fairport had agreed to play the village fete as a thank you to the locals for taking these young weirdos to their bosom.

After Pegg and co. 'entertained' the locals with the likes of 'Sloth' and 'Walk Awhile', Ashley and Ian Matthews joined the five-piece for nostalgic runthroughs of 'Blues In The Bottle', 'High School Confidential' and two songs which once defined the *What We Did* era, 'Mr Lacey' and 'Meet On The Ledge'. It would be sixteen years before all seven shared a stage again.

In the aftermath of an exhilarating afternoon, Ashley found himself sitting with Richard and Simon. Sensing kindred spirits, he blurted out, 'I really miss not being in the band anymore. I'd love to be involved ... Is there still a place for me?' The others shuffled uncomfortably, and muttered apologies. The message was clear: you can't come home again.

This longing – exacerbated by the demise of Steeleye Mk.1 – passed away in time, though not before he took Shirley to see Fairport play the Albert Hall in October. She spent most of the time watching him, 'It was really sad ... He obviously wanted to be there with them.' But Fairport were no longer his band and he was no longer their 'Tyger'. In grief, he turned to the reformed Steeleye Tim Hart had recently pushed him into (re)joining.

———

At this stage the other 'guest' Fairportee at the Little Hadham fete was in an entirely different place. While recording a second Matthews Southern Comfort album – the first by the band which bore its name – Ian had also recorded his band's next single, a Fairportesque interpretation of another Joni Mitchell song. By October, 'Woodstock' was sitting on top of the British charts, while the singer was wondering how the hell he got from Scunthorpe to here:

Ian Matthews: Musically, I knew I wanted a pedal steel guitar because through Fairport I had really gotten into The Byrds' [*Sweetheart Of The Rodeo*]. I really started being influenced by that sound of a contemporary country band and I wanted to try and move in that direction. While everyone around me was just screaming and hollering about The Band, I didn't get [*Music From*] *Big Pink*. I didn't get it at all. I was more into Ian and Sylvia. I was listening to what Eric Andersen was doing at that time. I loved that sound, and decided that that's what I wanted to try and do.

Where he was not so lucky was in his choice of managers. As he was 'thinking about whether I had a career or whether I was just going to pack it in, I hooked up with [Ken] Howard and [Alan] Blaikley. At that point not only were they songwriters, but they were high-powered managers, too. They were managing The Herd and Dave Dee. That swayed me into going with them.'

Under various pseudonyms – one of which ('Steve Barlby') would receive four credits and three co-credits on *Matthews' Southern Comfort* – the pair had enjoyed a number of notable pop hits, including 'Have I The Right?' (The Honeycombs), and were looking to take Matthews's distinctive voice in a poppier direction. At the same time, they realised the music scene was becoming more album-oriented, and were anxious to carve a niche for themselves before it was too late:

Ian Matthews: [They] took me on the understanding that I was going to do some of their songs, and we kind of sold ourselves to the record company on that basis. But then I started to change my mind … The initial concept was that Howard and Blaikley were going to write an album of songs for me, and consequently have their name associated with progressive pop music… You know, it would help them cross over… [But] I really kicked against that. I did not want a complete album of Howard and Blaikley songs because, quite honestly, they didn't have a complete [album in them].

In the battle for the soul of his debut solo album, Ian had enlisted some familiar allies. Still sharing that Brent flat with Richard Thompson, he asked the songwriter to write him a song. The result, 'A Commercial Proposition', was to Ian's mind, 'the ultimate post-motorway crash song. That's how I saw it. I think Richard just saw it as the most commercial thing he'd ever written. He wrote the song and [after] he listened to it ... thought, "Mm, that's pretty commercial." And he just threw a title on to it ... That's what Richard used to do. His titles hardly ever had any reference to the song at that time.'

Set to a chorus which repeatedly insisted, 'Everything's alright now, you don't have a trouble and you don't have a care,' Richard's verses suggested otherwise. He even slipped in a nod to his current musical direction, 'Bring in the fiddle you left out on the stair'. It was a perfect way to announce the new Ian, while serving to inspire the solo singer to impose himself on proceedings:

Ian Matthews: I ended up writing lyrics and having [Howard and Blaikley] write the music for the songs, and I brought in Richard's song. At that point I tried to influence the songs that they presented to me in a more folky light than the way they were presented to me, [which was] as heavy-weight pop songs. Some of them were not adaptable. There's a couple of them that just remained that.

The *Heyday* Fairport's involvement with the project did not end there. As the sessions began, Ian pushed all three founders to lend a hand, as they would do on albums by Marc Ellington and Al Stewart that same summer. The crash-scarred survivors welcomed any opportunity to make music with friends, while considering their options.

Ashley matter-of-factly states, 'We liked what [Ian] was doing,' even as he steered Fairport in a contrariwise direction. When Ian reiterated his need for a pedal steel-player, it was Ashley who suggested Gordon Huntley. Meanwhile, Richard's input kept the project on track until Ian had reached a point where he had enough confidence to take over the reins himself:

Ian Matthews: I hired Richard as producer, and we talked about who we were getting in to play on the album. We decided to get Ashley in to play bass … I think Simon played on it, too. What that does say to me … is that I was desperately trying to hold on to those relationships, and [that] there were no bad feelings from my side about what had gone down. I was just getting on with my career and they were the best players I knew … [Then Richard] decided that he didn't want to have his name on it. I don't think he wanted to be associated with Ken and Alan. He had an image to protect and that was his way of doing it. [There] was a combination of elements that turned Richard off. He wasn't there for the mixing, so … I just [took over].

Work on *Matthews' Southern Comfort* had begun in June 1969 – making it the Fairporters' first post-crash recordings. By the time he delivered the album it was very different to the one his managers had originally envisaged, and Ian had gained a far clearer idea of what he wanted and what he needed to make that happen. He now calls that solo debut 'a stepping stone … a Ken and Alan album, with me putting in my percentage of what I knew and what I was familiar with'. But he gave an altogether more caustic assessment back in 1971, 'I had to take other people's advice about what I should record and how I should record it. That's why it sounds such a mess.'

Yet patchy as it may be, *Matthews' Southern Comfort* has moments. And two of Ian's best early compositions, 'Thoughts For A Friend' and 'What We Say', both point the way forward. After much soul-searching, he was heading in an almost exact straight line from the country-rock Fairport once played, toward a sound that – according to his own contemporary description – was 'halfway between Area Code 615 and *Sweetheart Of The Rodeo.*'

It was a willing dissociation from his former band's aesthetic, one which led him to proclaim to *Disc* on the album's release that 'Fairport did influence me while I was with them. But … now I have found country music, and that's where it's at. I think it's the most moving type of music there is.' Elsewhere, though, he was inclined to admit that, 'in fact, I use the same rhythm sound as [Fairport] do, and people say theirs is folk – so how does one describe it? Volume wise they are louder – but basically it's [all] just electric folk.'

He knew he couldn't match Fairport 'volume wise', and he didn't really want to. In fact, Ian hadn't really thought about *how* he was going to go out and promote his own album. In the end, he decided he wanted the umbrella of a 'real' band around him. So he decided to create a band with the same name as his own (solo) album:

Ian Matthews: [The band] wasn't something I was talked into. It was definitely something that came from me and I decided that I wanted to give it a name … I was listening to Ian and Sylvia. And I thought the Southern Comfort was pretty applicable for what I was doing … and I liked the song [of that name]. It ended up being a stage song once the band came together, and it just had a flow to it, Matthews Southern Comfort. I felt a lot better about doing it then.

Still looking for his former colleagues' benediction, Ian Matthews' Southern Comfort made their live debut at Mothers on February 1st, 1970, with Fairport lending moral support to their support act. The very idea of sharing a bill with Fairport made Ian 'incredibly nervous', even if for now he had little idea what the band he had once been asked to leave now sounded like.

Nor did anyone else there that night. After all, this was only *their* third gig since Peggy replaced Ashley (and no one replaced Sandy). But Ian clearly remembers 'being stunned by how loud they were', as well as still a little in awe of his former compadres:

Ian Matthews: There were a series of shows that we all did together … It made me a little uncomfortable, because I felt at the time that I had to measure up to what they were doing. I just didn't have that sort of confidence in Southern Comfort. So it was kind of a bittersweet experience.

He knew he would have to make do with Southern Comfort for now, but perhaps that 'bittersweet experience' crystallized his musical goals. By the time he formed his next band, Plainsong, in 1972 he was openly stating that his intent was to put 'a bit more punch in [this band] than the electric sound which I had with Southern Comfort … Something like the old Fairport sound is what we're after.'

The influence had already begun to tell in his own songwriting, even as he continued to dollop pedal-steel across the multittracks. On the July *Second Spring*, Southern Comfort's true debut, Ian included a powerful Fairportesque arrangement of 'Blood Red Roses', spattered with the spirit of *Hark! The Village Wait*. Meanwhile, self-penned songs like 'Ballad Of Obray Ramsey' and 'Jinkson Johnson' suggested his Brent flatmate was not the only resident looking to tie together contemporary and traditional styles.

But Ian's fragile confidence meant he was rarely at ease, or embraced the spirit of friendly competition, real or imagined, former Fairporters exuded. When Southern Comfort went on tour with Fotheringay, all he could think was 'how eclectic they were. I just thought that they were a remarkably good unit, and [that] they were heading in a direction that maybe I could've gone in if I hadn't been so hasty to get a pedal steel player in.'

On the brink of latching onto his folk/country ideal with a band that was slowly learning to adapt to his musical ideas, the worst of all possible things happened – he had a hit record. And not just a hit, a number one single. Suddenly all the self-doubts Ian had been keeping at bay came banging at his door:

Ian Matthews: I just couldn't cope with everything that came along with a hit record. I didn't want to know about it, and it wouldn't go away – photo sessions, stupid questions all the time … I just didn't know what having a hit record entailed … [So] I [have] had a real love/hate relationship with that period. I loved the idea of having the number one song in the country but at the same time it forced me out of my shell and it just made me very uncomfortable. It took a lot of my songwriting time away from me. I was trying very hard to become a songwriter at that time and all I seemed to be doing was interview after interview after interview. There was always something else that I had to do that would take me away from what I wanted to do … It wasn't merely *Top of the Pops*. It's that whole grind of one-night stands that wear you down physically until it becomes just another job.

As so often when one is not thinking straight, the scale and suddenness of this success convinced Ian he hated the whole Southern Comfort sound, one he had been carrying in his head from the day he left Fairport but which he now decided 'was not the sound that

I wanted to be represented by ... I had become disenchanted with the dominant sound of a pedal steel guitar in a band. At the time, I thought that the band was musically shallow, but it wasn't. And it wasn't until after I'd left that I realised ... there could've been other options if I'd been thinking more clearly, if I'd really been dissecting what I was feeling.'

Instead, he walked out on a band cast in his own image in the middle of a tour to promote his third and their second album, *Later The Same Year*, during a sell-out show in the same Midlands city where they had made their live debut less than a year before. And this time he was not gonna let Howard and Blaikley change his mind:

Ian Matthews: I handled it so badly ... I just went into free fall. I was just so confused about what we were doing. I was so angry at myself for not having the nerve to address issues. I started walking out on the band. I remember doing a show in Scarborough and feeling, halfway through the show, that what we were doing was so desperately pointless and I just unplugged my guitar and walked off stage. The final straw was playing at the Birmingham Town Hall. We did the soundcheck, and it was just a crap soundcheck. But my head was in such a place that I projected the soundcheck on to [an] actual show to a roomful of people and I left the soundcheck and walked up and down the street and got on the train and went home without saying anything to anybody. And then locked myself in my flat for three or four days. My management took to pushing notes under the door.

At almost exactly the same time was Ian boarding the train from Birmingham, his erstwhile vocal foil in Fairport was convening a meeting with her own band to inform them she was breaking up Fotheringay. Her reason for pulling the plug? Too little success.

It had all started out so promisingly – even if Sandy's disagreements with her manager were as profound as Ian's with Howard and Blaikley. Yet Sandy, for all her mood swings, had absolute faith in Joe Boyd as a musical soundboard. Also, though she rarely admitted it publicly, she had always felt ambivalent about forming another band. Boyd was in no doubt she should become a solo artist and expressed these thoughts in typically forthright fashion in the immediate aftermath of her departure from the band she loved:

Joe Boyd: Sandy was nervous that … she wouldn't get a record deal. I said, 'You must be joking.' … During that conversation, she also expressed reservations about doing a solo record and said she might form a group … I told her all the best musicians would love to play for her solo record [and that] she would be worth more to A&M as a solo artist … Anyway, the question was not resolved.

There was another factor to now consider in Sandy's case – her live-in partner, ex-folk musician Trevor Lucas, who from this point forward would be a force to be reckoned with in the lady's life and musical career. An impolitic Boyd candidly admits, 'At the time I didn't have much sympathy for this [relationship]. With my single-minded view, I thought, "Oh come on, what's more important here?"' Trevor and Joe were never going to be bosom buddies even before Sandy informed her manager she was forming a band with Trevor:

Joe Boyd: I said, 'Please don't.' … Trevor liked the trappings, he liked the good life. Fairport were down to earth – get a decent place to rehearse, get a van that'll get you from A to B, and think about the music. They weren't interested in hanging out at The Scotch of St James.

Like Ian, Sandy lacked the innate confidence to front her own band, preferring to hide behind a collective, even one consciously cast in the image of Fairport. Once her beau informed her that he was disbanding Eclection, the next step was a done deal and a package deal, which came complete with Eclection's dynamic drummer:

Gerry Conway: [Trevor and I] were trying to keep together something that didn't want to be together … [Eclection] had lost its spark. I can remember having a conversation with Trevor and Sandy at Trevor's flat … chatting about musicians and music, and out of that by the end of the night it [became], 'Let's form a band.' We decided that we would all like to do something together, [which] left us to find a bass and guitar player.

Meanwhile, Sandy had arranged to go see Crosby, Stills, Nash and Young at the Royal Albert Hall on January 6th. She came away more than ever convinced that her own band should be free of such monstrous egos: 'I thought they were musically brilliant. But they seemed to have forgotten they had an audience.' The experience prompted Sandy to inform the short-lived *Music Now*:

> This will be a *group*. It's not just my group, everybody will have a say in what goes on ... I decided against going solo because I would have had to work with a backing group [and] I knew that relationship would have been no good. I couldn't have worked like that. I like to be part of a group.

By the time Boyd returned from California with an eye-watering solo deal for Sandy, courtesy of A&M, her new band – initially called Tiger's Eye – was a *fait accompli*:

Joe Boyd: A&M eventually came up with a $40,000 advance figure – twice what they had paid for the Fairport Convention albums – and an immense amount of money in 1970. [But] by the time I returned from California with this offer, Sandy had already begun rehearsals with Albert Lee, Pat Donaldson, Gerry Conway and Trevor ... I kept telling Sandy that she would need to tour to support the expense of the band – the very position she left Fairport [over], because she didn't want to be touring all the time.

Boyd, who could generally see trouble ahead, did his best to head it off at the pass. When A&M finally agreed to consider Sandy and 'her' band as one and the same, he begged Sandy, 'Can we at least structure it as your group, your deal and your name on the contract?' A headstrong Sandy refused: 'It had to be a five-way collaborative deal.'

That decision alone made the band untenable in the long term, while ensuring that decisions about future Fotheringay releases would be determined 'collectively', in this life and the next – hence the 'fake' *Fotheringay 2,* released in Sandy's and Trevor's names in 2008, and the highly disappointing 2015 Fotheringay boxed-set, *Nothing More.*

Lucas felt he now had license to go out and spend a large chunk of the initial A&M advance on a sound system out of all proportion to the band's status or needs. The set-up would confine the band to concert halls and concert tours at a time when Fairport played any venue that would cover their costs. A still-besotted Sandy sought to portray Trevor's finespun bull as business acumen:

> We can only play large dates because of the cost of moving equipment … Our roadies have christened the amps Stonehenge … But we need an amplifying system like that. Without it it's impossible to do the electric guitar work we do – and hear it clearly … Ours is a more intricate sound, and you need all those amplifiers to bring out the detail.

The sound system proved so big, they had to hire a seven-and-a-half tonne truck just to transport it. As a result, to quote roadie Gordon 'Doon' Graham, 'We never toured enough to cover the costs.' That was one unnecessary drain on the Denny bank account. Another was putting the whole band on retainer while they worked up a repertoire, pushing their account into the red before a note was even recorded. At least the music was worthwhile, and for the new bassist these rehearsals were a fond and abiding memory:

Pat Donaldson: We spent a long time playing through … the songs. It was a good band from that point of view. We were always arranging songs – it was a pleasant thing to do because everybody was in the same frame of mind. Nobody wanted to be the superstar of the group.

If the process of creating an entirely new set from scratch was challenging enough, it became greatly extended when Sandy's chosen guitarist, Albert Lee, reluctantly admitted he was in the wrong band and these songs were really not his cup of tea:

Gerry Conway: After a couple of weeks of rehearsals, [Trevor noticed that] Albert would sit in a corner … [He] said, 'I don't know if Albert's happy. We'll have to tackle him.' Albert had virtually not uttered a word in two weeks. So we asked him, and he said, 'Well, I've been meaning to say…'

It is hard to see what Sandy, who had personally travelled to Ireland to recruit Lee, had been thinking. He was a fine country picker, who had made a series of terrific country-rock singles for Bell – including a double-slice of Big Pink, 'Tears Of Rage b/w Too Much Of Nothing', but he should have been auditioning for Southern Comfort. He confided as much to an American guitarist of similar pedigree:

Jerry Donahue: I knew Albert didn't feel it was much of a vehicle for his style of playing ... but Pat Donaldson persisted ... He said they wanted a guitarist who wasn't strictly English in his approach and could cover the more country elements in Trevor's writing.[17]

Fortuitously, when Lee finally mustered the resolve to quit, he suggested Donahue as his replacement. The ex-pat, initially non-plussed by the folkier aspects of the music, persevered until he found a way into their faux-folk sound. Once again, though, there was a scheduling issue:

Jerry Donahue: I went to the audition as they were about to start recording. At the time I was due to go on a European tour with The Tumbleweeds ... I was already committed to doing it ... I even suggested that Albert Lee should do the recording, and that I'd join them when I got back. But fortunately for me they decided to have a break, anyway.

This break gave the singer the opportunity to write some more songs to beef up the newly-christened Fotheringay's set. Sandy needed all the help she could get. Trevor's one notable contribution was a folk-style ballad about Australia's most notorious outlaw, Ned Kelly (about to be played on celluloid by Mick Jagger, who used the worst Irish accent in movie history). If the album was not going to be mostly covers, Sandy was going to have to come up with goods to go with the gorgeous 'The Pond And The Stream' which she had written the previous summer.

Fleetingly in the frame for the fourth Fairport album, 'The Pond And The Stream' was about Anne Briggs, whom she openly described

---

[17] Those 'country elements in Trevor's writing' remained a distant speck on the horizon throughout the band's existence.

as 'the best girl singer of traditional music'. A song of longing for the simple life, it consciously eulogized someone who 'used to go off and live in woods when[ever] she felt like it'. But most of the new songs she brought to rehearsals not so much addressed what Sandy did on her holidays as evoked memories of an idyllic childhood in Broadstairs, Kent:

Sandy Denny: We were right on the sea. Down to the bottom of the garden and over a field and there it was. So I suppose it must have stuck … When I write songs I often picture myself standing on a beach or standing on a rock on a promenade or something. I just put myself there sometimes, and without even realising it I find myself describing what I'm looking at and often it's the sea … I really can't think of anywhere that's nicer than that. [1973]

The addition of 'The Sea' and 'Winter Winds' – both replete with coastal imagery – still left Fotheringay light of songs when they entered Sound Techniques for the first time on February 18th, 1970. But Sandy was anxious to make her own statement – and collect a much-needed album advance.

It would take an English folk ballad contemporary with 'The Bonny Bunch Of Roses' to demonstrate that Sandy's new band were no slouches when it came to interpreting tradition and could rein themselves in when tackling one of A.L. Lloyd's 'big ballads'. Their drummer remembered the heavily-rehearsed epic taking its own sweet time finding its kernel of greatness:

Gerry Conway: 'Banks Of The Nile' was [a song] we rehearsed, but it never really settled and when we got in the studio, it was still in a state of flux. We came to record the song … and it wasn't quite happening. It was a long song, a lot of verses … so we went to the pub and [had] a conversation. We decided that we were just gonna go in and busk it. And that's exactly what happened. It was a first take, everybody doing what they felt.

Even such an affecting reinterpretation of a traditional stalwart failed to convince Sandy doing such songs played to her or their strengths, while her chosen producer, Joe Boyd, made it clear he considered them no Fairport: 'It might have been that I was the wrong person for the job, because of my lack of enthusiasm for the basic concept.' In fact, Boyd found it 'painful ... to hear her working with a group who just weren't at the level of Fairport. Jerry Donahue was not Richard. Gerry Conway was not Mattacks.' The others quickly gleaned his 'lack of enthusiasm':

Jerry Donahue: [Boyd] never really had his heart in Fotheringay. He used to do the production, but he pretty much left it to the engineers. He would sit with his feet on the console reading a newspaper. We were all buzzing around, having a fantastic time. He just never seemed that interested. He'd make the occasional opinion – 'I think you ought to do that one again' – [but] he should have been a lot more involved.

Yet whatever birth pangs surrounded *Fotheringay*, they do not linger in the grooves of an album that still repays repeated listens. Sandy's four originals are a uniform joy, while two contemporary covers reflect the same sensibility as the post-accident Fairport. One of these was a *Basement Tapes* gem already covered by Albert Lee's Country Fever, 'Too Much Of Nothing', necessarily sung as a Sandy/Trevor duet.

The other country-rock standard Sandy wanted to record was 'Silver Threads & Golden Needles'. But democracy demanded that this terrific take make way for a lugubrious Lucas contribution, Gordon Lightfoot's 'The Way I Feel'. Even after slowing it down to accommodate Lucas's Aussie drawl, it was obvious filler, put there to preserve the fiction that Fotheringay were a cooperative. They could do better, as Sandy soon agreed. Within weeks of *Fotheringay*'s release she was telling the media the album was not representative of where Fotheringay were really at:

We have been doing the material on the album at gigs, but from now on we will be doing new things. Once something is done and recorded, it is pointless to do those same songs all the time ... The only problem is that the audience want to hear the album tracks. But you mustn't let that stand in the way. The new material will be more exciting for the band to play, so the audience will get a better performance.

The venues they were booked to play, and the expectations of paying audiences, presented another obstacle to mass acceptance. The formalized Fotheringay set was in stark contrast to the spontaneity of Fairport club gigs from yesteryear. These musicians were reluctant to play any song not previously rehearsed, knowing no one in the band could emulate Thompson's gift for extemporisation.

There was another way in which Fotheringay was not Fairport. Their solution to their financial predicament was not to play more gigs and win their audience over, but to play less gigs and rehearse more. It was a situation which infuriated at least one Fairporter. Bassist Dave Pegg admits he 'used to get pissed off about Fotheringay, because we'd be doing about two hundred gigs a year ... [whereas] I think they only did about six gigs. But we knew they were getting paid the same as we were getting.'

In fact, Witchseason were no longer handling Fotheringay on a day-to-day basis, and all that money 'they were getting paid' was being carefully tallied against the A&M advance. Sandy professed not to care. After a month-long national tour to promote *Fotheringay*, the collective retired to the country for the summer, renting a large farmhouse on the Sussex coast, because as Sandy insisted:

> Rehearsal time is very valuable to us, and since we've been living down in the country we rehearse an awful lot more ... In London we tend to spend more time drinking tea than actually working. But life in the country is far more condusive to work.

Yet, when a relocated Ashley came to call and see his old friend, with his new partner and stepchildren in tow, the comely Collins was shocked to find Fotheringay 'virtually ignored us. When they finished their game [of football], they went into the house, leaving us outside to play with my children ... [even though] we'd travelled some distance. I thought them a self-centered, rather graceless bunch, really only interested in themselves.'

The once-worldly Sandy seemed to Shirley to be building a band whose primary purpose was to serve as a buffer against the world and a balm to her fragile ego. If this was indeed the case, the bubble was about to be pricked by the most successful singer-songwriter of the seventies, someone Fotheringay seemed to think would make a

good support act for a much-vaunted relaunch at the Royal Albert
Hall on October 2nd:

Jerry Donahue: Elton [John], Pat, Gerry, I and Linda Peters [aka
Thompson] were all enlisted by Joe Boyd [that summer] to go in and
do fourteen [demos] in one day ... and the way [Elton] was playing
– he was a wonderful piano player – [seemed] sensitive enough ...
[So] we thought he'd be a really good opener for us. Be we had no
idea ... he was going to do the most incredible rock'n'roll show ever.
He pretty much blew us off the stage.[18]

The performance Fotheringay put on that October night
suggested that they had been on their summer holidays. They
sounded surprisingly under rehearsed and the new material – with
the exception of a blistering anti-war song, 'John The Gun' (perhaps
Sandy's answer to 'Sloth') – comprised folk songs like 'Gypsy Davy'
(Child 200) and 'Wild Mountain Thyme', a folk standard with
Scottish roots and a lovely Gaelic air that brought out the best in
singer and guitarist alike. Such a return to folk roots was partly
enforced. The economics of the band demanded another album
and advance by year's end but strong original songs were in short
supply.[19]

Both Sandy and Trevor were already distancing themselves from
Fotheringay's first offering, Trevor publicly complaining, 'The
trouble with the first album was that we hadn't played the songs
enough beforehand,' while Sandy insisted, 'The next album can't
fail to be better than the first ... [which] was all right for when it
was recorded, but it was the preliminary effort of the group ... [The
band] has got hardly anything to do with that [now].'

By this time, though, Fotheringay's London showcase had come
to be seen as the night of the big letdown and perhaps the beginning
of the end. Sandy granted Karl Dallas an interview to blow off steam
about the pressures to which she was being subjected:

[18] That fabled set of demos, half sung by Elton, half by Linda Peters, has been bootlegged
on CD as *The 1968 Demos* [sic] and released 'officially' in Japan as *Prologue*, in both cases
credited to Elton John.
[19] A fortnight after the Albert Hall, Trevor was insisting, 'We really are getting more material
together and we'll have five new numbers ready for our Autumn concert tour,' but four
were traditional arrangements.

I kept getting approached by people who were telling me things about this member of the group and that member of the group and [how] you'd do much better without him and him, and why don't you do this or that. These were all private intrusions to me. People kept approaching me and saying, 'Listen, you could be a superstar,' and this and that ... In the end I said to [these] people that I was just one member of a group and if they wanted me without the group then they could piss off ... [Because] that one gig was made into like the end of the group, nearly.

The only way out of this encroaching negativity was to deliver a second album which delivered on all the promise of the first, minus the filler and with Trevor firmly relegated to a support role. But in a joint interview in *Sounds*, shortly after the Albert Hall gig, Sandy seemed to suggest this was the last thing on her mind, insisting, 'I know I sing more songs than Trevor, but that's purely accidental.'

Two mid-November BBC sessions, both recorded the week before scheduled album sessions, included two songs which suited Trevor's vocal range and timbre. Both were traditional: the Australian outlaw ballad, 'Bold Jack Donahue', and an obscure Child ballad of elopement, 'Eppy Moray'.[20]

At least by December the lady had come up with the obtuse, but powerful, 'Late November', based on a strange dream she had the week before the Fairport motorway crash, which she subsequently convinced herself was some kind of prophetic foretelling, in the tradition of the popular ballads she grew up with.

Those very ballads – which had kept her own songs off *Liege & Lief,* prompting her to quit Fairport – now returned with a vengeance. During the BBC sessions she unveiled chilling versions of 'Gypsy Davy', 'Wild Mountain Thyme' and 'Lowlands Of Holland', the last of them a capella – as if matching the magnificent electric arrangement on *Hark! The Village Wait* might be too great a challenge for Fotheringay.

Meanwhile, they worked up a lovely understated electric arrangement of the English mystery-ballad 'Bruton Town', hardly indicative of the band Sandy described in a September interview:

[20] The only 'traditional' tune previously recorded for this song was provided by Ewan MacColl, who said he learnt the song from his family.

'Everybody's traits are coming out a bit, and the music is getting a lot louder ... [So] the next time you hear us I might be really blasting out with some incredible tone in my voice.'

Four of these songs were now recorded at the first two sessions for that all-important, break-or-bust second album. With such songs arranged in advance, Sandy was telling *Sounds* ahead of time, 'We [are] hoping to have it finished towards the beginning of November. I'm really looking forward to it.' As Donahue later observed, 'It was ... the peak of her enthusiasm with the band, the start of the second album.'

Once again, though, the twin challenge of finding a role for Trevor and writing enough original songs to suggest Fotheringay was not just a watered-down Fairport, slowly wore away at Sandy the optimist. A hiatus was called till mid-December, by which time she hoped to have more contemporary material. And indeed a December 18th session did yield a usable take of 'Late November' before Sandy resurrected a song she sang – and recorded – pre-Fairport, Dave Cousins's 'Two Weeks Last Summer'.

The producer, who had been played the original version by Sandy back in 1967, was fast losing patience with the process. He knew he had till the end of the year to complete work on *Fotheringay II*, because as of January 1, 1971, he was due to report for work at Warners in LA as music director for their film division. Witchseason had become a burden and Warners had offered him a way out.

After the December 18th session, Boyd, Sandy, Trevor and Pat Donaldson went for a bite at the pub opposite Sound Techniques. Boyd admits he was not in a good mood. Meanwhile, Sandy became increasingly emotional the more brandies she downed. The producer proceeded to repeat all of his previously-voiced concerns, one by one:

Joe Boyd: We hadn't finished our target for that day's recording ... Sandy was very upset. She was despairing of what they were going to do. The record wasn't going well, it was taking longer, so it was costing more, and the group was running out of money. Sandy was saying, 'What do you think I should do?' I replied that she should do what I had said in the first place: disband the group and be a solo artist. Sandy said if I did that would you stay in Britain? ... I recall that I said, I'd already sold the company and been appointed director of music services at Warner Brothers, [but] if there was anything that could make me want to undo those steps, it was what she'd just said.

In the version Joe gave *Rolling Stone* in 1973 – the earliest of many accounts of that drink-fuelled conversation, and probably the most accurate – he admitted, 'I said if she would break up the group I would think about staying in London to produce her. The next day I told her I couldn't; that I had to go to LA, and she shouldn't base her decision on me. The amount of time spent under that rash commitment was about twelve hours.'

It was apparently long enough for a now-sober Sandy to convene a meeting of the band for the following morning to inform the others she was disbanding Fotheringay. Those not party to the pub showdown were stunned:

Jerry Donahue: We'd reached a peak in our careers at that time. [But] Joe Boyd decided that Sandy should break into a solo career, so he aborted the second album when we were about halfway through recording it. No one really agreed with him that it was the right time for it, including Sandy herself. She was in tears when she told us. She'd never been happier. The way things were going, the second album was likely to do even better than the first. It was all so sudden and there were no warning signs. We'd been to a Christmas party only a few nights before Sandy broke the news to us, and she'd been really enjoying herself and saying how well things were going. I remember Sandy telling us that Joe Boyd had been offered a big job with Warners and that he [said he'd] turn it down if she'd go solo … Joe went off to Warners anyway. She was very bitter about that afterwards.

That lingering bitterness would effectively end Sandy's close friendship with Boyd. On the two occasions she was asked directly about that evening, in 1973 and 1974, she reiterated, 'He said he would stay in England and not take the offer to join Warner Brothers … And finally … I agreed to do it, [reasoning that] if he felt so strongly about it, then I thought he's got to be right … [because] he was a really good friend of mine.' Boyd thinks the financial realities had already begun to bite so Sandy was simply belatedly facing up to the inevitable:

Joe Boyd: I don't think she took great note of what I was saying because it was coming from 'the great Joe Boyd'. It was because I was only saying what she knew to be true. She saw [with] my departure that she was gonna be alone with these doubts and these fears ... about this group: creatively, financially, structurally, again and again ... [So] she leapt on an opportunity to get herself out of this mess ... [Because now it's] a year later, the money's running out and ... when this next advance comes in, all it's gonna do is wipe out your debts.

All of which remains assuredly true. The band *had* become untenable, and no realignment of the band's repertoire to something more folk-based would do anything other than delay the inevitable. Asked to explain her reasoning the following month, Sandy told an important media supporter, 'All the time I felt very responsible to the group for finding songs and writing songs. I was conscious that a lot of pressure was on me.'

Two weeks later, Fotheringay gave their farewell concert at the Queen Elizabeth Hall, attended by fans, friends and family alike. Yet even at this bittersweet leave-taking Karl Dallas couldn't resist taking potshots at the band's – and specifically Sandy's – ongoing lack of professionalism:

> Fotheringay's farewell concert at the Queen Elizabeth Hall on Saturday evening was exciting. It was also sloppy, under-rehearsed and of uneven quality ... Even if we disregard the necessarily spontaneous ensembles that were formed by the addition of such guest artists as Long John Baldry, Martin Carthy and Tyger Hutchings, about half the songs we heard were completely new material. One of them was so new that try as she might, Sandy Denny was quite incapable of remembering the first line, and had to start with the second.

Whatever Dallas's opinion, given the financial hole Fotheringay had dug for themselves, it does seem rather short-sighted not to officially record the show, which included a moving one-off encore of 'Let It Be' – the last Beatles single – sung by Sandy at the piano. It would have been a perfect contract filler, keeping the wolf from the door while she planned a solo career.

For a chastened Sandy, it was a brand new day. Like all those on the Witchseason roster, she was now an Island artist, pure and simple. As almost his last act before boarding the plane to LA, Boyd was passing the baton to Island boss, Chris Blackwell. Unlike Sandy, he had known for some time that with his own financial model, Witchseason had been living on borrowed time:

Joe Boyd: A crunch was coming; the debts were cross-collateralized … I went to see Chris Blackwell and worked out a deal where he would make good on all the debts … and I would get out of the middle of the whole situation. I had done a good job as a record producer, I'd built people's careers, but I hadn't done a good job as a commercial manager, 'cause nobody had any money – including me … [So] when Witchseason was sold to Island, there was a big toting up and there was a position arrived at for every individual signed to Witchseason. The idea was that everyone would do a new deal with Island directly, and their account balance would be transferred. Island was going to give each one an advance … giving them a clean slate going forward.

Blackwell wisely refuses to take any credit for the roster he thus effortlessly acquired, 'Witchseason was absolutely Joe's label, it reflected his taste … All I did was put the records out and support them in every way possible.' Witchseason, though, was no more and the onus was now on his label to maintain some kind of support structure.

Everyone in the now-disparate Fairport family – ex-singer, ex-bassist, ex-guitar wizard, even the rump which clung to Convention – would have to learn to fend for themselves. For Sandy it was the start of a career on the skids. As Thompson recently observed, 'After Joe left, Sandy was cut adrift a little. The people at Island didn't really see what was great about her, beyond how great a singer she was.' Even Thompson could not translate such a self-evident truth to the label.

8. Solo Singer, Needs Band

age 26—MELODY MAKER, September 19, 1970

SANDY DENNY

Voted No.1 Female Vocalist

I'll have to work with someone on the album that I know and respect musically. I've got a few songs written for it, but … I shall think about the conception of the album for at least a month or two.

—SANDY DENNY, *SOUNDS*, 16TH JANUARY 1971

[Matthews' Southern Comfort] just sort of happened, with a lot of friends helping out, but I hadn't got a very clear idea of what I wanted to do musically. I knew what I didn't want to do, which was why I left Fairport when they started moving towards traditional music – which is funny, since on my next album I want to do at least five traditional numbers … [This time] it won't be a case of people just playing because they're friends, like Richard [Thompson], but because I want them … Of course, I'd still want Richard!

—IAN MATTHEWS, *MELODY MAKER*, 16TH JANUARY 1971

Richard Thompson's January 1971 departure from Fairport Convention quickly brought him back into the musical spheres of the trio whose leave-taking preceded his. The next twelve months would see him record no less than five albums with his fellow Fairport refugees: Sandy Denny's *North Star Grassman*, Ian Matthews's *If You Saw Thro' My Eyes* and *Tigers Will Survive,* and Ashley Hutchings's distinct folk-rock projects, *No Roses* and *Morris On*; topping all this activity off with a collective sea cruise through rock'n'roll standards (The Bunch's *Rock On*) in tandem with Fairportees past and present.

The newly independent guitarist would also tour with the solo Ian Matthews and Sandy Denny, before joining Ashley Hutchings and his new bride, Shirley Collins, for a series of Advent gigs with another eclectic folk-rock band of Ashley's invention. Prior to these commitments he would produce Sandy Denny's first solo album, and play electrifying lead on Ian Matthews's first two solo albums. And in his spare time, such as it was, he would lend his guitar tone and timbre to a panoply of other artists' sessions.

These would include an eponymous folk-rock flit from chanteuse Françoise Hardy (her second and last 'London' album); Shelagh

McDonald's magical second album, *Stargazer*; Marc Ellington's underrated *Rains/Reins Of Changes,* and John Martyn's first fully-fledged masterpiece, *Bless The Weather.* Ellington and McDonald were both being produced by Sandy Roberton, under his September Productions umbrella, as Roberton regularly reached for Richard's number when he needed an A-list guitarist who could play both light and shade. Ellington, who had so fallen in love with Scottish tradition that he relocated to Towie Barclay Castle, was an old friend of Thompson's:

Marc Ellington: We had a mutual friend in Ian Matthews ... I got to know Fairport fairly well and sang [with them] on a couple of radio shows ... Richard ... has an extensive knowledge of many things which interest me, for example, Scottish literature and music, and traditions in general ... Before the war a three-piece Scottish band could play reels, bothy ballads and then the current big-band hit. Richard is very much part of that tradition.

Another old friend, who shared the odd bill with Fairport back in the day, was Gary Farr, whose idiosyncratic *Strange Fruit* – also produced by Sandy Roberton – Thompson would later claim, 'from a playing point of view, [was] the best [session. It was] with Ian Whiteman and Roger Powell and Ace from Mighty Baby in the rhythm section. It was really steaming stuff.'

It would prove to be Thompson's first connection with a set of musicians who would colour his beliefs permanently and accompany him on his most controversial musical odyssey. But at this point, Richard was, as future wife Linda states, 'just deciding what to do ... It just gave him some breathing space. He'd been touring since he was sixteen.'

According to the same lady, he also 'did quite a lot of sessions for The Seekers. He was very friendly with Bruce [Woodley]. I think they were drinking buddies ... Richard would play on the records but say, "Just don't put my name on it."' And he also certainly played on his own 1968 composition, 'No Man's Land', on the New Seekers' second album, *New Colours*, also uncredited. Evidently, the man who refused a producer credit on the first *Matthews' Southern Comfort* album was alive and well and living at The Angel.

One production credit he was happy to receive, though he would later disclaim any real technical input in the process, was on Sandy Denny's eagerly-awaited solo debut. Even before Fotheringay's farewell, Sandy was talking of working 'with someone ... I know and respect musically', and for her there was only one name on the list.

Having scrapped *Fotheringay II*, Sandy had decided to make a clean breast of it. Even the one backing track from those sessions to feature on her solo album, 'Late November', was embellished with Thompsonesque fills at the expense of the not-so-bold Jerry Donahue.

Fotheringay's undercooked 'John The Gun', the one other Sandy original recorded with Boyd, would be scrapped. One of Richard's favourite Sandy songs, he wanted something gutsier on an album featuring both of Fairport Mk.2's leading lights. Initially, though, deciding which songs to record took a backseat to finding an engineer with whom Sandy felt comfortable:

Richard Thompson: She couldn't quite face up to the idea of selecting a producer, so we [originally] rolled into the studio with Andy Johns engineering, and recorded a few things in a haphazard manner. It needed a litle more direction, so we brought in John Wood.

The brother of fellow producer Glyn, Andy Johns had worked with the likes of Jethro Tull, Free, Led Zeppelin and, most recently, The Rolling Stones on *Sticky Fingers*; later producing one of the greatest guitar albums of all time, Television's *Marquee Moon*. Any problems were therefore unlikely to be technical. It was a question of finding a more *sympatico* spirit.

The ultra-familiar John Wood gave them both someone who, by his own admission, liked to be 'in control of how the thing sounded, balance and things like that'. An engineer at heart, he was happy to leave it to Richard to choose musicians and provide the lady with a drinking companion when they would adjourn after (or during) a session.

Thompson vividly recalls 'an Indian restaurant on Westbourne Grove, where Sandy would finish off a couple of bottles of Mateus Rose. You wouldn't have guessed we were recording such melancholy songs if you'd been in the Indian restaurant.'

Perhaps surprisingly, the musicians to whom Sandy and Richard initially turned were independent of the band with whom they both made their names. The rhythm-section alternated between Fotheringay's and Mighty Baby's Roger Powell and/or Ian Whiteman, usually when they needed something 'steaming', as on 'Down In The Flood', 'John The Gun' and 'Let's Jump The Broomstick'.

Sessions began on March 11th, 1971 – after the label left Sandy to 'think about the conception of the album for … a month or two'. She still did not seem sure what kind of record she planned to make. A comment to Karl Dallas in May, just before the last set of sessions, suggested that, six months on from *Fotheringay II,* she was still struggling to strike the right balance between traditional songs and her own: 'There's far too much emphasis being put on "writing my own material". That's why so many bands are making bad albums. They think it's expected of them to compose the lot themselves.'

It was her way of saying she wanted a balance, but that was precisely what the final album lacked. Yet a great deal of time was spent on cover versions. Fine versions of Patsy Cline's 'Walking The Floor Over You' and country classic 'Losing Game', learnt from a Flying Burrito's recording, ended up on the cutting-room floor. Also lost was another Child ballad whose origins has been lost in the mists of time, 'Lord Bateman', a song she both demoed and cut as a backing track, presumably intending to make it a centrepiece in the mould of 'Banks Of The Nile'.[21]

The equally traditional 'Lowlands Of Holland' and 'The Nightingale', two songs she performed at a pair of BBC sessions set up between the album sessions and its release, were not even attempted at the sessions. Gone, too, were 'Gypsy Davy' and 'Wild Mountain Thyme', both covered sympathetically the previous November.

Instead, just one traditional song, 'Blackwaterside' – recorded on that first session – found room on the album, as Sandy pushed herself to write original songs. Once again, though, they came out all of a type. She later admitted, 'I thought, God, I've got to do this album, and I started rushing all these melancholy songs out.' The end-result was not the three-dimensional construct her producers – past and present – had been hoping for:

[21] The story of 'Lord Bateman' seems to date back to the 12th century and the adventures of Gilbert Becket, father of Thomas, but the earliest reference to the ballad itself is not until 1715.

Richard Thompson: [*North Star Grassman* was] slightly one-paced, unfocused, not well enough arranged. Probably not played well enough, in some ways ... Sandy would really [just] write a certain kind of song unless you pushed her to do something different ... It made for a lack of contrast. And she'd use sea images a lot ... On that particular record, there's about six tracks with sea images.

Joe Boyd: I was pleased when I heard that Richard was producing her solo record ... but [it wasn't] as transcendentally wonderful as I would have imagined a collaboration between Sandy and Richard to have been.

Sandy was as aware as her co-producer/s at the lack of joyful songs, a state of affairs she tried to joke about in interviews, 'I sit down to write, and I say, okay I'm going to write some jolly little songs, with none of that doomy quality about them, and as soon as I get my fingers to the keyboard, or pen to paper, out they come in their thousands – doomy, metaphorical phrases, minor keys, weird chords.' But it was no joking matter that the ways of her own muse were as much of a mystery to her as her fans:

Sandy Denny: I can't tell you about my songs. They're so strange ... They just come out like that. I do try to write a bit more cheerfully, but it doesn't always come off ... I don't like people to know what's happening in my head. And this is a fault ... My songs are a bit devious and perhaps weird. [1972]

If there seemed to be little she could do about the type of songs her muse offered up, it still lay within her powers to rein in one co-producer when he wanted to overgild the lily. She insisted she was on the case to Jerry Gilbert in June 1971, and was about to go to New York with Richard and John 'to mix the album at Vanguard', knowing full well that the appropriately-named Mr Wood 'is a terrible string freak ... That's why I'm going to New York ... because if I leave it just to him to mix it'll come back swamped with strings.'

Two *North Star* songs – 'Next Time Around' and 'Wretched Wilbur' – still came back doused in strings, arranged by the unsympathetic Harry Robinson. But at least the album was finished, just in time to debut eight of the songs at the prestigious Lincoln Festival on July 24th, backed by a three-piece pick-up band, one of whom, bassist Dave Pegg, had not played a note on the sessions or ever performed with the lady.

Thankfully, Thompson and Gerry Conway had worked on the entire album and seemed unfazed by an entire set of unreleased songs with 'doomy, metaphorical phrases, minor keys, weird chords' before a large open-air festival crowd.

Sandy soon let the cat out of the bag, prefacing 'The Optimist' by informing the large audience it was a song they hadn't as yet figured out how to play. She seemed tickled by the self-deprecating name the others had given this 'temporary band': The Happy Blunderers. And yet, a solo set was never on the cards – even at smaller shows. As she had told *Sounds* readers three weeks earlier, 'I'll always work with a band and I may join some band or get another band together.'

Even when Gerry Conway went on tour with Cat Stevens and Richard Thompson went to the States with Ian Matthews, just as she was due to play a September showcase at the South Bank's intimate Queen Elizabeth Hall, Sandy refused to go solo, a format she had used on two BBC sessions the previous month.[22]

Having set up the QEH gig around the release of her first solo effort for Island, Sandy refused to alter her plans, drafting in the current Fairport rhythm-section plus Jerry Donahue for a show that was bound to engender national reviews.

Robin Denselow, writing in *The Guardian* and married to Sandy's good friend, Bambi Ballard, did his best to put a positive spin on the evening, explaining that 'some of the Fairports have gallantly stepped in, [but] they haven't had too long to rehearse'. Reviewer Diane Easby was less forgiving, lambasting the contribution of one 'special guest' Fairportee:

> At the end of a song called 'Quiet Joys of Brotherhood' ... a fiddler began to play rather badly from the gloomy back part of the stage. Perception dawned in disbelief; incredibly it was the great Dave Swarbrick – was he nervous? Further horror followed with their miserably uninspired encore, 'Matty Groves'. I should have left three songs ago.

[22] The *One In Ten* BBC Two appearance (as in, one person for ten minutes) would be her one BBC appearance to survive the regular culls made by our so-called national broadcaster.

If the ad hoc nature of the band was enough of an obstacle, it was compounded by a Sandy consumed with stage fright. She later apologised to the audience via the pages of *Disc*, 'I hate putting people through that drama, with them all sitting on the edge of their seats, [wondering] is she going to make it. I really should get myself together.' But the damage had been done. Another showcase had failed to live up to its billing.

Even the economics of a first US tour failed to convince Sandy to just pack a guitar and a good microphone. A&M needed to shift some units, as their own press release for *North Star Grassman* tried to put a positive spin on the imminent tour, claiming that, 'Sandy Denny appears to be on the verge of gaining the audience her work has always deserved.' But the album disappeared with unseemly haste from American record shops, meaning, as her previous producer noted, that 'her solo career didn't pick up, or gather any momentum going forward'.

And yet, two headline-grabbing events that year suggested a status her sales belied. One was the award for Top Female Vocalist in *Melody Maker*'s Readers' Poll for the second year running, for which she posed on its front cover with Rod Stewart, winner of the Top Male Vocalist, an award he had taken off the previous recipient, Robert Plant.

Plant had the last laugh, though, recording the best-selling album of 1971 with his band Led Zeppelin, their fourth and the first to feature a guest vocalist. Sandy Denny, swopped vocal burdens with Plant – a devoted fan of Fairport and its brand of folk-rock – on Zeppelin's faux folk-ballad, 'The Battle Of Evermore'. It remains the recording for which she is best known despite the nominal acknowledgment she received on the famous sleeve.

She also flirted with a past association which seemed increasingly rose-tinted, sharing vocals with Ian Matthews on the title-track to his solo LP, 'Thro' My Eyes'. Like *North Star Grassman*, this underrated treasure would only hover on the edges of the charts. Yet it featured a far stronger set of songs than Sandy's, aligned to the musical talents of Richard, Pat Donaldson, and ex-Liverpool Scenester Andy Roberts. *If You Saw Thro' My Eyes* was everything Ian's Southern Comfort albums had aspired to be:

Ian Matthews: It was a reaction to what I'd been doing. I [thought] my infatuation with the pedal steel [had] got in the way of my career

... Had *Thro' My Eyes* come as my first album after Fairport, people would've thought, 'Yes, of course. That's what he needs to do.'

There was even a tip of his hat to Fairport. Ian finally put 'his' interpretation of Richard Fariña's 'Reno Nevada' (and an equally fine cover of 'Morgan The Pirate') on record, asking Richard to overdub his lead – another doff to yesteryear – to a basic track founded on the rock-solid Fotheringay rhythm-section:

Ian Matthews: ['Reno Nevada'] certainly went [on] longer ... quite a bit longer than the fade out. Tim [Renwick] played on the basic [track] and then ... Richard came in to overdub ... I don't think I told him I was going to do it, but that is what I specifically brought him in to work [on]; and then we just kept going and had him work on other things, too. Tim had that really boisterous rock'n'roll sound – the one he used in Quiver. And then [I wanted to add] Richard's electric folk style of playing... I just had this sound in my head of the two of them playing together on the same track and ... playing off each other.

Unfortunately, Gerry Conway's contributions at the first few sessions so impressed Matthews's original producer, Paul Samwell-Smith, he co-opted the drummer into Cat Stevens's band. Indeed, one day Conway and Samwell-Smith stopped coming to work for Ian, preferring to transfer their allegiance to the ultra-commercial Cat. As with that first Southern Comfort album, the singer simply wrestled control from his concerned managers and carried on regardless. This time it was Andy Roberts and Sandy Roberton who were enjoined as the (still-uncredited) co-producers:

Ian Matthews: When I started talking about making that album, we searched around for a producer. Ken and Alan ultimately came up with Paul Samwell-Smith. He was doing Cat Stevens already at that point. Paul listened to some of the songs I had and some of the cover versions that I wanted to do, and I explained I need[ed] a righthand man to be able to transfer my ideas into actual music and he knew Andy. Andy was recuperating. [He] had also been in a road accident where people had died. So Paul's phone call came at just the right time and Andy and I put the whole thing together to take into the studio. We talked about which players we wanted and I basically went for people that I knew and admired, [like] Keith Tippett ... We started the sessions, the tracking sessions, the first two days went very smoothly. The third day Paul was late and we sat around waiting for him. The fourth day he was late again and we just got on with it. The fifth day he called in and said, 'I'm sorry I'm having problems here at home and I just cannot come in today.' And we decided that we could do it without him, and at that point we let Paul go. From there on, it was Andy and I ... That's when Sandy Roberton, who was a friend of Andy's, started dropping by and offering suggestions, and I really liked the ideas that he had. Sandy began staying longer and longer and talking to Robin Black, the engineer, and saying, do this, do this, do this .... Sandy really should've been credited as the producer of the record.

The five traditional songs Ian had mentioned wanting to record back in January were consigned to the backburner. Perhaps they had fallen by the wayside after an unlikely potential collaboration with his old friend Ashley came to naught:

Ian Matthews: Before I made [*If You Saw Thro' My Eyes*], Ashley and I got together at my flat in Hampstead to talk about doing something together ... We actually talked about having Tim [Renwick] be part of it, too. We thought that Ashley and myself and Tim could be the nucleus of something. But the idea turned out to be a little bit too rock'n'roll for Ashley. I think he was thinking in other directions ... He [was] still in Steeleye, but he wasn't happy in Steeleye.

If You Saw... was what Ian came up with in the aftermath of that conversation, Ashley came up with *No Roses*, also with Sandy Roberton at the helm. For Ian, the idea of an album that was half folk, half rock, receded as soon as the songs started to flow:

Ian Matthews: I was really writing at that point. The faucet was turned on and it was flowing freely, which is why after leaving Southern Comfort I was so able to make another album so quickly.

Although seven of the ten songs on that ostensible solo debut were Ian's, there was an air of collaboration with Ian and Roberts 'working on stuff together ... [Andy] was great at arranging stuff and coming up with acoustic guitar licks'. Also happy to swop acoustic for electric was Richard, who 'played acoustic on the basic [tracks and] overdubbed his electric'. Sandy Roberton found himself *unofficially* 'producing' another album featuring Richard the session guitarist. Ian now needed to convince Richard to join him and Andy on an American tour, his own big push to announce a genuinely radio-friendly solo debut:

Ian Matthews: [Richard] just wanted to get back to America. He committed to it not necessarily 'cause he wanted to work with me, but ... he was quite happy to make money and not have any real responsibilities apart from turning up, just there to be in the band ... He was a loose cannon in many ways in those days ... We played a week at the Bitter End, a week at the Troubadour. We were supposed to play a week in Vancouver, but it was such a horrible venue that we pulled out after the first night and just spent a week in Vancouver. Andy and Richard just went and played pool. When we were in California, we were at Joe [Boyd]'s house one day in the back garden, laughingly messing around with 'Da Doo Ron Ron', just pissing around, and we liked it so much we just did it that night. It got a great reaction.

Richard was secretly rather enjoying disappearing into the background. In fact, Andy Roberts recalls, 'Ian was having to work – he was doing press – Richard and I were [just] the band. Nobody cared about us ... He was a drinker [then]. And a man who would chase women. We shared all that – we played a lot of snooker as well.' The highlight of each gig – if one discounts a particularly raucous deconstruction of 'Da Doo Ron Ron' – was 'Genesis Hall', a song Ian had not been allowed to record for Fairport.

Ian later suggested the whole 'tour was basically designed to see whether there was any hope for me over there. But I don't think the agent was really into what I was doing ... We were being booked into all sorts of rock clubs ... [I thought,] I'm not really good enough to play by myself, and I'm not sure if I want to join a band, so the only other alternative is to get other people to work with me.' By the time the trio returned to Blighty, Ian was convinced this combination should become a long-term unit.

Richard did not, though he agreed to play on a second Ian Matthews album, *Tigers Will Survive*, recorded in the immediate aftermath of America, even though the sessions had less intensity and camaraderie and Ian had less quality songs.

Ironically, this album nearly resulted in another novelty hit when Vertigo insisted on issuing 'Da Doo Ron Ron' as a single. When it garnered airplay, Ian was asked to make a return appearance on *Top of the Pops*, inducing a full-blown panic attack akin to the one that had caused him to leave Southern Comfort standing at Birmingham New Street station:

Sandy Roberton: It's funny, Ian didn't want to be successful. I remember I went round to his flat in North London and he wouldn't open the door. I was screaming through the letterbox, 'cause we'd got *Top of the Pops* for 'Da Doo Ron Ron'. He didn't want to do it.

This reaction to the prospect of renewed success was treated by the label as a display of pop star petulance. As Ian told *Melody Maker* the following year, 'After [that], they got very fed up with me … They hardly promoted the album and then they withdrew it … Eventually I got them to release me from my contract.' Ian had decided to enter into a formal collaboration with Andy Roberts and make music that would be lost on the likes of Vertigo, but would have been perfect for a now moribund Witchseason.

Meanwhile, Richard was renewing his US work visa for a second American trip of the year. This time it was the turn of Sandy Denny, solo artist. Without Gerry Conway or the two Daves, Mattacks and Pegg, she needed Richard to help her put together her third makeshift band in six months. If she called Pat Donaldson herself, drummer Timi Donald was surely a suggestion of Thompson's, who would soon use him on his own solo debut.

The prospect of another combination with whom she had never previously played failed to dissuade Sandy from introducing a smattering of rock'n'roll covers or referencing a tradition she continued to mine live, but rarely on record. If she again tackled 'Bruton Town', a song 'under consideration' for her last two albums, the loudest cheer of the evening was invariably reserved for 'Matty Groves', still the commercial benchmark for English folk-rock Stateside.

The mixture of rock'n'roll songs, folk songs and solo album tracks was a disappointment to fans hoping to hear more of a cross-section from her Fairport and Fotheringay albums – all released Stateside by A&M. The experience left the singer disappointed, 'We [just] hadn't rehearsed enough, and the pressure is so much more over there to be really tight and professional.'

The pressure to go solo continued to build all through the spring, even as she told successive journalists, 'I prefer travelling with people, and also playing with them on stage'; 'I've never said I was going solo – it was everyone else that told me I was'; and, finally, 'I could be making a lot of money if I was working on my own ... but I really like to be with a band.'

Sandy seemed oblivious to the possibility of a mass defection, even after Barry Dransfield declined to join her band on a permanent basis because 'he wanted to do more than just play fiddle'. And Richard certainly now wanted to do more than just play guitar.

If playing with Sandy (and Ian) had been a stop-gap while he found his own voice, by the beginning of May 1972, Richard felt he was 'treading water ... I wanted to do something a bit more for my own music'. He had fallen in love with Sandy's best friend, Linda – who joined the pair onstage in Eltham that month for a version of the Buddy Holly song, 'When Will I Be Loved?' – which was perhaps Richard's way of giving notice.

His departure would be the straw that broke the camel's back – and just in time, because Sandy's band-or-bust policy was about to break the bank. It was time for her to go solo, no mistake. Meanwhile, Ian Matthews simply carried on with his plan to form the ill-fated Plainsong. Richard was ready to present the world with *Henry The Human Fly*, his maverick alter-ego with a touch of Crazy Man Michael about it. And Ashley and Simon, who had been doing their damnedest to persuade him to join their joint crusade – a new band for all Albion – couldn't have been more expletive delighted.

9. Albion Sunrise

The first lady goes electric

IF SHE'D asked me for my opinion, I'd have advised her against it. Fortunately, she didn't. And Shirley Collins' version of "The Murder of Maria Marten" on h e r forthcoming album is not merely an incredible dramatic feat; it also indicates that electric folk has reached a new stage in its creative development.

I've just had a preview of the album, and I have no hesitation in nominating it as folk album of the year, and "Maria Marten" as the best track of the year.

The song begins with a fade-in of a really wailing folk rock band that could have been Fairport Convention in its heyday. In fact, it is, for the lead guitar is Richard Thompson, the bass is Tyger Hutchings, the second guitar is Simon Nicol.

Then Shirley begins singing the song with the fifth and sixth verses, the ones about William Corder arranging to meet Maria Marten at the Red Bar and going there to dig her grave. Her voice comes swooping into the ensemble like that of a hardened band-singer, topping all the instrumental action with ease.

Just two verses from the middle of the song, and the band fades out, giving way to a pair of fiddles, one playing drone, the other a slowly meandering counter-melody. It has the mind - blowing impact of the psychedelic sounds in Sgt Pepper, though actually it reminded me of a hurdy-gurdy.

Then Shirley starts the song at the first verse, the usual "come all ye"

SHIRLEY COLLINS: sounds of Sgt. Pepper

Shirley's (which is nice now that she has become Mrs Hutchings) although he appears officially only as a bass playing member of the Albion Country Band which accompanies her.

And what a band! Forget the folk supergroup connotations for a moment and concentrate upon the way in which such unfamiliar instruments as the Northumbrian pipes, the serpent honking away rather like a sax in early woodshed rock and roll, the crumhorn, the melodeon, the concertina, the jew's harp, and the gorgeous hammer dulcimer have been blended together. There is even a chime of bells at the climax of "Poor Murdered Woman."

I've been waiting for a long time for the electric folkers to discover the remarkable tone colours available in the instruments of the English tradition, and it's finally happened.

Above all this embarrassment of musical richnesses, Shirley's voice floats, sound and serene, making meadows sound like meadows and mountain streams sound like mountain streams. On two consecutive tracks she is joined by Mike and Lal Waterson and Royston Wood producing a sound which is refreshingly different from the old Waterson-YT effects, and yet clearly related to what they were doing then.

On the best of these, "The White Hare," Shirley sings no solo, but is part of the vocal ensemble throughout. The words she sings to "Hal an Tow" are slightly different from the familiar Young Tradition version.

The other tracks on the record are "Van Diemen's Land," a rather sunny version of the bitter transportation ballad, in which the agony at its heart is conveyed better by Colin Ross's pipes rather than by Shirley's vocal, "Just as the Tide was Flowing," which has a double-tracked chorus from Shirley and some slightly incongruous phasing on the instrumental, a much livelier version of "Claudy Banks," a song which I often think might be better entitled "Ploddy Banks," it's usually sung in such a spiritless fashion, "The Little Gypsy Girl," a really gay piece in which the melodeon dulcimer

[In the] music business now ... the discard rate is phenomenal. So you have a situation where quite a talented band only get one shot to make a record, and if it doesn't work, they go back to the sticks ... Thankfully, we were given the chance to actually develop and sell pretty crappy numbers of records for the first three or four albums – and [actually] five, six, seven, eight, nine, ten records.

—RICHARD THOMPSON TO BRIAN HINTON, CIRCA 2002

Island Records' willingness to continue releasing records bearing the Fairport imprimatur meant they would keep making them, come what may. If anything, another near-death experience made them keener. Four weeks after Thompson's bombshell, another kind of bombshell struck The Angel, this one leaving much the same devastation a real bomb would.

On February 20th, 1971, at around eight in the morning, a driver fell asleep at the wheel at the top of the hill and his lorry ploughed into the former public house, piling straight into the room in which a slumbering Swarb slept, killing the driver outright. (Simon thinks, 'The chimney stack came down on the roof of his cab.') This time, though, everyone inside the appropriately named Angel escaped unscathed. Swarb sat up to see desolation all around him. An absent Richard, who had the room above Swarb, escaped the carnage completely:

Simon Nicol: It was what I always dreaded happening ... I could hear the lorries double declutching at the top of the hill ... It was a 'straightaway'. Down one side of a valley then straight up, but there's a kink in the bottom where it goes over water, where the houses were, and eventually a Dutch truck driver did fall asleep at the top of the hill ... When the fire brigade arrived, Swarb was sitting up in bed ... listening to the moans of the co-driver. What was astonishing was that the room was completely full of rubble, bricks from the front wall, which had completely collapsed, and the chimney stack

which had fallen on top of that, but there was not one single brick
on Swarb's bed. The bricks in the room were up to the level of his
bed, all around him... [Richard] was in London that weekend. His
room was all right, it's just the walls fell out of it. The floor was still
in place. Anyway, all the contents of Richard's room came [fluttering]
down from the upstairs room.

Dave Pegg: Richard's stuff was hanging out of the building ... his
bed, his hi-fi, everything. We were trying to figure out how to try
and salvage things for him when we became aware of all these oblong
bits of paper blowing out from the room. They were cheques from
sessions.

The four-piece Fairport included a philosophical Nicol, who wisely
interpreted it 'as a message to migrate elsewhere'. The days at The
Angel were officially over, memorialised in the title of their sixth
album, *Angel Delight*, itself a case of unfinished business which evolved
from an attempt to give the label – and themselves – a hit single.

Peggy was, by his own admission, 'surprised when the chaps said
we'll keep it going'. At least they already had a completed 'Lord
Marlborough', plus fully worked-up arrangements of 'Banks Of The
Sweet Primroses' and 'Bonny Black Hare' they'd been playing for
months, and two fine Swarbrick/Thompson songs previewed on BBC
Radio One and French TV's Pop-2. As Pegg notes, it made for 'lots
of tracks, ... none of 'em ... strong enough for singles in the record
company's opinion. But there was a collection of songs there.'

Sure enough, *Angel Delight* was an album with enough meat on its
bones to force feed the faithful. Though it was no *Full House*, it was
a worthy consolation prize. Pegg, for starters, was happy to see Swarb
take over the reins. In fact, he has 'no bad memories of that period
at all'. However, Fairport's new lead guitarist was quietly struggling:

Simon Nicol: I did feel like a fish out of water [having to play lead
guitar], but the others were incredibly encouraging ... I had totally
the wrong type of guitar and amps, designed to play behind Richard
... [We had] no [real] musical direction. [We were] just getting the
material we had done with Richard into a four-piece line-up. We had
the gigs and we had to do an album ... [Fortunately,] there was a lot

of energy in that band, that we [had] inherited from the *Full House* line-up, [even if] we weren't developing a new repertoire.

That energy is there on a recent archival CD release from a show in Finland; although as one online review rather cuttingly put it, 'Well known Fairport tunes, often played at breakneck speed ... [as] an exhibition of technical skills rather than musicianship.' Energy wasn't the only thing they'd inherited from the *Full House* line-up. The band also continued to imbibe on an industrial scale – with occasionally hilarious results:

Dave Pegg: We did a festival once in Frankfurt, and we got on stage, all paralytic, and Simon went up to the mike and it was just total darkness out front, with bonfires burning all around the perimeter where people were camping, and Simon said, 'Good evening. We are Fairport Convention. I see you've got your fires lit. Going to burn a few more tonight, are we?' And that was it. It was total silence for a whole hour.

Fairport live could still blow away a receptive audience, but like the post-*Last Waltz* Band, it seemed at times like they were merely trading on former glories until a man called Blackwell brought the curtain down. It soon became clear, though, that Island had no intention of pulling the plug. The C.O. stood full-square behind this Convention, whatever its constituent parts:

Simon Nicol: We were niche marketing before the expression even existed. The way that things were run at Island [back then] was incredibly fortuitous. They were so supportive and yet hands off, and they remained so faithful to us ... And it wouldn't have happened without ... the way that Chris ran his company. His whole managerial team came to gigs and they had personal relationships [with the musicians], not just with the Stevie Winwoods ... The commercial support [remained even] when most of our releases were disappearing into the bargain bins. They were still putting out Fairport records seven or eight down the line. In 1974 they felt so bad that we hadn't had any kind of party for a gold disc, they did a number-crunching exercise and added up all the sales ever, in all formats, and presented us with a gold disc with miniatures of all the album sleeves [for] aggregate sales. They didn't have to do that sort of thing.

The label didn't even throw its hands up in despair when Dave Swarbrick announced their intention to record a folk-rock opera about 'The Man They Couldn't Hang', Babbacombe Lee, who in 1885 had been tried and sentenced to death for the murder of his landlady, Emma Keyse, but when it came time to be hanged, the trapdoor of the gallows refused to work on three separate occasions and his sentence was commuted to life.

The idea soon consumed Swarb and Fairport in turn; largely because as Dave Pegg observed in 1973, 'Without Richard, Swarb's influence appeared to become greater, because he then got into songwriting a lot and he was also the singer.' Here was a project Swarb could really sink his teeth into. He began putting it together even as they worked on *Angel Delight*, as a way to keep the band going and adopt the contemporary fashion for concept albums, dating back to *Sgt Pepper*, mother to a million imitations yet a concept album in name alone:

Simon Nicol: We were at The Angel when Swarb came across the bound copy of the articles from *Lloyd's Weekly News*. We'd all heard the story about the man they couldn't hang, and assumed it was apocryphal … but there it was in gaudy Edwardian tabloid prose. Initially, he was just gonna write a song about it, but he stuck to it. He came up with a structure and distilled [it] down to a concept album. John [Wood] didn't want to produce it on his own and I was quite happy to be both sides of the glass. At the time I really enjoyed the process of recording. And it helped to have a [more] objective view, as well as [being] involved with the music.

The following year Swarb informed *ZigZag*, 'By the time I presented the idea to the others, I'd already got the rough ideas for three songs,' which tallies with what Pegg told *Melody Maker* in June 1971, 'We are rehearsing for … an opera thing with no change of tracks, and we're hoping to do it on stage. [But] we don't really know what it's going to be about yet. We've only got three songs.'

The whole project remained Swarb's baby, with Pegg recalling, 'He was full of energy and working eighteen hours a day on it. That's what you need when somebody like Richard goes.' But Swarb never really developed the idea much further, and in these circumstances one needs enough ideas to create an entire album. Fairport were at least one songwriter short.

When the lavishly-packaged album *Babbacombe Lee* appeared, at year's end, it was on the receiving end of the most lukewarm reviews to date. Indeed, it became a rod with which to beat its bandleader, one Charles Shaar Murray was happy to wield on the fourth estate's behalf:

> Ever since Fairport's epoch-making *Liege & Lief*, they've become more and more Dave Swarbrick's band. The ads for their last tour featured a large photo of Swarb in solitary grandeur, and with Sandy Denny and Richard Thompson long gone, it's for better or for worse, the Dave Swarbrick Experience ... [So, although] the idea behind *Babbacombe Lee* is fine ... it's disappointingly executed.

Though very much his baby, Swarb was soon deflecting much of the criticism in the direction of its producers. Once the whole thing had been mixed and readied for release by John Wood and co-producer Simon Nicol – adhering to the band's request for no track separation (making radioplay out of the question) – a listening session was organized. The rest of the band, and Swarb in particular, seemed underwhelmed by what they heard and rather conveyed the idea it was, somehow, *Simon's* fault:

Dave Pegg: While we were in America, we got the final [*Babbacombe Lee*] tapes and there was a bit of a lack of interest from certain members of the group ... [after] Simon ... had taken all this on ... and working incredibly hard.

Simon Nicol: In the end, I wasn't best pleased with the reaction of the rest of the band to my efforts. I was fairly wrung out by the time they got to hear it. What with one thing and another, ... that was when I decided it was time for me to leave Fairport.

If ever there was a time to bring the curtain down on this remarkable band, this was it. The last founding member wanted out, leaving a (consistently great) rhythm-section and an erratic fiddler to carry the load. When Simon broke the news, he remembers, 'DM was upset, but the other two were fatalistic.' Yet ever the company man, he did not leave the others entirely in the lurch, agreeing to see the thing through till the end of the year:

Simon Nicol: Chris [Blackwell] happened to be on that leg of the [US] tour. [As] we were touring with Traffic, he was ultimately underwriting our being there. The tour was going well, it was a good fit. Fairport were a very good opening act for them. [But] we came off the stage at San Antonio and I told the others, I've had enough of this Fairport lark ... It was partly to do with their attitude to the finished [*Babbacombe Lee*] when they heard it. Swarb was unhappy with it. I felt like I'd suddenly become an outsider ... And I thought, I've been in this band for a quarter of my life. [So] I went to see Chris ... There was a UK tour [due] to start. He [asked if] I['d] see that through to the end. That's what happened. It felt like the end of term.

Like Ashley and Richard before him, Simon had had enough of Swarb and the direction the band was going in under his tutelage. Finally, it just became too much and he quit – without making the slightest provision for what he was going to do next.

———————

It was too late to lend a hand on an album of traditional morris tunes his two oldest friends had just completed (*Morris On*). However, the prospect of a longer-term association was not entirely out of the question. Much to Simon's delight, Ashley and Richard were working together again after a two-year hiatus, during which Ashley had made three albums under the Steeleye Span umbrella, the second of which, *Please To See The King*, had become the first electric folk album to breach the Top Ten.

The Mk.2 Steeleye had finally united Ashley with Martin Carthy. It was Tim Hart who, Ashley admits, 'wouldn't let it rest, and believed it was worth pursuing. He was the one who contacted Carthy and [suggested], why don't you come into a reformed Steeleye Span? And he did. That's the one time I wasn't at the helm.' Hart also took it upon himself to explain the *raison d'être* behind this revamped combo:

The new group was formed specifically to get on the road, whereas the first band would have just made albums. We all still work separately as well and within the group everything is fine, because we have all known each other a long time. We are mainly working in universities because we are stipulating a sitting audience. Our music is intended to be listened to. In some ways it is demanding. To get the most out of the songs you have to listen to the words. There are no long solos, in which the audience can allow their minds to wander.

Once again Ashley threw himself into work; as Simon suggests, his way of 'claw[ing] his way out of whatever black hole he was in ... and the more he worked, the more work he created'. The black dog was still at his heels. But much to his initial relief he found that the 'reformed [Steeleye] with myself, Tim and Maddy, Peter Knight and Martin Carthy, it worked. If I had imposed my ideas then, we may have had a problem in sounding like Fairport. As it happens, everyone had very strong ideas of their own.' Those 'very strong ideas' took the band in a distinct, drummerless direction which required Ashley to learn a whole new way of carrying the bottom end:

Ashley Hutchings: No one had tried to play British folk music in an electric context without a drummer, and so I was filling in lots of areas. That was fascinating. It was very unusual ... I listen to those records and I think, 'I can't play like that now!' I was able to concentrate on those bass patterns because we were doing traditional song ... Within a year or so people started to say that Steeleye were in opposition to Fairport ... [If there was a difference] Steeleye was a folk group that was electrified, whereas Fairport was a rock group playing folk music ... [Steeleye Mk.2] were quite 'Celtic'; Scottish ballads and Irish fiddle-tunes and stuff like that. Peter brought the jigs and reels – and we were happy doing it. [It was still] traditional music with electric instruments.

As *Hark*'s false dawn was now quietly forgotten, Hart, Carthy and Hutchings all went on a charm offensive with the media. Worryingly, they each seemed to have different ideas of what the band should be. While Hart saw it as a touring troupe, the avuncular

Carthy claimed, 'I don't have any ambitions, except to stay sane. I would like to see the group make sense.' If that was always asking a lot, Tyger felt they were part of 'a quiet revolution going on. There's Fairport, Fotheringay and Trees and us doing these things. Traffic are doing an old British number, "John Barleycorn", and I heard East of Eden doing a medley of reels the other day.' Was the folk-rock revolution nigh?

Reinforcing the sense of comrades-in-arms, the new Span made their 'official' live debut – after an unbilled session at the Cambridge Folk Festival and an impromptu 'secret gig' at Salford University – sharing a bill at the Royal Court in London with Fotheringay, three weeks on from Sandy's Albert Hall meltdown.

This newfangled Steeleye had come together after 'innumerable rehearsals in the front parlour of the vicarage of St Saviour's in St Albans, where they are living with Tim Hart's father'. The one carry over from *Hark! The Village Wait* was 'The Blacksmith', the new arrangement of which was so radically different it opened both their first BBC radio session and their second album. All change.

At least Steeleye Mk.2 and Fairport shared one key aesthetic. As Carthy recalls, 'We all played bloody loud! It was a loud band, and if anybody suggested that we turn [it] down, I'd tell them to get stuffed.'

Indeed, an actual battle of the folk-rock bands nearly took place on Ainsdale beach in July 1971. Fairport and Steeleye had both been booked to perform during a Granada TV folk-rock special, during which nigh on ten thousand locals came to hear who was making such a racket. Having soon got into proceedings, when the bands ended their sets abruptly, because the cameras had stopped running, there was almost a riot.

But Steeleye's real War of the No Roses came six months earlier, on their first national tour, supporting Jethro Tull. Tull were performing the material from *Aqualung*, an album that almost defines heavy rock, while Steeleye preferred singing about the bonny boys of Bedlam, 'The Lark In The Morning' and 'The False Knight On The Road'. Not surprisingly, some audiences refused to sit still or keep quiet. The (South) *Shields Gazette* reported on a show at the Sunderland Empire where 'the constant barracking caused Span to repeatedly ask parts of the audience to channel their noise into something more constructive'.

And yet, a healthy percentage of Tull's audiences seemed to not only enjoy Steeleye, but were inspired to rush out and purchase their new album, *Please To See The King*, which charted at tour's end. Yet Ashley seemed slightly dismissive of the results, calling it 'a good document of the music we've been making for the past six months and that's about it'. As far as the demanding Tyger was concerned:

> We've only just scraped the surface of what we can do. The main problem is that we don't get a chance to practise much because the others are still doing their own solo gigs ... [which means] the group, as a group, isn't as tight as it should be ... [but] I don't have any particular thoughts about getting our music to a wider audience – we are thinking purely along one line of traditional music and we'll be carrying on as we have been.

Not only were Tim and Maddy still touring as a duo, they were recording as one, completing *Summer Solstice* – with Sandy Roberton again at the console – in the downtime between Steeleye activities. Ashley knew he had no real grounds for complaint. The pair had made it plain at the outset, 'Yes, we'll be in the band but we want to continue [gigging].'

As it happens, the part-time nature of the revamped Steeleye project afforded Ashley an opportunity to construct a more single-minded vision of electric folk, the singular *No Roses*. And once again he turned to the only producer who could make this kind of project happen:

Sandy Roberton: I pulled the money together. We both produced it. It was a nightmare to organize. [Steeleye] had three date sheets, 'cause [the others] wanted to keep doing the clubs ... [with] Steeleye fitting in between them. While they were going off, we [decided to] do *No Roses*. We did some of it at Morgan [Studios] with Roger [Kweskin]. He wasn't a folk engineer, so he gave it more of a rock sound. B&C put up the money. We didn't have to go and play them demos or anything. I just said we're gonna make this record. They said great.

No Roses actually began life as an unnamed Shirley Collins project, first mentioned in *Sounds* shortly after the April release of *Please To See*

The King. It made no mention of a role for Tyger, though it suggested Collins 'will be featuring Richard Thompson, Simon Nicol and Dave Mattacks on her next album'.

Richard had been keeping tabs on Ashley, recognising, 'the work [he] did with the early Steeleye Span was very important ... The textures on the first album in particular are still beautiful.' Now Hutchings had time to reconnect the dots. If those 'textures' were no longer woven by Steeleye, perhaps the Fairport folk-rock contingent would agree to stitch together another traditional tapestry.

All it would take was the necessary budget, which Sandy Roberton convinced B&C to provide, and a crew of like-minded musicians, which Ashley supplied. B&C probably did not fully understand what they had agreed to, but they signed off on the grandiose project. Roberton fully admits, 'I have no idea what [*No Roses*] cost to make, but the session fees would soon have added up!' Somehow, Ashley found a way to unite the elements in Fairport which had first forged a folk-rock trail with the ones he continued to blaze:

Simon Nicol: *No Roses* was ... conceived and executed as a one-off project. And it embraced a cast list of hundreds. Everybody [from] Ashley's black book ... I was delighted by its range. With *Liege & Lief* we'd done it with less imagination. But with *No Roses*, Ashley had really drawn back the curtains [on tradition] into a broader panorama.

Fronting this 'Fairport reunion' of sorts was the consummate traditional singer to whom Ashley was engaged. Shirely Collins, as producer Sandy Roberton recently observed, 'had a great knowledge of [English folk] songs ... and a true feel for them ... [But] it was quite an adventurous record for her [to make], heading in a more rock direction.' Not that the daringly open lady didn't already have form, having recorded the equally groundbreaking *Folk Roots, New Routes* seven years earlier with guitarist Davey Graham, a jazz-folk album that influenced everyone from Jimmy Page to Neil Young.

But it seems unlikely even she envisaged needing twenty-five musicians to make a thirty-five minute album. If her memory serves her well, the whole process was largely serendipitous:

Shirley Collins: We went into the studio and it just sorta built every day. People would come in and play on the song they were supposed to play on, and then say, 'Can I stay?' It didn't feel like a responsibility ... You don't set out with the idea of 'I'm going to make a seminal album!' It just grew in the studio and ... everything conspired to make it work well.

The album was certainly a more dynamic fusion of folk and rock than *Please To See The King*. In particular, 'Claudy Banks', 'The Murder Of Maria Marten' and 'Just As The Tide Was A-Flowing' proved that there was nothing intrinsically incompatible about a singer of tradition fronting the best that English (folk and) rock could supply. Shirley herself made it clear, in an interview the month of the album's release, that this was a conscious co-mingling:

> One thing I was pleased about this record is that it sounds totally English ... That was the one thing we set out to do ... That's one thing I care about from here on, that the music sounds English.

Mrs and Mr Hutchings were speaking with one voice, something they consciously reinforced with the album's inner sleeve – a fold-out that captured Ashley and Shirley arm in arm strolling through the English countryside.

Yet anyone searching for a joint credit on the album-cover would have looked in vain. Ashley was merely identified as one of two dozen musicians accompanying the first lady of English folk, a member of the first (and largest) ensemble to be called the Albion Country Band. Karl Dallas, though, was having none of it. In an August 1971 feature in *Melody Maker* – headlined 'The first lady goes electric' – he went to town:

> I've just had a preview of [*No Roses*], and I have no hesitation in nominating it as folk album of the year, and 'Maria Marten' as the best track of the year. The song begins with a fade-in of a really wailing folk-rock band that could have been Fairport Convention in its heyday. In fact, it is, for the lead guitar is Richard Thompson, the bass is Tyger Hutchings, the second guitar is Simon Nicol ... [In fact,] this is Tyger's album as much as it is Shirley's.

The curtain rises on Fairport Convention.
St Michael's Hall, Golders Green, May 27th, 1967.

A rare photo of the five-piece Fairport Convention Mk.1, summer 1967.

Fairport grace the cover to issue one of England's finest fanzine, 1969.

Two classic Fairport line-ups, a year apart, autumn 1968 and autumn 1969.

From *Liege & Lief* to *Full House* in six months, as faithfully recorded by *Jackie*.

Richard 'Henry' Thompson twists the knife again.

Fairport minus Thompson, and Thompson minus Fairport, circa 1971-72.

A pensive Sandy Denny on and off-stage, solo and with Happy Blunderers, 1968 and 1971.

The Steeleye Span line-up that released two albums in 1971 and
the Albion Country Band line-up that released no albums in 1972-73.

Shirley Collins and Ashley Hutchings in full costume
for a turn at nobody's wedding, 1973.

Philippa Clare as the bride and Dave Swarbrick as the groom at nobody's wedding, 1973.

'I feel for you, you little horror...'
Richard and Linda parenting and performing in 1973.

Fairport Mk. 10 *Rising For The Moon*, June 1975.

Richard & Linda Thompson do the hokey pokey
at the Cambridge Folk Festival, August 1975.

The Albion Band/s at the time of *The Prospect Before Us* (above) and *Rise Up Like The Sun* (below), 1976 & 1978. All change!

Linda Thompson at a friend's wedding, 1980,
and singing of heartache, July 1982.

While B&C prepared *No Roses* for release – packaged almost as lavishly as Fairport's *Babbacombe Lee* – Ashley returned to the Steeleye cooperative refreshed enough to complete a third album, *Ten Man Mop*, which the *Disc* review suggested 'gives a true picture of what Steeleye have been doing onstage for the past few months'.

In truth, though, *No Roses* served as the death warrant on a band with too many cooks working from an Anglo-Irish recipe book. It was a recipe for conflict. As masterchef Hutchings observed, on his departure, 'I would like to play more English songs as opposed to predominantly Irish, which was what we were playing.'

Another character in the Steeleye kitchen was secretly relieved. Tim Hart told *Sounds*, 'We were starting to go round in circles. The thing is, Martin and Tyger had a musical policy, which was largely the musical policy of the band.' Tim Hart wanted Steeleye to follow his course. He always had. Which is why Ashley's wish 'to concentrate upon making English music' coincided with the realization, 'I really didn't want to be in a band with [Tim] anymore.'

A stoic Sandy Roberton, having produced exemplary product for both parties in the same year, took the view that Ashley was simply done with one project and felt the time had come to move onto another: 'Basically Tyger want[s] to get into a fresh, different type of music because he is one of those guys who when he isn't building something, then it isn't worthwhile.'

Sadly, it signalled the end of their own fruitful working partnership – one which had produced two remarkable albums, *Hark! The Village Wait* and *No Roses*. When Carthy took Ashley's resignation as his cue to quit, it marked the end of Roberton's association with Steeleye. But he was not out of work for long. His services as a manager-producer were needed by another ex-Fairporter, looking to experiment with his own brand of Plainsong.

For Ashley, there was nary a pause between the final shows with Steeleye and a three-date tour of south-west pubs; the very places where Sabine Baring-Gould collected some of England's greatest folk songs, the perfect place to promote *No Roses* and resume working with Richard.

While *Disc* gleefully reported, 'Hutchings [is] play[ing] bass for wife Shirley Collins ... Also in [this] temporary band are guitarist Richard Thompson and John Kirkpatrick,' Shirley was telling Karl Dallas, 'Ideally, I would like to be part of a bigger group with other singers and musicians. I just don't want to go around being Shirley Collins and her group ... The only snag for me is that I don't want to sing anything else but traditional music.'

Yet when the *Melody Maker* folk columnist scurried down to South Molton to catch this Albion Country Band's first Devon date, Collins took him aside and brusquely warned him, 'You're not going to write this up as the beginning of something much bigger, are you? They've just come along with me in place of [my sister,] Dolly.'

Despite the shows capturing the fragile spirit of *No Roses*, Collins admitted to the still-attendant Dallas, 'I have a feeling that if they [were to] keep the Albion Country Band going, it would never be the same.' And nor would it. Thompson was unsure what had just happened, having imbibed 'an amazing drink called Mahogany. There was one show about which I have no recollection at all. It totally blasted the brain cells.'

For all of Collins's coyness, though, and the rather low-key nature of the gigs, something *was* afoot, even if no one wanted to jump the gun. Questioned about reunion rumours the following week, Tyger hedged his bets:

> I have been working with Richard for a couple of weeks and I will inevitably be involved in another electric folk band. But we couldn't call ourselves Fairport ... We don't want to duplicate what we've done already. I left Steeleye because I just decided I wanted to change again ... Richard, Simon and myself have just stopped working and need a holiday to think things out.

As it is, these three otherwise undocumented *No Roses* shows would inform Ashley and Simon's future plans, but not Richard's. It was a show the previous week at London's prestigious Rainbow Theatre which provided more of an impetus for the next chapter in the Thompson story.

On November 27th, 1971, Fairport Covention played the official London date on Simon Nicol's 'farewell' tour with the band. Sensing that this could be the last time, the *Angel Delight* Fairport were joined by both Richard and Sandy, fresh from their recent joint provincial tour, for the most extended encore the fabled old theatre had heard in many a rising moon.

A cross-section of songs from the *Liege & Lief* era – 'Matty Groves', 'We Need A Whole Lot More Of Jesus', 'Down In The Flood' and the *Liege & Lief* instrumental medley – vied with like-minded favourites from the *Full House* pick'n'mix – including 'Country Pie', 'Sweet Little Rock'n'Roller', 'Blues In The Bottle' (in the form of a duet between Simon and Richard), 'Wipe Out' and 'High School Confidential' – before being topped off with Richard and Sandy duetting on 'Something You've Got' and 'The Weight'. It was a cogent reminder of the diversity of styles this band could command.

But these occasionally off-key harmonies were for one night only. By the following week, Richard was in Devon downing Mahogany, and Simon was saying an unofficial farewell to Fairport, appropriately enough at Cecil Sharp House. This time the four-piece was joined by Sandy and her beau, Trevor Lucas – previewing the line-up which would threaten to revive the band's fortunes in a couple more years.

For now, these London shows served to remind everyone just how much of Fairport's core repertoire had gone unrecorded, a state of affairs Sandy's unemployed partner now decided to do something about. All he needed was for Chris Blackwell to sign another blank cheque, made out to 'The Bunch'.

10. The Splinter Group In Action

*We talk about the [Fairport] family ... [but] it's [all] too fragmented now. We've
all got different ideas, we've all gone in different directions ... There was a time in
history when we were all pulling together, consciously ... Henry The Human
Fly, Morris On, No Roses, the Albion Country Band album: we were trying
to commune with tradition, our background history, mythology, magic – the whole
thing ... There was a kind of conscious movement.*

—ASHLEY HUTCHINGS TO BRIAN HINTON

I saw Fairport doing a gig at the Rainbow. It was the Babbacombe Lee *line-up,
and Sandy and Richard got up and did some rock'n'roll things. And I thought
it would be a nice idea to get that down on record – things that groups play that
knock audiences out, but never get recorded.*

—TREVOR LUCAS, 1973

As 1971 petered out, the musicians who had bailed on Fairport and
Steeleye during the past twelve months were all pulling in the same
direction – backwards. In one case it was to the birth of rock'n'roll;
the other pushed things back a few more centuries, to the origins of
English folk dance.

Almost the only thing the two distinct projects had in common
was that both were pitched to Island, and each was given the green
light. There really did seem to be a vast vat of goodwill at the label,
which no amount of consumer apathy could tarnish.

The one constant in both projects was Richard Thompson – for
whom 'High School Confidential' and 'Old Woman Tossed In A
Blanket' existed along the same continuum. Ashley, asked to do a
cameo on Trevor Lucas's rock'n'roll album, vented his abiding love
for Chuck Berry with 'Nadine', but otherwise left 'em to it. He was
too consumed with the idea of an electric album of morris tunes to
ignite another rock'n'roll revival.

Said 'Morris Project' had been preying on his mind since at least
March 1971, when he told Jerry Gilbert, 'There are so many more

things to try – for instance, all the tunes [Steeleye Span] have played have been Irish, and the same goes for Fairports. But English morris dance tunes haven't been touched at all, and this is a major field that could be tackled by somebody.' By the name of Tyger.

Once again, it had been a trip to Cecil Sharp House – repository of the English Folk Song and Dance Society archives – which had opened the door to another element of tradition he barely knew existed:

Ashley Hutchings: The penny dropped when I discovered morris music at Cecil Sharp House. I walked in and there was a record playing. It was William Kimber doing morris tunes. It was [like], 'Wow, what's this?' There was a little shop just inside and they were playing it there. It was on vinyl. 'Have you got anything else?' 'No, there isn't anything else.' From that moment on I [decided,] 'I'm gonna be the next one who does this.' I contacted John Kirkpatrick and … he said, 'You're mad.' … [But] *Morris On* has been very successful. In its own way it was as groundbreaking as *Liege & Lief*. [It] completely blew open the dance side … Mike Harding told me once he was driving along the road and he heard a *Morris On* track on the radio and nearly crashed. He could not believe what he was hearing … People [can] get very weird when morris is involved: 'You must do this. You mustn't do that.' I just went ahead and did it.

By November 27th, 1971, with his departure from Steeleye still news, the *NME* was reporting that Ashley 'has plans for his own group, and hopes of doing an album of morris dance music'. All he needed was another record label who asked very few questions, and another set of musicians he could press gang into joining his pilgrimage, because, if *'No Roses* was a labour of love … *Morris On* was a crusade'.

John Kirkpatrick: I wish I'd kept the letter where Ashley outlined the idea for *Morris On*. I remember he said he'd done Fairport and done Steeleye, and was talking to Royston [Wood] at the time about having a specifically English band.

This time Ashley would keep the budget manageable, sticking to a handful of helpers, with Thompson and Mattacks representing the Fairport brand of folk-rock. Accordionist John Kirkpatrick and fiddler/singer Barry Dransfield filled the other musical blanks. Aside from a couple of a cappella cameos from the missus, it was an album which put dance at the centre of English folk (rock) – again.

With *Morris On,* Ashley reinforced an abiding belief one did not need to be an apostate from rock to play folk. Or vice-versa. After two tiring years trying to keep up with Swarb's ferocious fiddling night after night, Mattacks was in heaven, 'I was going through a phase where I'd had it with jigs and reels at a million miles an hour [so] doing [*Morris On*] was a great joy.'

Morris On was not just another electric folk album. It was a blueprint for another band. At the time of the sessions at the turn of the year, an ongoing involvement from all five *Morris On* musicians seemed like a possibility. A January 1972 piece in *Disc* reported 'Tyger is still working on getting his own group together … He's been working with Richard Thompson and Royston Wood, but would like to have John Kirkpatrick join them.'

In fact, even as Young Traditionalist Royston Wood was agreeing to provide vocals, accordionist Kirkpatrick had turned the gig down for the love of a woman: 'Sue [Harris], to whom I was married, had just packed up her full-time job so we could work as a duo.'

If the January 22nd *Melody Maker* reported Kirkpatrick's withdrawal from the project, it suggested everyone else remained on board, though there was no plan to start 'serious rehearsals until April'. Ashley had already decided to appropriate the name of the 'band' from the critically-acclaimed *No Roses*, without necessarily representing that sound or singer:

Ashley Hutchings: I was still in Steeleye [when I started] thinking … I want to be in a band that's making English music, that has the English sound, with morris at the heart of it. So I left and formed the Albion Country Band. That was after we made *No Roses*, [where] the name was used to credit all the various musicians. Then Shirley gets very miffed when I [decide to] use the name Albion Country Band … She was saying, 'I made this album, why aren't I in the band?' But I [just] felt: it really isn't [her] thing. It's an electric band with Mattacks on drums. I know they're on the [*No Roses*] album, but it's a bit different when they're on stage and you['ve] got monitors. She's an unaccompanied singer, to a large extent. It was never on as far as I was concerned.

For a month or two, it really looked like Ashley, Simon and Richard might be working together again. Yet even at this juncture, Simon urged caution, telling one music weekly, 'I won't deny that Richard and Tyger and I have talked about working together again. [But] we've just finished two very long tours ... and the last gigs ... had a feeling of nostalgia about them.'

Sure enough, just as everything seemed rosy in Simon's country garden – where provisional rehearsals were under way – Thompson informed the others he did not want to tie his future to anyone else's vision, even Ashley, who became the third Fairportee to be rebuffed by a resolute Richard in a matter of months.

At least Ashley had an additional guitarist, currently their drummer, in the form of Simon Nicol, inspiring him to ask, what about recruiting the little drummer boy who had such a blast making *Morris On*? For DM, the call couldn't have come soon enough: '[It] came at a point when I was particularly pissed off with the way things were going with Fairport.' DM quit Fairport on February 3rd, 1972, severing yet another link with the glory days of *Liege & Lief* and *Full House*.

That Fairport was kaput. Long live the Albion Country Band. This band, however, would most definitely *not* be revisiting its former glories. It would instead seek to recapture a different yesteryear even as Albion rocked 'n' reeled to its own authentic sound. Richard had opened the door for them with his own freshly minted clarion call, 'The New St George', the burden of which – 'Leave the factory, leave the forge/ And dance to the new Saint George' – suggested a quite conscious intent. It became the Albion's own come-all-ye.

It was not lost on Ashley that he had formed 'a band with three ex-Fairport members, [while] concurrently there was a band running with no original Fairport members in it'. Simon, who had kept a careful watch on his friend's activities since departing the fold, welcomed the opportunity for a new start:

Simon Nicol: I'd watched what he'd done with the Steeleye thing, once he'd come out of his mope, and created this amazing repertoire

of the kind of music he would have wanted to concentrate on with
Fairport. The first two [Steeleye] albums are astonishing – particularly
the first one, where he's got Mattacks and Conway playing on it. And
the song choices are inspired. I [had] just become a homebody for a
while. Then the phone rings, and it's Ashley. He's come to the end
of his time with Steeleye, and [already] he's got his running shoes
on straightaway and [wants to] start another band. [He's still] on the
rebound from his depressive mind-set after leaving Fairport … he's
on his own, and he's still got the fire burning to make new stuff. And
there's all these musicians he knows who haven't met, so he says [to
me], 'What about forming not a continuation of the *No Roses* album,
but we'll use the name and keep the identity? I've been talking to
Royston from The Young Tradition and Steve Ashley, this young
songwriter. Would you like to see what develops?'

Thompson's decision not to commit himself to Ashley's vision for an
English brand of rock founded on a common musical heritage was
not made on aesthetic grounds. Broadly speaking, he shared Ashley's
vision. But like Kirkpatrick, he gave it all up for the love of a woman
– and an underlying belief it was time he ploughed his own furrow.

A chance meeting at the sessions for the rock'n'roll record Trevor
Lucas had convinced him to make, would turn his world upside down.
That album was recorded at a new live-in studio in Oxfordshire,
The Manor, the brainchild of Richard Branson, overseer of a new
independent rival to Island, Virgin Records. Remarkably, the prospect
of using a producer without a single production credit did not dissuade
Blackwell. Trevor was soon raiding Sandy's little black book/s to
round up every folk-rocker who had ever been weaned on rock'n'roll:

Gerry Conway: We went in as guinea pigs at The Manor studio –
the first group ever to go in there. It was then just a barn. We were
more than willing participants in recording and then trying out this
live-in studio lark with the food and everything. There were two
drummers, DM and I, in this long barn with him at one end and me
at the other – some tracks we did together, [on] some tracks one of
us would play tambourine.

Of the musicians on stage that November night at the Rainbow, Sandy, Richard and DM were promptly co-opted into The Bunch – as this set of raggle taggle folkies would be duly dubbed. Dave Pegg would also have participated, had he not been laid low with the mumps. So it fell to Fotheringay's Pat Donaldson to lend a hand.

It was Richard – despite some sniffy statements after the fact – who seems to have largely dictated the choice of material, the songs recorded at initial sessions reflecting almost entirely his own taste, and his elder sister's record collection: Buddy Holly, Chuck Berry, Jerry Lee Lewis, Everly Brothers, Hank Williams and Dion DiMucci (a terrific Thompson arrangement of 'My Girl The Month Of May'). The general good humour which pervaded proceedings was also reflected in a tongue-in-cheek press release some wiseacre penned:

> The songs played don't sound like religiously remade rock and roll songs. True they mimic and occasionally laugh at the styles of the time … but no one gets hurt in the process … [And] Richard as a guitarist plays rock and roll perfectly, accentuating his notes with a roughness that is often mistaken for bad playing. That roughness is more emotion than technique, and at the same time more technique than emotion.

Not every reviewer seemed to share the joke. Fred Woods, in his *Folk Review* review, reverently prayed, 'I *hope* it's a spoof. It would be sad to think that these talented musicians could delude themselves into thinking that this was a good record.' One thing was for sure, everyone had a good time making it. Perhaps too good a time. One girlfriend invited along recalls, 'In the control room they were drinking Fosters [lager], and Trevor made a complete steel curtain with these [pull] rings.'[23]

One lesser-known singer who had received the call because she was 'a long-time friend of Trevor and Sandy … [and] the most under-rated girl singer in the country', remembers recording her vocal for 'The Loco-Motion' 'when Sandy and Richard were in their respective loos in Island being sick. He literally couldn't stand up.' The singer in question was understandably nervous about singing with her closest friend. Thankfully, a smitten Richard insisted:

---

[23] A full-page ad for The Manor and its facilities in the music weeklies noted proudly that it had ample 'room for producers, wives, girl friends'.

Linda Thompson: In those days [Richard] was very supportive of me. I was always terrified of singing with Sandy, and he'd say, 'Don't let her [intimidate you].' He was a meek-mannered Clark Kent in those days. And Trevor … would be very helpful with my vocal. When Sandy wasn't around, he'd say, 'Let's nip in and do this vocal.' … She was definitely competitive. She wanted to sing everything.

And yet, Linda more than holds her own, not only on 'The Loco-Motion' but more tellingly on her sisterly duet with Sandy on 'When Will I Be Loved', having been immersed in the Everlys' music from a tender age. As Linda confirms, her parents 'were country music fanatics. Fanatics. All the Hanks. Hank Williams, Hank Snow, Hank Thompson. It's a Celtic thing. It's the same music … and I think Richard's sister turned him on to a lot of that stuff.' The pair soon realised their exposure to the same sounds growing up was part of a mutual wavelength they shared across the entire musical spectrum:

Linda Thompson: 1966-67, I was singing in folk clubs in Glasgow and [in London]. I went to the Scottish Academy of Dramatic Arts but I left after … one of my teachers said to me you'd be a great comedienne. And I said, 'I don't want to be a comedian. I want to be a great tragedian.' [Anyway,] I preferred music. I was born [in London] and I went to Glasgow when I was very young. Five or something. But I always wanted to come back, so I just came when I left school. I was eighteen actually. I got into University College … modern languages and business studies or something. I left after five minutes … It was just nice to get out from the constraints of parents. I did mostly traditional and mostly unaccompanied. 'Twa Corbies', lots of Scottish traditional stuff.

The fact that Linda was as passionate about folk and country music as Richard and could convey that passion effortlessly, it seemed, made him evaluate the former fiancée of his ex-producer/manager in a completely new light. In fact, the next thing anyone knew – even Warners' new music exec – Richard and Linda were almost inseparable:

Joe Boyd: [Linda] came back from LA. And then we almost got back together again when I came to London, following her return. And then we didn't. And a few months after that, she wrote to me [about Richard]. It surprised me, it was [so] unlikely ... But we got a singer out of that. She would not sing around me. She felt I was too judgemental, or that she wouldn't live up to my standards. Yet she ended up singing with Richard, who has very high standards.

Love at first sight, it wasn't. Richard and Linda had first met back in October 1969, during a break from the *Liege & Lief* sessions. The latter wryly recalls it was 'in a Chinese restaurant in King's Road ... I sat beside Richard and Joe was at the head of the table. I was sat next to this kind of dull vegetarian and we were all passing the food and he's not having anything ... I think he tried to tell me why, and I was like, "Spare me. I'm eating sweet and sour pork here."'

But despite Linda's abiding friendship with Sandy and her close relationship with Boyd, it would be some time before their paths crossed again. Quite simply, as Simon matter-of-factly states, 'Joe never brought his girlfriends to work. There was never a bored girl sitting on the sofa waiting to be taken to Annabelle's. He had a clear defining line.' When the star-crossed pair met up again, at The Angel, Linda left convinced her friend Sandy did not know greatness when she heard it:

Linda Thompson: I did go to Little Hadham a couple of times, but I was with Joe; when you're young, you only notice the people you want to notice. I don't know why I didn't notice Richard, but I only had eyes for Joe. He wasn't really on my radar. I remember Sandy ranting on about him. I [just] went, 'Really?' ... I was friends with Nick [Drake] and John Martyn. I thought they were better, actually.

Linda had been spoilt by a fortuitous proximity to great guitarists and singer-songwriters from an early age. In fact, she had known John Martyn since the age of twelve, when he delivered newspapers to the family home in Glasgow. As she says, 'Sandy was truly exceptional. As was Richard. [Yet] John is probably my favourite of them all ... Mad as a snake. But I loved John.'

Lacking any sense of awe at the way Richard wielded a Fender may have worked in Linda's favour, but even after she fell for him, she still had to do most of the heavy lifting to get the relationship airborne:

Philippa Clare: [Linda] had a thing for him for a while before [they hooked up]. Richard was quite a challenge. He always used to sit with his toes together with odd socks on, being vegetarian and quiet.

Simon Nicol: Linda's extrovert side was a very good match for Richard's introverted one. She could talk the back legs off a donkey – in a lovely way – whereas he was dodgy-eyed and stuttering ... She opened [Richard] up like an oyster – he had no choice. He didn't have a chance. She turned him round – with a strong rope.

Linda Thompson: Richard was unbelievably introverted [back] then. Basically, he went out with women who picked him up, put him over their shoulder and took him home. [1985]

Fortunately, the twenty-something Richard still had a penchant for Dutch courage in a glass, a weakness he referenced in a number of contemporary lyrics, one of which ('Twisted') included the couplet, 'Sitting at the bar with my face in the jar/ Something tells me I'm twisted.' As he told *Uncut* recently, 'I was probably drinking a bit in those days. Or a lot. Perhaps I just thought that was what you had to write [about].' He was altogether more open about his former drinking in a 1982 conversation with fellow singer-songwriter, Tom Russell:

Richard Thompson: I used to drink to excess ... You have to do something to satisfy that bit inside you that wants to get out of there. If you're drinking you want to get lost in something. If you're playing music, you want to get lost in something. ... I find the people in bars are the most interesting people in society. They're the ones who can't stand it. They're the ones who see something terrible about what goes on, and they want to kill the pain of it.

In 1972, he still considered himself at one with the 'heroes, patriots, martyrs, reformers in the great sense' that Thoreau championed for their civil disobedience, whose societal conscience saw them

'commonly treated as enemies'. Such outsiders inhabit most of his
best songs.

In his case, it took a lot of drink to 'kill the pain'. Fortunately, as
Linda soon found, Richard 'could drink anyone under the table …
His sister was exactly the same. But I could never take it. I'd be sick
for three days throwing up. Obviously by the time I met Richard I
did drink, but not very much. Sandy was a big drinker, but … you'd
just sit there sipping your drink while she went through [several]
bottles of wine.'

However soon the formal courtship began, it was only a couple of
weeks after the initial Bunch sessions before Richard invited Linda to
share a studio again. He started recording his own album of original
songs – *Henry The Human Fly* – the second week of Janaury 1972,
and Linda was contributing backing vocals.[24]

Perhaps these sessions were part of the courtship. Certainly, when
Richard produced out of thin air songs like 'The Poor Ditching Boy',
'The Angels Took My Racehorse Away' and 'Nobody's Wedding',
it made Linda reevaluate his place in the pecking order of English
singer-songwriters, cementing a deep admiration (nay, adoration) in
the impressionable lass.

If she made little immediate progress figuring out where such
songs came from, when Richard was called on to explain himself
by a couple of music journalists that May, he seemed to imply they
were merely the tip of some vast internal iceberg of doom and gloom:

Richard Thompson: The songs are between a year and two years
old. You really have to … weed out all the bad stuff. That really
takes a long time. The stuff I've written in the last year isn't on it …
[*Henry*] shows what I think English music should sound like. [1972]

Richard Thompson: I like to sit on things for a while. They're
between a year and two years old. The stuff I've written since then
… I wasn't sure enough … to include on the album … [But] I keep
writing throwaway songs. It's very annoying – stuff I don't want to
write … It's usually awful, or it's a country song. I write hundreds
of country songs. [1972]

---

[24] Presumably both Sandy and Linda were readily available because they were concurrently
obliged to do overdubs for The Bunch album at Basing Street.

Wherever they had been fermenting, the songs came in a torrent once Richard entered Sound Techniques, on or around January 12, 1972. On that 'first' day, he recorded at least five songs: 'Amazon Queen' (which went unused), 'The Old Changing Way', 'Shaky Nancy', an acoustic 'Roll Over Vaughn Williams' and 'Painted Ladies'. He returned to 'Roll Over Vaughn Williams' four days later, multitracking a legion of electric guitars, while working on at least two other songs, one of which was 'The Poor Ditching Boy', which did indeed 'cut through to his blood'. And hers.[25]

The session on the 16th may well have completed *Henry The Human Fly*. Or perhaps he laboured on for a few more days. But by the end of the month he had sent a finished master to Island, exchanging it for a plane ticket to America, accompanying Sandy on her second US tour.

The album had come together very quickly and cheaply. Although over the years Richard has enjoyed giving the impression it coalesced in a somewhat haphazard manner, in 1974 expressing amazement that 'anyone put it out. It was done in a hurry. I'd like to do it again. The songs and the ideas were very good, but it wasn't very well executed.'

Four years later, he was claiming he made the whole album 'on spec' and 'then approached Island with it. I'd figured that if they weren't interested, I could probably sell it somewhere else.' Not so. The original studio reels clearly indicate Island Records were the 'client'. In 1988 Richard finally admitted, 'I went into the studio and recorded [the album] and ... sent them the bill ... They very graciously put it out.' And put it out they did – alongside *Morris On* and *The Bunch Rocks On*, party to a familial folk-rock movement of sorts:

Richard Thompson: Conceptually, Ashley and Fairport and myself and Sandy – we were developing this fairly fragile style of music that no one else was particularly interested in – this British folk-rock thing ... [so] The Bunch was rather a retro-step ... *Morris On* was the kind of record we should have been doing.

Henry The Human Fly came out of nowhere, and it went straight back there. A brave gesture on both the artist and label's part – perhaps

---

[25] In subsequent live performances, this magnificent song was usually sung by Linda.

the most courageous of Thompson's career – it was a work that bore deep into the darker side of the English pysche. Perhaps too deep. And all of this he then buried beneath guitars as treacly as Marmite.

The end product was too multi-layered for most musical palettes. When asked to explain his thought processes, Richard resorted to paradoxes. 'Mary And Joseph' was 'a religious song – and it's not. It's a credo I believe, but I don't know what I believe in.' 'Nobody's Wedding' originally 'started out as ... a really nasty song, and then in the course of time I wasn't angry anymore, so I chopped out the really vicious verses'. Even with the evidence now on public display, he couldn't bring himself to explicate in conversation just how bleak and blighted his vision of Albion was:

Richard Thompson: The style of [*Henry*] was very clear in my mind ... What actually came out was a bit different from what I thought, but it was still very English. [1975]

One listen to *Henry* brings home why he had spurned so many opportunities to remain in the shadows. He had something important to say, and was determined to do so with his own voice, whatever its limitations. It was the very point he made to the press on its release:

Richard Thompson: My temperament's changed since I left Fairport ... I can't see myself ... being in a band and devoting myself to it 100% of the time ... The *Morris* [*On*] record was really enjoyable to do, but if I had to play morris music all the time I'd go bananas ... Traditional music is [probably] 50% of what I play on my record player but I don't want to perform it all the time. I want to play whatever British music is ... But it ... isn't there yet ... I'd like to grow towards a music which expresses me, what I feel and what I go through. Traditional music doesn't really do that for me ... I enjoyed doing Shirley's album, but it doesn't satisfy my soul .... [*Henry The Human Fly*] is an attempt, it has a traditional feel but it's contemporary music. [1972]

There was blood not only on the tracks, but between the cracks. So imagine the hurt he felt when he read the review by the usually sympathetic Andrew Means for *Melody Maker* which concluded,

'Meaningful lyrics are marred by bottled-up vocals, uninspiring guitar phrases and a general lack of conviction in performance … That's the general impression of the album – beautiful, even brilliant ideas half-hidden and half-exploited.' As a review, it sailed a full five fathoms wide of its mark.

And yet, Thompson would allow himself to become half-convinced this way-off critique made some kind of sense. He later informed *Hokey Pokey*'s Colin Davies, one of his most persistent cheerleaders, 'The vocals are so bad. I was having a very terrible time singing at that point – tortured with self-doubt.' Indeed, he has rarely wasted an opportunity to put *Henry* down over the years, usually when brought up by a lifelong fan of the record:

Richard Thompson: [I'd like to] do the vocals again. The unfortunate thing about that was that I did the backing tracks without realizing that we'd done them all in the wrong keys, so we had a few problems that way … [And] the performance on my part was pretty bad. [1974]

Richard Thompson: The performances are dreadful, but the material is interesting. They're not representative of my current interests, though … *Henry* is a bit labyrinthine. I wouldn't make it again. [1978]

Richard Thompson: The negative criticism of that record was 50% absolutely right – it wasn't a very well-performed record, and I sang it really badly, because I wasn't a good singer. The other 50% was probably wrong … People just didn't understand it. [2014]

He never quite got over the critical roasting it received. As Linda points out, 'He was very young and it was his first solo album, and it got slated. I remember we went for a walk on Hampstead Heath … and he got *Melody Maker* and he … couldn't believe it … I don't think he was ever going to make another record [ever again].'

The record still received an American release. Warners – now tasked with distributing his records – gamely tried to find a way of marketing it. And they almost found a way, drafting a press release inserted into promotional copies of the album – still far more common than the few 'stock' copies shipped to stores – that insisted:

The lyrics, like many good things, must be studied to be appreciated ... [while] the guitar work, all Richard's, is as dense as it is deft. Layers upon layers are combined to form ever-changing patterns and harmonies, supporting, reinforcing and adding to the vocals.

At least Yankee rock scribe Ken Barnes, writing for Boston's *Fusion*, recognised the album's sheer originality. In fact, his review teetered on the brink of hyperbole as Barnes called *Henry* 'the best album I've heard all year' and singled out for the most fulsome praise, 'Thompson's vocals, strongly accented, oft-times cracked or strained and rather plain by conventional standards, [yet] manage to invest just the proper amount ... of rough poignancy.'

Barnes duly made *Henry* his album of the year in the end-of-year *Fusion* critics' poll, by which time its *auteur* knew full well he was very much in the critical minority. The critical consensus may have turned 120 degrees in the intervening decades, but the whole sound of the album still remains a barrier for some – much like another classic album released the same week, Nanker/Phelge's equally murky masterpiece, *Exile On Main Street*.

What would have cut Thompson to the quick, if he had been there to witness it, would have been the occasion in the late eighties when his ex-wife attempted to re-record one of the album's centrepieces, 'The Angels Took My Racehorse Away'; asking one of her (and Richard's) guitar-heroes, James Burton, to play on it. Unfortunately, 'when I first played *Henry The Human Fly* to James Burton, he said, "What language is that?" I said, "James, it's English." He said, "Is it at the right speed?"' Linda never did get to redo the song – a personal favourite – in the studio.[26]

The cruel reception these twisted songs received probably did for several other ditties in a similar vein which Richard had been stockpiling over the past eighteen months. He was taking the whole thing personal. How could he not? As he explained, the month of *Henry*'s release, 'Any song's personal ... Obviously you can't write a song at an impersonal level because it just doesn't happen. Whatever you do is related to you very immediately in some way, even if you're writing about something happening in Australia.'

---

[26] As partial recompense, Linda sang the song as an occasional encore at her 2007 shows.

Two particular songs from this period – 'Dragging The River'
and 'When I'm Prime Minister' – he played repeatedly, but never
recorded in an Island studio. Both seemed to delight in the kind of
working-class hero who would willingly murder and maim those
who had once bullied him. They remain quintessential examples of
Thompson's select body of 'chip-on-shoulder' songs, reflecting the
skewered working-class consciousness of a resolutely middle-class
man:

Richard Thompson: Among the [English] working classes you
often find this monstrous chip on the shoulder, which stops them
from enjoying themselves a lot of the time. They want to feel that
they've been hard done by a lot of the time …. In the middle class
you don't have the social stigma, but you do have this thing called
extreme boredom … You have to get out of the suburbs. The suburbs
are death. [1982]

The embracing of feelings he would subsequently suppress
presumably explains why in later life he not only disavowed these
songs, but seemingly wiped all memory of them from his brain; so
much so that when, in the year 2000, he received 'a tape in the post
that was very cryptically labelled … it took me two minutes to realise
that I was singing in a folk club, with the Ex, singing some song that I
haven't sung since 1973 … It was … as if it were coming from Mars.'

Other discards came even closer to the knuckle. 'The World Is A
Wonderful Place' was another tongue-in-cheek song he let Linda
demo on his behalf, while two other period pieces – 'You Got What
You Wanted' and 'Someone Else's Fancy' – were so misanthropic that
they were passed directly to Ashley, as possible fodder for the folk-
rock band he and Simon had been obliged to assemble without him.

If Ashley was still hoping to make an Albion Band album that
could replicate the critical impact of *Hark! The Village Wait* and *No
Roses*, Richard also remained convinced he had something to prove.
It had taken him some time to get over the reception his own record
received. Thankfully, he had also gradually come to realise just how
sympathetic a singer his girlfriend could be, and began sculpting new
material that suited a duality of voices:

Linda Thompson: I think [*Bright Lights*] was always going to be a Richard and Linda album. 'Cause we'd started it together, and he had been wounded by the notices for *Henry The Human* [*Fly*] … He was really hurt and he thought, 'I'm not going to sing anymore. I'm with a singer, so we'll just do it together.'

And in October 1972, the opportunity arose – during another of those spasms of regime change Hutchings endlessly instigated on the Albions – for Richard to temporarily resume an alliance with his erstwhile bandleader. A series of autumn 1972 Albion Band shows in tandem provided an ideal opportunity to test Richard and Linda's vocal interplay against what, for Linda, was a baptism of electric folk.

Here for a season only was the Country Band Ashley had wanted all along, but could not have. Lasting only a couple of months, it would provide a springboard for the next significant reinvention of English folk-rock – just not from Ashley. It was Linda who came to the fore, wringing every ounce of emotion from three brand new Thompson originals, 'Shady Lies', 'Has He Got A Friend For Me?' and 'The Little Beggar Girl', and freeing 'The Poor Ditching Boy' from those 'strongly accented' *Henry* vocals.

The addition of the Thompsons also meant Ashley now had singers who could really put the middle-C in Country, as evidenced by a rambunctious rendition of John Loudermilk's 'Break My Mind' and ragged-but-right covers of the Everlys' 'All I Have To Do Is Dream' and 'So Sad To Watch Good Love Go Bad'.

However, when the rest of the Albions decided to celebrate New Year's Eve at Roy Guest's Howff club with another endless encore of rock'n'roll standards, its leader pulled the plug on the gig and the band, complaining, 'The final night [at Howff] descended, and I use that word advisedly, into a ridiculous jam, past closing time, of Chuck Berry-style rock'n'roll. I'd had enough and didn't want to know anymore.'

Another Ashley experiment had been curtailed by the curmudgeon in him. Richard and Linda's artistic alliance, though, had only just begun. After their enjoyable Albion Country Band 'interregnum', they resumed touring as a duo, playing the folk clubs Linda knew well, and Richard did not. For him, it became part of the healing process her presence was already accelerating:

Linda Thompson: He'd never worked acoustically before. Although people think of him as a folk-orientated artist … he'd never really played acoustic guitar. He's a rock'n'roll musician, that's all there is to it … He said to me, 'Do you fancy doing [some] folk clubs?' Which was incredible to me, because I thought he's a star. [1980]

Richard Thompson: At the time I left Fairport I was very divorced from people. Playing music is always a ritual but it became like a very speeded-up film. We'd turn up, play, go back to the hotel, drink all night &c. It was very empty. So going back to the clubs was really an attempt to get closer to people, and draw people closer to us. [1977]

From the first, there was an audible spark to the shows. As Linda says, 'It was, no pun intended, electric. It really was, because we did have this great chemistry … And we also liked *exactly* the same things. It was spooky.' This was reflected in their choice of covers, everything from an a capella 'Once Brave Napoleon' to country classics like 'Angel Of Death', 'The Train That Carried My Girl From Town', 'Life Is Like A Mountain Road' and 'The Wild Side Of Life'. Even when they brought Simon Nicol into the fold – on an enforced break from Albion Band duties – the vibe remained ever upbeat and positive, even if the songs were not:

Simon Nicol: I remember the three of us forming a trio … [for] folk club gigs. What a joy it was to be included in that, and never be made to feel like a gooseberry with this newly-married couple who were madly in love. It would be very easy to [feel left out]. And Richard was starting to reveal a part of himself we'd never seen. With Linda's prodding he was revealed to be a very funny man [onstage]. And he'd always been an electric guitarist, [but] now [he revealed he was] an inventive acoustic guitarist. A lot of significant Thompson songs are also on the table – 'End Of The Rainbow' [for starters] … one of the most devastating songs ever written.

If the songs rarely mirrored the onstage bonhomie, the comedic edge evident in some of Richard's earlier efforts re-emerged in songs like 'Dragging The River', 'When I'm Prime Minister' and 'Little Beggar Girl', which on occasion he suggested was 'about taking money from people under false pretences – rather like this evening'. Most of the new songs went Linda's way to counterbalance the fact that Richard generally continued to take lead on the *Henry* songs.

Magic was in the air even before two minor masterpieces were slotted into the set in the new year: 'The Great Valerio' – previewed on a BBC session in January – and the utterly bereft 'Withered And Died', both Linda lead vocals. But when it came to 'End Of The Rainbow', Richard took the lead, perhaps because a pregnant Linda might not have been overly inclined to embrace its sentiments:

Linda Thompson: I did a sharp intake of breath when I heard 'End Of The Rainbow' ... because this was a child he didn't want me to have. When she was born he was fine, but I did [gasp]. In fact, Simon and I were the first people to hear it, at a gig with four people there. We were playing as Hokey Pokey and Simon and I were both sitting at the side of the stage and he [says,] 'I'm going to sing a new song.' We both sat there and [just] went, ['Oh my] God.' And of course he goes, 'It's all poetic licence.' Bullshit. It was a shock to the system. But I think it's a wonderful song! Even Muna loves it and it's about her!

The idea that a father-to-be would whisper to his unborn child, 'I feel for you, you little horror, safe at your mother's breast/ No lucky break for you around the corner ... There's nothing at the end of the rainbow/ There's nothing to grow up for anymore,' remains chilling still. But the notion was not wholly original. (Jimi Hendrix had tackled the very same subject from the point of view of the foetus – on 'Belly Button Window', released on the posthumous *Cry Of Love* in 1971.)

Though Richard was fully aware his wife was about to give birth, he showed a similar lack of sensitivity when scheduling a week of album sessions as she entered the third trimester. Even if she had been the healthiest of women, expecting the heavily-pregnant Linda to muster her full range and power at such an advanced stage of her pregnancy shows the 24-year old Richard was still living in a world of his own.

What he couldn't have known was that Linda had a rare medical condition, dysphonia, which would in the fullness of time rob her completely of that angelic singing voice. It peeked its head over the parapet for the first time at the sessions for *I Want To See The Bright Lights Tonight* in spring 1973:

Linda Thompson: I was pregnant with my first child. I was twenty-five and we were making *Bright Lights*. And John Wood kept saying to me, 'You're moving off mike, you're moving off mike,' which I wasn't. So that was when [the dysphonia] started. [So] I had to take [my] time in the studio. It started just after I got married and just after I got pregnant. Richard … didn't want me to get pregnant. He was not keen on this. I think it was hard [for him]. He was very … distant during that pregnancy. So I think that was part of it … It was a mixture of psychological and physical components.

Despite such obstacles, the *Bright Light* sessions came together as quickly as *Henry*. Richard claimed in 2014, 'We did it in three days. It cost £2,500 to record: the whole thing – studio fees, session musicians, gear rentals. Those were the days.' The session tapes have been long mislaid so there is no way of confirming such a recollection, but even if it took a little longer, one would be hard-pressed to hear a singer in crisis on the finished record, which long ago acquired the sheen of a fine cut-glass decanter.

Richard even addressed his penchant for a wee dram himself. When asked in a press interview if 'Down Where The Drunkards Roll' was autobiographical, he replied, 'I'm only a potential alcoholic, but I'm working at it.' He also repeated the assertion that 'The Little Beggar Girl' was 'about us … We squeeze money out of people for playing for just an hour … The musicians are the beggars, and the audience are the others.'

As for 'When I Get To The Border', that was intended as 'an overture for the rest of the record: everybody on the record play[ing] a little bit'. When 'The Calvary Cross' – the stunning second track that segued from 'When I Get To The Border' – came up he openly admitted it was 'about a muse, or … a drive that you might not want, but it's there, and you're a slave to it'.

Here was the first hint on record that Thompson might not be entirely happy with the preternatural musical gift he had been given. The impulse to disappear remained, it having taken Linda to rescue him from it. The birth of Muna and a mystifying reluctance on

Island's part to fast-track the album – using an 'acute' vinyl shortage as an excuse – now gave him the option to opt out again.

As the Thompsons disappeared for six months, Richard wrote about everything but fatherhood and his ongoing search for a belief system. Still in his English phase, he continued writing about other people's lives and the British weather, the two subjects that obsessed his island race. But even as he defined that sensibility for all time, a change at the record label threatened the privileged position the Witchseason acts had previously enjoyed. They had a new A&R man, and he wasn't a fan:

Richard Thompson: The A&R [man] was [now] Muff Winwood who was very rhythm & blues, with the Spencer Davis Group connection, and he absolutely hated that record … We thought it was a good record, but I think it took almost a year to come out … It's probably what *Henry* … should have been – the singing's better and the arrangements are a bit more coherent.

––––––––

While something as perfectly tailored for an English folk-rock audience as *Bright Lights* utilised the best of Thompson's back pages, Ashley Hutchings now found himself left scratching around for material which was in a traditional vein but had a contemporary dimension, having previously thought he had found it. Writing in *Melody Maker* at the dawn of 1972, Andrew Means had stated, 'The [Albion Band's] contemporary material will come from Steve Ashley, Lal Waterson [and] Richard Thompson.' And initially it did just that:

Ashley Hutchings: The reason I started the Albions in the first place was I wanted to form a rock group who played what I believed would be English rock music. Influenced very strongly by morris music, but also by Richard Thompson and a few others. And so initially the repertoire in 1972 was very overtly trying to be English. We did 'The New St George' and, later, 'Albion Sunrise'. To a certain extent, Richard was [also] in that mood … We were trying to reassert our Englishness.

However, once Thompson supplied Ashley with a six-song demo tape that spring, including 'Rainbow Over The Hill', 'Time To Ring

Some Changes', 'Albion Sunrise', 'You Got What You Wanted' and 'Someone Else's Fancy', he felt he had done his bit. Meanwhile, Mike and Lal Waterson were busy demoing songs for the irridescent *Bright Phoebus*, and were naturally keeping their songs to themselves.

They still cordially invited Thompson to add his distinctive guitar-tone to the record and let the largely-unemployed Ashley co-produce (anonymously). It became one of Thompson's favourite sessions, while providing Ashley with a further benchmark on which to write in the popular style and retain a distinctive English sensibility.

If the release of *Bright Phoebus* four months after *Henry The Human Fly* confirmed a common vision, it left the Albion Country Band trailing in their communal wake. It may even have helped convince Ashley he was not quite there yet. For most of the summer, the formative outfit had been reliant on the young Steve Ashley to come up with contemporary songs which 'displayed an understanding of the English traditional form':

Simon Nicol: Eventually the [Mk.1 Albion Country] band did develop a repertoire. Steve [Ashley did] bring some of his offerings to the table, some of which were traditional, some of which were his own songs. I remember 'Fire And Wine' and 'Lord Bateman' being the two strong[est] songs. [The band] was unlike anything else. It was authentic and very folky and fun. [And] Royston had a lot of experience as a frontman. I didn't realise what a good fiddle-player Sue was.

Unfortunately for this Ashley, excepting 'Fire And Wine' – which proved something of a showstopper – The Albions' older overseer seemed to prefer working up electric arrangements of Richard's songs. *Henry*'s 'The New St George' and 'The Poor Ditching Boy' duly appeared alongside the unreleased 'Albion Sunrise' – which announced 'a most illustrious sight ... a country band, playing hand-me-downs'.

As Simon suggests, the other highlight of those early Albion Country Band shows was more traditional. Steve Ashley's triple-ply rearrangement of 'Lord Bateman' owed something to the *No Roses* 'Maria Marten'. It was precisely the kind of material which delivered on Royston Wood's boast, to Andrew Means, 'What we have done is pull a lot of English folk songs into the thing ... but we're giving them our treatment, which doesn't sound like anybody else.'

Yet just six months into another daring electric folk experiment, the Albions' bandleader decided the line-up would never surpass its predecessor/s and called it a day. He still had yet to lead an outfit with a lifespan of more than a year. The abruptness with which Ashley pulled the plug on Albions Mk.1 convinced Royston Wood 'the three ex-Fairporters have decided that they can get on without the rest of us'. To him, it was all about personalities. This time it was not:

Ashley Hutchings: It didn't really work. We did quite a number of gigs, but we didn't make an album ... [And] when Royston and Steve left, we had these gigs and Simon and I couldn't exist, nor could the roadies and the management, without fulfilling the gigs and getting the money ... So [I thought,] 'Let's ask Richard and Linda to come along and do them.' But we all knew it was just an interim thing, [even if] we were all singing from the same hymn sheet.

The fleeting resumption of a Richard and Ashley alliance hinted at a future direction for both of them. Both, though, would be stymied by the power-shift at Island. When Ashley, after a largely frustrating 1972, set about forming the Albion Country Band Mk.3 with two musicians he had wanted from the outset – Martin Carthy and accordionist John Kirkpatrick – he found that all the uncertainty had unsettled Mattacks. By the new year, DM had been persuaded to return to his former Fairport berth, even as Ashley finally began recording a full-blown Albion Country Band album, *Battle Of The Field*:

Simon Nicol: *Battle Of The Field* is recorded quite early on with the third [Albion Country Band] line-up. This is the line-up coming together. 'John meet Martin. Sue meet Simon. This is Roger. Let's work on these songs and record them.' That's how it was done. [There] was a rehearsal place somewhere like ... Stourport. I think John and Sue live[d] in that area. [It was] a recording project with every intention to be a touring band ... We made the record before we did any gigs.

The now-departed Steve Ashley intended to use both his own songs and the impressive Albion Country Band arrangement of 'Lord Bateman' on his own album, which appeared in 1974 as *Stroll*

On,[27] making this one element of the original Albion Country Band completely absent from their debut album.

At least Ashley was permitted to include whatever Richard songs he wanted. 'Albion Sunrise' duly became the second Thompson song that year to serve as 'an overture for the rest of the record, [with] everybody on the record play[ing] a little bit'. 'The New St George' was also put to service, segueing into the traditional 'La Rotta' as Ashley continued his interweaving of traditional styles galore.

In fact, its sheer diversity of traditional styles would be part of the album's charm, Ashley sandwiching a Morris Medley between a broadside ballad and Thompson's calling song. 'Battle Of The Somme' concluded an album that, although it lacked the dulcet tones of Maddy Prior or Shirley Collins, took up where the original Steeleye left off.

But before Island could even muster a marketing plan, Ashley began pushing for them to finance two distinctly different projects: *The Compleat Dancing Master* (a reference to John Playford's 17th century collections of folk tunes) and *Rattlebone & Ploughjack*, an album which combined music and spoken word in a way seemingly more suited to radio than a record:

Ashley Hutchings: I can't remember why [Island] allowed me to make these albums. [But] I made the three albums in one year: *Battle Of The Field*, *The Compleat Dancing Master*, *Rattlebone & Ploughjack* – three completely different albums. [The last of these] was like a documentary;[and] the most expensive album I'd worked on to that [date] ... It was David Betteridge [at Island] who very much supported me, even though he wasn't a musician. He was a money man and a contracts man. But he let me make *Rattlebone* for Island. How bizarre is that?

At the same time as he was recording this vinyl 'radio documentary', Tyger decided to further push his luck by asking to make a(nother) collection of dance tunes, à la *Morris On,* but drawn directly from John Playford's *English Dancing Master*, first published in 1651 and comprising 104 tunes, some of which remain unidentified even to this day.

---

[27] The original Albion Country Band actually reformed for a day to help him re-record 'Lord Bateman'.

Ever the iconoclast, Ashley decided an album which 'cover[ed] seven centuries or thereabouts of "traditional" dance music in England using a combination of old instruments and modern electricity', was still not ambitious enough for him. And so he 'set the pieces up and link[ed] musical items with historically suitable spoken word. Thus, a piece of Dickens [would] lead into two polkas; a Puritan [would] rant against dance prior to a 17th century Playford tune; a late 16th century discussion by pupil and dancing master on etiquette in court dancing [would] be followed by a stately Elizabethan consort of viols.'

Perversely, of the three albums Ashley delivered to Island by the end of 1973, *The Compleat Dancing Master* was the only one the label deigned to release at the time. The other two were quietly filed alongside *I Want To See The Bright Lights Tonight*, marked D.N.U., in a cupboard with a sign on the door that read 'Beware The Leopard'.

The most commercial offering, *Battle Of The Field*, had fallen victim to Ashley's own restlessness. For the fourth time in four years he wilfully disbanded an outfit that had just completed an album the label expected him, and the band in question, to promote:

Ashley Hutchings: We were still in debt to Island ... We [had] made the album and at the end of the year we said, 'Let's call it a day at the end of these gigs.' There was no dissenting voice ... even though we knew we were playing good music. So ... Island didn't put the album [out, which was] logical business practice. We weren't there to promote the record.

Perhaps he was unconsciously looking for an out. Fronting and managing an electric folk band was again becoming too much for his fragile psyche. As he told Karl Dallas in 1974, 'It was a constant battle keeping the Albions afloat from beginning to end ... Finally, it just ground to a halt.' He had been pushing himself too hard.

After producing three albums in a single year on three separate occasions in the past four-and-a-half years he was at breaking point psychologically, and wrung out physically. It now prompted talk of retirement from music at the venerable age of 29: 'After the problems I've encountered with recordings in the past year, I've no inclination to make another record in any form. I don't want to get involved ... I've had enough of the aggravation ... of making a record.'

Even the thought of failing to make ends meet with a wife and a family to feed could not persuade him to continue pouring product into an apathetic world. His decision was symptomatic of another minor breakdown brought on by overwork (and maybe some congenital overambition). Tellingly, the June 1974 release of *The Compleat Dancing Master* failed to even replicate the modest success of *Morris On*.

For now, the workaholic needed some rest and recreation. Meanwhile, honorary Albion Country Band members Richard & Linda Thompson received the welcome news that their album was finally being readied for release, signalling their re-emergence into the world of popular music when they were needed most. A necessary reorganization of the Island hierarchy had turned the wind of change in their favour again. With an album as good as *Bright Lights* to promote, it was surely now or never for the part-time recluse and his bonny bride.

FOLK

BY CO

Hutchings: the age of Steam

ASHLEY HUTCHINGS AND SHIRLEY COLLINS: tremendous relief

THERE'S something very English about Ashley Hutchings. Neat. Dapper. Phlegmatic. Organised.

He might be a banker, or an accountant, perhaps, who lives a quiet life in Sussex with his wife, and spends much of his leisure time gardening.

It comes as quite a shock to think this man has played a major role in influencing the course of the folk movement. In fact he's been possibly the most important single person in the whole experiment of integrating folk into rock music.

A founder of Fairport Convention, then of Steeleye Span, then of the Albion Country Band. Ever the pioneer, Ashley Hutchings was always much more than simply a bass player in a rock band with folk connections. He had brains which sought horizons way beyond the view of most musicians.

So what's he doing at the moment? Trolling round the folk clubs backing his wife with an acoustic group called the Etchingham Steam Band, that's what. And he's happy.

No more rock bands for Ashley—for the first time in his career he's directly involved in the folk scene and he's finding it a tremendous relief after all the high power and the pressures that revolved around the electric bands.

Hair

He's quite adamant. He'll never play in the rock field again. If pressed he'll even admit to a certain bitterness about what's gone before.

"I don't like being bitter, and I don't like using the media to air any bitterness I might have. But yes, I suppose I am bitter. I'm bitter that one has such a rough ride in order to do something which in the end product is so simple. I'm also bitter that I've impaired my health through it."

The Etchingham Steam Band is turning out to be a much happier story. It was formed around the turn of the year and at the time

Ashley had no intention of joining them.

Shirley Collins was no longer to be accompanied on gigs by her sister Dolly so the Etchinghams were formed out of a Sussex group called the Country Cousins to back her, as she didn't fancy performing solo.

The Albion Country Band had slithered to a halt some months earlier, so Ashley was at a loose end, but it was an eleventh-hour decision that he should join them.

"I was still languishing after the demands of Albion, it took a long time to get over the final break of Albion. I don't know what I

was going to do. I think it was just listening to them rehearse made me want to play again.

"When the Albions broke up I didn't touch my instrument until I heard the band rehearse. I just lost interest in playing. I was totally fed-up and I had no inclination to carry on playing at that stage."

He was totally drained by the experience of the Albions and even now it's too soon for him to make any rational conclusions about it.

"It was a constant battle keeping the Albions afloat from beginning to end. Just keeping it going was a battle

Oh hell. I've been rumbled. Last month's Folk Review *contained the exposé I have been dreading every waking moment of my life since I threw up rock music to try my hand at the Big Money circuit – the British Folk Scene. I feel honour-bound to confess all in the hope that … I may be judged mercifully. Firstly, I do admit that in 1969 I enticed Dave Swarbrick into Fairport in order to give the group a more widely-appealing money-spinning folk image. This was achieved faster than my accountant's wildest dreams, so I immediately left to see what money could made closer to the real folk-scene itself. Spectacular results were achieved with Steeleye Span, but I wasn't going to stay with a group that had hopes of adding a heavy rhythm section – and thus would move away from the folk-scene I so yearned to make my fortune in. The Albion Country Band was next, a spectacular revue featuring a remarkable turn-over of well-known folkies, together with a team of morris dancers, road crew and sick vehicles. Of course, we were really coining it in now, as you can imagine…*

—LETTER FROM ASHLEY HUTCHINGS, *FOLK REVIEW*, **AUGUST 1974**

Ashley might be interested in recognition, but … as soon as he achieves any kind of success, he'll go and do something else, which I think is quite admirable.

—RICHARD THOMPSON, *NME*, **8TH MARCH 1975**

No matter how high-minded Tyger's stance seemed to his friend Richard – who always envied Ashley's unwavering self-belief – his way of working could sometimes resemble career-suicide. Simon rather thinks *Battle Of The Field*'s non-release was, at least partly 'to do with the fact that Ashley did not have a manager and sometimes he is not his own best representative. It's like, the man who represents himself in court has a fool for a lawyer.'

By the end of 1973, Hutchings had run out of options. The industry was more and more about shifting units. Rather than adapt to its changing ways, he retreated. In fact, his next musical project was a symbolic recreation of the Ethnic Shuffle Orchestra – the 1965 quasi-skiffle band which had been a mid-sixties starting point for all his musical explorations.

According to Ashley, the Etchingham Steam Band – as the new outfit was called – came about because he was 'listening to [Shirley and her band] rehearse, [and that] made me want to play again … The idea was just to have a nice, relaxed band playing traditional songs. It's a tremendous relief … I can't envisage going in a band playing in [the] rock field again.' Or indeed getting another record deal.

Once again this was music as therapy, reflected in the idealistic way Ashley talked in a June 1974 *Melody Maker* article about trying to recreate a 'close relationship with an audience and … being in control of one's sound, and not relying on amps and mikes'. The Etchingham Steam Band was a conscious uncoupling of any folk/rock synergy. The all-acoustic outfit would be fronted by Shirley, a traditional voice that seemed like it pumped forth from a crystal spring:

Ashley Hutchings: When the third line-up of the Albion Country Band broke up … we went away and licked our wounds because we really wanted that one to work. What followed was the Etchingham Steam Band. I was really able to get deeper and deeper into traditional music, and dance as well, [even] getting an acoustic bass guitar for the first time in my life. [I] just wanted to support Shirley and her music.

For Shirley, it healed some of the fractures their relationship had suffered as a result of her exclusion from the Albion Country Band. She had her husband back again, and was doing what she loved most – singing traditional songs. Quite how long her partner's restless spirit would be quelled was unclear. Probably not for long:

Shirley Collins: It was fun, it was unassuming, it was light-hearted. It wasn't trying to be 'art'. We did play a lot of those first gigs actually by candlelight in pubs. That was at the time of the power cuts … which is why it was formed. It was Ashley's idea that we did something that totally didn't need electricity at all … We only played in small venues – well, apart from the Albert Hall.

That Albert Hall gig was a part of the short-lived Folk Proms. Held on September 27th, 1974, it was the most fitting place for a Dylan nut like Ashley to become reacquainted with the part of the folk constituency that considered even an all-acoustic band anti-folk. He still remembers being 'barracked at the Folk Proms', some shouting, 'This is not folk music. Get off!' The more trappings of a rock sound he jettisoned, the more he seemed to cop flak. Hence his riposte to a review in the *Folk Review* of an Etchingham Steam Band show earlier in the summer (see this chapter's opening quote).

One ill-directed charge from the dyed-in-wool finger-in-ear brigade was that he was commercialising their beloved ballads, most of which were first published as 'penny' broadsides by commercial printers. Ashley still recalls an occasion the previous year, when 'Carthy and I were at a folk festival .... It was like a workshop on electric folk music. [There were] hundreds of people, and we had to justify ourselves – [to prove] we weren't in it for the money.'

For all the strides he had made bridging the divide between folk and rock, there seemed to be no welcome mat at either door for the eclectic music-maker. The Folk Proms convinced him another rethink was required. Once again, he beat a retreat back to Sussex, planning to sit out another hard winter and regroup in the spring, when the electricity might be back on and his friend Simon in a position to return his calls.

If 1974 thus became something of a lost year on the Hutchings CV, it was the year Richard & Linda Thompson finally announced themselves to the world at large. This time Richard grasped the poisoned chalice and held on, even as he loudly bellyached about how 'the music business is awful ... It's terrible from every aspect ... a really ugly place, a nasty country to be in ... And it can't be changed ... To be a professional musician is a strange thing. It has to drive you mad eventually. It has to unseat your mind.'

For all his protestations, the best kept secret in the Thompson household was that he really wanted hit records – on his terms. As Linda avers, 'He tried to be more commercial. He *really* tried.'

So when Richard received a call one day from a namesake he already knew, saying that he would like to put out the album the Thompsons had recorded the previous year, he was hugey relieved, if a little confused. How exactly was a *Melody Maker* journalist going to facilitate the album's release?

The explanation: former music journalist (and future award-winning sports journalist), Richard Williams, had been appointed head of A&R at Island, and almost the first artist he wanted to know about was the guitar-vocalist, who could now sing halleluiah. The Muff Winwood era was officially at an end:

Richard Williams: David Betteridge, who was managing director, offered me the job ... Muff Winwood was moving from running A&R to become Managing Director of the Basing Street studio, one big studio, one smaller studio and very much a going concern ... I knew a lot of people at Island [already] through [my association with] Roxy [Music] and [King] Crimson. I knew [all] the E.G. people ... I liked Richard [Thompson] a lot. [So] one of the first things I said when I got [to Island] was, 'What's happening with Richard?' [No one knew, so] I asked Muff. He said, 'Well, him and Linda made this record and nobody thinks much of it.' I rang Richard and said, 'Can I hear it?' He came in and I listened to it and thought it was ... a fantastic record. Everything you could want, very polished, great songs, sounds like a proper record and has something that sounds like a single ... So I said we should release this and release it as is. Everything was immediately put into [motion].

The news triggered a resumption of touring from the husband-and-wife team, initially as the same acoustic trio – with Simon – that had given a smattering of intimate live performances the previous autumn. Yet, no matter how keen the Thompsons were to get *Bright Lights* into the shops, Richard preferred to preview the next album, which did little to tone down the dark side of *Bright Lights*. Meanwhile, every vestige of *Henry* was removed from the set.

If 'Withered And Died' and 'End Of The Rainbow' were already out of season, they had been superseded by five songs the duo had yet to record – 'I'll Regret It All In The Morning', 'Never Again', 'Georgie On A Spree', 'The Sun Never Shines On The Poor' and 'Hokey Pokey' – the first four of which were as bleak as any mid-winter.

A fortnight into February 1974, BBC DJ John Peel gave the Thompsons an opportunity to do some advance promotion for *Bright Lights*. The pair played three new songs instead, a taster for two dozen acoustic shows they were booked to play in the next six weeks. After all, it was these shows which were keeping the wolf from the door:

Richard Thompson: While we worked acoustically we were earning a good living; but a band isn't the place to earn money unless you're extremely successful … If we wanted to earn money we'd have stayed in folk clubs – because if you're successful there you can do very well. And we did very well – both Linda and I together, and when we were playing with Simon as well. [1974]

By May, though, Island were asking for something more product-friendly from the duo if they were to provide tour support for a sixteen-date sortie supporting Traffic. This required the acquisition of a rhythm-section – Willie Murray and Steve Borrell, on the back of just two days' rehearsals – a resumption of Richard's electric guitar playing and the assumption of a new band name, Sour Grapes (later preserved for the Richard, Linda and Simon trio).

It meant a first live outing for 'Calvary Cross' and a pulsating full-band preview of another guitar masterclass, 'Hokey Pokey'. As far as rhythm guitarist Simon Nicol was concerned, 'It was obvious that they were making compromises … [From] being a trio with a rhythm section, [it] started to move towards a rhythm section accompanying a couple.'

Although they included five *Bright Lights* songs in their forty-five minute set, Sour Grapes' support slots drew little attention at the time, for which *NME*'s Thompson apostle, Bob Woffinden, offered an explanation of sorts:

> The day I saw Sour Grapes they took a time to warm up, and strangely elected to play their trump card – the irresistible title-track from the album – first of all. But they were certainly good value as a support act – for God's sake … and after a while Thompson and Nicol were trading licks with a confidence that recalled the finer days of Fairport. Linda Thompson sang well, though she doesn't yet have … confidence in her stage presence.

Perhaps Linda's mind was on other things. Whatever emotional distance had developed between her and Richard during her pregnancy, she was back to playing the field and singing her heart out – as much to impress the headliner as her husband:

Linda Thompson: That was quite enjoyable, actually. Opening for somebody is fantastic because you're finished at half past eight and I could be [there] for the kids, so it was good. And I had a little flirtation/fling with Jim Capaldi which was fabulous. I was mad about him. I was [just] married. I mean, how awful. But I was absolutely insane about Jim Capaldi and so he and I had a good time together when everybody's back was turned. Maybe that's why I enjoyed it.

For Richard, the return to concert halls was a mixed blessing. The experience prompted him to bemoan 'the big barrier [because] of the stage and the lights', while admitting he preferred 'playing electric guitar because it gives more scope'. He continued to insist he was 'not a soloist. I play off whatever else is going on. I just pick up things off drums and bass – it's called cheating.'

Former fans of Fairport refused to be fooled. They were overjoyed to hear Richard had not lost his ability to transform songs with dazzling displays of six-string pyrotechnics. An electric set also allowed more light and shade than an album – particularly one as unremittingly bleak as *Bright Lights*, for which Richard showed a surprising need to apologize in contemporary interviews:

Richard Thompson: It is a bit of a down record, but that was accidental. We tried to balance it, but something obviously went wrong somewhere…There are a lot of slow numbers. But … it's still enjoyable, there are some optimistic songs. We're not a doomy band – we try to cover aspects of our experience. [1974]

Richard Thompson: We should have taken out a slow track and put in a fast one, but we didn't really have one at the time. Those were the best songs we had to put on a record at that time. [1975]

His American label took the view, once bitten, twice shy. They decided not to take their lead from the almost universally positive reviews, one of which called *Bright Lights* 'one of the hottest albums of the year' (Jerry Gilbert in *Sounds*). The classic LP would not be released Stateside for another two-and-a-half years, when it would form half of a schizophrenic double-set called *Live (More Or Less)*, accompanying a version of 'Calvary Cross' that took a blowtorch to the studio prototype.

Meanwhile, *Bright Lights'* original title – *Hokey Pokey* – was transplanted to the next album, which he and Linda began recording that summer. The title-track signalled a return to plugging in. Asked that June about the likely direction for *Bright Lights'* successor, the guitarist described it to a tee: 'The new album will be more electric, and the songs will not be … as wordy … More just a rock'n'roll record. But an English rock'n'roll record.'

Recorded in two sets of sessions, the new album took up where the live performances left off. Unfortunately, still-unidentified problems with Linda's singing this time *did* call a halt to proceedings mid-sessions. Though no actual explanation was forthcoming, the following year Richard made a cryptic reference to having to take 'three months off because of a purely physical thing. It was Linda's voice.'

By the time they resumed work, the songwriter had gone cold on the material already recorded: 'There was a whole new perspective on it, simply because to us it wasn't a new record by then. If I listen to it now, I can hear the split down the middle.'

Of the five songs on *Hokey Pokey* not debuted at the spring shows,[28] Thompson seemed to most like 'Mole In A Hole' (a song by the Watersons), 'A Heart Needs A Home' and 'The Egypt Room' – which was 'supposed to be … half way between The Coasters' "Little Egypt" and George Formby,' but came out sounding like The Krays meet *Electric Kool-Aid Acid Test*.

He had also now written perhaps his ultimate 'chip on shoulder' song, 'Smiffy's Glass Eye'. Though it pastiched a number of rock'n'roll clichés, the song had a serious subject at its core – bullying:

Richard Thompson: 'Smiffy's Glass Eye' was originally called 'Herbert's Glass Eye'. And then we met the real Smiffy – he works at Sound Techniques studios. It's just about cruelty and how people destroy each other through being very superficial. The kids hate him, and pick on him and destroy him. It's terrible when someone is disliked because of his appearance; you should only see what is in

---

[28] 'Smiffy's Glass Eye', 'The Egypt Room', 'Old Man Inside A Young Man', 'A Heart Needs A Home' and 'Mole In A Hole'.

someone's heart. It's an amalgamation of childhood memories and various playground horrors. [1975]

If 'Smiffy's Glass Eye' drew on his own 'childhood memories' to strike back at those who mocked the afflicted, the album's highlight was 'Never Again' which laid bare the man's nerve ends. The oldest song of all, it dated back to the dark days of 1969. Though he had not finished it at the time, it continued to address the aftermath of the motorway crash:

Richard Thompson: Eventually I convinced myself that I ought to write a third verse ... But funnily enough it still expresses the same emotion. It's strange. I don't really think I wrote it [as such]. It just came from somewhere. [1974]

Not surprisingly, it was left to Linda to sing the new words. Her virtuoso vocal fully held its own with those of Sandy on 'Farewell, Farewell' and 'Crazy Man Michael' – the other sides of that sundered triangle.

But as with *Henry*, the production on the album version sometimes got in the way. No one in attendance seemed to have noticed there was a superior alternate take of 'A Heart Needs A Home', later released on *(guitar, vocal)*. Perhaps the choice of Simon Nicol and John Wood as co-producers was intended to leave Richard calling the shots. Certainly, the other Fairportee makes light of any technical contribution he might have made:

Simon Nicol: I was happy to do that and it gave me a sense of being more than a rhythm guitarist. I've had my name attached to a number of albums, but unless a disagreement breaks out between part of the band and you have to do a bit of firefighting, what does a producer do, anyway?

In fact, nobody at Sound Techniques – even that consummate sound engineer Wood – seemed to know what sound they wanted. As far as the *auteur* of this quixotic quilt was concerned, it was simply 'not that important. Ideally, you just do something until it happens to sound right, and sometimes it sounds right straightaway.'

He would soon change his mind, but not soon enough to alter the sound on an album stuck somewhere between the muck and mire of *Henry* and the melodious clarity of *Bright Lights*. By the time they completed recording, Thompson was already detaching himself from the results, dismissing all (but one) of the songs:

Richard Thompson: Nine [of the songs] are my own compositions, and eight of those are old ones – the only new one is 'A Heart Needs A Home'. Because they're old, I don't feel much connection with them. The album was started last year, but the material comes from a year before that. [1975]

It was all part of a major psychological, or spiritual, volte face. By the time *Hokey Pokey* finally appeared the following spring, both Richard and Linda had been changed from the creatures they were, having embraced a particularly cerebral, rather ascetic strand of Islam.

With his conversion, Thompson's songwriting turned away from his once burning ambition to make a definitive 'English rock'n'roll record'. And that was not all. He began to denigrate his earlier work, suggesting it lacked a spiritual dimension:

Richard Thompson: I recognised something that I wanted, decided I'd been moving towards it and when I identified it for what it was, I accepted it. Music … doesn't have a life of its own … It's the state of one's own being that's conveyed through music, and [where] Islam [is involved], the only thing you can communicate is the affirmation of it, the unity of existence, a belief in [the] prophets and Mohammed was a prophet. [1978]

Adding to the mounting irony, it was a group of rock musicians who brought Richard – and ultimately Linda – into the Sufi commune they joined in the second half of 1974. Richard later suggested he found his spiritual calling after attending a speech on Sufism by Shaykh Abdalqadir as-Sufi (the former Ian Dallas) at a church hall in Belsize Park. He forgot to mention that the members of Mighty Baby – with whom he had played on a number of sessions, including Gary Farr and The Bunch – had joined this sect first, led by Martin Stone, who in his usual contrary way quit as soon as the others joined.

When Ian Whiteman and Roger Powell talked to Richard about
their new-found faith, the guitarist says he saw 'something … that I'd
never seen before, something I wanted for myself. It was a quality.' After
he had 'read straight through the Occult Bookshop in about two years,
I was looking for [that] something'. For such an intellectually curious
individual, this particular vision of Islam connected all the dots:

Linda Thompson: Ever since he was in Fairport, he was the airy-
fairy one: never ate meat, never wore leather. He read Gurdjieff and
Madame Blavatsky while everybody else was reading *The Beano*. I
always thought when he was forty, he'd live on a mountain. I [just]
didn't think it would happen as young as it did.

Richard Thompson: I always felt there had to be more than this.
When I was at school I started to read books on Zen Buddhism,
yoga, astrology, everything. I reached the decision that Islam was the
means of access to knowledge of the universe, and at the same time I
met some friends who were musicians and who were Muslims, and I
recognised in them a quality that I wanted for myself. [1978]

Richard Thompson: I was heading in a particular direction at
breakneck speed, and then heading at breakneck speed the other way.
Becoming a Muslim, I found that a lot of things you wanted suddenly
fall into place: they're suddenly right there. [1975]

Like most of the major religions, the Muslim faith was – and is –
riven with dissent regarding the one true way. Richard chose one of
the more ascetic. Thompson himself depicted his faith in later life as
'like a pure version of Islam, the inner core of its teaching, the spiritual
hub. It's derived purely from the Koran and the prophet Mohammed,
in a direct line.' If Sufism has a Christian equivalent, it is Gnosticism.

Quite why this required the Thompson family to join the commune
is less clear. But Linda confirms that the two really did happen
almost in tandem, 'When Muna was a few months old, Richard
and I converted to Islam, and [we] left the flat in Hampstead for the
commune soon after.' There was precious little joy to be found there,
even for a new convert and his wife:

Linda Thompson: [Sufism is about] Oneness, about going toward your higher self … One of the maxims is that if you turn to the world, it'll run away from you and if you turn your back on it, it'll come to you … [But] we went to it in a very punishing way, no laughing, no drinking, no talking, no loving – nothing, you know. We denied ourselves everything, hoping that outer contraction would cause inner expansion … We just basically gave all our money away. Or he gave all our money away … and if you talked to a man, you had to keep your eyes down … He wanted to turn his back on the world. And he did. [1985]

It signalled another seismic shift in the dynamic of an already rocky marriage, one which Linda looks back on ruefully, 'Men are very much supposed to be the dominant force in Islam. I thought it was very good for Richard, it made him come out of himself a bit – a lot actually. [And] I thought, well, it won't do me any harm to play a subservient role. In fact, I think it did.' The transformation stunned a visiting friend, freshly arrived from LA:

Joe Boyd: Starting in the summer of 1973, I was back and forth … And little by little … I saw more and more of Richard and Linda. I went over to their house once in Hampstead … after they'd left [the] Bristol Gardens commune, but they were still very involved. I remember Cat Stevens came over for dinner, and he and Richard and I all ate rice on the floor with our hands, [while] Linda waited in the kitchen with a scarf on.

When, in the autumn of 1974, Richard and Linda's enthusiastic A&R man arranged a meeting to discuss the release of *Hokey Pokey* – an album he liked a lot – he was invited to the communal home. He found that the leader of the commune had already been working on Richard and Linda to renounce the evils of electricity:

Richard Williams: I went to see them when they were living in some grand Sufi squat in Maida Vale – a row of beautiful stucco houses – and there they were squatting. It seemed to have turned Richard away from electric music a bit, which I thought was a pity. What I really loved about Richard was his playing. The Richard Thompson that I love is the one on [the *(guitar, vocal)* versions of] 'Calvary Cross' and 'Night Comes In'.

Fortunately, the leader had yet to fully achieve his joyless goal: convincing the Thompsons to abandon their true calling. The guitarist duly agreed to promote an album which Island were hoping might break the Thompsons' commercial dam and bring the husband some of the recognition his work to date deserved.

For the remainder of 1974 and the whole of 1975 he would continue to recognise the worth of what he (and Linda) had previously wrought, promoting and celebrating *Hokey Pokey* (as well as select parts of *Henry The Human Fly* and *Bright Lights*).

While that battle for the soul of his music-making was ongoing, he would also find the time and inspiration to record perhaps his richest album, while performing the most electrically charged music of his career. For one eventful year he would continue to ply his wares in the shadow of the Calvary Cross, at the mercy of a wilful muse, even as he was telling friends and foes alike, 'I'm a Muslim, and the influence of that is in everything I do.' Only then would he fully succumb to Sufism, and begin dismissing the three glorious albums he had made between 1972 and 1974 as the work of a dilettante:

Richard Thompson: I never listen to my old records now. Even the albums with Linda were just leftovers from old albums; we were just finishing up old material. [1977]

Some leftovers.

12. Rise Up With The Moon

Ideally – and this is the truth – I'd like to be in a band so that I didn't carry
all the responsibility … I think the ideal situation is being in a band [with]
everybody having their own ideas and calling it something else.

—SANDY DENNY, *SOUNDS*, 8TH SEPTEMBER 1973

What I would really like to do would be just to join a band again. Not to be a
star with a backing group, but just the singer with the band. Like it was in the
Fairport days. In a way, it's a drag that I started with such a good band … The
best things that Fairport did in those days were never issued. That's why I've
found it so hard to settle down with any group of musicians since I left Fairport.
I keep trying to recapture the feeling, not the sound, but the wonderful feeling we
used to have between Tyger and Richard and Sandy and me … in those old days.

—IAN MATTHEWS, *MELODY MAKER*, 1ST JANUARY 1972

Both of the singers from Fairport's vocal heyday began 1972 in a
similar state of mind. Ian Matthews and Sandy Denny – the former
on the back of a big hit record, the latter not – had both disbanded
post-Fairport configurations in January 1971. Each spent the rest
of the year trying to build solo careers with bands built around the
endlessly versatile Richard Thompson. But when he made plain his
desire to forge his own path, both singers resigned themselves to
recreating their folk-rock fusions without him.

In Ian's case, the band he now put together was conceived from
the outset as a collaborative outfit – 'like it was in the Fairport days'
– based around the duo which had toured America, *minus* Richard,
who they discovered 'didn't want to be in a band'. Ian found himself
in limbo, while Richard returned to the States with Sandy, and Andy
Roberts – his trusty righthand man – embarked on his own solo tour.
Soon enough, though, Ian got a call from Roberts's manager saying,
'Andy's losing his voice! Can you come … and help him out?':

Ian Matthews: So I went up and did about three quarters of the show
with him … and it felt good, just working together in England, with

a different bass player. Then I went along to another gig at a college in South London ... just to see Andy as a friend, and we talked then about putting Plainsong together ... We set ourselves the task of taking a song and arranging it into a Plainsong piece in an afternoon and if ... at the end of the afternoon, we had something that was pleasing to all of us, we were going to be a band. [So] we took 'Along Comes Mary' and we were pretty happy with it by the end of the afternoon, and at that point we decided to be a band.

There was a couple of problems. Firstly, Ian was tied to a management contract with two individuals he had outgrown, though, as he says, 'It wasn't until Plainsong that I realised that Howard and Blaikley weren't necessarily that good for me, and that I needed to have people that thought more progressively than they did.' He was also signed to a contract with Vertigo, who ever since the *Top of the Pops* no-show had pretty much washed their hands of him. But they still wouldn't release him:

Ian Matthews: Vertigo were making a fuss about wanting a third [album] and I just didn't want to make another solo album at that point. I remember Ken and Alan having a meeting with them, and coming back and saying, 'Vertigo feel that they already have one third of Plainsong under contract, and they don't have to negotiate.'

Extricating himself from management and label was not going to be easy. Fortunately, Ian had a valuable ally in Sandy Roberton, who knew how to play the game and had a vested interest in delivering Ian from limbo so that he could take over the reins of production and management. He returned to Vertigo with an offer they could hardly refuse:

Ian Matthews: Sandy and I agreed to do one more solo album for them for like £5,000, instead of the £50,000 they owed [me], and that was their payoff. Then they didn't release it. They put that one track on the sampler, which wasn't [even] on the album. And called it by the wrong name. Apart from that, they did a great job.

That album, *Journeys From Gospel Oak*, would not be released until the summer of 1974, only appearing at producer Roberton's behest

after he extracted the tapes from Vertigo and sold them to B&C.
Unexpectedly, this contractual obligation album still stands up:

Ian Matthews: I didn't cut any corners. The only thing I didn't do
was use my own songs. I put two songs on there that I knew Plainsong
would not want, and then I just chose tasty covers that I'd wanted to
do for a long time. The country thing was there, [just] not as strong
as it was in Southern Comfort, not by a long shot. I don't know why
they didn't want to put it out. Maybe they just had had enough of
me at that point.

Having Sandy Roberton as his official producer for the first time
made recording a breeze. According to a contemporary comment
from Ian, the whole thing was completed in five days, and even
though he 'knew that there was going to be Plainsong [and] wanted
to save my best songs for that ... the songs on there turned out pretty
damn good'. At last he was free to negotiate a new deal with Elektra
Records, just as soon as he got two other monkeys off his back:

Ian Matthews: Andy and Sandy [didn't] want a chunk of their
earnings [going] to people that they hadn't chosen as representatives.
We were adamant about being Plainsong, and we would do whatever
it took to not only get out of the Vertigo thing, but also get out of
the Howard and Blaikley thing.

Ian arranged a meeting with Elektra's founder Jac Holzman in
New York. According to Roberton, 'Holzman secretly wanted Ian
and [took the view that] if he had to take this band first, he would
get him in the end.' A major-label advance from the flush Elektra
label allowed Ian to rob Peter to pay Paul, buying out Howard and
Blaikley with a quarter of the £30,000 Elektra advance.

With the way finally clear, Plainsong could at last begin work on
their debut album, *In Seach Of Amelia Earhart*. All the constituent parts
– including bassist Dave Richards and guitarist Bob Ronga – were of a
single mind. The result is an album that effortlessly combines the best
of Crosby, Stills and Nash, the Flying Burrito's and Ian-era Fairport.

Despite journeying to Gospel Oak, Ian had singularly failed to get
country-rock out of his system and the album was all the better for

it. In fact, as he admitted in June 1972, 'The songs are getting more and more country. We tried to fight it for a while but we decided to just go with the flow, let it come out the way it wanted to.'

It was an album which with the right promotion and the requisite breaks could and should have been a hit. Unfortunately, partly to keep a sense of déjà vu at bay, Ian had come up with a theme of sorts, only for it to backfire on them. Fascinated by the story of Amelia Earhart, Ian had devised a three-song suite about her – 'Amelia Earhart's Last Flight', Albert Brumley's 'I'll Fly Away' and his own 'True Story Of Amelia Earhart'. He soon found that, once folk saw 'the cover art ... people [just] presumed it was a concept album'. It proved an unwelcome distraction from a set of quality songs, which needed no such crutch.

Deemed neither fish nor fowl, the album crashed and burned. But rather than re-evaluating their goals, the musicians – reduced now to a Ronga-less trio – set to work on a second album in a year. Having given his all to *Amelia*, Ian relinquished control, allowing the others to introduce a more democratic spread of songs, while gamely trying to inject his usual blend of folk and country (reflected in covers of the traditional 'Old Man At The Mill' and a misty-eyed 'Miss The Mississippi And You', taken from the folksinger who invented country, Jimmie Rodgers). But the unity of sound on its predecessor had vanished in the mist, and an uneasy truce ended with the final fractious session:

Ian Matthews: There was already internal conflict within the band when we were making [the second album]. Bobby [Ronga] was gone. It was just the three of us. Andy was into his Merle Haggard kick. So there was just a conflict of influences. We finished the album and I took it to Holzman in New York. He played it and said he wasn't very interested in putting it out. He didn't think it was as good as the *Amelia Earhart* record ... During the conversation he said, 'You know I signed Plainsong because of you. I want you to think about this. I'd really like you to make a solo album for me. ... There's a producer out in California. I'd like you to go out there and see if you would work with him.'

Once Ian found out that the producer Holzman had in mind was ex-Monkee Michael Nesmith, such a prospect – combined with the idea of relocating to California – pretty much turned his head. He set about trying to extract himself from a band he had gone to so much trouble to create.

He later claimed he was largely reacting to how unahppy he was 'with that second Plainsong album. There was just no direction on it, no cohesiveness … I didn't want it to come out.' And nor did it, until 2005.[29] In 1972, though, Plainsong's premature dissolution led to legal threats from those members who gave up part of *their* advance to help Ian out. But for the singer, the lure of la-la-land proved simply too great:

Ian Matthews: I certainly cherished the idea [of going to California], because all the music I was listening to at that point was coming from the West Coast. And I saw that as a way to move forward. [But] I didn't handle [the break-up] very well.

In fact, Nesmith turned out to be a less sympathetic producer than Sandy Roberton – who had done such a fine job on both Plainsong albums and *Journeys From Gospel Oak* – and it would take Ian a while to realise that his best work invariably put the Anglo- in Anglo-American artist.

His preferred producer would also end up in California, though long after his own career had nosedived and major labels stopped returning his calls. Even a spell at Columbia would not reverse that commercial decline and eventually, in the eighties, he returned to the country that was his creative wellspring.

———

By then, Ian would hardly be the only Fairporter left longing for a time when a Joe Boyd or a Sandy Roberton block-booked a week at Sound Techniques and came out with a strong album. The other Sandy, a fellow Fairportee, would not live long enough to fully rue her decision to stay put in England and resume her solo career with a new producer of limited experience.

After the aborted second Fotheringay album and the protracted sessions for her first solo album, Sandy Denny had come around to the notion that her longterm boyfriend would be an ideal sounding-

[29] By then, Andy Roberts and Ian had revived the Plainsong brand (initially with Clive Gregson, fresh from a five-year stint in the Richard Thompson Band).

board for her ideas in the studio, a view he tried to validate in an
April 1972 interview:

Trevor Lucas: Sometimes [working together] makes our relationship
difficult, [but] it's good for a producer to know someone so well that
they see them as both a person and an artist. [Someone] like Sandy
tends to be fairly introverted and sensitive in her writing and lyrics,
so it's easier for me to understand what they are about.

When her original production team heard that she had thrown in
her lot with her boyfriend, they were both concerned. Boyd (then and
now) takes the view that Trevor was simply not 'a strong personality
as a producer. He had ideas which were okay, but you don't feel that
there's a really strong vision unifying the records from beginning to
end. It's not a consistent feeling.'

John Wood, who would work with both men, suggests there was
'no real common ground between Joe and Trevor in the studio.
They have totally different ideas about making records. Joe's a great
believer in people getting on with it and getting something very
immediate, the record being a performance. Trevor was obsessed with
the deconstruction method, doing things piece by piece.'

Worryingly, Trevor's first deed was to book a set of sessions for
Sandy's second album at The Manor, the country retreat that had
made recording The Bunch such a hoot. Those sessions had been
so unfocused that Lucas and his motley crew of singers had needed
four more days at Basing Street Studios to turn their jam session for
swingin' lovers into the concept-album Lucas sold to Island.

One might perhaps expect such an outcome to have set off alarm
bells at the label, especially given the demands of working up new
material with a 'fairly introverted and sensitive' singer-songwriter.
But in the post-Witchseason world, Island were content to let Sandy
call the creative shots:

Richard Williams: It was a very self-indulgent time and record
companies had [decided] that you could trust artists to know their
audience better than anybody at the record company, but often to
their own detriment. Sandy [was] allowed that degree of freedom.

Perhaps they had believed Sandy when she told the papers she was going to 'prep' the new songs on the road, 'tak[ing] all the new material over to the States and do[ing] it for about a month, and then com[ing] back and record[ing] it. Usually I go straight into the studio and do all the stuff, and then we go out and do it on the road and improve it a thousand fold. [So] the record [ends up] an inferior thing to what you're doing on the road.'[30]

Predictably, once again a week of Manor sessions in early March (6th–12th) found the Lucas method of recording wanting. Sandy – never the most disciplined of recording artists – simply racked up recoupable recording costs she could ill-afford, with little to show for it at sessions' end:

John Wood: We [originally] went to The Manor to do it, and we had a great deal of technical difficulty, and it was basically a total waste of time. Sandy wasn't a disciplined worker … [and] there wasn't an urgency to get on with anything. If you didn't start at two, you could start at six … So not much was achieved, and I think the only things we kept were maybe 'Bushes And Briars' and 'Sweet Rosemary'.

Even Lucas admitted, the following year, that time spent 'at The Manor … was nearly wasted. We got maybe one or two tracks out of it.'[31] As for the idea that Trevor's presence might be a calming influence on the volatile artist, the opposite seemed more the norm:

John Wood: She did have mood swings, to put it mildly. Sometimes, if Trevor was in the studio she'd be so uptight, it would end up in some domestic fracas. A lot of it was a lack of self-confidence, which is very common in people who bluster.

Sandy had actually arrived at The Manor with an album's worth of strong songs ready to record. And according to Island tape-logs at least eight songs were pulled to a mix reel. From which, neither her

[30] In fact, the only new song definitely debuted at the February 1972 shows was 'Listen, Listen'.
[31] A number of those Manor recordings now clutter up the Deluxed-to-death, two-disc edition of Sandy on CD. They generally bear out Wood's withering verdict. Hopelessly annotated as the set is, ensemble versions of 'The Lady', 'It'll Take A Long Time', 'For Nobody To Hear', 'The Music Weaver' and 'Listen, Listen' all appear to date from the Manor sessions. The majority lack any real musical urgency, making for outtakes with a capital Oh.

interpretation of Anne Briggs's 'Go Your Own Way My Love' nor 'After Halloween' were revisited that spring. Only 'Sweet Rosemary' and possibly 'Bushes And Briar', a song she wrote on the spot after a visit to an ill-attended church nearby, proved to be to the Manor born.

Once again Sandy began an album intending to include songs which gave folk-rock fans a frame of reference, but ended up with a more diffuse mix of styles, on both her originals and covers. Neither Briggs's folk-club favourite nor 'Bruton Town' – performed in the States – were short-listed.

Perhaps Sandy decided they were simply too downbeat. Before work resumed at Sound Techniques, on April 30th, she informed a journalist her new material 'definitely has a much more cheerful note than the last album. And that is because I'm more cheerful in general.'

Yet neither of the covers recorded in May could be considered 'more cheerful'. Both were, in fact, cut from Conventional cloth. Dylan's 'Tomorrow Is A Long Time' – covered successfully by Rod Stewart the previous year – came from the same Witmark demo as 'I'll Keep It With Mine' and 'Percy's Song', while 'The Quiet Joys Of Brotherhood' took a lief or two from Fairport's 1969 arrangement.

At least a new original recorded at the same sessions was among her very best. 'It Suits Me Well' adopted the voice of a traditional troubadour framed in terms of a New Age traveller, and a male one at that. It suggested working with Thompson had once again rubbed off on Sandy's songwriting.

It was a direction she would have been well advised to pursue. Instead, she and Trevor sequenced an album supposed to be all things to all potential fans. And the ten-song collection does sound terrific in isolation, while failing somehow to be more than the sum of its disparate parts in an era when albums worked as a totality or not at all. Sandy did her best to put on a brave face on its September appearance but *Sandy* sold less than the weaker *North Star Grassman*. The lady seemed inured to the fact that her work was something of an acquired taste:

Sandy Denny: I don't particularly want to be rich and drive around in a Rolls-Royce – I mean, shit, I wouldn't mind, but it's not my ambition, and it does get very harrowing having to scrape the barrel all the time to pay for things … I seem to have lost a lot [of confidence] in the past couple of years, been undermined by a lot of things, and I felt I needed to do it just to give myself the confidence to get out there and sing, and know that people really wanted to hear me. [1972]

Reviewers both side of the pond were as kind as they could be, with *Rolling Stone*'s Stephen Holden unwittingly prophesizing, 'If this can't do it for her, nothing can.' He meant it as a positive statement. He considered *Sandy* 'the year's finest album by an English singer'. But Sandy drew only negative vibes from the commercial failure of her strongest solo album:

Linda Thompson: After the *Sandy* album, it got her down that her popularity didn't suddenly increase in leaps and bounds, and that was the start of her really fretting about the way her career was going.

Island, too, began to fret. They had pulled out all the stops this time to promote their favourite diva, paying for an exquisite David Bailey photo-shoot and a beautifully packaged foldout sleeve. But when the sales figures came in, Fred Cantrell, head of sales and a self-confessed Sandy fan, recalls, 'We began wondering, where are we going wrong?'

———

The Island folk were already voicing similar concerns about the songbird's parent band. A Mattacks-less, Nicol-less Fairport Convention had again delivered an album when there was no actual band to promote it, after wasting a lot of time and money making a different album at The Manor with musicians whose connection to Fairport and English folk-rock was less than zero:

Dave Pegg: Roger [Hill] came in ... He was in The Uglies ... I took Swarb to see him play ... So we rehearsed for a couple of days, but then Dave Mattacks didn't think it was going to work out ... So Dave left, and we [had] got all the tours booked, and we weren't going to blow it ... so we got one of Roger's mates, Tom Farnell, in and went off and did the tour ... It was like going on holiday with your three best friends ... We never went down badly ... [but] it didn't feel like a Fairport band ... Anyway, when we came back ... we didn't feel confident about recording with that band, and David Rea ... was one of the guys who had been on at the [LA] Troubadour with us ... So we got Dave to ... come over, and we made the *Rosie* album at The Manor ... It was a bit of disaster ... We worked [on it] for about two months and we played the tapes, and everybody knew that it wasn't on. As far as Swarb and I were concerned it was all over.

By 1974 Pegg was openly admitting that *Rosie*, 'cost £16–17,000, which is an incredible amount of money ... [and it was] because we did it all wrong in the first place ... *Angel Delight* and *Babbacombe Lee* together were made for under £6,000.' The initial results were not only unrecoupable, but unreleasable. Finally, the Brummie brothers hit upon the idea of asking Sandy's boyfriend to salvage something from the tapes:

Trevor Lucas: Dave and Peggy had made a record with David Rea at The Manor which didn't come off as a group, and really didn't come off as a recording either. So they took it up to Sound Techniques to listen to it up there ... At the time I was just finishing *Sandy* ... They'd decided to re-record it ... [and] asked me to produce it ... So we [decided we] were going to make a 'Fairport' record with Dave and Peggy, and [get] some people who had been in the band – like Richard and Dave Mattacks – [to guest on it]. [1973]

The resultant album – save for a title-track which was one of Swarb's best – was a dog's dinner even after Lucas cobbled something together from the others' reheated leftovers. Some tracks, like Lucas's own 'Knights Of The Road', sounded like the work of another band – in this case, Fotheringay, having once been earmarked for that band's aborted second album.

The following year Swarbrick offered a partial apology, suggesting, '*Rosie* [never] had much to do with Fairport ... I only wish I had kept a lot of the tracks for a solo album.' He would later try to lay (some of) the blame at Island's door, claiming, 'It started out as a solo album but Chris Blackwell had other ideas.'

In fact, the supreme fiddler wanted all of the commercial opportunities that came with a successful folk-rock act, just none of the responsibility when he delivered – for the second time in a year – a resounding dud. For his Brummie sidekick, *Rosie* offered not so much one more chance as one last chance:

Dave Pegg: We got ... Dave Mattacks, and Jerry Donahue and Richard Thompson on guitars, just for the album sessions. At the time Trevor Lucas was [just] going to produce the album, while Jerry Donahue and Dave Mattacks were [hired as] session men. We thought we'd ... have one last go at getting the group off the ground. We didn't want the group to end, but we also didn't want [the record] to be bad. [1973]

Once again, though, those recuperative powers which clung to the Fairport name began to weave their magic as Lucas and Donahue – both at something of a loose end – agreed to join a revamped Fairport. As Pegg says, 'Jerry was just doing sessions. I didn't think for a minute that he would join the band ... I had been to his place in London, this luxi-plush flat, [and] thought there's no way he's going to rough it ... [But] he was into it.'

For the next three years this new line-up would revel in a cloud of Fotheringport Confusion. In fact, Donahue and Lucas joining Fairport put the kibosh on a potential Fotheringay reunion. After Sandy returned from a dispiriting solo tour at year's end, a reunion dinner had turned into a discussion about whether to reunite the original band.

However, a reformed Fotheringay was always a non-starter. Gerry Conway was making a good living playing with Cat Stevens, and the prospects of finding someone to refinance Fotheringay on a viable basis were minimal. Both Donahue and Lucas correctly concluded they would have an easier life in the new improved Fairport. Now they just needed to convince the rock-solid DM to rejoin:

Jerry Donahue: I was really happy in Fairport, as was Trevor ... It was just too hard to walk away from ... [especially as] we'd asked Dave Mattacks to stand in for a few gigs while we were looking for another drummer. It was a bit sneaky really, as it gave him the chance to listen to what we were doing, and he liked it.

Even having to promote the dissolute *Rosie* failed to dissuade Fotheringport from taking to the road – something they assuredly needed to do. As Pegg admitted, shortly after the new line-up was agreed, 'We did like 30 gigs in 1972, which isn't enough to keep a band going. By the end of that year … we were up to our necks in debts.'

Naturally, there was a down side. Trevor going on tour after tour with Fairport meant that the woman who had left this band at its creative and commercial peak to be with *him* was stuck at home chewing the carpet and thinking dark thoughts. Some of those dark thoughts turned into songs – and rather good ones at that. Indeed, Sandy's description of the inspiration behind three songs on her third solo album, in a Japanese tour programme, confirm a common inspiration:

> *Like An Old Fashioned Waltz* – Two dancers alone in an enormous deserted ballroom.
>
> *Dark The Night* – About lost love … and being alone with your memories.
>
> *At The End Of The Day* – Anyone who has ever been away from home for a long time and has felt a little homesick will understand … this song.

After Sandy's concerted efforts to sustain a relationship with Trevor, it was he who now left her to her own devices, prompting her to suggest, in a March 1973 interview, 'Things aren't going as well as I feel they should be. That's as far as I'll admit it's going wrong, the fact that it isn't going right.' In fact, some of her new songs were refreshingly direct, leaving Trevor in no doubt as to 'what they are about'.

Nonetheless, Sandy arrived in Los Angeles the first week in May to start recording her third solo album at A&M studios, anxious for her Trevor to again wrap her in sonic wool. He had kindly brought along 'his' band to help the music weaver on the four songs she had ready, three of which directly addressed deep-rooted feelings of loneliness and doubt: 'At The End Of The Day' and two songs she had yet to perform, 'Solo' and 'Friends'.

When Joe Boyd came to see her in LA, hoping to heal wounds, she told him the last of these 'was about Pete Townshend. 'Cause he used to come hit on her when Trevor was away.' In fact, the song was about a single evening when she and Pete went back to her place and she refused to sleep with him *unless* he stayed the whole night:

Pete Townshend: Sandy and I were both drinking a lot, but she seemed, like me, able to handle it physically. I feel very dim not to have realised that she was reaching out to me so urgently, in need not only of some physical love, but also some … of my spiritual strength … She rang and told me she'd written me a song.

While Sandy portrayed 'Friends' to Boyd as 'a real attack' on someone she considered a friend, 'Solo' was a no less direct attack on someone she still thought of as her soul mate. The fact that she could pen a line like, 'Right now, I think the things you say are liable to confuse,' says a great deal about how conflicted the lady remained about the love of her life. Yet any such concerns faded away the night she was joined for an extended encore by a five-piece Fairport:

Sandy Denny: When I was at the Troubadour, Fairport were in town and they got up on stage with me and did five or six of my songs, and we did some looning about and stuff, and I felt a sudden sense of relief when they started playing, it was just really nice to have them all behind me. [1973]

That 'sudden sense of relief' was partly because she had just spent three largely miserable weeks on the road promoting *Sandy* solo on the bottom end of bills to the likes of Loggins and Messina, the Steve Miller Band and Shawn Phillips. After a particularly frustrating support set to Loggins and Messina in Washington, Sandy rather undiplomatically informed a *Village Voice* reporter, 'If this is what it means to get three thousand people to come and listen to you, I'd rather go and play to my best friends.'

When asked about the tour later that year by a sympathetic scribe, she admitted she 'found it very heavy. There were only three of us … travelling all over America, [which] puts a lot of strain on everybody.' Her two travelling companions were brother David and an old friend,

Miranda Ward, a former pop reporter who had agreed to take time
out from a teaching career to babysit the singer through her first solo
tour of the heartlands.

All too soon it became apparent there would be no great
breakthrough Stateside. The experience left Sandy, by her own
admission, 'a bit numb about the way things are going at the moment.
When you're a bit indecisive about some things, it becomes such a
strain to make a decision.'

The big decision to which she alludes, concerned whether to
rejoin Fairport Convention, for the very reason she left in the first
place – to be with her man. Trevor had already stoked the rumours,
telling *NME* in July, 'It's not totally off the cards – it could happen.
Musically it'd work. But I think Sandy's got some things to do first.'

By September, she was starting to buckle, confessing, 'We're away
from each other an awful lot – I mean, he's off on the road again for
a couple of months at the end of September, then he's off again after
that, so it's obviously a bit of a strain … [And] I miss that really warm
feeling we used to have with Fotheringay.' In a misguided attempt to
strengthen their loosening bond, Trevor and Sandy finally tied the
knot at Fulham Registry Office the same month.

To compound her own growing sense of inertia, Sandy had to stand
idly by as a rejuvenated Fairport went from strength to strength. The
line-up had just made their strongest album in years. *Nine* – recorded
that summer – was the ideal blend for ex-folkies in folk-rock disguise.
Fairport were on another musical mission. This time the plan was
to edge away from tradition and towards a more contemporary
consensus, lest they be struck down by sickness and disease:

Trevor Lucas: Galloping Folk … attacks rock musicians at a great
speed. Tyger, for instance, had been into country music and rock'n'roll
… and then all of a sudden he met Sandy, started getting involved
with folk music … and it gets worse and worse until you can't sing
anything else except songs from Somerset. It gets you like that. And
that's what … I and Swarbrick have been trying to get away from
… [We want] to try and use what [we]'ve learnt musically from the
traditional way of playing music and translate it into contemporary
types of songs. [1973]

Nine actually opens with 'The Hexhamshire Lass', a song so traditional and toe-tapping it could have come from *The Compleat Dancing Master*; being followed by another of Fairport's traditional recalibrations, 'Polly On The Shore', before the equally hoary 'The Brilliancy Medley'. So much for a sea-change. But then the band entered uncharted seas as Donahue contributed an off-kilter instrumental, 'Tokyo', while Lucas brought in 'Bring 'Em Down' and his own retort to 'Solo', 'Possibly Parsons Green'. With lines like, 'Don't try to use me or cry to confuse me', it plainly addressed someone who had the same London postcode.

Swarb, enjoying being part of a creative collective again, offered his own powerful recasting of Richard Lovelace's 1642 poem, 'To Althea From Prison', which had entered tradition via the back pages of Percy's *Reliques Of Ancient English Poetry*. All in all, a band that a year earlier had looked for all the world like it would go down in the flood, had been restored to an even keel:

Dave Pegg: I think that five-piece band, had it stuck together, would have gone on to do greater things ... Trevor was a bit arty compared to the rest of us but he was always shouted down ... But [with] that line-up ... we started from scratch ... and it was good ... It was different from any of the other Fairport line-ups because it approached a lot of different kinds of music ... Trevor loved singing and so Swarb could concentrate on the fiddle, and everybody was doing what they really wanted to do.

Determined to keep busy, they also continued to attend the album sessions of their alumni, and in August 1973 Sandy completed her third solo album, recording another five tracks, including the wistful title-track, 'Like An Old Fashioned Waltz', with Trevor at the console and the Fairport rhythm-section in the room. Sandy now delivered on a threat from the previous October, to make her next album another departure of sorts:

I think the days are gone when you could label things. I wouldn't like to mislead the folkies by saying the new album was a folk album, and I wouldn't mislead rock fans by saying it was a rock album. I like romantic songs. I'm a romantic at heart.

Once again, though, there were worrying signs that Sandy had come to these summer Sound Techniques sessions short of songs, evidenced by her decision to rewrite an old song of hers, 'Carnival', and ill-judged covers of three standards, 'Whispering Grass', 'Until The Real Things Comes Along' and the again discarded 'Walking The Floor Over You'.[32] The album delivered to Island in September sounded like it had been stuck together with paper and glue then dipped in a vat of strings:

Richard Thompson: She was feeling pressure from within. And the tendency is to move towards the middle of the road, which is a mistake. *Like An Old Fashioned Waltz* went too far in that direction.

It was not what the record-label had expected, and there was no one at Island who really knew what to do with an artifact like this. Meanwhile, her biggest supporter and label boss was busy pursuing his strategy to make Island a multimedia company, turning *The Harder They Come* into Island Films:

Richard Williams: Everybody [at Island] loved her. The company could not have been more supportive in terms of effort. It's just, she was not very biddable most of the time, and [yet] sometimes too biddable. And there was Trevor … Chris was very involved, but he was spending a lot of his time in Jamaica and Los Angeles, so he'd tend to come in every couple of months, which is not ideal. He sees things he doesn't like and changes them, and then goes off again. It was not a great way to run a company.

David Sandison: She was making good records but nobody was channelling it properly … Island were doing their bit … but there wasn't anything constructive going on in career terms … And my knowledge [from] meeting her off and on socially was that increasingly she was a wreck … In A&R terms … getting decisions made [had become] impossible, certainly crucial artistic decisions … [because] Blackwell was away most of the time.

---

[32] 'Walking The Floor Over You' was actually a *North Star Grassman* outtake she revisited in 1973.

Uncertain how to handle the lady in Blackwell's absence, Island's staff simply shifted the release of Sandy's difficult third album from late November to early spring. Suddenly, Sandy – who had provisionally assembled an interim band with the Fotheringay rhythm-section 'until we get something else happening' – found herself without a promotional purpose to what would be another loss-leader of a tour.

When Conway was again whisked away by the ever-commercial Cat, she drafted in drummer Willie Murray – who had survived Sour Grapes – and embarked on half-a-dozen November dates while previewing four new songs at a BBC session.

Those BBC versions of 'Solo' and 'Dark The Night' suggest this band had potential as a concert vehicle, but her confidence seemed to be draining from her nightly. When she turned up at the Rainbow, the last day of November, for another Fairport onstage reunion, the writing was on the crumbling Astoria walls. With the Fairport name on the marquee, the pressure was off as she was transported back to yesteryear, wailing her way through 'That'll Be The Day'. For one night only, she was again a singer in a band called Fairport Convention (in public, and Fotheringport Confusion in private).

With a Far East Fairport tour beckoning in the New Year, and no sign of a release date from Island for *Old Fashioned Waltz*, Sandy decided to stowaway on the plane, something she admitted she 'wouldn't have done, actually, if it hadn't been for the fact that the release of my album was late. I decided that the gigs I did hold for myself were a bit superfluous.'

Once in Tokyo, Lucas made her sing for her supper, 'It seemed silly to have her sitting in the wings and not on stage. Once she was singing with us, it made sense for her to rejoin.' By the time they got to Australia for two sold-out shows at the prestigious Sydney Opera House, the *Nine* five-piece line-up was engaged in an internal debate about whether to restore Fairport to a six-piece, just like in its heyday.

The Fotheringay contingent needed no convincing. As Donahue said in 1975, 'There hasn't really been a [Fairport] singer, male or female, as good as Sandy since she previously left the band … [But] Swarb and Dave Mattacks were the last to come round to the idea, I suppose as they'd been in the band when she left, first time around.' Swarb would later challenge the accuracy of Donahue's account:

Dave Swarbrick: I wasn't anything but pleased to be able to work with her again. She improved the group tenfold. Despite all that has been said about … our relationship. I was, with the exception of Trevor, the closest to her. I guess I was worried in case I wasn't going to get as easy a life as I'd been having. I don't know whether I made those worries vocal, but [truth is,] the group … didn't have a singer.

The commercial logic to restoring the six-piece was inescapable. It meant three-fifths of the band responsible for the influential *Liege & Lief* would be together again; while Fairport acquired a great singer *and* a gifted songwriter, having persevered for three long years without either. But Sandy's recruitment also raised the stakes for a band who had become content with life in the slow lane:

Dave Pegg: We were quite happy as a five-piece. But there was a bit of domestic strife in their household because Trevor was always away and we were working more or less non-stop … Eventually we [decided] we'll really have a go at it this time, because Sandy's up for joining the band, which we were all obviously pleased about. But we knew we would all have to make a serious effort at doing it and doing it right.

The most immediate problem was how to subdivide a live set which had evolved in less than a year from a less-than-rosie runthrough of faded glories into a show in which Galloping Folk had its place, but was returned to the stables when the band unbuckled 'Sloth' or dipped into the world of Fotheringay for Lucas's 'Ballad Of Ned Kelly'.

When choosing which of Sandy's songs to insert into the *Nine* set, there was a more practical concern – which songs they had the time to knock into shape for the pending Sydney shows, having agreed to record them for a live album:

Dave Pegg: We were doing Sydney Opera House, and we were the first kind of rock band to play there. We did two shows in one night, which were sold out … We got John Wood to come over, who did a brilliant job [recording them] … We wanted to do some things with Sandy, [but] it wasn't rehearsed so much … It was very much thrown together.

The Sydney album, released as *Fairport Live* – their first official live outing – generated the usual generous reviews, another game attempt from an ever-positive music media to present the latest Fairport in a glowing light. But it already suggested Sandy and the *Nine* band might not be such a snug fit.

Aside from the opener, a less-than-transcendent 'Matty Groves', Sandy's contributions to *Fairport Live* were two songs from *North Star Grassman* – 'John The Gun' and 'Down In The Flood' – both of which lacked the necessary fizz, and a duet of 'Something You Got', whose more natural home was on a reel of Bunch outtakes. In fact, the album referenced *Full House* more than either *Nine* or *Liege & Lief*, giving workouts for 'Dirty Linen', 'Sir B. McKenzie' and an epic 'Sloth'.

Rather than filing the tapes away or filling the album with better recordings of the band made when Sandy had fully bedded in, Island rush released *Fairport Live* in July 1974, an unchacteristic misjudgement which would have long-term repercussions. They did not even bother to recover, let alone review, tapes the band had made barely a week later at a three-night residency at the LA Troubadour:

Jerry Donahue: The Troubadour recordings were intended to contribute to that [live] album, but we ran out of money and couldn't pay for the tapes. They were held for a long time by Wally Heider's Mobile, until Island eventually bought them back.

If the label had exercised a bit more patience – or indeed, foresight – they would have discovered a week can be a long-time in folk-rock. The intimacy, exemplary acoustics and familiarity of the setting would have made a *Live At The Troubadour 1974* album far more viable as product (an assertion ultimately validated by the 2013 release of sixteen performances from that residency on a Deluxe edition of Fairport Ten's one studio album, *Rising For The Moon*).

In particular, the band's decision to cede the microphone to Sandy long enough for fans to get a glimpse of what might have been had Sandy stayed put in 1969, and allowed Fairport to apply their patented sound to 'Crazy Lady Blues', 'It'll Take A Long Time' and 'Solo', three of her best songs from that solo interregnum. LA versions of

'John The Gun', 'Matty Groves' and 'Down In The Flood' also beat the pants off Opera House prototypes.

And when the band of drinkers turned the stage over to the lass to get in a round, it allowed her to deliver a 'Like An Old Fashioned Waltz' which showed just how much a waste of money all those strings lathered over the album version had been. It may even have convinced A&M attendees to get behind the album when it was released, both sides of the pond, alongside the underwhelming *Fairport Live*.

When *Old Fashioned Waltz* did finally make it to the shops in June 1974, it was lost in the shuffle. Island had finally taken the bolt off the D.N.U. cupboard, wondered what happened to the leopard, and dusted off master-tapes for no less than four records by the Fairport family of folk-rockers: *Like An Old Fashioned Waltz, Fairport Live, The Compleat Dancing Master* and *I Want To See The Bright Lights Tonight*.[33]

It was a veritable tsunami of product from the Fairport stable. However, rather than signalling the long-awaited commercial breakthrough for their brand of English folk-rock, it sounded the last reveille on a stillborn musical revolution. Everyone involved had ventured some distance from their communal starting point, making punters take their pick:

Richard Thompson: Folk-rock became a very blinkered thing. It went up this alley and couldn't get out. It seemed rather absurd. It had one particular approach and in the end it never varied. It became so cliché-ridden ... The same rhythmic patterns, the same stops, the same types of songs. It didn't move. [1978]

It had been two and a half years since the band that continued bearing the name contained even a single contributor to that eponymous 1967 debut album. While Ashley kicked at the ashes of electric folk, Ian had stayed put in LA, working on a second solo album for Elektra, leaving just Richard – with a little help from Simon and the wife – to carry the baton Fairport themselves had temporarily tired of brandishing.

At the end of 1974, the inspired guitar-vocalist finally delivered the third instalment in a trilogy delineating the most musically vital way

[33] Meanwhile, over at B&C, Sandy Roberton had persuaded Lee Gopthal to resurrect Ian Matthews's equally worthy 'lost Vertigo album', *Journeys From Gospel Oak*.

ahead. Once Island gave the green light to *Hokey Pokey*, he would once again lead the way. And maybe, just maybe, a new Fairport album – with Sandy lending it lyrical lustre – would also deliver the goods. 'Twas time to dispel the miasma of Fotheringport confusion and forge a new sound for St George.

Richard Thompson

PART III
NIGHT COMES IN
1974–1982

(guitar, vocal)

A Collection of Unreleased and Rare Material
1967-1976

Double album with a Recommended Retail Price of £3.49

Album ICD8. Also Available on Cassette

13. Why Don't You Love Me Like You Used To Do?

[With] Sandy's second stint ... the live work ... was great: a real band, working together, all mates. Good times. Fans were overjoyed to see Sandy back with us; it gave us a chance to revive some older songs that we hadn't done in a while, [and] Sandy and Trevor together made a great frontline team.

—DAVE SWARBRICK TO NIGEL SCHOFIELD

If you'd taken the music away from Fairports, all you would have been left with was one very fucked up band. Personalities, management, business, finance, record company. There are a few lights in the wilderness, but basically the whole thing was just fucked.

—DAVE MATTACKS, *MELODY MAKER*, 12TH OCTOBER 1975

I'm not Richard Thompson. That's just a reputation. It's difficult, because in a way if it's expected of me, it traps me.

—RICHARD THOMPSON, *STREET LIFE* #3, CIRCA NOVEMBER 1975

As 1974 drew to a close, folk-rock's many supporters at Island were praying that 1975 would be the year a rebooted Fairport Convention and a reinvigorated Richard and Linda Thompson recouped on all the good press and glorious music which preceded their latest offerings.

Richard and Linda had already delivered the third instalment of their 'English rock'n'roll' trilogy, the multi-faceted *Hokey Pokey*, while Fairport remained ensconced in the studio with an A-list producer working on their 'comeback' album, due in the new year, Both had committed to promoting their respective records with all the strength they could muster. Surely, this time, Island could just wait for the plaudits – and pennies – to roll in.

But in the Fairport camp all was not well. Even after welcoming Sandy back into the fold, band finances were a mess. As Pegg had admitted back in September: '1973 was a really bad year [financially] ... We did a lot of work, but our business just got totally screwed up and nearly put an end to us.'

A series of elementary mistakes by then-manager Phil Sterling-

Wall – of which sending the sound system to Japan as excess baggage, not freight, takes the cookie – meant, as Pegg says, 'We'd spent five times more than we were going to earn from the tour.'

Once again Island bailed them out – 'against our vast royalties' – but by the summer of 1974 the strain was starting to tell on everyone, including their highly-strung singer, who admitted, 'The past few months have been a very heavy time. It's been hard for everybody to even survive and just smile through it … Whether [the band] can withstand any more of the stress that's being pressured on it is up to the individual members, and how liable they are to crack at any given moment.'

There was another problem – an aesthetic one – as far as their high-strung singer was concerned. Sandy couldn't wait to jettison much of the set they had been performing in the Far East and on the West Coast. Top of her personal hit-list was 'Matty Groves', which as she noted, 'People in the audience would expect me to do, [but] it felt like a lot of them knew it better than I did.'

Determined not to let the band turn into a nostalgia act churning out greatest hits, the lady set anyone straight who expected otherwise. As early as March 1974, she was informing the press that 'Matty Groves' and 'Sloth' were in her sights, 'We're basically going to do what we feel happiest with – new songs, things that Swarb's written, and me, and Trevor, and perhaps other people outside the band – with some traditional stuff, perhaps.'

Perhaps not. After all, she had bluntly stated as recently as September 1973 that 'there are people who spend most of their time getting the traditional stuff out and reviving it … [but] I quite like writing my own stuff'.

It sounded like Fotheringay all over again. At least there was a well of original songs with contemporary significance – for her, at least – readily available. As she was at pains to point out, Fairport had been her 'backing band on a lot of *Like An Old Fashioned Waltz* [and] by the time it came out, I was touring with them … playing several of the songs.'

However, this was not the case. 'Solo' was the only song from *Old Fashioned Waltz* regularly featured in the Fairport set. The others considered the rest of the material on her album too far removed from what a Fairport audience expected, and the disappointing sales figures seemed to bear this out. Instead, they wanted her to write the kind of song which did appeal directly to that audience. It had been a long, long while.

As songs from the dried-up ballpoints of Trevor and Swarb remained in short supply, the burden once again fell almost entirely on Sandy's shoulders. And everyone knew it was now or never:

Dave Pegg: We all feel the next album is important, so we've taken last month and this month off, and have been doing a lot of rehearsals – the people who write have been working on songs. We want to get a good choice to select from. One of the problems with the band in the past has been that there's never been an excess of material, but just enough to fill [an album]. We don't want to make that mistake again. So although we [were] hoping to finish it before we go to America [in] October … we won't be able to. We'll just record what we've got … We'll take another month off in January to record more, to get a really strong album … The next one will be the first with Sandy back, so it can't be a filler; everyone feels it has to be a monster. [1974]

The first new Sandy song to feature in the live set proved promising. 'Rising For The Moon', previewed on a BBC radio session in July, had first appeared in April. A rousing come-all-ye to Fairport's long-suffering fans, it was a perfect way to announce the new era. Two other songs demoed at the same time – 'The King And Queen Of England' and 'One More Chance' – were cut from more singular cloth. Indeed, by the following June she was openly admitting, 'I set off by thinking I must write with Fairport in mind. I consciously tried to do that, but I often go right back into my own style, whatever that is.'

'The King And Queen Of England' was another of her elliptical lyrics. Extant only as a beautiful 1974 demo, it was a song the new Fairport – perhaps in deference to their new producer – decided to leave well alone. Thankfully, 'One More Chance', originally called 'Goodnight World', was simply too strong for Fairport to pass up, proving to be the highlight of those first album sessions.

Island had once again opened their chequebook, signing up as Fairport's new producer legend in his own lunchtime Glyn Johns – ex-Beatles engineer, producer of Clapton, Led Zeppelin (albeit uncredited) and The Who. It seemed like a good fit. But on the damning evidence of the album he proceeded to produce, Johns was as wrong-headed a choice as could be; evidenced by a comment one Fairporter recalls him making on day one of the second set of sessions, 'Right, let's hear what you've got, and I don't want to hear any airy-fairy folk bullshit.'

At some point a momentous decision had been made: there would be no traditional songs on the new Fairport album. In a statement at the time of its release, Sandy implied it was a conscious decision on the band's part, 'Steeleye are the masters at digging up the old material. We could do something like that, but the group want to move on, taking their roots with them.'

Swarbrick kept schtum for now but later wondered aloud, 'Why didn't we open a few books? ... We didn't really have any material for *Rising For The Moon* ... I think that shows.'

A (partial) explanation seems to be that Johns thought they should get away from such an association – perhaps because Swarb was right and he 'didn't know bugger all about the tradition'. Someone else was simply relieved to be told what to do:

Sandy Denny: He's very strict in the studio. It took all the weight off the rest of us, especially Trevor, who'd done the last two and was finding it really difficult to say or even suggest something without us all jumping down his throat. Glyn just put himself by the console and told everybody to shut up. [1975]

The other survivors from Sandy's first post-Fairport combo agreed with her that looking to England's musical past could put the band's long-term future in doubt:

Trevor Lucas: We're getting farther away from more traditional music [and] into contemporary stuff ... We're getting more into soft rock. In a way, the Fotheringay side of the line-up is coming out stronger. [1975]

Jerry Donahue: Fairport was not always a folk thing. It went through that stage, but it shouldn't be expected to stay there just because it made that experiment. [1975]

The Fothering in Fotheringport embraced Johns's approach. The Fairport component remained altogether less convinced. In fact, one essential element was not just unconvinced, he'd had enough of Johns, the rest of the band and their whole hand-to-mouth existence:

Dave Mattacks: The day I pick up a newspaper between takes ... it means I'm not enjoying it anymore. The last time I did that was when we were recording *Rising For The Moon* ... when [I knew] I was leaving the band anyway ... [Glyn and I] did have a wee falling out towards the end of the recording, but that's not why I left. I got tired of earning £100 a week and feeling, post-Joe Boyd's management, that we weren't going anywhere.

Dave Swarbrick: [Johns] wanted Mattacks to play like a country and western drummer, [all] nice off-beat rim shots, and they had words and Mattacks got on his bike.

———

A drummer as good as DM was never going to be out of work for long. By April 1975 he was gainfully employed accompanying Richard and Linda Thompson at London's Queen Elizabeth Hall, alongside Dave Pegg. The *Full House* rhythm-section were lending a hand for a show Island were recording. The South Bank showcase also confirmed that the Thompsons had placed their business affairs on a sounder footing, after taking on a new manager for the first time since Witchseason:

Richard Williams: I remember [Richard] saying he was thinking of going with Jo Lustig for management. I knew Lustig ... [and] his background: Broadway in the fifties, New York showbiz, working with Nat King Cole and Frank Sinatra. But Jo worked very hard for them. And [he] understood artists like that. Then they turned Sufi, which was [already] happening when Jo came in.

Unfazed by the couple's new-found faith and new-found earnestness, Lustig set about organizing an extensive acoustic tour to coincide with the March 1975 release of *Hokey Pokey*, culminating in a one-off semi-electric London showcase – the duo's first electric excursion since Sour Grapes.

Acoustic appearances on John Peel's *Top Gear* radio show and on BBC Two's weekly concession to rock, the *Old Grey Whistle Test,* were intended to push the duo's new album into the public consciousness. Once again, though, Richard preferred using BBC facilities to 'document' his and Linda's predeliction for country favourites, recording one-off versions of 'Wishing' and 'I'm Turning Off A Memory' for *Top Gear* in February, while the *Whistle Test* appearance saw them debut the as-yet-unrecorded 'Jet Plane In A Rocking Chair'. The only promotion the current album received was a double helping of 'A Heart Needs A Home', the one song Richard seemed to rate.

But whatever type of reverse promotion was provided at the Beeb's expense, the spring 1975 shows saw Richard and Linda devote nigh on half of the sets to the new album; another quarter slice going to familiar country-rock fare like 'Love Hurts', 'Dark End Of The Street' and 'The Wild Side Of Life', where Linda's throat-catching vocals had optimum opportunity to shine.

On a couple of occasions the duo even resurrected 'Shady Lies', a song from the Albion Country Band era, perhaps a tip of the hat to the belated release of Marc Ellington's *Marc Time*, an album Richard and Linda both worked on back in 1972. *Henry The Human Fly* and *Bright Lights*, though, were treated with scant regard, with 'Nobody's Wedding', 'Bright Lights' and 'The Great Valerio' the only three songs referenced nightly in the provinces.

As the London date loomed, though, the pair decided to display a broader cross-section of the guitarist's post-Fairport career, something their bedenimed roadie rightly welcomed:

Bernard Doherty: The crunch date was the Queen Elizabeth Hall when suddenly Richard said he would play electric … There was all this mystique about whether he would play 'Calvary Cross', because it had all these religious overtones. Everyone wanted him to play it. And he did, it was so great. He went back to plugging in.

With three-fifths of a *Full House* Fairport, Richard didn't just plug in for 'Calvary Cross' – an electrifying eight-minute excursion that travelled all the way from Reno, Nevada – there was also a chilling electric 'Withered And Died' and three songs from *Henry The Human Fly*: 'Poor Ditching Boy' (sung by the missus), 'Nobody's Wedding' (with John Kirkpatrick doing an accordion-led waltz) and 'Shaky Nancy'. All were greeted with warm applause. Richard even gave a solo debut to the newly-penned 'Beat The Retreat', an early warning to all those present that he was 'burning all my bridges'.

The climax of the whole evening was a good-humoured exchange between a pesky punter in the front row who kept requesting 'Meet On The Ledge' and Linda. When Richard offered to play it if she'd sing it, the lady clambered up onstage. It was Sandy, who proceeded to join Linda for a spirited 'When Will I Be Loved', complete with one last guitar solo as Richard's wife called out, 'Take it away, Hank.' Everyone cracked up.

As a conclusion to the *Hokey Pokey* tour – and the Thompson's 'English' era – the Queen Elizabeth Hall experience could scarcely be bettered. Unfortunately, only the five acoustic songs from the show have been preserved by Island, another missed trick on Island's part.[34]

Rather than putting out a live album of their own, the Thompsons were already making plans to visit Basing Street, to get a head start on the next album, even though Richard seemed to think he had little new to offer his fans or the label:

> I haven't got any words. [I'm] dried up. I suppose it could always be an instrumental album … If I ever get any words written, it should be very interesting … I'd like to do something really passionate, about real things and what happens in this twilight world … [But] if we record one next month, it won't be out until the end of the year, so … we may as well make it then … The contract asks for two a year – though if we actually produced two a year, I don't think the record company would be able to handle it.

In fact, the next album would be in the can by August, as under Richard Williams's A&R aegis Island prioritised the prolific penman's latest bulletin from the 'twilight world'.

---

[34] Thankfully, a fine complete audience tape does exist and is in circulation.

In another part of Basing Street that spring, Island had been gearing up for a new Fairport album, finally completed in February 1975 after a brief European tour had replenished funds and a new drummer had been found who could be the long-term replacement for DM:

Dave Pegg: We had this European Tour lined up [so] we had one of our roadies, [Paul Warren], play drums on it … We had auditioned about thirty drummers in London, which was one of the worst weeks of my life. Some of them were good, but the group was so untogether. There were dreadful things going on. It was mainly Sandy who was at fault. She was getting difficult to work with at the time.

Bruce Rowland had first crossed Fairport's radar back in 1972, when they were stuck in *Rosie*land. He had a rock-solid pedigree, having been a founder member of Joe Cocker's Grease Band, thus proving that he could more than hold his own in any hard-drinking, hard-working band. But for Fairport it was another move into rock orthodoxy, much to Glyn Johns's delight.

One high-strung hurdle remained. What would Sandy think of Bruce's time keeping? Because if she *wasn't* happy, the second set of *Rising For The Moon* sessions would be a baptism of nitro-glycerine for Rowland. Even after Cocker, the drummer was slightly taken aback by the volatility of Fairport's frontperson. Thankfully, there was someone on hand who knew how to handle her:

Bruce Rowland: What made Trevor invaluable was that Sandy would play endless mind games with you and take you to the brink of making her cry, but Trevor was just that little bit better than her at that, and he [also] made her laugh. And he kept her in a very good place to work.

Unfortunately, the producer who had (temporarily) taken Trevor's seat was inclined to countermand his methodology. Dave Pegg recalls, '[Sandy] got upset with Glyn a few times. But that's the way Glyn is. She always got very nervous before doing a vocal in the studio. John Wood could push her too, but she was used to him.'

At least the lady had done her work assignments, bringing one new

and two not-so-new originals to the sessions. The newest of these was
another character study of someone close to her. 'Stranger To Himself'
was a masterpiece of encapsulation, depicting perfectly the person
quietly fuming as Johns wrestled the band's direction away from him:

Sandy Denny: Someone – it could have been Peggy – remarked that
no one really knew who Swarb was; in fact, he doubted if he even
knew himself. That's what inspired ['Stranger To Himself'], which
began as a series of images.

Songs of commensurate quality, though, were in short supply. A
worried Sandy resorted to trawling through earlier demo tapes, from
which she rescued *Sandy* discard 'After Halloween', and a December
1973 demo for the stillborn successor to *Old Fashioned Waltz*, 'What
Is True?' Both had been written by a Sandy who thought she was
developing her own career, making both self-conscious examples of
her 'own style, whatever that is'. But time was short and other options
few. As Jerry Donahue later observed, 'We didn't have a lot of material
to choose from and … there was no time to sit back and say, "Let's
finish it when we have some better material."'

If Sandy's offerings seemed ill-suited to the Fairport *Nine* line-
up, the pair of songs Swarb and Trevor brought to this second set of
sessions – 'Let It Go' and 'Night-Time Girl' – highlighted just how
few alternatives they had.

Knowing it was produce or die, Swarb toed the line for once, trying
his best to put a positive spin on the experience by claiming, 'The
group is moving towards Sandy all the time, and she towards us …
The new album will be a compromise between pleasing us and [what]
we feel the audiences want to hear.' But this wasn't a view Swarb held
for very long. His subsequent description, to Nigel Schofield, was
more acerbic, 'The words "baby" and "bathwater" spring to mind
whenever I think of that era of Fairport.'

Even under his own wayward stewardship, Fairport had never
made an album as unrepresentative of the Fairport brand. When
review copies of *Rising For The Moon* were sent out, some recipients
were taken aback at how few compromises had been made and how
little the finished album resembled previous Fairport artifacts, let
alone its immediate predecessor, *Nine*.

Once again, it was a *Melody Maker* journalist and a long-standing champion of the band who suggested the empress needed new clothes. The salient part of Colin Irwin's review read:

> [*Rising For The Moon*] certainly falls short of the promise of A Major Work muttered from the Fairport camp ... [Sandy's] presence has injected the band with some of their old spirit, but it's too Denny-oriented for it's own good and it would be easy to mistake the whole thing as a record of Sandy Denny with backing musicians.

Irwin did not have to wait long to find out what the singer herself thought of his critique: 'I had this interview arranged with her through Island ... and the paper got me to review the album that week, and I actually didn't like it ... Anyway ... she'd arrived at Island and while she was waiting for me to come, she read my review and threw a wobbler, just stormed out.'

Now the sympathetic scribe knew how Trevor felt. Two weeks later Sandy did agree to a promotional interview, but with *Sounds'* Jerry Gilbert, which she used to berate anyone who wanted more of the same from the band she had made her own, 'There's an incredible number of people who are very disappointed when they come along and find that, although the musicianship is better than ever, we're not going to do the same kind of stuff ... they've been expecting us to do.'

Driving her point home, Sandy led Fairport's fans a merry dance at the Royal Albert Hall launch of *Rising For The Moon* on June 10th. She was determined to do few of 'the old songs they've been expecting'. Instead, her backing band let her perform three songs from *Sandy* – 'The Quiet Joys Of Brotherhood', 'It'll Take A Long Time' and 'Listen, Listen' – and three songs from their collective heyday, 'Tam Lin', 'Mr Lacey' (a song she had always yearned to sing solo), and the evergreen 'Who Knows Where The Time Goes?'

Fairport also debuted almost the entire new album in a two-hour show which was not quite the triumph their 1969 Festival Hall set had been, but was nonetheless proof that its spirit lived on. As part of her own forward-thinking, Sandy debuted a brand new song, dedicated to her father, called, 'I Won't Be Singing Any More Sad Refrains' which she prefaced by sending up the very idea of such a song, asking the audience rhetorically, 'Can you believe that?'

Any problems within the band by now were largely personal. After witnessing his first blow-out from Sandy during their pre-*Rising* return to Oz, the newest recruit sought an explanation from his partner in rhythm:

Bruce Rowland: In Australia, Sandy was pie-eyed for about three gigs on the trot, and it edged her performance. I thought it was riveting ... [But] the more tight-assed members of the band took exception to it ... So I asked how come ... [Peggy] said, 'The happy drunks we don't mind. It's the paranoid ones we can't cope with.'

Those April antipodean shows and their marathon performance at the Albert Hall were both raised digits to all the carpers of this embattled band. If the album reviews raised hackles, they had also made Sandy temporarily raise her game. But by now, Swarbrick had come to feel that deferring to his favourite diva had made Fairport a band he no longer recognised. He now began to raise his voice in dissent, often in earshot of the lady herself:

Sandy Denny: Swarb and I were always somehow a very fractious couple of people to have in a band all in one go. He's always had a mind of his own and so have I. We were quite often conflicting, not to the point where we got to fisticuffs or anything, but it was a pressure ... I feel like perhaps he didn't enjoy some of the songs that I liked and that I'd written. [1977]

To make matters worse, the new management Fairport had taken on board – presumably after consulting Richard and Linda – was no more business-like or honest than Sterling-Wall. In fact, by the end of a September tour of the States, the band – almost to a man – were on the verge of mutiny, and Jo Lustig was cast in the role of Captain Bligh:

Dave Pegg: There were billboards up on Sunset Boulevard for *Rising For The Moon* ... [while] we lounged around for the first week doing nothing, 'cause Jo Lustig [had] said, 'Oh, you'll be doing press ... for the first week.' But there was nothing ... By the time the first gig came around ... we could have been on the road for three months.

Jerry Donahue: After Jo Lustig took over as manager we ... did a tour of the States, where we had half of the promoters pulling out, apparently because Jo hadn't secured signatures to all the gig contracts. We ended up over there on a tour with a load of unconfirmed dates ... We lost a lot of money over it ... It was a king-size mistake and we didn't end our relationship with him on the best of terms.

Dave Swarbrick: That Jo Lustig tour, we travelled all over the coldest part of America, for months ... We did gig after soddin' gig after soddin' gig, got back to England and I got four-pence. I wanted to chew out his jugular vein ... [But] it's hard to keep tabs when you're lying on the arse-end of the bar with a drink in your hand.

Dave Pegg: There was such a backlog of outstanding things that had gone wrong that nobody who came in and tried to sort things out [could]. We owed a lot of money. We weren't selling records. It was getting to a dodgy stage in the music business ... Jo [Lustig]'s tour, which he put together, was a bit of a disaster ... The previous year, we actually made about £5,000 ... Whereas Jo's lost £12,000 ... It was our seventh [US] tour, and it was make or break ... We had got the record company [on board]. And they did spend a lot of money on it.

By now, the Fotheringport vessel was lurching from one port to the next without any real let up or prolonged respite from the financial storm. As for Sandy, the endless personal problems had gone straight to her larynx. None of the handful of tapes extant from shows in September and October, come close to the standard of the June showcase.

On soundboard recordings from two September '75 Chicago gigs, Sandy can be heard painfully croaking her way through proceedings. And if her voice was increasingly fragile, a once hardy constitution was not far behind. Yet, still she continued to push her body to the brink, determined to match, or even outdo, the lads in the band:

Dave Pegg: Sandy would injure herself quite often, I remember. She'd fall over ... I can remember her going through airports in wheelchairs in America on several occasions. Usually it was drink. Dark nights and Guinness.

Linda Thompson: Sandy liked go-faster drugs and she got heavily into cocaine in America, after she had rejoined Fairport ... and it didn't stop back home. Other times it was tranquilisers and sleeping pills, a real cocktail of uppers and downers ... all stuff that made you paranoid and caused heavy mood swings. Which Sandy [already] had, in spades.

Dave Pegg: She did sometimes get a little over-refreshed, [but] we were all guilty [of that] in the Fairports ... She would play badly some nights and ... she would have hysterics, 'cause she'd played this really bad note. But the next night, if it happened, we'd all have a snigger and she'd throw a wobbler. You never really knew where you stood. One minute she was like a bundle of joy, the next minute ... really down.

A month-long tour of America was followed almost immediately by a tour of Britain. This was really not what the doctor ordered. By the end of it even Pegg admits, 'It got very difficult ... There was the occasional punch-up and people went storming off and disappearing. We had a good crack at it. It was the hardest we ever worked. Everybody had stuck in 100%, and they all did their best and we thought the record would do quite well, but it didn't.'

———

By October's end, Fairport's long-suffering bassist couldn't wait to hightail it to a band of teetotal tea-drinkers for an altogether more sedate sojourn through the same sceptered isle. The only moments of madness which came his way on the three-week November tour with Richard and Linda – a reunion of the same line-up that had made Queen Elizabeth Hall a landmark gig – were onstage.

This kind of musical mayhem Mr Bassman liked, as the Thompsons ticked every box in their treasure chest of tricks, delivering a show that was as rock solid as St Paul's and still a carousel of 'some thing[s] really passionate, about ... what happens in this twilight world'.

Three nightly workouts in particular wrung every ounce of intensity from the band. Two of these developed on prototypes recorded in August: 'For Shame Of Doing Wrong' and 'Night Comes In'. If the former was little more than a superior pop song on the album, in concert it became a frenzied assault on the senses, the like of which had not been seen by fans of this Thommo since the *Full House* gigs.[35] The latter just fired ever more precise darts of sound at its awestruck sitting targets while Babylon fell down.

For now, Richard seemed almost apologetic about the dramatic shift when a journalist decided to raise the matter, 'There's more guitar, yes. It's a funny sort of guitar really. [But] it's not so strident or aggressive, it's more spacey.'

Of the other new songs, 'Streets Of Paradise' was both stark and unforgiving: 'The tears fall down like whisky, the tears fall down like wine/ On an island made of cocaine, in a sea of turpentine.' It was starker still on the album converts rushed out to buy. Indeed, the sound on *Pour Down Like Silver* was generally sparse, something Thompson later claimed came about 'by accident ... We were intending to have Simon come and play rhythm guitar and he wasn't available.'

Without Nicol, the only guitars on the album were Richard's. His preferred rhythm-section – from *Full House* – was also only available for three songs. Still, at least 'Streets Of Paradise', 'For Shame Of Doing Wrong' and 'Hard Luck Stories' all poured down like bitter.

On 'Night Comes In', though, he had to make do with Timi Donald and the ever-professional Pat Donaldson, who now noticed that Linda was again being 'given short-shrift from the other side of the glass, and not given the time and consideration that Richard was necessarily given'. Thankfully for Linda, the song from this period which still means the most to her, 'Dimming Of The Day', had been recorded the previous October at Olympic, on a day when her voice rang with an almost religious purity.

As for her husband's previous threat to deliver an instrumental album, all that remained of such a notion was a guitar-piece (originally for bagpipes) by James Scott Skinner, commemorating those who fell at the battle for the Heights of Dargai in 1897.

Sandwiched between one-off band performances in Cambridge and London with these two distinct rhythm-sections were the handful

---

[35] The mix on the 2007 CD is so askew that I recommend interested parties seek out the excellent audience tape of the Oxford show for a real sense of how it sounded at the time.

of sessions needed to deliver an album that had everything the folk at Island – Richard Williams in particular – were hoping for. They could even afford to leave unfinished two songs Richard had brought to the sessions as possible stopgaps.[36]

If Pat Donaldson was required to 'sub' for Dave Pegg at a September Roundhouse show, Pegg was back in Blighty for a full-blown November UK tour, and got to play five of the songs from the forthcoming album – 'Streets Of Paradise', 'Hard Luck Stories', 'Jet Plane In A Rocking Chair', 'For Shame Of Doing Wrong' and a 'Night Comes In' from the twilight zone.

Lucky attendees heard nothing at the shows to make them suspect that Richard and Linda were saying farewell to the evil muse who made the man play music this dark, this powerful, this unrelenting, or were planning a prolonged musical sabbatical. Yet the guitarist had already warned readers of *Melody Maker* six months earlier he resented the grip this music still had on him:

> Music, in that way, is too strong, too powerful, to fool around with ...
> The only reason I go out on tour is because I haven't really grasped the
> reality of music. The day I do that will be the day I stop playing music
> in that way. I'll then just pick the time, the place and the company.

At least Richard Williams took note of such hints, dispatching an Island mobile truck to three shows, no less, on that November tour. By this time Thompson was being quoted in *Melody Maker* saying he was trying 'not to be involved in the actual business ... because it is completely artificial ... The music is there and it'll go on, but I don't want to be a part of the business.'

A period of retrenchment beckoned. Richard even recalled the time he 'used to make stained-glass windows. I've sometimes thought I could do that again.' At least Island had something for a rainy day.[37]

The Thompsons were not about to issue a press release announcing their sabbatical from song. They simply returned to the London Sufi commune, where they were soon packing their few belongings and

---

[36] Only 'Wanted Man' was left in something approximating to a releasable form. Yet it was still overlooked when Williams compiled his own Thompson double-album anthology the following year.

[37] As it is, a 'full' record of these historic shows would not appear until 2007, when its release was overseen by figures with nothing like the same musical empathy.

heading for Norfolk, where a new Sufi commune was being forged in outlands where even angels feared to tread:

Jo Lustig: Richard came to me and said, 'Look, my Mullah doesn't want me to play electric guitar. I don't know what I'm going to do about my guitar. Do you still want to handle me, because I'm not going to be working?'

———

Dave Pegg, meanwhile, having recently relocated to a hamlet just outside Oxford, returned to find that *Rosie* had left her calling card. Fairport Convention was once again a three-piece. The husband and wife team in Fairport Mk.10, having sown dissension in the ranks, had decided to admit the jig was up:

Sandy Denny: I think everybody had just about had it by that time … We were in terrible trouble financially … All the money we were making was going straight into the hole … Dave Mattacks [had already] left because he couldn't handle it anymore, and then Jerry decided to leave. Trevor and I just thought, 'Fair enough, knock it on the head.' … It just didn't spark off the way it might have done had everything been going smoothly, the finances and everything … like it did in the old days … Most of the time we were so bloody worried about everything and you lose a lot of enjoyment from that. [1977]

The numbers had never added up and, unfortunately for them, the business they had entered many moons ago when it was a cottage industry was increasingly being run by accountants. Perhaps their friend Richard had the right idea. Sandy, though, gave no thought to retirement, only how to resurrect the solo career she left on hold to rejoin Fairport.

At least the break-up wiped the slate clean, while the release in September 1975 of a four-album boxed-set called *The Electric Muse: The Story Of Folk Into Rock,* by Island, in tandem with Transatlantic, seemed to simultaneously offer a particularly lavish epitaph to English folk-rock's halcyon days.

The set, which weighed nearly as much as a headstone, included 'holy grail' lost recordings from the Island vaults, including the *Full*

House version of 'Poor Will And The Jolly Hangman' (with a newly recorded vocal by Richard *and* Linda) and the Albion Country Band's clarion call, 'Albion Sunrise'. Perhaps appositely, the set was such a great success it was never re-pressed:

Karl Dallas: I [had] approached Nathan Joseph, then head of Transatlantic Records, who contacted Chris Blackwell, whose company then controlled much of the non-Transatlantic material, and between them the joint product was agreed ... Ashley Hutchings and Ewan MacColl ensured that companies like EMI and Decca were 'persuaded' to allow their material to be included ... The set sold out immediately [but] Island didn't produce any more, because the lavish production costs meant they lost money on every copy sold.

At the same time as these two record labels were reminding fans how rich this vein of rock had been, an itinerant ex-musician turned postman was selling, mail order, a crude cassette compilation of BBC radio sessions he had played his part in creating between May 1968 and February 1969, when a six-piece folk-rock band called Fairport Convention, who never quite delivered on their commercial promise, recorded these priceless radio sessions:

Ashley Hutchings: I was getting some royalties from Fairport Convention, but not much because Island Records stopped paying us royalties. Shirley and I were really struggling through the mid-seventies to make ends meet ... [so] I put together the *Heyday* tape – [mainly] because I was proud of the stuff.

Simon Nicol: Guess who managed to horn-swoggle tapes out of all the BBC engineers at the end of every session? And then they turned up later. The original cassette he brought out was like a personal bootleg. And who should be roped in to duplicate them but Judy Dyble's husband.

Heyday it was called, and *Heyday* it would always be – even after the original concept was bastardized not once but twice, first by Hannibal Records in 1987 and then by Universal in 2002. The original fourteen-track cassette compilation – which sold hundreds and was then dubbed by thousands – consisted solely of songs recorded by the Denny/ Matthews/ Hutchings/ Thompson/ Nicol/ Lamble line-up.

With just three originals – two of which were previously unreleased – and eleven of the covers which had made them such an exciting live act, *Heyday* sampled everything from Simon's 'Shattering Live Experience' to Sandy's one-song Jackson Frank tribute ('You Never Wanted Me'). Finally, two particularly popular early Fairport favourites – Richard Fariña's 'Reno Nevada' and Leonard Cohen's 'Suzanne' – were also released in slightly truncated guises.

To many lucky recipients who received *Heyday* direct from the mailman, this music must have already seemed more mythic and untouchable than the genuine folk songs Ashley now listened to, and which once again at the end of 1975 he was gearing himself up to revive. For him at least, the heyday of English folk-rock was long past but the revival of Electric Folk was just around the corner.

In those days we took it for granted [that] there was unlimited studio time. We'd be in the canteen, sitting chatting to Bob Marley, and then he'd go into one studio and we'd go into another. He'd sell eighty million records, and we'd sell eight.

—LINDA THOMPSON TO AUTHOR

It was into this end-of-days climate that Island decided to hurl the 'lost' Albion Country Band album, *Battle Of The Field*, and that expensive folly, *Rattlebone & Ploughjack* – both recorded in 1973 – on St George's Day 1976. Evidently, a clearing – or cleansing – of the vaults had been ordered, with a Richard Thompson anthology and a *Full House*-era live album also in the pipeline.

It was certainly high time *Battle Of The Field* entered the fray, even though the commercial climate was against it. The reviews, as Ashley notes, uniformly asked 'why hasn't this come out earlier – this is great'. Angus McKinnon, in *Street Life*, suggested that, 'three years after its recording, [it is] as important a contribution [to English folk-rock] as *Liege & Lief*.'

Even if it seemed like this battle was already lost, time to muster a new army to a new tune – as Ashley explained during a rousing rally call to the troops in the fortnightly *Street Life*:

I feel that electric folk has somehow bypassed a considerable amount of indigenous English material. I've nothing against other sources ... I love black American blues, R&B, also country music, but English players don't always sound entirely convincing when imitating American styles. At the same time, so much American rock is worryingly bland ... [and] I'd rather try for music that is more substantial, and one way of achieving that is to take the traditions, write the songs and build on that base.

By this time, the Etchingham Steam Band was slowly evolving into something else, an electric dance band, the avowed intent on Ashley's part having now become 'break[ing] down that static relationship between performer and audience'. The process by which the Albion Dance Band emerged from Etchingham was, to his mind, 'totally organic'. By the end of the process he had something akin to the nine-piece Fairport he had envisaged back in 1969:

Ashley Hutchings: [The Etchingham Band] just didn't fizzle out, it became the embryonic Albion Dance Band. The repertoire didn't change that much. We'd got the dance bug … We [just] became more and more amplified. We added Mattacks on snare drum and hi-hat, just a small kit and added Simon Nicol strumming an electric guitar. I picked up my electric bass again. When we started to play for dancing properly, that's when I got an electric again … There wasn't really a cut-and-dry 'that's finished, this starts' [moment]. I've got some photos of the Etchinghams playing for a dance and there's Simon Nicol there and Dave Mattacks on a snare drum. So it's four Etchinghams plus three Fairports … It had virtually two of everything, like the Noah's Ark of folk-rock groups. God knows how we could afford even the expenses, let alone the fees … [But] 1976 was very much the year of the Albion Dance Band. It just got bigger and bigger. You blink and it's got two drummers, two squeeze boxes, two everything. It's a massive band. [And] no one else is doing it.

Ashley was still consciously operating below the radar of the record industry, 'just doing the stuff for enjoyment and live performance. I certainly couldn't see the point in making a record. I was probably alone in the group in thinking that but my arguments held sway.' Yet the audience the resurrected Albions were reaching was a young one, open to the energy of the band and prepared to embrace the experience when Tyger suggested you can all join in: 'A lot of the gigs we did … were universities and colleges … At some point someone said, why don't we get a Morris dancer in, to dance [along].'

Thankfully, Ashley's determination to operate on the margins dissipated as soon as his wife Shirley pointed out that the Albion Dance Band, circa '76, was 'a wonderful band … Loud, electric and quite Fairportey, with Simon Nicol on crunchy guitar.' By December of that year, her husband was telling a regional newspaper, 'We've become more of a rock group, but the developments in the band have all happened naturally, that's the great thing about it. We're taking dances to a wide audience: students, rock fans, people of all ages.'

An album that captured the experience while it was still vital was the obvious next step. But with whom? Island was a non-starter, if the first royalty statement on *Battle Of The Field* was anything to go by. Fortunately, at least one ripple from this new brand of electric folk had reached the other side of the industry pond:

Ashley Hutchings: Marc Rye was at EMI and he was a great fan of the music, and he made it all happen. Boyd had gone to America, John Wood had moved up to Scotland, so it seemed right to go to Harvest. And John Peel was behind it, too. He loved our music. I can't remember [even] going back to Island. Muff [Winwood had] come in and didn't like us.

Harvest were hip, cash-rich and surprisingly open to the idea of multiple projects, the first of which would be a genuine sequel to one of Hutchings's more successful Island projects, 1972's *Morris On*:

Ashley Hutchings: *Son Of Morris On* was the first one on Harvest. The idea came from me. I was in the bedroom with Shirley. [I said,] 'Why don't we make another *Morris On*, 'cause that [first] one only scratched the surface?' ... So I record *Son Of Morris On*, immediately followed by [the] Albion Dance Band [album]. This is where John Tams comes into the picture ... He guested on *Son Of Morris On*, and I realised he had a very crusading [type of] mind.

Tams, who had been playing with acoustic folk combo Muckram Wakes, was a multi-instrumentalist as comfortable with the fiddle as the concertina. He would prove an ideal foil for Ashley for just as long as he remembered, when it came to the Albions, the former Fairporter was first among equals. The pair would find a way to work together for five productive years on both commercial and wholly uncommercial projects.

Son Of Morris On would fall into the latter category, having nothing like the impact of its parental predecessor – lacking as it did the invigorating interplay of Thompson and John Kirkpatrick. The people at EMI, Harvest's parent company, still did not bat an eyelid when Ashley relayed his plan to record the first Albion Dance Band album, *The Prospect Before Us*, almost immediately afterwards. Nor did they interfere when he laid out his vision of the broad church of traditional styles he wanted the second Albion album that year to contain:

Ashley Hutchings: *The Prospect Before Us* is a good representation of what we were doing at the time. It's not just country dance stuff. It's got medieval music, it's got songs, it's got a bit of everything.

Unfortunately, this is the insurmountable problem with *Prospect Before Us* — it lurches from pillar to post to pylon like a man three nights drunk. Starting in glorious fashion with the polka-dotted 'Jenny Lind', it proceeds to wander rather aimlessly through minuets, wassail songs, masques and choruses. Indeed, almost the only traditional song-forms the Albions forsook were carols and ballads, those traditional templates with which Hutchings had previously seemed at home.[38]

Like Island of yore, Harvest pulled out all the stops on the album's release in February 1977, with full-page ads (see chapter heading) and a fold-out sleeve whose front cover was the statement of a bold musical marauder: Britannia — electric guitar in hand — staring across a brown and pleasant land. When the record registered as little more than a blip in the lower reaches of the BRMB album charts, Harvest took the stoical view: better luck next time.

———————

At Island, though, where good music had always made its pink and white logos go round, an unexpected financial crisis had made its decision-makers look again at the bottom line and wonder if it wasn't time to let some other label underwrite the folk-rock revolution it had once largely bankrolled:

Richard Williams: We bought a pressing plant. Great mistake. But Island was growing very fast. We were not only a record company, we were a distribution company for Virgin, Chrysalis, Charisma

[38] 'On Christmas Night All Christians Sing' — an outtake to *The Prospect Before Us* could have given the post-Ashley Steeleye a run for its money in the Christmas singles stakes.

[&c.] And they got our sales force, who really loved music. They would go into the good record shops and [the owners] would listen to them. David Betteridge thought [it] a very obvious [next step], to have our own pressing plant to guarantee [product]. So they bought EMI's Park Royal plant. I don't think Chris thought it was a good idea. It was David's project. [Other] things were changing. Clive Banks came in as head of promotion and he was a much more commercially oriented person – he had come from Warners. And the mood changed. My mood changed – I was looking for the hits. I wanted to sign [New York punk band] Television in 1975, but there was such a lack of enthusiasm for [them], it extinguished a bit of my enthusiasm. Nobody could see it at all, and I felt my influence was waning. It was changing when I left ... It [now] needed a Roxy, a Sparks, a [Bob Marley & The] Wailers every year.

The acquisition of the pressing plant was a particularly disastrous move. As another Island A&R man, Tim Clark, told Mick Houghton, it only 'made sense until we lost manufacturing rights for Virgin, Chrysalis and EG'. When that happened, everyone, Clark included, feared the worst: 'At one point we had to do a license deal with EMI just to stay in business.'

So when the rump of the once-mighty Fairport Convention – having temporarily dropped the Convention part – approached the label in the spring of 1976, pleading for one more chance to fire up the fans, the reaction was non-committal and the budget miniscule:

Dave Pegg: We got the feeling it was going to be the last one ... You [could] see what's happening down in the office ... We went to [Fowey in] Cornwall ... just Bruce, Swarb and I, and a guitarist called Ian ... It was going to be a Swarb [solo] record and in the process of doing that, we realised that we [might] get away with one more, so we thought, 'Fuck it, it's probably the last thing we'll ever do – [let's] have another Fairport line-up.'

Simon Nicol: *Gottle O'Geer* was something Peggy and Swarb got Island [to agree to. They] were prepared to let him play around with the tape[s]. Peggy and Swarb had already brought some tapes from an earl[ier] project: 'When First Into This Country' and a couple of other songs ... were already recorded elsewhere for a Swarb solo project. Anyway, we listened to them and [thought] it was a starting point for an album. '[So] how can we make forty minutes of music out of this, because if we can deliver forty minutes of music, they will give us a cheque?'

When initially approached, Simon was still a member of the Albion Dance Band – though he now admits he 'wasn't sure whether I wanted to be part of the things they were about to do'. Asked to lend a hand on what he assumed would be the last Fairport album for Island, and maybe for all time, how could he say no?

Although it had been nigh on five years since he had been a card-carrying member, he again manned the console on what was a strictly low-budget affair, with John Wood nowhere to be seen and the main Island studios firmly under lock and key:

Simon Nicol: I was engineering. [Bruce Rowland] was producing. It was a Dave Swarbrick record initially, but it morphed very quickly into a band record. I don't think at the time Island had underwritten it. [But] they had said you can use the demo studio under the Island office buildings in St Peter's Square, Hammersmith. We had the run of the place and we worked at night. Not that it was overused, but we had the keys to it. It was free, and we were using our own money ... We're all free and we've got this studio for nothing. That's how I met Bruce. He was prepared to be the producer. Swarb and Peggy were prepared to be the talent and to bring such people as they knew to help with it. It was a very odd way to make a record. We'd work through the night, and I'm not that kind of person. [But] there were a couple of occasions when they said, 'You should play on this.' No organization, no planning, just shooting from the hip.

If there was a comparison between *Gottle O'Geer* and a previous Fairport album, it was *Rosie*, the one made after Simon first quit. Indeed, this was the very comparison *NME* made about the finished artifact on its release in June 1976: 'Like *Rosie*, generally regarded as the low-point of the band's recording history, [*Gottle O'Geer*] was begun as a Dave Swarbrick solo album ... Like *Rosie*, this isn't a very good album.'

Unlike that dud, though, the handful of tracks completed when still conceived as a solo Swarb project remained largely intact. These included a pleasing stroll through 'When First Into This Country', the album's opener. But as Pegg later admitted, 'There were too many people with so many different styles or approaches to music. The only things that did work ... [were] things that Fairport were always good at – [the] things that naturally happened.'

Not surprisingly, this damp squib did nothing to stoke the diminishing flames of idealism which once burned bright at the Island offices. On that metaphorical morning after the reviews came in, the label threw Fairport out with the ashes of folk-rock:

Dave Pegg: When Island started up it was a bunch of guys, they were all into the music, they'd do anything for Fairport. They were really good to us, though nobody else in the band would say that. They never ever recouped ... [But] all of a sudden you had to justify the fact that you were spending so much making records, and nobody was buying them. The music industry suddenly became a business.

So underwhelming was Fairport's eleventh and last Island album that one worthy contribution to the Fotheringport canon went largely unnoticed: their interpretation of a song their erstwhile frontperson deemed surplus to requirements for her next solo album, 'Take Away The Load' (or as it was called on *Gottle O'Geer*, 'Sandy's Song').

For once, the lady had a surfeit of original material, and rightly surmised her old friends needed all the help they could get. The song may even have always been intended for the family. As she later said, 'When I began, I was writing things for the next Fairport album. Some of those weren't what I wanted to do once I left the band.'

Any rancour regarding her sudden departure had passed quickly as she rekindled the one friendship which predated the band. As Swarb told me, 'Sandy used to come round every day. Or I'd go over there. I knew her walk. I wouldn't even look out the window, I'd just let the door open and let her in.'

Sandy was delighted to have her opinionated friend as a sounding board for the new tunes she was writing, some of the best songs she would ever pen. 'No More Sad Refrains' – debuted at the Albert Hall

the previous June – was already earmarked as a possible title-track
to her fourth solo album, which had again been rubber-stamped by
Island, who continued to be treat her with kid gloves, even as doubts
about her career trajectory lingered:

Tim Clark: There was no A&R person within Island giving her
direction, and we had faith in Trevor, although I'm not sure who else
we could have brought in to produce Sandy at that time; she could
be a real handful, a real, real handful.

What no one at Island had yet to realise was that the songs Sandy
was writing mapped out the battleground of her marriage to her
chosen producer. The state of mind expressed in these songs was
one she rarely shared even with her closest friends, isolated as she
increasingly was in the country, holed up in a Cotswold cottage
underwritten by the ever-generous Blackwell. As Linda recalls,
'She'd never call up and say help! She'd call up and go blah blah
blah, and you would sorta think, she's handling this the way she
handles everything.'

But Sandy poured all those nagging doubts and insecurities into
her notebooks, which contain drafts of numerous new songs, as well
as occasional marginal rebukes, like one in which she chastises herself
in the second person because 'when you are with the one who loves
you, you want to get away somewhere, yet no one else is quite the
same when you do, so you run hell for leather home to him, and
swear to yourself you'll never leave again'.

When this album of introspective songs finally appeared – in the
spring of 1977 – she talked about her decision to change course and
become the songwriter she'd always aspired to be; one whose folk
roots only showed through occasionally:

Sandy Denny: I'm not writing in the folk style and I haven't done
[so] for a long time, and I wish people would wake up and knock all
these labels on the head … I did try recently to be a little more down
to earth about things but I do find it rather difficult, because I'm a
bit shy of people knowing me. I mean, I adore Joni Mitchell but I
do think she went around wearing her heart on her sleeve. I adore
listening to those songs, but I wouldn't like it to be me whose painting

it around for everyone to know. The last thing I'd want everyone to know is my business. [1977]

The naked honesty of the songs she demoed in winter 1976 suggested a new Sandy was emerging from its chrysalis, but it was still something Sandy was determined to mask in the studio, if necessary with the usual lather of strings. She all but admitted as much on the album's release, 'It might be a bit [too] schmaltzy in places even for my liking, but ... I'm a bit of a sucker for that.'

At least this time she eschewed overdubbing them, where practical, accompanying the string section live in the studio, not burying them beneath an unsupervised overdub. Three songs were recorded this way at a single session at Basing Street on April 25th: 'I'm A Dreamer', 'Full Moon' and 'No More Sad Refrains', all of which in demo form stood comparison with her very best. There had been nothing half-baked about those Byfield versions.

In fact, she had never been more prepped to make an album than when she arrived at Basing Street for the first session on April 23rd, 1976. Nor had she ever written so many originals beforehand, six of which she cut in the first four days of sessions – including the three layered with strings. But after she sang 'I'm A Dreamer' to a string section live, it was still subject to further second-guessing. It was a process her producer liked to encourage, leaving her chosen guitarist, Donahue, to ruefully remark, 'the original version ... was a lot simpler, you could really hear the full melody.'

The mollycoddled couple seemed determined to run up as large a studio bill as Island would countenance, even with songs that merely needed the deftest of touches. After four sessions in which the focus was firmly on originals – save for a second attempt to capture 'Losing Game' (previously recorded by James Carr and the Flying Burrito Brothers) – May Day saw Sandy rip apart Thompson's song of infidelity, 'For Shame Of Doing Wrong', while a recalcitrant Richard tried to remember how it went. The engineer secretly yearned for more of the same:

John Wood: I think Sandy drifted away from some of the more rootsier and gutsier feelings that she'd started with both in Fotheringay and in the next couple of solo albums ... [It] started to get a little more pandering to the middle of the road … She'd lost some of her individualism … I think it's a shame that she didn't pick one or two other songs by Richard … to have a go at.

Work remained ongoing through June as Trevor coaxed Sandy into overdubbing perfectly good vocals, adding layer after extraneous layer to basic tracks. And Island continued to pick up the tab, even when Sandy scored and arranged an eight-minute choral version of 'All Our Days', to serve as a reprise of the album's pseudo-classical centrepiece. But she was fast running out of room, and Island's largesse did not extend to a double-album.

Nor was the extravagance of Sandy's vision confined to the studio. When the album was finally delivered in early July, she began to conceive a nationwide tour with the kind of band only a cash-rich record label could afford to subsidise, in the name of tour support. Imagine her shock when Island made it plain they would do no such thing:

Sandy Denny: The album was finished about July last year, and I was supposed to go on the road in October with a band and everything. I had a big band lined up with a lot of good people in it: Jerry Donahue; 'Rabbit' [Bundrick]; Dave Mattacks; Pat Donaldson; Andy Roberts; about eight people. I put the project to Island and they just didn't seem to want to invest an awful lot of money to put the show on the road. [1977]

Island knew not it would be their last pitch before punk swept Sandy's audience aside with one concerted swat. They also seemed not to know this was something worth promoting. Despite some unnecessary post-production, the last minute addition of 'Silver Threads And Golden Needles' and another godawful sleeve design by Trevor's sister, Marion, the album Sandy delivered in July was her strongest collection to date. But it sure didn't sound like the work of an ex-folksinger.

Rather, it sounded like someone planning to relocate to Laurel Canyon. Even the working title of the record – *Gold Dust* – was a nod to the West Coast lifestyle and the singer-songwriters who lived there. She had written its title-track about her friend Miranda Ward, who had fallen under the spell of Little Feat's Lowell George and, with this dalliance, acquired a taste for cocaine that would make her a dangerous friend to have around for as long as she remained mistress to a musician hellbent on having his friend Charlie on retainer. It also placed a wedge between Sandy and her favourite couple:

Linda Thompson: We had to give up [on] Sandy, and people like that. However misguided it was, we were trying to better ourselves [and] find a spiritual side, and we couldn't hang around people who were sinking brandy and snorting coke.

If a brandy and coke lifestyle was rife in la-la-land in 1976, it was not one which Sandy's English label were keen to countenance – or fund. In fact, Brian Blethyn approached another old friend of the singer, designer Bambi Ballard, trying to convince her to take over Sandy's personal management from brother David. As Bambi says, 'Blethyn's attitude was: We can't handle Sandy anymore. Island is thinking of blowing her out, because there's too much friction. She's baulking at certain gigs. Trevor is too much of an influence, and Sandy needs serious management.'

Bambi shared Blethyn's concerns but felt ill-equipped to provide the requisite iron fist in velvet glove. Island's next gambit was even more bizarre – encouraging their favourite folk-rock chick to plant herself firmly in the middle of the road with a blatant play for radioplay. Trevor in 1985 insisted it was Island who 'asked us to record "Candle In The Wind", which Sandy liked as a song but [had] never considered recording. We felt a little let down by the songs we left off the album to accommodate that.'

An immediate loss was a terrific Sandy original called 'Still Waters Run Deep', for which Sandy apologised, 'In the end I did incorporate another track on it and take one off but … that's more of a result, rather than a cause, of the [album's] delay.' John Wood was mystified by the substitution, coming after the loss of 'Full Moon', a song which featured on the *Gold Dust* sequence but would be omitted from the nine-track *Rendezvous*.

It was February 1977 by the time Sandy returned to the studio to do Island's bidding. She found Richard and Linda recording some demos and set about trying to convince Richard to play for his supper again. Sandy later recalled, 'He was relieved to get back on the electric guitar and start wailing away.' But this was hardly the right song, and the guitarist sensed someone artistically adrift:

Richard Thompson: I feel Island Records were not entirely sympathetic to Sandy's style or needs, and were either unaware of the great talent she had or were unable to channel and market it to those many people who would appreciate it. [1986]

Rendezvous' delay only further knocked the stuffing out of Sandy. The release dates relayed to her were ever changing. Originally it was 'coming out in October, then November, then December … there was always another date … [until,] eventually, it ended up being May 14th'.

By the time it finally appeared, a year on from the sessions, she admitted, 'I haven't listened to it that much for such a long time now. I've got to get back into the way I felt when it was finished.' To further her own heightening concerns about label support, master tapes had been dispatched across the Atlantic to A&M, without any word as to whether they intended to release *either* version. Having made an album almost tailored to the American singer-songwriter market, she was being rebuffed by the very label that had been so supportive.

If Sandy thus spent the second half of 1976 fretting about her next career move, her erstwhile musical sounding board, Richard and his partner Linda had taken a sabbatical, doing almost nothing in 1976 to facilitate their musical careers. And yet, at year's end, Island fast-tracked a double-album anthology of largely unreleased Richard Thompson recordings, called *(guitar, vocal)* – seemingly at *Rendezvous'* expense.

The project was very much Richard Williams' brainchild, a personal indulgence he was determined to push partly because he knew he was heading for the Island exit, and a return to music journalism:

Richard Williams: I'm sure *(guitar, vocal)* was my idea … I went to [Jo] Lustig and said, Why don't we do something like this to make people appreciate Richard in a different way? … Richard took an interest. I'm sure that 'Throwaway Street Puzzle', 'Mr Lacey' and

'Poor Will And The Jolly Hangman' were his idea ... 'Night Comes In' and 'Calvary Cross' were definitely mine, because I'd taped those at the Oxford Poly ... I thought those two long things were the best he'd ever done. He just tore the guts out of them ... [But] I certainly never thought of releasing the whole concert as an album at that point. I just wanted those tracks. It was a nice way of keeping his career going ... I knew that [the alternate] version of 'A Heart Needs A Home' was there. I put [the album] together, but I asked him, 'Have you got any interesting bits'n'bobs?' He said, 'I'll go and do these [instrumentals].'

If the two instrumentals – 'Flee As A Bird' and 'The Pitfall/The Excursion' – were perhaps tunes Thompson had earmarked for the all-instrumental album he had talked about the previous year, they were his only studio activity in 1976 – save for a single session with Sandy. And yet *(guitar, vocal)* was one of the most incendiary releases of the year, featuring Thompson the guitar-hero.

The guitarwork on the BBC 'Mr Lacey', *Full House*-era workouts of 'Poor Will And The Jolly Hangman' and 'Sweet Little Rock'n'Roller' and the live versions of 'Calvary Cross' and 'Night Comes In' suggested just how few peers he had when wielding a Fender. But whatever input he had on the unprecedented archival project, his general view on his work to date had now hardened into one of disavowal, bordering on disgust:

Richard Thompson: Music's a very transient thing ... and looking back I don't find them very interesting records. It's difficult for me to retain any enthusiasm for things I wrote then ... I'm writing songs now that aren't caught up in that direct emotion ... It's nice that people are interested in the music, but it's something I would try and be detached from. [1977]

Richard Thompson: The previous albums have been too one-dimensional. All people would get from them is a kind of recognition of a mood or emotion; like, if you're feeling despondent you put on a despondent record and relate to that. But those kinds of emotion in music aren't interesting to me anymore. [1979]

His level of dissociation from the distinctly English style of rock music he had peddled for the past six years was laid bare by one extraordinary exchange during an interview for *Dark Star* magazine in May 1977, while undertaking a tour, the set of which would feature exactly two songs from his oeuvre to date – a near unrecognisable 'When I Get To The Border' and an epic 'Night Comes In'. A distraught journalist/fan asked the apostate from Albion:

> **Dark Star:** Would you [consider] includ[ing] more familiar older material to make it 'better' for the audience?
> **Richard Thompson:** I might do if I thought it was up to standard, but I don't think it is.
> **DS:** What about the stuff on *Bright Lights*?
> **RT:** It's like moribund, listless … It's rubbish.
> **DS:** Presumably you'd be just as critical of *Hokey Pokey*?
> **RT:** More critical. It's the worst I've done.
> **DS:** How about *Pour Down Like Silver*…
> **RT**: It has still got some older songs, but the performance is lifeless. It still sounds [too] English to me.

To those once close to him, Thompson now appeared almost detached from music itself. The following year, as a first new album in three years finally beckoned, he was still talking as if he couldn't wait to discard the mantle of musician and assume the position of preacher:

Richard Thompson: I got cheesed off with playing, that's all. It's very hard to live your life according to music, I refuse to do it. I think music has to be a hobby for someone like me … I don't want to be an artist. I don't want to be this chap in the blank canvas and the rain coming in through the broken skyline. [1978]

Having shut out the world, there was very little those on the outside felt they could do about Richard's new-found calling. The time for intervention only finally came when Linda began to haemorrhage blood after giving birth to her son, Teddy, in the North London Sufi commune in the spring of 1976:

Philippa Clare: [When Linda] went off to that commune I was very accepting of what she wanted to do, until she was in danger and then my nose was above the parapet. That was when I broke down the door because she was having Teddy, and she was there on wooden crates, about to give birth. And there's Richard [just standing there]. I'm going, 'We've got to get her to a hospital.'

Linda Thompson: I gave birth in the squat in London, no doctors, no nurses, no nothing. I ended up in hospital. After I'd given birth, [I was] not right. It was four days later. They wouldn't let me go to hospital. They said, 'No, no, no. You're all right. You've just had a baby.' But I wasn't all right … The [hospital] fixed me up and they stitched me. They [had] freaked out [at what they saw]. The leader of the commune said, 'Oh, [it's] just attention seeking. That's all it is.'

Actually, Linda nearly died. When she did finally regain her health, she began to demand changes, pushing Richard to take up music again, whatever the wishes of the leader of the commune, who seemed to view anything which required electricity – whether it be a guitar or a delivery ward – to be anti-Islam.

Out in the real world, Island continued producing damning audio evidence that this guitar-vocalist once played follow the leader in a band which took English folk-rock to the Pacific rim, making *Full House* converts of the West Coast's club-going multitude.

Live At The L.A. Troubadour appeared in January 1977, and even though Simon Nicol rightly feels 'the sleeve gave you no impression as to what it was about', this budget-priced album was a welcome reminder of a time when Fairport's brand of folk-rock put the folk in prog.

In a pincer movement of sorts, Island and Linda prompted Thompson to pick up his electric guitar, not to replicate the music on any archival artifact but to make the kind of music he had described in a series of interviews he gave leading up to the duo's first national tour in eighteen long, dark months.

Cryptic at the best of times, he informed one interviewer that the words to all these new songs 'have come from various [Arabic] sources. I'm sort of an editor, really.' Two terrific new songs – 'First Light' and 'Strange Affair' – purported to be translations of old

Arabic poems, the former by Muhammad Ibn-al Hamid, the latter by Si Fudul al-Huwari. And as Linda says, 'We were both studying Arabic, [so] if he says that [some lyric] comes from a thirteenth century translation of the Koran, you can trust me, it did.' And yet when both songs appeared on 1978's *First Light*, they were deemed Thompson compositions.

Whatever the truth, he had his work cut out selling such material to an audience whose most recent purchases were *(guitar, vocal)* and *Live At The Troubadour*. In fact, one of those May interviews, conducted after a particularly frosty reception at a half-full Birmingham Town Hall, revealed just how much of an uphill struggle it was proving to be:

Richard Thompson: There's nothing at all in the Koran against music. [But] I can't sing songs about going out with my best friend's wife … One has to be selective … [The reaction] has been varied, but mostly good. Telling people they're going to die all the time can't make them happy … We're feeling our way. It's very exploratory. I don't know where it's going or where we're going to end up. [1977]

At the same mid-tour point, Thompson admitted 'our audiences go into a coma after the second number, because the subject matter is very shattering'. Thankfully for such folk, a thirteen-minute stun-gun 'Night Comes In' came next. It was worth the price of admission alone. But as live experiences went, the May 1977 concerts were not so much 'shattering', as mystifying.

Melody Maker's Colin Irwin was certainly in the latter camp, writing about the tour, months later, 'Playing with a band of unknowns, he barely acknowledged the audience, concentrated almost exclusively on new, unfamiliar material, some of which was plain weird, and gave little indication of a regained thirst for performing. An object lesson in introspection.'

The shows which diminishing numbers witnessed were nothing like those seen by the same fans on the now-hallowed tour to promote *Pour Down Like Silver*. Even the inclusion of this extended 'Night Comes In' and, on night one in Brighton, an acoustic 'Beat The Retreat' did little to dispel the sense of dislocation. Yes, Thompson was playing more electric guitar than ever before, but the band behind were playing the kind of meandering soul-blues he had previously disdained.

The core from Mighty Baby – who had disbanded in 1971 after a two-album career, interspersed with sessions for Gary Farr, Shelagh McDonald and Keith Christmas – had been co-opted by Thompson, whose own route to Islam had crossed theirs, albeit three years later. But it was hardly a marriage made in Mecca, with the rhythm-section flaying away, like sailors lost at C, and Ian Hammond organ providing almost as many sonic brush strokes as Thompson's guitar.[39]

The audible disorientation was hardly alleviated by the titles to some of the new songs: 'The King Of Love', 'The Fire In The Garden' and, opening the show, 'The Flute Tells A Story', a part-spoken piece on which Ian Whiteman played the same flute Guy Stevens had thrown across the studio at the first Mighty Baby session in 1969, shouting, 'I don't record fucking flutes.'

The Middle-Eastern influence – something Whiteman had acquired on a trip to Morocco and a pilgrimage to Mecca – was particularly overt on 'The Bird In God's Garden', an eight-minute piece that originated on the 1972 album *If Man But Knew,* credited to The Habibiyya, an alias Powell and Whiteman adopted for this experimental project.

When the Thompsons' long-standing road manager, Bernard Doherty, turned up for the first rehearsal, he remembers coming 'up the stairs. I could hear them all banging away, and I thought, This isn't Richard ... They had ... all those congas. I call it his Santana period.'

And yet, the guitar-playing that May was, if anything, the apotheosis of what Richard Williams extolled as 'the Coltrane [influence] ... the swirling guitar, the real heavy doom'. As for Linda, she had been set free. Released from her silent Sufi prison, she was looking to use the old songs 'as a [necessary] reference' even as Richard baulked at songs he didn't find 'interesting anymore [because] they're like spin-offs really, from one's energy – the energy you put out to get through life'.

So removed did he feel from the earlier material that three 'old' songs he allowed into the set – each previously featuring Richard on lead vocal – were now given to Linda,[40] even if one was immediately dropped:

---

[39] Whiteman himself had a long, distinguished career as a session musician even before Mighty Baby, playing on the original Ben Carruthers 'Jack O' Diamonds' 45 back in 1965.
[40] That one-off 'Beat The Retreat' on opening night in Brighton was sung by Linda, as were 'Night Comes In' and 'When I Get To The Border'.

Linda Thompson: I had completely forgotten that [I sang most of the songs on that tour], but I think our Sufi leader wasn't very keen on us doing it. Certainly Richard would've wanted to be in the background. I don't think he felt singing was very Sufi or something. I felt I was singing too much on that tour, but obviously he just didn't want to sing ... It was good to be out of the commune at least, [and] on the road ... [But] he was always worried about his singing.

Some of the 'new, unfamiliar material' which constituted the rest of the ninety-minute show had already been recorded in the studio back in February, including 'Layla' and 'Strange Affair', two songs which would appear on the couple's 'comeback' album the following year. Semi-acoustic in its studio guise, the former became a blistering retort to the unGodly in concert, proof positive that the electric guitar could be put to the service of the Prophet.[41]

However welcome such guitar workouts were, the underlying message in the new songs was unsettling to fans. They suggested Thompson was looking to make a Sufi-like statement akin to *If Man But Knew*. A pre-tour report in *NME*, the week before Brighton, had already suggested Richard 'and Linda are due into the studios in May to start recording the new album, for which half a dozen songs are ready, which [they]'ll be previewing on the tour'.

Yet the plan to take this material off the road and straight into the studio would fall at the first hurdle. On May 29-30th, the devout duo attempted to cut three songs from the live set, 'The King Of Love', 'Rescue Me' and 'Strange Affair' and two others, with the tour band in tow. At the console was an old familiar, back from LA and raring to go. However, he was no fan of Mighty Baby:

Joe Boyd: [Richard] and I and John Wood went into Basing Street with these Muslim guys who he was playing with. We did a day, maybe two in Basing Street. I thought it was awful ... You know, when you [have] play[ed] with Mattacks and Pegg and you're suddenly hearing Richard play over this rhythm section... I said, 'Richard, come on, be serious.' ... I think John and I were going to

---

[41] The February recording of 'Layla' – the one song from those sessions to appear semi-officially on Flypaper's *Doom & Gloom From The Tomb* cassette – barely qualifies as a prototype.

co-produce ... a record ... It [soon] became clear that it just wasn't working ... I think Richard knew. I mean, he could hear [it]. I think [Island's view] was, 'Let's see what happens. Here's some studio time, let's see what it sounds like.'

The Thompsons' 'Sufi' album was quietly scrapped, never to be heard (of) again. Nor was this all the bad news the wind of change carried. Shortly afterwards, Linda remembers, 'Chris Blackwell ... came to us at a party and said, I love you guys but I'm gonna have to let you go. And we thought, that's fair enough ... [But] we were so blasé about Island. We were with Island for seven, eight years at the time ... Nowadays you're only with [labels] seven, eight minutes.'

The Richard who had grumbled about the industry repeatedly, now had his wish granted. With Richard Williams no longer at Island, keeping the A&R department motivated, the duo were heading for a spell in the wilderness, literally and metaphorically. And they were not alone. Unbeknownst to Sandy, she would not be far behind.

How ironic, then, that in the fullness of time – as Linda confirms – 'The record company got their money back ... I think they thought ... "How are we ever going to make any money off these two?" But they recouped long ago.' It turns out Richard Williams was one of the more far-sighted foremen at the Island coalface. Most of the records the Fairport family made in a nine-year association with Island would keep selling steadily, year on year.

Thompson the breadwinner, whatever his own assessment of his pre-Sufi canon, was going to have to rethink his relationship to music and Mohammed's teachings if he was ever going to reclaim his place in the world of men. That would take a further retreat into the wiles of Norfolk and another kind of intervention, at the behest of a former lifesaver, Joe Boyd.

15. Without Prospects

Sandy Denny

What we were doing, even though it was only on a small scale, will stand the test of time. It has far more worth than the entire pop output of the seventies. Very, very broadly speaking, there are three types of pop-rock music in the seventies. There's overblown prog-rock, there's Glitter rock and at the end of the seventies, there's punk – which although it … was a reaction against certain music, such as Pink Floyd, which is fair enough, … has almost no worth as music.

—ASHLEY HUTCHINGS TO BRIAN HINTON

There will be a breakthrough … I'm convinced that music made up of all the elements of British tradition will become widely accepted in the country. It may take the form of a more or less straightforward rock music, it may not.

—ASHLEY HUTCHINGS, *STREET LIFE* #17, JUNE 1976

In fact, an Anglo reaction to American-style rock music was already revving into gear when Ashley made his 1976 prediction to *Street Life*. Unfortunately for him, its name was punk-rock, not folk-rock. Founded on a fiercely anti-American aesthetic set to a bedrock of Britbeat, it evolved into forms of rock and pop that were angular and Anglophile to the core. It just contained less than zero in the way of folk tradition, doing for English folk-rock what Dylan going electric had done for the American folk revival eleven years earlier.

Whatever its worth 'as music', punk certainly provided a much-needed jolt to the system, one with which the old guard took its sweet time coming to terms. Now, Linda Thompson insists, 'The Sex Pistols were brilliant. But at the time I didn't get it at all.' In this, she was in good company.

Sticking one's head under the covers and hoping they would go away was the default reaction of most of the musical Establishment, the majority of A&R men and the entire prog phalanx. But in the end, with a great deal of prodding from a galvanized and all-powerful music press, the labels realised punk rockers were the future – *if* there was one.

For the Fairport brand of folk-rock, though, the future looked decidedly bleak. By the summer of hate – as the press labelled 1977's peak season of discontent – there wouldn't be a folk-rock berth at Island.

For Fairport itself, options seemed few and far between. But the determination to soldier on in adversity was in the band's DNA. Pegg, defining that attitude, informed the others, 'Right, we're never going to make it, forget record companies, forget all that. We'll do whatever we want, we'll play music we like.' Remarkably, he also managed to persuade one Fairport founder who had spent most of 1975-76 reviving the Albion Band – now enjoying a multi-album deal at Harvest – to give the parent band mouth to mouth:

Simon Nicol: We formed a quorum at that point, [because] we knew there [were] gigs out there for a band called Fairport Convention. The four of us seemed to be of a mind, 'Let's do it.' ... It just happened – nothing was planned. We'd just been dropped by the largest independent – who had seen which way the wind was blowing ... [But] it was a good line-up, and lasted longer than any previous line-up – three-and-a-half years. As soon as we started gigging together, it was a return to form, in the sense that it was rough'n'ready, highly energetic and [saw us] having fun before your very eyes – [which] is when Fairport was at its best.

Ashley's ad hoc approach to the Albion line-up had begun to unnerve even Simon, who would continue to offer his services, just not on a full-time basis. The inclusion of guitarist Graeme Taylor in the nine-piece line-up made for what Taylor himself called, 'Ashley['s idea of] a flexible line-up ... I didn't quite know what I was doing – whether I was playing rhythm guitar, lead guitar or what – because it [always] changed.'

Simon gives a blunter assessment of Albion band politics, 'I felt relegated by Graeme. His electric guitar parts became far more significant in the finished sound. They were there on *Prospect* [*Before Us*], but they became much more central to the sound.'

Simon had been around Ashley long enough to know the power balance could shift any time, anywhere. He just wanted to get back to enjoying making music. After five years away, Fairport welcomed him back like the prodigal son. In fact, the others – Swarb, Pegg and Bruce

Rowland – had been plotting his return ever since he lent a hand on *Gottle O'Geer*. Now all they needed was someone capable of managing a band with this many crusty personalities, and preferably someone who knew how to keep Swarb on a leash. There was only one candidate:

Philippa Clare: Swarb and I [had] got together through Trevor Lucas. Sandy and Trevor had gone to Australia [and] come back. It's about midnight. Doorbell rings and it's Trevor, 'We're going down the Greek [in Earl's Court]. I got a present for you in the car.' And out steps Swarb … He was dressed to the hilt and he had these amazing bell-bottom trousers on with brass studs down the side. When it came to home time, Trevor's saying, 'Swarb's got nowhere to stay.' So I put him in the spare room and I tell him, 'I'm locking my bedroom door.' The door knob is rattling all night. He stayed for three days, and [I] cracked eventually. Next thing I knew, he'd been to Birmingham and returned with his Mercedes van full of all his belongings and moved in. There was no discussion.

That relationship had run its course by the end of 1973 after both parties straying, but Philippa's abiding friendship with Sandy and Swarb ensured a continuing interest in Fairport right through the *Rising For The Moon*-era. By the time the band found itself singer-less, manager-less and label-less, Philippa's career had turned to Mud – the glam chart-toppers, that is. She 'was working with a company called Evolution, [where] I learned about promotion and putting on things … looking after Mud'. It was a good way to learn the ropes. And though she was new to personal management, she knew Fairport's foibles and folk-rock follies well:

Philippa Clare: I remember Jo Lustig coming up to me once and saying, 'You should be knighted. How do you control that band?' I said, 'You look after the chequebook and you have your signature plus one other, so no one else can put a cheque through.' [But] they wouldn't [have] trusted him. And you can understand why. I basically ripped myself off by managing them. If I got an endorsement deal for equipment, [say, a] new stereo, I never thought that I should have one, too … I [also] told Swarb, 'You're gonna get the worst treatment because of our past. I want everyone to feel [it's] even-stevens.' …

Whenever we went on tour, I put half the money in the bank and [gave] half the money to them. So there would always be money in the bank. Rehearsals weren't their strong point, so I [started] fining anyone who was late, and it was like a fiver a minute.

Not only did Philippa's work ethic soon whip the band into shape, she also secured them a new record deal, and not with one of the indie labels who had followed in Island's lucrative wake. The band still had a fan base inside the industry, and it was just a case of targetting the right 'rube' at the apposite moment – when the pubs shut:

Philippa Clare: I negotiated this record deal for Fairport which was unbelievable. I did the deal when I was still at Evolution, and then I left. Ken Maliphant [was] at Phonogram. I knew he was a great fan, and he was also a great drinker. So … I made an appointment to go round and see him at three o'clock. We got a record deal where we had freedom of artwork and total freedom [musically]. The only way they could turn us down was if the tapes were technically not up to standard … I think it was a five-album deal. But it was definitely because Ken was a fan and he'd had a few.

Phonogram were parents to probably the last prog-inspired label still standing. As Simon observes, 'The Vertigo label was supposed to be looking back at proggy bands, and we just about fit into that.' The twelfth Fairport album would now appear on the same spiral label as Black Sabbath. After the financial constraints of its predecessor, Simon and the band duly found themselves back 'at Basing Street proper – because we had a budget'. With the business-like Philippa on hand, even Swarb was finding it hard to act out:

Philippa Clare: I knew when Swarb was not on it – even though I didn't play a musical instrument. I'd be like, do it again, do it again, and he trusted me. We had that connection, which was very strong.

The album Fairport finished in the winter of 1977 would be an unexpected return to form and a most unlikely resurrection of the spirit that had imbued the blessed band in its heyday. With good reason. From the outset the album's centrepiece – and title-track – was a twelve-minute reworking of the *Full House* arrangement on 'The Bonny Bunch Of Roses'. Sung once again by Swarbrick to the same sombre accompaniment – at odds with the sentiments of the original ballad, which lampooned Napoleon's failure to defeat the British – the song celebrated an 'England [which] has a heart of oak'.

To further the sense of déjà vu, the album also included the 'English period' Thompson classic, 'The Poor Ditching Boy', at a time when its author had disowned the whole bally catalogue. Meanwhile, 'Adieu Adieu' (a.k.a. 'Well-A-Day'), a Georgian last-goodnight broadside the *Full House* line-up dabbled with but then discarded, was disinterred.

Here was a band consciously looking back. In fact, as Pegg later said, 'You could almost imagine *Bonny Bunch* as the follow up to *Angel Delight* and *Babbacombe Lee*.' So well did the quartet already know this material that, according to Pegg, 'We only ever rehearsed the album for three days, which was mainly spent in the pub playing darts.'

Released in July 1977, *Bonny Bunch Of Roses* was greeted with an audible sigh of relief by reviewers and label alike. And unlike the two departed mainstays from Fairport's glory days, this Fairport were looking to play and play, promoting the new album the same way they had *Full House*, converting concert-goers gig by gig.

———

While Fairport recommitted themselves to the road, Sandy's plans to hit the road to promote the release of *Rendezvous* had hit the buffers the minute she learnt she was big with child. Increasingly prone to depression and emotionally fragile, she told herself she would not take any chances with this child.

Having had a backstreet abortion after becoming pregnant with Jackson Frank's child shortly before the practice was finally legalised, Sandy had become convinced she would never be able to conceive. As Richard recalls, 'She was desperate to have a child. But [when it happened] I think it was something that emotionally was almost too much for her.' With Trevor suddenly no longer there for her, she found herself cast adrift in a sea of sorrow:

Linda Thompson: Neither of them was particularly faithful to each other. But this was the … seventies. She loved Trevor, but the people she really adored were people where the relationship was never consummated. She adored Richard, and whatever he told her to do, she'd do … Trevor was like her anchor … She loved him, but it wasn't the fierce thing that she had for [others].

Jerry Donahue: They would part company for days and they had regular spats, but would always come back to each other. They were suspicious of what the other one was getting up to, sometimes … without foundation, but often for good reason.

In these less-than-ideal circumstances, Sandy's initial determination to ensure the baby made it to 'term' was never going to last the full nine months. With Trevor frequently AWOL, she was left to her maudlin thoughts – crystallized in perhaps the last original song she ever wrote, 'Makes Me Think Of You'. All too soon she turned to the same crutches she had leant on for most of the past decade:

Philippa Clare: Smack, coke, dope, serious drinking, Pernod, absinthe – that was what she did when she was pregnant. [When Georgia was born prematurely that July] she was in such a state – no booze, no drugs, no nothing, her body's in complete … heavy withdrawals.

To compound Sandy's fogged-up sense that opportunity – if not life itself – was slipping away, news came that she had been let go by the label. Heavily pregnant and unable to tour, she was no longer even the critical darling of a music press increasingly preoccupied by the shit storm a new version of 'God Save The Queen' was creating. When *Rendezvous* received almost universal apathy and A&M decided to hold back on a US release (which never came), Sandy's provisional plan to relocate to LA vanished in a puff of smoke.

Yet she was not without options. Fairport and the Albions had both shown there were pockets of appreciation for pre-punk forms still. She remained confident she had enough of an audience to undertake a UK theatre tour in November 1977, albeit without a record label, let alone tour support. It was a gamble she needed to take to reaffirm her performing credentials and record her first solo live album, with a little help from a 'friend':

Karl Dallas: I'd gone to Edinburgh [sic] to see the opening concert, and it was very impressive. I mean, the band was a great band. It was a bit loose and I don't think it got much better. I thought it would. So I said to Marcel [Rodd], 'Let's record Sandy.' ... We hired the Island mobile and John Wood to engineer it, and went to the Royalty Theatre and recorded the whole concert, [but] there was a whistle right across all the tracks ... She was not well. Trevor moved heaven and earth to stop it ever being released ... [Eventually] he got Island to buy it.

As Dallas suggests, the seventeen-track document of Sandy's November 1977 tour came from the wrong end of proceedings, a show at London's Royalty Theatre on the 27th, not the superior show at the same venue three weeks earlier, which actually opened the fortnight tour.

This added London date actually came a week after the end of the tour proper, thus negating the usual reason why one records a final show – everyone is on their game by now. A week off meant not only that her voice was again a little weatherbeaten, but her nerves were worn and frayed. *Melody Maker*'s Colin Irwin remembers seeing her before the show, 'and she was just pacing up and down, an absolute nervous wreck, shaking ... She was in a terrible state ... When I first saw her with Fairport, she seemed totally in control. [Now] she was holding the stage, but she'd actually dissolved into this wreck.'

Another person stunned by her jittery demeanour at the Royalty was her old friend Linda, who arrived for that final show in the company of husband Richard and Ashley Hutchings, only to find 'her singing wasn't good ... and she looked awful ... We were all shocked. Her voice was really shot by the end.' Which is presumably why 'Trevor moved heaven and earth' to suppress the tapes.

Yet even here there is much to enjoy from the rough mix – partly released on an Australian-only CD, before it was unnecessarily embellished by the same man who perpetrated the *Fotheringay II* atrocity, Jerry Donahue. A single album of the best performances from a band which was essentially Fotheringay bolstered by DM and Pete Wilshire's pedal steel, would have been a smart way to bring the curtain down on the Island years.

Ashley had not seen or heard from Sandy in years even though he was living in London once again – carrying on an extra-marital affair that would end his marriage. At the same time he was coaxing Linda into spreading her vocal wings again. When she expressed a willingness to sing for the ever-evolving Albions, Richard refused to permit it, only to realise he couldn't stop her:

Linda Thompson: Richard got so cross [when I joined the Albion Band]. He told the sheik, who summoned me up to his huge, stately home. He said, 'You can't do this. You can't go against your husband.' ... It was a real number. I didn't speak to Richard for about six months. [1985]

By this time, the Sufi commune had relocated to Norfolk, representing an even greater retreat from the modern world. In Hoxne, Linda found to her horror that there was 'no phone, no television, no record player, no electric light, no hot water ... You didn't buy anything store bought, so the women would make bread in the morning – and cakes. You were always cooking and there was no washing machine or anything, so it really was a full-time job ... [A life of] drudgery, really.' Not surprisingly, she quickly tired of the life her husband seemed to think would bring them nearer my God to Thee. There was also a pressing need for some basic hygiene:

Linda Thompson: At least when we were squatting in the [London] commune ... we had our own spaces. But when we went to Norfolk, we were all living together ... There wasn't a lot of cleanliness and I got really sick ... It was awful. I hated it. I hated Richard. I hated the commune. I thought, how can I get out of this? I did leave, and went back to my parents. My father was dying and they said in the commune, 'You can't see your parents.' That's part of [the] brainwashing. They cut you off from your [family]. I just left. Thank God I did. I wasn't as brainwashed as Richard, so I managed to leave and get out ... But [in the end] I went back, like a schmuck.

By the time Linda returned to Hoxne, even Richard was tiring of the isolation, the orthodoxy and the 'drudgery', even if he sought to justify his original decision in a 1979 interview, 'We [were] try[ing] to establish ... a very pure thing, and theoretically a very sane society, but in order to do that in our age it seems you have to completely isolate yourself.' Linda takes a more jaundiced view of this futile gesture, 'It was fine idealism, but in reality it's very hard to unplug from the system. You probably have to go a lot further than Norfolk.'

Finally, her husband remembered his marriage vows and reconciled their views of Islam, while Linda agreed to erase their differences from the public record, even denying earlier reports in the papers that suggested they had parted: 'We've had our ups and downs but we've never split up. Truthfully, I mean, I've run home to mother a couple of times but it's never been for more than a week.'

In fact, she *had* left Richard – hence the line in her Grammy-award winning song, 'Telling Me Lies', 'Should never have come back for more' – at the time when Richard was approached by two old friends in autumn 1977, hoping to persuade him to resume a once-lucrative career as a session musician.

The co-conspirators were Joe Boyd and Simon Nicol, the former having been enlisted to record a single with a new pop diva who had a number one album (*Rock Follies*) and a number one single ('Don't Cry For Me Argentina') under her belt and an unspoken yen to be a folk-rocker, something she kept under her hat until Virgin offered her the deal of a lifetime:

Joe Boyd: I was going out with somebody who was a close friend of Julie Covington. She introduced me to Julie, [who was] telling me how much [she] loved Fairport and [the] McGarrigles ... She'd just had this huge hit with 'Don't Cry For Me [Argentina]' and Virgin had [made] this no-expense-spared [request for] an album. And I said to Julie, 'You should sing show tunes, that's what you should do. I'm probably not the guy for this.' But she was like, 'No. That's too obvious. That's not what I want to do. I don't want to sing Cole Porter. I want to sing Kate McGarrigle.' And so we agreed to try doing a single. She wanted to do a song that I just thought was such a weird idea, 'Only Women Bleed'. I had ... [the] idea of getting John Cale to arrange it. I can't remember how many, if any, Fairport[ers], played on 'Only Women Bleed'. Maybe none. But the B-side was 'Easy To Slip' by Lowell George. When she said she wanted to do

'Easy To Slip', I thought, 'Well, this is a job for Fairport.' At the time, Richard had taken the position that for religious reasons, cultural reasons, whatever, he wasn't playing electric guitar. And Simon said, 'Well, let's ask Richard to play guitar. I think this would be great for him, because I know they need work. If you offered him the session and say he had to play electric, this ... [might] be a break through.' I had a conversation with him on the phone. Eventually he agreed to come and play electric on 'Easy To Slip' ... I got Simon and Mattacks and Pegg, and we went to Olympic ... this was the first time Richard had played electric guitar for ... years [sic]. Simon was almost in tears ... saying, 'I just can't believe that this guy is going to give this up.' ... [But] from that point on it was like, 'I'm back to being an electric guitar player.'

If Boyd's welcome intervention seemed to have worked, there was suddenly plenty of work for this session guitarist extraordinaire. It was like old times. Even a recalcitrant Richard was quoted as saying, 'I enjoy my independence. [But] I'd like to do ... some more session work, which I quite enjoy in small doses.'

The 'small doses' grew and grew as he now committed himself to two ambitious projects, both with Boyd ostensibly at the helm. One of these would be the album Virgin were even more keen for Julie Covington to make after her cover of Alice Cooper's 'Only Women Bleed' became a smash hit in the lead-up to Christmas 1977.

The other was more like it, an ambitious project which for the first time in five years brought all three Fairport founders together again. Ashley Hutchings and his recently revived Albion Band were set to make their first folk-rock album in half a decade, much to one former sidekick's pleasure and joy:

Richard Thompson: I haven't heard anything interesting in [English folk-rock recently] ... apart from The Albion Band, who are sort of an eccentric version of it. What they're doing is very interesting, but then Ashley's always. [1978]

Never short of ambition, Ashley once again found he had the means to enlist a real producer and co-opt all the musicians he desired, including both Thompsons and Simon Nicol, on a sabbatical from the band he had rejoined. A generous working budget also appealed to the producer responsible for Fairport's finest vinyl volleys, looking to kick-start a second folk-rock revolution with old friends and new acquaintances:

John Tams: We auditioned the album to Joe Boyd in Room Two at the National Theatre, one night. Joe sat in a chair in the middle of the room, the only member of the audience and we just stood and sang him the album! And he said, 'That will be all right! When do we start?'

Ashley Hutchings: I was in such a bad state with the broken marriage that I [had to] say to [Tams] at the beginning of the sessions, 'You're gonna have to take the reins here.' And he produced it with Boyd. The irony is that [what is] probably the best album The Albion Band ever made, I was only part of. I wasn't at the helm.

Simon Nicol: The Albion Band that made *Rise Up Like The Sun* was a large and essentially loose team which was 'led' (or perhaps 'marshalled' would be a better verb) by a trio of Hutchings (naturally), Tams (stretching his wings) and Boyd (the professional mediator). It worked for precisely that reason: the balance of Indians to Chiefs.

Ashley Hutchings: Harvest was a solidly great label. And we were lucky enough to get a guy [who] didn't know at the time, when he gave us a fair amount of money, that he was about to get the sack. So we spent all the money, easily, by which time he'd gone ... It turned out to be a very good album ... And it was a rock album! ... In fact, Joe now says the late seventies Albion Band were as groundbreaking as Fairport. ... The two most expensive albums I've been involved in are *The Compleat Dancing Master* and *Rise Up Like The Sun*. But Harvest [were] happy. And the *Melody Maker* [carried] a four-page feature.

Released in March 1978, *Rise Up Like The Sun* was a highly collaborative artifact, on which the Albion Band were augmented by a stellar crew that included Kate McGarrigle, Richard and Linda Thompson, Martin Carthy, Julie Covington and Andy Fairweather-Low.

As with the equally ambitious *No Roses*, this was so much more than just some Namedroppers' Convention. As Ashley elucidates,

'Some of the cameo appearances were crucially important. Like ...
Richard Thompson. I'd [consciously] created an Albion Band that
was encouraged to produce such a breadth of material.' If Ashley was
always hovering nearby in spirit, the album also benefited greatly
from his little black book:

Ashley Hutchings: My major work was done before we decided to
make the album. The building blocks were in place ... [notably] the
long-term relationship with Mattacks and Simon. It's a celebration
of musical culture in England, both past and present. It takes in
everything: church music, early music, music hall, rock, folk, jazz
even. An English musical celebration.

Perversely, though, an important link to the Albion Country
Band-era was left off as one of *Rise Up*'s producers chose to omit
Linda Thompson's exquisite rendition of 'Rainbow Over The Hill',
which was instead earmarked for a single that never happened.[42] But
even without this lost Thompson classic, the album provided for a
remarkably coherent 'English musical celebration'. With the choral
'Lay Me Low'/'Gresford Disaster' song-suite and bookended by 'Time
To Ring Some Changes' and 'Ragged Heroes', the album represented
a core electric folk aesthetic that was beyond vogue.

Tams suggests 'it was built behind closed doors, slowly and in
some detail', while acknowledging Ashley's presence 'quietly in the
background, keep[ing] the engine running'. In fact, Ashley had played
a subsidiary role in its realization. Still, the untamed Tyger was keen
to proselytize the end-product, suggesting to the *Yorkshire Post* on
its release, 'Some folk-rock fans will not find this acceptable, in the
same way that some traditional folkies found folk-rock unacceptable,
but we are hoping a new, wider audience will appreciate what we
are trying to do.'

He still believed a 'new, wider audience' was just a blind step,
and a couple of glowing reviews, away. The music papers were even
prepared to do their bit. The reviews were positive, with Angus
MacKinnon, now at the *NME*, leading the way:

---

[42] It was later added to the CD edition, along with the 45 version of 'Lay Me Low'.

Once in a green moon, an album crosses the great divide between minority and majority appeal with complete confidence and conviction. I'd recommend this album to anyone, whether they like or dislike folk-derived music, in much the same way as I'd lay Miles Davis's *In A Silent Way* on the anti-jazz lobby.

Dark Star's Nick Ralph was no less fulsome in his praise, targeting those among its readership who 'mourned the passing of Fairport as a potent musical force' to 'move heaven and earth to obtain this little goodie … [which] carries on from where they peaked'. Ralph was not alone in placing *Rise Up Like The Sun* in a direct lineage from the great Fairport albums of yesteryear.

With Richard and Linda at last recording as a duo again, and Fairport putting the finishing touches to a successor to the well-received *Bonny Bunch Of Roses,* there was genuine optimism that a third wave of English folk-rock may soon be upon the land.

An Albion Band performance at the Astoria on March 10th, 1978 represented the high-water mark of such hopefulness, the evening opening with a nod to past glories, a full ensemble performance of 'Albion Sunrise', with guest singer Linda Thompson – formerly of The Albion Country Band – there to lend a hand.

A month later, a Linda-less Albion Band entered BBC's Maida Vale studios to record a session for John Peel's late-night Radio One show, these days usually frequented by the latest one, two or three chord wonder. Yet Peel felt no shame – and nor should he have – as he unabashedly championed the Albions, either side of the latest Adverts 45.

––––––––––

Sadly, less than a fortnight later the legendary DJ was obliged to introduce a new wave of listeners to another ex-Fairport singer at the precise point when that voice had been permanently stilled. It was the night of April 21st, 1978, and Sandy Denny had died from an undiagnosed embolism, the result of a fall at her parents' house in Devon three weeks earlier. It had gone untreated because her mother, Edna, was too ashamed to take her drunk daughter to the A&E for an X-ray that may well have saved her life:

Philippa Clare: She [had gone] down to Cornwall to her parents, and she fell down the stairs onto the York paving stone, and Sandy went, 'I really need help, Mum,' and her mother actually said, 'I'm not having you seen drunk.' ... When Sandy came back, she was going, 'I've got terrible headaches.'

Dave Swarbrick: I do remember her having a bad cut on her head ... She pointed it out to me. But she was drunk at the time. It was April 5th, my birthday. She took my hand and rubbed it across the top and said, 'Look at that.'

Sandy's spiral downward had continued even after she stopped writing those 'miserable songs' which had only served to perpetuate 'a vicious circle'. As she had confessed eleven months earlier, 'Being on my own, I tend to think of sad things and so I write songs that make me feel even sadder. I sit down and I write something and it moves me to tears almost. I'm fed up with feeling like that.'

Her solution, such as it was, was to record other people's songs again. She had anticipated Julie Covington – who was due to record Sandy's wistful ballad, 'By The Time It Gets Dark' – by recording her own cover, hoping to have a hit single and maybe sign a record deal on the back of that. Bryn Haworth's 'Moments' was a song she had heard him play in an adjoining studio in 1975. It was perfect for the slightly throaty vocals her lifestyle had now given her.

Recorded eleven months before her death, it would have been the perfect epitaph had Island been on their game. But what it did not capture was the pit of despair into which she was slowly sinking – and which hanging out with The Who while they recorded *Who Are You?* only made worse. Drummer Keith Moon was digging an even deeper pit and, unlike Sandy, he had the income to indulge his deathly lifestyle. Born within five months of Sandy, he would be dead within five months of her, another victim of one midnight misadventure too many.

And still Sandy continued to play the party-girl. On one brandy-fuelled jag, she phoned Pete Townshend, 'very drunk, and said that she loved me, she needed to see me, then and there. It was in the early hours.' The gifted guitarist was in bed with his wife.

Sandy continued to seek out fellow musicians, confusing the intimacy of music making with that sense of personal closeness she perpetually craved. Ex-Fotheringay bassist Pat Donaldson was one such lover with whom she maintained a long-distance liaison – although he was in New York now – searching for a connection she had once felt with her husband.

Several of the references to intimacy on *Rendezvous* were directed at Donaldson, not her wandering Aussie. Trevor, to her mind, was never there. And there was a reason. He had found a new love, one who was interested in something more permanent than a roll in the hay at Philippa Clare's flat.

Throughout those fateful final months, Sandy's whole support system had been on the fritz. As Linda candidly admits, 'I had left Richard and took the children. I thought, I can't stand this, I've had enough. So I had my own problems. My father was dying, and ... I went back to live with my mother and helped nurse him. So I don't think I had time for Sandy's problems.' Philippa was off managing Fairport; while Bambi Ballard was in the throes of divorcing journalist Robin Denselow.

No one, a sozzled Sandy had started to notice, was picking up the phone in the middle of the night. When she crashed the car in a nearby ditch on her way back from the local pub, as she did with annoying regularity, the locals were growing tired of pulling her out:

Dave Pegg: She would sometimes turn up at our house in the middle of the night ... or you'd see her car in a lay-by and she'd be in it, off her face. I mean, I've done that, but when you see it happening on a regular basis, and the village community is very small, and everybody knew what Sandy's car looked like ... We would go out and help Sandy. Everybody did whatever they [could]. But we had our own existence.

Bruce Rowland was another former comrade with whom Sandy had recently enjoyed a wee lowland fling before the veil had fallen from his eyes, 'If you gave her an inch, you were trapped. She could really make you feel bad about ignoring her.'

As Trevor'n'Sandy dissolved their decade-old co-dependency before knowing eyes, daughter Georgia was inevitably caught in the crossfire. The other Fairport wives and girlfriends were now just keeping their heads down:

Christine Pegg: Deep down we knew it had all been going wrong. We knew Trevor was thinking of going, but we'd got into the habit of keeping our heads down while the storm passed – and this time, it didn't.

After one too many occasions coming home to find the baby sitting in her baby chair in the car, Trevor finally decided to act. He rang the enabling Philippa Clare 'from Byfield. Trevor was very rarely in tears, and he was in tears: "I don't know what to do. I can't cope. She's dropped the baby down the stairs. She's driven [the car] into a hedge. I'm gonna take the kid to Australia.'"

Philippa, who had been providing Trevor and his new girlfriend safe haven at her flat, knew how to keep a secret. But Trevor remained wracked with guilt. As his second wife, Elizabeth Hurtt-Lucas, told Sandy's secondary biographer, 'He felt it was Georgia who had to come first, because Georgia couldn't look after herself at all ... He said he was no longer "in love" with Sandy, which is not the same as not loving her.'

Trevor may well have claimed as much to Elizabeth. Certainly he seems to have already been planning a new life with the daughter of Philippa Clare's upstairs neighbour. Once he formulated a plan to return to Australia with Georgia *and* his new love, there were only a few people he felt he could confide in, lest they immediately convey the news to Sandy. But at least one other girlfriend knew he was preparing to take flight, Georgia's well-being on his mind:

Bambi Ballard: She certainly didn't know that Trevor was leaving. And I did. Trevor had intimated at some point over the phone ... He [told me], 'I've reached the end of the line.' ... When she died, I thought, 'Thank God she never knew that Trevor wasn't coming back.'

It was sister Marion's partner, Nigel, who drove Trevor, Elizabeth and Georgia to the airport for the flight to Sydney, having been 'party to several conversations he had with Marion about [leaving]. He wasn't intending on coming back, that's what he told us.'

Such was the bubble she existed in now, Sandy had not seen it coming. Nor had her close friend, Miranda Ward, who was startled one Thursday evening in April when Trevor had called her from a telephone box and bluntly informed her he had left Sandy and taken Georgia with him – though he omitted one salient detail, that he was taking Sandy's daughter to the other side of the world. Prophetically, his last firing shot to Miranda was, 'You say you're her best friend – so prove it. You look after her.'

And look after her, Miranda did. But not for long. An eleventh hour phone-call from Sandy in Byfield revealed that she now knew something was up as she asked Miranda, with an unfamiliar tremor in her voice, if she had heard from Trevor. Miranda told her what she knew and offered her shelter and solace at her flat in Barnes. She even drove down to Byfield in the middle of the night to scoop her friend up, fearful of what she might do when she finally awoke to that nameless fear.

Again, Sandy felt the need of a crutch and believed her friend Miranda could supply both a physical and a psychological one. Even after Miranda drove to Byfield, picked Sandy up, and drove her back to her flat in Barnes, no one was saying anything about Trevor's whereabouts, either through misguided loyalty or plain ignorance:

Miranda Ward: Every night, after Sandy had gone to bed, I was desperately trying to track down Trevor … I needed to know, as the person who had been given responsibility for Sandy, what to do if she got in an accident. My very words to people were, 'What if she ends up in hospital in a coma?'

Throughout that final lost weekend, Miranda did her best to keep Sandy's spirits up, to keep her off the spirits and to restrict any medicine to the painkillers from her cabinet that she steadily fed to her friend for the increasingly bad headaches she had been having for the past three weeks.

Indeed, on the Monday morning, Miranda was awoken at six by a Sandy who 'wanted Painocil' as a 'very bad headache had woken her'. Unfortunately for all concerned, Miranda had now taken a day job as a schoolteacher and, as she later wrote in her diary, 'Somehow couldn't leave, but did.'

It was the last time she would see her dear friend *compos mentis*. Later that morning, Sandy was found slumped at the foot of the stairs, near the door of the bathroom, unconscious. But it was not Miranda who found her there. It was her near neighbour, musician Jon Cole, whom Miranda had asked to call in to check on her friend. He immediately called an ambulance, and then Miranda, who began to call around Sandy's friends with the worrying news that she was in a coma. When she reached Linda, at her parents', the vexed singer snapped, 'Oh, what's Sandy done *now*?'

Linda and Miranda made for a disconsolate sight as they trundled to the hospital together, only to find Sandy 'wrapped in silver foil. I sat and talked to her, the way you do with people in a coma.' Initially taken to Queen Mary's Hospital in Roehampton, the still-comatose Sandy had been transferred to the Atkinson-Morley, which specialised in brain injuries. Meanwhile, the word had gone out, find Trevor and tell him what has happened.

The message reached him at his parents' in Australia, a doctor having phoned him up in person and informed him that if he got on a plane immediately, he might just get back in time to see his wife alive. There was only one problem – Trevor had bought himself a one-way ticket.

Only by borrowing money from his father was Trevor able to make the return journey, with a heavy heart and a lifetime of memories, arriving on the Friday morning only to find there was no hope, and no opportunity to say farewell, farewell. As he sat by her bruised and beaten side, wrestling with the decision whether to let them turn off the life-support, Sandy passed away at seven-fifty that evening, barely thirty-one years of age, having been living life on the edge for too damn long. She had written her last sad refrain.

16. A New Day?

I think [Sandy] was always torn between fame and its pursuit, and the perceived freedom of lifestyle that she envied in her friend, Anne Briggs.

—RICHARD THOMPSON TO PAM WINTERS

It was like some reference point was gone, and you could never achieve certain things because of [her death].

—MADDY PRIOR TO AUTHOR

We had already been thinking about what might happen to Fairport: with Sandy gone, it felt like a piece of the jigsaw would always be missing.

—DAVE PEGG TO NIGEL SCHOFIELD

Trevor was beside himself. Whatever he'd said to his new love, his feelings for his old love had never entirely died. Now there was bound to be a police investigation into the circumstances of his wife's patently premature death. No one wanted the truth to come out, least of all him. And so the story that Sandy had fallen down Miranda's stairs became the Authorised Version, even though she could not have done so without taking several stacks of books with her.

Indeed, no one who testified at the hastily-convened inquest offered, or was able to offer, first-hand knowledge of the crucial fall at her parents' house in Devon back in March, although everyone knew that the lady had become increasingly accident-prone. A toxicology test demonstrated there were no drugs in her system. Nor was there enough booze in the house to have precipitated her collapse. And yet…

As it is, her parents would go to their graves blaming Trevor, seemingly unaware that if anyone had delivered the final blow, it was her own mother, Edna, when she decided propriety took precedence over her daughter's well-being; refusing to take her to hospital when she fell and banged her head.

It would make for a particularly bleak funeral service, which ended, as Island publicist David Sandison later recalled, 'when the damn piper walked in playing "Flowers Of The Forest". And at that

point ... we all just fell apart.' Originally penned to memorialise the
fallen at Flodden Field, the moment provided an affecting tribute
to another noble spirit who would remain forever young. However,
not everyone present at Putney Vale cemetery felt the events of the
previous month were just a series of terrible accidents:

Richard Thompson: That was the way it was going to happen and
there was nothing you could do about it ... The world was too much
for her ... I do feel that life had gotten to be too much for Sandy to
bear. Accident or not, I don't know how she would have continued
beyond that point.

Not surprisingly, impotence and guilt melding with an all-
consuming sadness enveloped everyone who had necessarily distanced
themselves from the falling comet. A keen sense of loss cast a pall not
only over proceedings at Putney Vale, but the future itself.
    As Linda told Pam Winters, 'I have known a lot of people who
have died in my life. But Sandy is the person I think of most ... For
years after she died, I thought of her every single day.' Swarbrick, who
had known the lady longer than even Linda, was consumed with a
despair which carried over to the next tour:

Philippa Clare: When Sandy died, we had to go on this tour to
Ireland. It was absolutely appalling, because the whole band was in
terrible grief and they all act[ed] out in different ways. I had Simon
on one side [of me] and Swarb on the other in the back and Swarb
started playing all Sandy's stuff on the tape machine, and of course
a fight broke out. And I'm the one ending up with a bloody nose.

There was one notable absentee at the cemetery. Ashley 'couldn't
go to the funeral. I was doing the play, *Lark's Rise* [*To Candleford*]. I
hadn't seen Sandy for some time, and the one time I'd seen her [was]
in a cafe and she was drunk.' She had offered Ashley her hand to kiss
as if he was some supplicant and, regretfully, he had refused to share
in the joke.
    Like Sandy and Linda, Ashley had been wrestling with his own
failing marriage for some months, along with a career change that few
had seen coming, effectively putting The Albion Band as a gigging

entity into mothballs in order to take the role of musical director at
the National Theatre:

Ashley Hutchings: I get a call from Bill Bryden, director of the
National Theatre, [ask]ing would your Albion Dance Band come and
do the music for *The Passion* – it wasn't called *The Mysteries* then –
which was an updating of medieval mystery plays by this great writer,
Tony Harrison. John Tams loved the idea. One or two people were
not sure about [it, and said,] 'Count me out.' [So] we do it and we
absolutely love it. One [kind of] marriage begins, another marriage
ends. Artistically, it changes everything. The nature of the Albion
Band changes forever ... Whoever is in the Albion Band that night
is in the Albion Band. From that point on, no manager. My whole
personal life is in turmoil. I'm living in London [again]. I'm going
to see plays. I'm meeting actors and TV people. The Albion Band
drops the dance and we do other plays – and we stay for four years.

The transition was not quite so smooth, or as pre-ordained, as
Ashley suggests. Both *The Mysteries*, an attempt to modernise the
Easter passion-play which would eventually take on a life of its own,
and the National's adaptation of Flora Thompson's *Lark's Rise To
Candleford* – which would consume Ashley on-and-off for the next
three years – were initially conceived as short-term projects to keep
the Albion Band active 'between projects'.

Actually, they had never been busier. *Lark's Rise* was in rehearsal
(not performance) the afternoon Sandy was buried in Putney Vale,
in preparation for a three-night stint in Milton Keynes, after a
successful run at the Cottesloe Theatre, part of the National's South
Bank complex. When the play was temporarily placed on hold,
the Albion Band took off for France to continue promoting *Rise
Up Like The Sun*. Indeed, the promotion of this welcome dose of
unabashed Albionesque folk-rock spanned the summer, culminating
in a potentially vital set on the main stage at the open-air Reading
Festival.

Here was Ashley's opportunity to convince punk-rockers who
had come to see The Jam, Patti Smith and the Tom Robinson Band
that they were missing out. Instead, as one receptive attendee wrote
in a letter to *Melody Maker*, 'John Tams and the band were a sound

for sore ears, but the audience did not appreciate this.' The response rather reminded the bassist of the one Steeleye once received from Aqualung's acolytes:

Ashley Hutchings: Some bright executive at EMI put two and two together and thought….festival, mud, outdoors….we'll have Albion Band [doing] *Rise Up Like The Sun* [in] green wellies … We really pulled all the stops out at Reading to try and do a great show. And yet cans were thrown at us. There was a stroke of genius from John Tams, he was singing a song as a can whizzed past his ear and he put out his hand and caught the can and carried on singing. Which brought a cheer from a section of the audience. But it was fairly disastrous and I think that was the end of the honeymoon as far as I was concerned with the rock scene. I wasn't sure whether we were going to go back to it after the theatre work and I didn't want to know after the Reading experience … That was probably the end of the rock world for us. After that, it was the theatre and the folk scene for me.

Reading served to convince Ashley that the battle for English rock's soul was lost. He began to batten down the South Bank hatches. Having retired to his London pied-à-terre to lick metaphorical wounds, he began rehearsing for a series of performances of *The World Turned Upside Down*, Keith Dewhurst's theatrical projection of Christopher Hill's disquisition on the radical groups that sprung up during the English Civil War.

And still Ashley tried juggling all his musical chairs. The play's October opening at the National was immediately followed by another full-blown Albion Band UK tour, appositely billed as The Winter Sun Tour and featuring an unexpected resurrection of 'A Sailor's Life'.

Two benefit shows at Hammersmith's Riverside Centre in December were confusingly billed as 'Julie Covington/The Albion Band', when as far as Ashley was concerned the chart-topping Covington was simply temporarily co-opted into another amorphous Albion Band, as were Richard and Linda.

Covington sang 'I Want To See The Bright Lights Tonight' and 'By The Time It Gets Dark' with effortless ease. In fact, her performance of the latter was so good, and Julie's love of Sandy Denny and Richard

Thompson's work so profound, that Ashley began to hatch another Albion Band project – a tour which would present the songs of two folk-rock leading lights to his own post-Fairport sound.

But that tour would have to take a backseat to yet more performances at the National at the start of 1979. It took till the following June for theatre-work to dry up long enough to allow this incarnation of the Albion Band to take to the road for a nine-date national tour.

Drafted in for the duration was Andy Roberts, someone who had enjoyed a previous association with Richard, as well as being in line for Sandy's aborted 1976 tour-band. He had never played with Fairport's father-figure, but the way it was explained to him, 'Ashley wanted to put together more of a rock band, like the early Fairport – [and] he wanted to feature Sandy Denny songs. He was going to get Julie Covington in to sing, but she cried off at the last moment.'

Covington's replacement, Melanie Harrold, did her best but she was no Julie – or Sandy. Nonetheless, the show provided a welcome reminder of both the power of the songwriting and Ashley's gift for electric folk arrangements, notably on a dramatic medley of 'North Star Grassman' and 'It'll Take A Long Time':

Ashley Hutchings: It was a great band. We did a 'sea medley' using three songs by Sandy Denny, as a tribute to Sandy. It was about fifteen minutes … It started with the sound of waves over the PA, and from under that we'd bring in the guitars. I've always thought of the sea as a metaphor for Sandy.

Actually, the bulk of the set celebrated the songs of Richard Thompson, with versions of 'Nobody's Wedding', 'Rainbow Over The Hill', 'Farewell, Farewell', 'Time To Ring Some Changes' and 'Meet On The Ledge' all featured. Also in the mix was the one song Sandy and Ashley wrote together, 'Come All Ye', and a Dylan song on which all three had excelled, 'Percy's Song'.

The shows were a great success – so much so that they were fleetingly revived the following year – and a welcome reminder to those, like Martin Carthy, who by 1980 began voicing a collective concern that, 'Albion seem to have set up shop at the NT …[but] they could walk out if they wanted to. They're a fabulous band and

if they could use that four years of being subsidised, just imagine
what they could do if they opened the door. I wish to God they
would.' For Ashley, it was all part and parcel of that unremitting
work ethic:

Ashley Hutchings: We were working six nights and two matinees.
They kept coming up with great plays and you can't say, yeah, we'll
do it but mark us out for two weeks [to tour an album] ... But by the
end there's a clamour for us to get back on the road.

Early in 1981 Ashley's hand was finally forced by John Tams, who
had been none too happy to be left with the detritus at the National
when Tyger toured his Albions-do-Fairport show, and began plotting
a breakaway band:

Ashley Hutchings: I [had done] a short tour with a completely
made up Albion Band [while] John [Tams] held the fort. They didn't
challenge [my right to do this, or ask,] 'Why have you done that?'
[but] shortly after Dispatches they formed Home Service.

A May 1981 *Melody Maker* report detailed the mass defection of
'virtually all the established Albion members'. This coup left 'Albion
guru Ashley Hutchings without a group'. It would be 1982 before
he revived the Albion Dance Band name. From this point forward,
Hutchings's path would ever be the one least travelled.

Where he missed a trick was in not releasing some sort of artifact
representing the 1979 Albion project, a rich celebration of that period
when English electric folk had a cutting edge.

Ashley was not alone in failing to memorialise the loss of Sandy
in official form. Richard and Linda had been performing 'It'll Take
A Long Time' at their 1979 shows, before cutting a heartbreaking
version of 'I'm A Dreamer' for the original, unreleased version of
Shoot Out The Lights. Neither appeared on record. Nor did an equally
heartfelt tribute from Thin Lizzy's Phil Lynott, intended as a solo
A-side called simply 'Sandy'.[43]

---

[43] The lovely track features on a European Thin Lizzy bootleg CD called *Rare Tracks Vol. 2*.

As the shockwaves from Sandy's death continued rippling below the oft-shallow surface of popular song, the band with whom her name would always be synonymous addressed the dying of the light. The very man who had wrestled the reins from Ashley in 1969 had started to tire of the touring treadmill.

A four-album solo deal with Transatlantic, which Philippa Clare had negotiated on Swarb's behalf back in 1976, meant he could indulge his love of folk music with anyone who took his fancy, while retaining the gig-generating capabilities of the folk-rock brand he had driven into the ground. He admitted as much in a *Melody Maker* interview he gave to promote his third (and best) Transatlantic solo album, 1981's *Smiddyburn*:

> Having been with [the band] for ten years, I didn't have any more ideas left [that would work] with that sort of electric set-up … Probably Fairport should have split maybe six years earlier … [After that,] you're down to three or four tracks off an album that are good and the rest are dross.

Swarb's retrospective quotient of good v. bad was overly generous. There was no escaping the fact that the two albums which had really done for Fairport's good name – *Rosie* and *Gottle O'Geer* – had both begun life as solo Swarbrick projects, only to mutate into lesser Fairport albums.

There was even less left in the locker when Swarb and his fellow survivors convened in February 1978 to record a successor to *Bonny Bunch Of Roses*. The fiddler had just recorded two albums' worth of traditional tunes for Transatlantic and the well was dry.

Tippler's Tale, Fairport's second album for Phonogram, would prove a slap in the face for anyone who thought the band had turned again a corner creatively in 1977:

Philippa Clare: *Tippler's Tale* was the beginning of the slide, [although] they were earning more money than they [ever] had before. They were working and it was going into their pockets. Germany loved them. Denmark loved them.

Further hastening Fairport's dissolution was the unresolvable issue of Swarb's hearing, which had become so damaged from years of electric amplification that he was given an ultimatum by the specialist he consulted at the end of 1978, 'Basically ... I had two choices – stop playing regularly with a loud electric band or go deaf.' The band manager, as concerned as anyone, was now infected by the band's growing fatalism:

Philippa Clare: Swarb already knew he had problems with his ears – sometimes he was so deaf, he would press the fiddle up so hard into his jaw, [just] so he could hear the music through the bones. He had various ear operations and it was getting too much. [And] I think everyone had just had enough. It was getting fractious.

When Clare was summoned to Phonogram to discuss Fairport's future plans, it was made plain that they really didn't have one, at least not on a major label: 'They wanted to drop [us. But] they had to pay [us off] because we could make an album [out] of stuff we'd rejected from other albums – it all technically passed the test.' As it is, they were contracted for another four albums:

Dave Pegg: They said, 'Please don't make any more albums.' ... We said, 'Sorry, we're going to send you another four, one a month if necessary.' In the end, they paid us not to make any more.

It was probably the best payday the band ever enjoyed, and once again it was thanks to Clare. But it also meant no other label would touch them with a ten-foot pole, let alone subsidise another Swarb-led project. The time had come to knock it on the head.

The final blow to the band's shaky equilibrium came when Bruce Rowland turned up to rehearsals with his new wife, Birgitte, who once designed the *Full House* album sleeve. At this time she had been the young bride of Fairport's frantic fiddler:

Philippa Clare: Bruce was living with Swarb's second wife. So that had its moments. No wonder they had to have a woman manager! We did have a rule – no wives or girlfriends on tour – but Bruce and [Birgitte] were like John and Yoko. And they would bring the dog and the picnic basket, [even] book into another hotel. Bruce and Swarb were pretty tight at one point, but it got a bit furry round the edges when Birgitte came on the scene. Fairport is a very dysfunctional family, and after a bit it gets very wearing. There are periods when they fall out and periods when they fall in, but Bruce wasn't easy. I always had to check his hotel room, [in case] he'd stolen the TV or the curtains.

By spring 1979, the band – to a man – agreed it was time to end the masquerade and, if not go out in a blaze of glory, at least stop embarrassing themselves. The same view was reflected in Colin Irwin's *Melody Maker* review of their very last London show, at the Theatre Royal:

> As they drift off into the sunset it seems irreverent to chide them now, but … well, we wouldn't really have lost any great contribution to art had they quit three years ago, when Sandy left for the second time. And despite the unswerving loyalty of a following which brought them back for numerous encores, and the obvious emotion of the occasion, there was very little in Saturday's show (opening their farewell tour) worthy of climaxing such a distinguished tradition.

A sense of relief was palpable, especially from those band members who still recalled the *Full House* era, to which the first half of most of the shows were now devoted, featuring 'Walk Awhile', 'Dirty Linen', 'Journeyman's Grace', 'Adieu Adieu', 'Sloth' and 'Flatback Caper':

Simon Nicol: [After] three-and-a-half years with that line-up, we'd had enough. 'Cause Swarb and I divided into one camp; Bruce and Peggy [were] in the other. Quite often, it felt like there were two bands onstage. Sometimes it was difficult getting through the evening musically.

Dave Pegg: Everybody was too old and set in their ways to try anything new … We'd got an audience back [but] we moved into doing Civic Halls and stuff, and we were doing very middle of the road gigs; it was more like a cabaret show.

If the quartet's avuncular musicality was no longer sufficient to sustain the artifice that this was the same band responsible for *Unhalfbricking, Liege & Lief* and *Full House*, they retained the well-earnt regard of some musicians from the same milieu with a few more million in the bank.

And so it was that Fairport found themselves invited to open an outdoor show in the grounds of Knebworth House on August 4th, 1979, which also signalled the return of their old playmates Led Zeppelin to an English stage for the first time in four years. Zeppelin themselves, unbeknownst to its members, were less than a year away from being deflated for the last time.

The huge crowd's reaction to Fairport's greatest hits set was largely one of bemusement. But it was, as Simon says, 'A splendid pay-off day. We had to go on first. And [we were the] first away. 'Cause we had another gig … but it wasn't [to] 120,000. I'd never seen a PA that big – there wasn't a PA that big in the UK. The Clair Brothers had flown one in. The forty-five minutes flew by, [we] said ta-ra to everybody and set off up the A41.'

Determined to play their final set to the faithful, the four Fairporters still standing had organized an altogether more exclusive show later on that summer's day in the field of a local farmer, near the village of Cropredy, a name soon synonymous with Fairport's now-annual Convention. In 1979, Karl Dallas took the view, 'With eighteen albums behind them, … Fairport ha[ve] certainly earned their [rest]. Time, at last, to move on to something new.'

Quite what this something new might be, no one knew, as everyone flew off in distinctly different directions. Dave Pegg had recently joined the swelling ranks of Jethro Tull, who continued to command arena-size audiences, while the other Dave still had two solo albums left on his Transatlantic deal.

As for Simon, he was gainfully employed again as the onstage foil to a reinvigorated Richard and Linda Thompson, who had a new label and a new album to promote. And the final Fairport line-up had product, a posthumous live album from the last tour, fittingly called *Farewell, Farewell* and overseen by the business-like bassist:

Dave Pegg: When we knew we were splitting, rather than just go out on nothing, [we thought] we'll just do a farewell record, and we'll

put it out ourselves … So we just pressed up three thousand of them
and sold them from here.

The first pressing soon sold out, and it continued to sell whenever
it was repressed by the label Pegg had formed as a potential outlet for
Fairportees' side projects and archival releases, Woodworm Records.
But the actual music on the album confirmed that the band had called
it a day just in time, being one of the least rewarding artifacts to ever
bear that once-proud name.

———————

Perhaps artifacts like this were preying on Richard Thompson's
mind when he was asked – the same year *Farewell, Farewell* appeared
– whatever happened to the English brand of folk-rock? He brusquely
replied, 'Folk-rock music came to a dead end.'

Thankfully, he and his chanteuse-wife would still find a way to
carry folk-rock's flickering torch the last few steps to Babylon, even
if they were finding 1979's musical climate almost as challenging as
the Fairports.

Having unexpectedly resurrected his fast fading career at the end of
1977, after two years adrift in a miasma of inner-doubt, torn between
a sincere faith and a God-given gift for making music, Richard
sensed himself being pulled under by the tides of post-punk even as
his manager threw him a lifeline: a two-album deal with Chrysalis
Records that resulted in the underrated *First Light* (1978) and the
patchy *Sunnyvista* (1979).

After the Julie Covington 'Easy To Slip' session in October
1977 rekindled the guitarist in him, he had informed Jo Lustig the
dynamic duo was ready to record again. All he needed was a label
that believed his gifts were undiminished by daily prayer; preferably
one fattened by the surge of new wave sounds yet retaining a
penchant for past times.

In December 1977, the couple drew up a list of songs to demo
before pitching their new, spiritually-tinged material to a brave
new world. Wisely, Richard put the Mighty Babies out with the
bathwater, cutting three songs acoustically, two with Linda on lead
– 'Strange Affair' and 'First Light' – both songs debuted live the
previous May.

By the time Chrysalis entered the frame, most of the longer, soul-fused songs from that tour, like 'Rescue Me', 'The King Of Love' and 'Fire In The Garden', had been jettisoned (along with the magnificent 'Madness Of Love', later revisited by Graham Parker, Polly Bolton and John French). In fact, just three songs from the 1977 live set would make the album – one of which Linda was not so keen on:

Linda Thompson: Yeah, we did talk over things but he was very autonomous – if that's the word – [about] having a finished song. Occasionally he'd play me things that I didn't like and he'd say, 'Tell me the truth,' and I'd go, 'Oh, I don't like that very much.' Then he wouldn't speak to me for three days. [That happened with] a couple of the songs on *First Light* – maybe 'Layla', [and] a couple of those Sufi songs. But he was funny. He'd go, 'No, I don't mind at all.' 'But you obviously do. You're not speaking to me…' [And] the stuff that he threw away… Oh my God! Because if anything was a little schmaltzy, [forget it].

As a return to recording beckoned, Richard agreed to keep his hand in – and renew his own relationship with the producer he trusted most – by playing lead on a Julie Covington album, which had finally come together after much toing and froing between producer and diva about choice of songs and musicians.

Her nominated producer remained convinced she should tackle the kind of show tunes that suited her strident voice. Even after she showed she had (half) a folk-rock album in her, Boyd never did feel he got the balance right:

Joe Boyd: The Julie Covington record suffered [because although] the tracks all sounded great, and it was well produced, it didn't suit Julie. The material wasn't really right for her.

The end result was certainly an odd mix of folk-rock and soft pop, contemporary and nostalgic. And the album did very little on its release, with the Kate Bush and John Lennon covers simply not working. Yet her versions of 'I Want To See The Bright Lights Tonight' and 'By The Time It Gets Dark' prove that her instincts weren't wholly awry. An album of folk-rock might have worked. As it is, the most folk-rock aspect on other tracks was Richard's playing, which left some other musicians speechless:

Joe Boyd: ['Only Women Bleed'] triggered an album with Julie, and we could've used Richard and Simon and Mattacks and Pegg, but we decided to use Andy Newmark, [Willie Weeks] and the guy from Little Feat, [Neil Larsen], on keyboards. [So] I said, 'Let's put Richard in that. That's a rhythm section.' I was just wanting to prove to him you can play with the best. Don't settle. By that time Jo Lustig had Chrysalis cued up as a label [for Richard and Linda]. Andy and Willy and Neil [had] never heard of Richard Thompson. I remember each one of them coming in the control room at a certain point on the first day and [whispering,] 'Who the fuck is this? Where did you get this guy from? He's unbelievable.' ... [So] I started hatching the next part of the plot ... 'How much time have you guys got?' 'We could stay another few days.' I went to Joe Lustig and I just said, 'If you don't get Chrysalis to fund going in the studio with these guys and making a record, you're a total fool.' I probably [offered to] produce it. But they didn't ask me. Jo Lustig ... was always a bit hard to get along with, for me. I didn't care. [I thought,] 'John Wood can do it. I'm just pleased that they've got this band.'

A slight whiff remains of some financial sleight of hand that allowed the American rhythm-section on Covington's album to also work on Richard and Linda's 'comeback' LP. If Virgin did unwittingly pick up a larger part of the tab for bringing the Americans over, it was unnecessary. Chrysalis were hardly hard up, having recently struck platinum with Blondie. Yet Simon Nicol's memory is that 'the Julie Covington album ... was a way of affording the American rhythm-section. One album underwrote the other.'[44] The Americans certainly wanted the issue of their fee resolved at the earliest opportunity:

Linda Thompson: Andy Newmark ... used to say, 'Are you paying me single scale, double scale or triple scale because I have different jokes for every [rate]... If you're paying me triple scale – fantastic

[44] According to the usually reliable Boyd, the Richard and Linda sessions were slotted between the Covington sessions when 'it became clear that Julie's voice wouldn't be up to working every day'.

jokes. If you're just paying me single scale, [not so good].' We said, 'We're hardly paying you at all.' He goes, 'No jokes then. No jokes.'

When the Yankee interlopers found Linda to be another first-rate torch-ballad singer, they probably expected more of the same. But she was a very different personality from the perpetually edgy Julie, grateful for the opportunity given her by the label Tull manager Terry Ellis and Chris Wright formed to populate another Island but hardly looking to the long-term:

Linda Thompson: Chrysalis gave us [the] money to make that record. We had a budget. I guess [it was] a professional record ... but [by] then, music was more of a hobby for me. You know, I was looking after kids and doing stuff and blah-blah-blah. The songs were different because they were religious type songs, so I maybe didn't like them as much ... although I did like 'Pavanne'.

Quite how much sessionwork the new rhythm-section even did on the fourth Richard and Linda album is a matter of dispute. Richard told *Swing 51* a decade later, 'The worst stuff I did was where a lot of time was taken in the studio ... [like on] *First Light*.' Yet at the time he was insisting the basic tracks were done in the blink of a TV eye:

Richard Thompson: We only had the rhythm section for three days, we had to be very specific. We tried DM but everybody seemed to be working at the time. We were thinking of people like Steve Gadd, but Andy Newmark and Willie Weeks were coming over anyway. It was a risk using them, but it's given it a slightly different feeling. [1978]

The ex-Fairport contingent was represented by Simon Nicol, who found the time amid the busy touring schedule Philippa Clare had drawn up for the year. Indeed, Clare herself found time to contribute backing vocals, as did Covington herself, Andy Fairweather-Low and Maddy Prior (taking a break from Steeleye, at the height of their post-Ashley commerciality). Also providing a cameo was Ian Matthews, trying to resurrect his career in Britain after deals with Elektra and

CBS in the States had taken him nowhere special. It seems he had not been keeping tabs on the Thompsons:

Ian Matthews: The Julie Covington LP was happening, and he just invited me to sing. I didn't know what he'd been doing. I didn't know he'd been through a conversion. But it wasn't a shock, knowing Richard.

While Linda was happy to leave 'Layla' to Richard and Ian, her singing in the studio was never better. The decision to use the Americans on the basic tracks meant that the practice of recording mostly live had to be abandoned and the tracks built up from basic track to final mix. This gave Linda a real chance to shine vocally. And for the first time she contributed lyrically, inventing the beautiful but deadly 'Pavanne', a *femme fatale* who took the phrase all too literally. The result of a strange dream she had one time, Richard pushed her to finish the lyric herself, only to meet unexpected resistance:

Linda Thompson: Who would bother to write songs if you've got Richard Thompson writing songs for you? Although Richard was fantastic with me. If ever he'd hear me humming a tune he'd go, 'What's that?' And I go, 'I don't know. I'm just humming a tune.' He'd go, 'No, that's great.' But mostly I didn't do it, because why would you when somebody is saying, 'Do you want to sing this? It's called "Dimming Of The Day"' – [still] one of the best songs I've ever heard.

This was a very different artistic relationship to the one John and Beverley Martyn 'enjoyed', even if Linda sees 'a lot of parallels with me and Richard and John and Beverley. You know, they're solo players, Richard and John … They [both] wanted to be just doing it on their own with other musicians in the background.'

If Beverley had been a fine songwriter in her own right before she ever met John, there were other parallels. Although John and Beverley would make only two albums together, the span of their marriage almost exactly mirrors Richard and Linda's, lasting a decade and ending in angry recriminations, set to an album that seemed to chart an inevitable collapse (the 1980 cult classic, *Grace And Danger*).

And if Martyn lost his way musically in the second half of the seventies, with the indifferent *One World* the only album Island issued between 1975 and 1980, Richard would later suggest he was guilty of the same charge:

Richard Thompson: In the seventies, I just wasn't thinking tightly enough to make a difference. Especially the later seventies, where I made really indifferent records. I just didn't have my mind on the job … *First Light* sounds like it's trying to be commercial in a really kind of pathetic way … It was trying to be something to please other people, which I'm very bad at doing.

In fact, Thompson has gone out of his way to impose his rather skewered view of the 1978 album's merits on rock critics, 'dissing' it at every turn and allowing it to drift out of catalogue (like its successor, *Sunnyvista*).[45]

In concert he has also treated this underrated record with scant regard, rarely – if ever – playing any songs. Yet no matter how often Richard dismisses the duo's 'comeback' album, it represented very much a return to form. One of the most overlooked records of the era, *First Light* belongs in the first rank of English folk-rock, even if musically it belongs only by association.

The one pukka folk-rock excursion on the whole record is the six-and-a-half minute 'Died For Love', which sounds like a traditional cover but was actually Thompson returning to the well, crafting something in the idiom for Linda to sing.[46] The result is a sight for sore ears even if held down by a rhythm-section with as much feel for English tradition as its countrymen had for punk-rock.

As a preview of sorts for that all-instrumental album he was still threatening to record, Thompson addended his original (based on the 'Railroad Boy' family of songs) with traditional instrumental, 'The Choice Wife'. It allowed listeners to take an acoustic break from the on-the-beat calisthenics of the Americans, most evident on the previous track, 'Don't Let A Thief Steal Into Your Heart', one of a

---

[45] The two Chrysalis albums are Thompson's only records unavailable on CD, save in the collectors' market.
[46] The original demo for the song was actually sung by Richard.

number of songs from the period which seemed to address romantic love but was really a call to *believe*.

One suspects Thompson's ambivalent feelings about the end results are inextricably bound up with his feelings about the whole so-called Sufi period, much as Dylan has all but dismissed the songs from *Slow Train Coming* and *Saved* from his mind (and set-lists) since 1981, having toured those two albums into the ground in 1979-80.

The Thompsons did much the same, returning to the road in November 1978 and staying there for much of the next fourteen months, pushing and peddling both albums Chrysalis signed off on. And although Richard and Linda's return to the boards passed much of the post-punk music media by, their reemergence was greeted with relief by those who had seen Sandy fade to black and heard Fairport's and the Albion Band's steady decline into comfortable musical niches.

For Richard, the prospect of resuming touring eighteen months on from the 'Sufi tour' brought up all the old issues of what to play and, more importantly, what to ignore from his impressive back catalogue. Once again, he seemed determined to alienate a diminishing fan base by telling the papers he couldn't relate to his earlier albums:

Richard Thompson: I've been listening to some of our old albums but I can't subscribe to the emotive content of them anymore … They're emotions I don't like to keep churning up, I'd rather chuck them away. The problem was, they were self-evoked, which is something I no longer consciously want to be. I'd rather it was more directed and more detached. All the best music is un-self-evoked and detached. [1978]

The impending tour seemingly filled him with a nameless dread. Even before it started, he was talking about the less than a dozen dates as a 'huge tour … four polytechnics in all. Salford [University] is terrible, it's a khazi,' before depicting touring as 'a very hard way of life. If I didn't have a family, perhaps I'd still be doing it'.

One can't help but wonder where he developed this aversion to seats of higher learning, and Salford in particular – a place he had never previously played (though his description of Maxwell Hall was certainly apposite). His concert-going audience, such as it was, generally resided in such places.

Given his non-existent commercial profile, a theatre tour was certainly out of the question. Even the London date was the relatively plush, but hardly capacious Drury Lane Theatre. Nor was Thompson helping to put bums on seats when he made it clear that certain songs from the canon were strictly out of bounds – 'Calvary Cross', for starters:

Richard Thompson: One thing I consciously avoid these days is recycling a particular emotional state in the music. I don't want to go through that thing of rehashing one's own dramas. If you sing a song every night, every night you look into that song. I'm more careful now which songs I look into ... The woman in 'Calvary Cross' was music; a view of music as something that can possess you – [until] you're working for it, rather than the other way around ... I used to feel very enslaved by music. [1979]

If 'Calvary Cross' was out, so were 'For Shame Of Doing Wrong' and 'Night Comes In', the two other guitar workouts that had once bolstered the *Pour Down* set-list and threatened to blow the fuses of a fair few 'khazis' of higher learning.

At the first night of the *First Light* tour – at that khazi of khazis, Maxwell Hall – the set-list was almost a return to the Sufi tour. There were just two nods to the man he once was: 'Bright Lights', the nightly opener, and a moving 'Genesis Hall', sung by Linda as part-tribute to her friend Sandy, with even Richard succumbing to its charms, unleashing a guitar solo straight from Revelation.

The rest of the set was either post-Sufi songs (nine of them) or covers – one of which referenced Fairport's heyday, Ricky Nelson's 'Things You Gave Me'. At least this time the new songs were theoretically available on the duo's new album. Indeed, save for the title-track, the album he would later brand as 'trying to be commercial in a really kind of pathetic way' was featured in its entirety.

Once again, Richard seemed determined to test the tolerance of his fan base for new material – and his record label's willingness to provide tour support. There was still one question he failed to articulate nightly – save in the music, which was once again a joy to hear: Did he really want to be doing this? He was doing a damn good impression of not wanting to be treading the boards in the couple of sitdown interviews Chrysalis arranged pre-tour:

Quite frequently [I felt] I didn't want to come back to [touring].
If you're knocking your head against a brick wall, what's the point
of doing it? …. If I can go somewhere else in music, that's fine. As
long as it's interesting, it's fine. When it stops being interesting, you
wonder why [bother] … I don't care that much.

But it didn't take long for that old witch from Calvary to weave
her spell. The music slowly began to possess this past master of the
electric guitar. A radio broadcast from Drury Lane demonstrated
that 'House Of Cards' and 'Layla' had as much potential for musical
pyromania as any sign on the cross; while a second encore of 'Then
He Kissed Me' suggested he had dusted off a Bunch of old records.

It helped that the pair had enlisted a familiar crew to tour the toilets
of England: John Kirkpatrick and Dave Pegg signing on along with
Dave Sheen, Graham Bond's ex-drummer. (DM continued to eschew
the road.) And far from disappearing from view after that initial tour
failed to create a chink in the charts, they resumed touring duties
the following February, with more universities opening their doors
to the duo.

This time around the set-list was more familiar to the faithful.
'Night Comes In' was resurrected, 'Then He Kissed Me' retained and
a double dose of country-rock restored to favour (including 'Your
Cheatin' Heart'). As a tribute to Sandy, Linda even sang 'It'll Take
A Long Time'. All vied with the recent songs, one of which was so
new it had yet to be recorded.

'You're Gonna Need Somebody' confirmed that the next step in
the duo's musical rehabilitation would involve a degree of brow-
beating, now with a socio-political dimension. The previous October,
Richard had informed the ever-supportive *Melody Maker* – now edited
by Richard Williams – that he knew which aspect of modern living
he wanted the next album to address. It was the same target as punk:
a generation's alienation:

[Thompson] says that much of the music he's written since recording
[*First Light*] has been overtly political, which has led him to a
dilemma. It's dangerous to become political, and he's not sure if he'll
sing these new songs in public because they are so political: 'I don't
know if it's the right time to say those things … I'm not very good at

explaining things, and rather than explain them in a clumsy way it's better to hear the songs ... [But] if you look at the world outwardly then it's madness. It's chaos. You have to look somewhere else if you want to find anything at all. Any meaning in life. Any calm.'

Six months later he would again warm to his theme in an interview with *Rolling Stone*, who for the first time in nearly a decade had remembered its former fondness for this folk-rock favourite. Ostensibly promoting *First Light*, which was struggling to gain any solid Stateside distribution, the singer-songwriter still refused to candy coat the message:

Richard Thompson: What's more interesting ... is beyond emotions, or to say things of a social or even political nature ... If you don't believe in anything beyond the solidarity of this world, then the world is a terrible place ... All you can do is get out of it. And the way to get out of it, as far as I can see, is to look inside yourself. [1979]

The political dimension on songs like 'Civilisation', 'Sunnyvista' and 'Justice In The Streets' could not disguise the fact that they were three of the weakest tracks to ever spume forth from his quill. If the last of these never made the live set, the satirical title-track was soon hastily dropped. Only 'Civilisation' survived into 1980, segueing into The Chantays' 1962 instrumental hit, 'Pipeline'.

By now, the couple knew neither reviewers nor longtime fans enjoyed the joke. Nor did some of the targets for their ire. The album cover – which used the logo of well-known package-tour operator Thompsons to lambast modern councils' housing policy – resulted in a writ.

At least 'You're Gonna Need Somebody' and 'Why Do You Turn Your Back?' demonstrated that Richard's politico-posturing wasn't just a covert attack on the infidels. Elsewhere, too, Richard Thompson was telling an uncaring world it was living on 'Borrowed Time', which used the same quasi-traditional imagery found on 'Genesis Hall', a decade earlier, to identify the enemy:

> There's riders in the country,
> They're taking heads for bounty,
> Wake up Corrine, they come to ride us down...

This was more like it, as was an inflammatory guitar-break he invariably addended to this tale of hard times. But after the promise of *First Light*, *Sunnyvista* was a worrying retreat into a black and white world. And once again, the little lady had been returned to the shadows – as if Richard had gotten Linda to tow the line and could proceed accordingly.

On the first side of the album Linda is largely a bystander. Even the second side – which includes the three songs that almost salvage the album, 'Lonely Hearts', 'Sisters' and 'Traces Of My Love', all featuring Linda on lead vocals – had the injudicious 'Justice In The Streets'.

At least Richard had the wit not to use his mocking rewrite of The Kinks' 'Lola', 'Woman Or A Man'. What on first listen seemed like a witty vignette about a man who falls for an individual who is so androgynous the suitor wonders 'if she was a woman or a man', hid a far more deep-rooted aversion to the blurring of gender in this modern world. When Joe Boyd raised the issue with Linda, she professed her complete ignorance:

Linda Thompson: I'm an idiot. Joe was saying to me, 'You know, [there are] so many misogynistic songs of Richard's...' Honestly I never even thought about it. Perhaps I just didn't want to look at it. There's none as blind [as she] who will not see. And that was me.

If 'Lonely Hearts' – one of just three *Sunnyvista* songs to survive in the live set until the final Richard and Linda tour in May 1982 – also suggested an underlying contempt for those destined 'to remain outcasts in love and the losers in gain', fortunately, the emotion conveyed in Linda's delivery rescued the song from moroseness and imbued it with a real yearning.

But even some of her most affecting vocals could not salvage one of her husband's more misguided career moves as the album was savaged critically and ignored commercially. And unlike Phonogram, Chrysalis had no need to pay off the puritan in Sufi clothing to end their brief association and close the book on the great seventies English folk-rock experiment. They just needed to terminate the peripatetic pair's recording contract, for the second time in three years.

NEW MUSICAL EXPRESS

THE THOMPSONS & SON. Pic: PENNIE SMITH

A CONVOCATION WITH AYATOLLAH THOMPSON

Yayha and Ruqayya (alias RICHARD and LINDA THOMPSON) discuss Amputation, Stoning People To Death and The Destruction Of The Touareg over a working breakfast with Infidel reporter GRAHAM LOCK

After he did Tubular Bells, *Mike Oldfield called up Richard and said, 'Let's do an album together.' I said, 'Richard, you've got to do it.' And he said, 'I would if I could. I'm not being difficult here. I can't.'*

—LINDA THOMPSON TO AUTHOR

It has been put to me that I could have sold more records if I did this or that, joined certain bands at certain times, used up-market record producers or toured more … but I'm a very perverse person … If someone says, 'Oh, terrific guitar playing', my first instinct is to think I should take up another instrument.

—RICHARD THOMPSON, *ROLLING STONE*, 5TH APRIL 1979

If *Sunnyvista* sold Linda and the label short, the ensuing shows proved to be everything the imperfect platter was not. A ninety-minute concert in Hamburg, partly broadcast on the Europe-wide syndicate *Rockpalast* in January 1980, caught the live band – now featuring Fairportee Simon Nicol and a troubled Pat Donaldson – at their blistering best.[47]

As per usual, the presence of Simon seems to have calmed Linda's nerves and soothed her larynx as she delivered impassioned interpretations of 'Pavanne', 'Strange Affair', 'Lonely Hearts', 'Sisters' and a version of Sandy Denny's 'I'm A Dreamer' life-enhancing enough to raise the dead, at least *in memoriam*.

As for Richard, three months of plugging away at the electric had convinced him to plug in for good. 'For Shame Of Doing Wrong', 'Night Comes In' and 'Borrowed Time' were all edge-of-the-seat musical rides. Even 'Civilisation' now had a direct pipeline to the witchy muse of electric music.

It was November 1975 all over again, save that Chrysalis had neither the wit to record one of these live shows for potential product, nor to retain the pair's services for a third album. The eight demos the couple recorded at Dave Pegg's home studio in June – including

---

[47] The full concert was broadcast digitally in the nineties. The original WDR broadcast ran to 35 mins.

'Walking On A Wire', 'Wall Of Death' and 'Just The Motion' –
suggested it could be their best collection since *Bright Lights*.

By the time Richard and Linda Thompson had returned to the
road in March 1980 for another national tour, the writing was on the
khazi walls. Another day in the sun seemed to be drawing to a close,
leaving them reduced to playing support to a contemporary of theirs
who had recently ridden the gravy train.

As it happens, this eleven-date tour appeared to prove that some
people really were lucky in life, unlucky in love. The headliner was
Gerry Rafferty, of Stealers Wheel fame, whose recent 45 'Baker
Street' had been a worldwide phenomenon, topping singles charts
both sides of the pond. He had followed up that success with a
fine album, *Night Owl*, on which Thompson thrice lent timbre
and tone.

The spring shows also reunited Simon Nicol and Dave Mattacks
with Richard, edging ever nearer to a reformed *Full House* line-up,
minus Swarb. Sadly, Pegg was still too busy to busk along, leaving
bassist Andy Brown to preserve the sonic status quo with a little
folk-rock à la mode.

The tour gave the headliner pause, too, as he witnessed the pair
win over his own crowd with new songs like 'Just The Motion' and
'The Wrong Heartbeat', both demoed in June. In fact, Thompson
had been writing up a storm, so much so that a number of the songs
demoed that month would have to make do with inclusion on solo
live albums, fan club cassettes and/or latterday Fairport albums (in
the case of 'How Many Times Do You Have To Fall?', all three).

At the end of the spring tour, the cash-rich pop star approached
his fellow ex-folkie Richard with a proposal, unaware that there was
at least one other producer waiting in the wings, with whom the
Thompsons had a more symbiotic association:

Joe Boyd: When I started at Hannibal, Richard was still very much
under contract to Chrysalis. Right around the time that I was severing
my relationship with Island and setting out as an independent – the
summer [of 1980] – I got word that Chrysalis wasn't picking up
Richard's option. Neither record had sold. They dropped him. [So]
I spoke to Richard and said, 'Come on. I've got a label. Let's make
a record.' ... And he said, 'That sounds like a good idea.' Anyway, I

[then] called Jo Lustig and he said, 'We don't want any independent deal. We want a major label deal. And I've got one.' 'Really? With who?' He said, 'Gerry Rafferty and Hugh Murphy are setting up this production company. They have a deal with United Artists. They're going to produce Richard and it's going to come out on UA.' So then I spoke to Richard and I said, 'Gerry Rafferty and Hugh Murphy? Really??' And he said, 'Yeah. It'll be different. I think it'll be a challenge. It'll be fun.' … Richard's always had this idea that he could make a pop record.

The guitarist who railed against the music industry's shallow sensibility and obsession with success had a secret he was reluctant to share with anyone but his nearest and dearest. After five years in the wilderness, and without a record label for the second time in three years, Richard was looking to make a hit record. He thought he had the songs to do it – and Rafferty agreed:

Linda Thompson: I know from when I was with Richard, he wanted to produce commercial records. He wanted people to buy his records. I mean, he really did. He wasn't in it to be obscure. I love being obscure. There's no pressure. And all these years later … the records are still selling … He tried to be more commercial. He really tried, but … he [also] managed to not say that very much.

Perhaps the married couple should have interpreted events at their first show that 'summer' – the live debut of those recently demoed songs with a full rock band featuring DM *and* Simon – as a sign all might not go to plan. The Bedford College Folk Society – of which esteemed body the author was a member – decided to spend most of its annual budget putting Richard and Linda on at the Open Air Theatre, across the Inner Circle from the co-ed college, expecting a crowd to turn up on the day and fill a venue more used to Shakespeare than folksong.

Instead, it poured and poured, prompting Linda to recall, 'The rain! It was biblical. Another portent of doom and gloom.'

The show still took place, just under a tarpaulin cover with the small crowd huddled in a circle around the musicians, assigned a couple of amps each and a hi-hat, snare and bass drum for DM to play. Hardly an auspicious unveiling of the proto-*Shoot Out The Lights* set! Nonetheless, there was room for powerful versions of 'Borrowed Time', 'Wall Of Death' and 'The Wrong Heartbeat', and the welcome return of 'Dark End Of The Street' and 'Hard Luck Stories'. The lucky few had no way of knowing that what they had seen was a form of rebirth.

Richard and Linda followed this not-so-dry run with a return to a folk club, a semi-secret acoustic show at the Black Horse Folk Club in Amberley. Reverting to their roots, the duo busked their way through 'The Train That Carried My Girl From Town', 'Break My Mind', 'Crying In The Rain' and 'Blues In The Bottle'. Almost like old times.

It was just a one-night-only nod to the past. Richard was firmly focused on the future, working up the material he needed to make that 'pop record'. Hence, the inclusion of a single new song in Amberley, 'Just The Motion'. The other tunes he intended to include would need a familiar band of musical brothers.

Four festival dates made up the rest of the summer schedule – a late July appearance at the South Yorkshire Folk Festival, two sets at the Cambridge Folk Festival in early August and a full electric Thompsons set at the first Cropredy Fairport reunion.

At these shows, Richard and Linda would be backed by Dave Mattacks, Simon Nicol, husband and wife team John Kirkpatrick and Sue Harris, and for three of the four, multi-instrumentalist Pete Zorn (who was obliged to make way for Pegg at Cropredy). Here were all the essential components of the band that would make *Shoot Out The Lights* – twice! – and then tour it till the wheels came off.

The plan appears to have been to work up the new material live in readiness for entering the studio in early September to start the album. At the Cambridge Folk Festival, a nine-song set broadcast over the BBC World Service comprised two songs from 1975, 'For Shame Of Doing Wrong' and 'Jet Plane In A Rocking Chair', and seven unreleased songs, five of which would end up on *Shoot Out The Lights*.[48] The promotion of their sixth album had started a year and a half early.

---

[48] 'How Many Times Do You Have To Fall?' and 'Speechless Child' – a song about an abused child – would not, though the latter would feature on a BBC World Service broadcast of the Cambridge set.

At the end of August, the Thompsons' fully-serviced musical vehicle moved to a field on the outskirts of Oxford for the first Fairport reunion, a day-long event bolstered by stand-alone sets from Ralph McTell and Richard and Linda. Given that this was an audience which accepted no substitutes, Pegg stepped in on bass.

Zorn and Peggy would trade places a few times more while Richard and Linda's sixth album came to life and their marriage died a death. Had he attended the 'Rafferty' sessions, the Fairport bassist would not have had to travel far. At least recording the album at Chipping Norton Studios suited another long-term collaborator:

Simon Nicol: I think the [Rafferty-produced tracks] are charming, and it brings back that time. That was done in Chipping Norton, which is where I was living. So I used to walk to work. The others were all staying residentially. [I guess] I was missing out on all the bonding between the band and the producer, [who were] all living together. I was just clocking off. [But] there are some very interesting comparisons to be made with the [released] version. I wouldn't write off the Rafferty version – I think there are some very worthwhile, tweaked arrangements – 'Don't Renege On Our Love' for one. And Zorn's bass playing is outstanding.

If Simon retains fond memories of these sessions, for Linda the protracted process took its toll. Initially, though, she seemed delighted with the way things were going, telling Patrick Humphries, 'Gerry has been selective about the material. He has a great feel for continuity, whereas the last record was terribly disjointed and a lot of the songs didn't go together … Gerry's more of a perfectionist than we are, and he's made us work a bit harder.'

The 'perfectionist' part certainly rang true. As the sessions ran into October, still there was no finished record. Rafferty tried changing the arrangements and even the lead vocalists around.[49] He was not only 'selective' about the new material, he convinced the duo to reinterpret 'A Heart Needs A Home' (which was never under serious consideration) and 'For Shame Of Doing Wrong' (which made it

---

[49] A rough mix exists of a Linda lead vocal on 'Back Street Slide', a song generally associated solely with Richard. Also – oddly enough – a Rafferty lead vocal was recorded for 'The Wrong Heartbeat'.

to the Mk.1 version), believing there was radioplay in these songs recorded right.

'For Shame Of Doing Wrong' was one of two songs from a 1977 Island album reinterpreted for the 'Rafferty' *Shoot Out The Lights*. The other selection from Sandy's farewell platter was 'I'm A Dreamer', which was recorded both acoustic and electric, with an exquisite Linda vocal ringing every ounce of emotion from it. Richard went along with its inclusion but was not a happy man:

Linda Thompson: Richard does not like recording other people's songs ... I'd [have] like[d] to record Sandy's and Nick's, but he'd never hear of it. Maybe it would bring back memories for him, which he doesn't want to dredge up. [1982]

She was determined not to let one of her friend's finest worksongs die. She had singled out the self-same song for a two-hour Radio One show called *Star Choice*, earlier in the year. And on the first anniversary of Sandy's death, Linda had placed an In Memoriam notice in *Melody Maker*, only for Richard to 'go apeshit, 'cause I put his name on it, too'. Linda had personally always preferred singing someone else's song but was rarely allowed rein:

Linda Thompson: It's always easier to sing ... songs that aren't to do with you. Songs you've written, or you're known for singing, are somehow harder to sing than 'Dark End Of The Street' ... [where] the pressure's off. You didn't write it, you're just singing it and it's not associated with you.

With Gerry's invaluable technical aid, *Shoot Out The Lights* looked set to be an album which put Linda's throaty vocals at its very heart. For most of September/October 1980, she rose to the occasion. But in the notes to *Dreams Fly Away* (1996), she confessed to being 'monumentally unhappy during this record – I felt bogged down and I knew things would [only] get worse and worse. I stuck very close to Gerry Rafferty, but he was even unhappier than I.'

The dysphonia threatened to return with a vengeance, so getting a good vocal took time and patience, neither of which Richard had in any abundance even when the producer shared his approach to making a record. And Rafferty did not. Soon enough, the Thompson who refused to sing 'Jack O' Diamonds' or release 'Poor Will And The Jolly Hangman' came to call, digging his heels in at almost the exact time Rafferty decided he would complete the record his way or the highway:

Linda Thompson: I quite like the smoothness of some of it, but it was a difficult record to make. You know, Gerry was difficult, Richard was difficult. I think we did all the basics live. We did all the rhythm tracks live, and we did vocals afterwards. Richard did some live vocals. But he didn't like it. I quite liked it. I didn't prefer it or not prefer it, but those guys were two control freaks. So whatever Gerry said, Richard would say, 'No way.' Whatever Richard said, Gerry would say, 'Oh no...' It was absolutely a dick thing ... But I liked Gerry a lot more than Richard did. I stayed friends with Gerry.

Richard would later insist, 'The main problem [with Rafferty] as a producer, [is] that he was more like the artist. He really wanted control over absolutely everything. When he got to the mixing, I just didn't bother turning up for the mix ... and that was the last time I spoke to Gerry Rafferty.' That is not the way Boyd remembers it. He believes he was told by Thompson that Rafferty banned him from the mixes – not the smartest move:

Joe Boyd: They [had] started working on the record and I went about my Hannibal business. Every once in a while I would check in with Linda or run into Simon somewhere ... and I heard it wasn't going so great. And then I heard that Richard wanted to pull out of the whole thing. So I called him up and I said, 'What's happening?' ... Richard [was] get[ting] more and more uncomfortable with the way that the thing's being made ... He realises it's not so much fun as he though it might be and Gerry won't let him sit in with the mixes. He's like, 'No, no, no. You can hear it tomorrow. I don't need you around now.' And that was the final straw with Richard.

None of which explains – or excuses – Richard's failure to see it coming. He later claimed he was 'attracted to the idea of doing it with Gerry because it was a way we'd never done it before – to go in and make an album which was viable for the American market'.

Lest we forget, he had already worked with Rafferty on *Night Owl,* alongside the long-suffering Pete Zorn, who had no illusions about Gerry's methodology, 'Rafferty only knows one way to make records: lay down a good, solid rhythm track, overdub all the solos, overdub all the vocals.'

He, at least, was not greatly surprised when the Rafferty version of *Shoot Out The Lights* ended up 'sounding very clean, very polished – it didn't have any of the raw edge [Richard thought] the songs warrant[ed]'. The artist, though, felt let down and profoundly disappointed:

Richard Thompson: [*Shoot Out The Lights* Mk.1 took] a really long time. That was really taking it to bits and sticking it back together again. Not my cup of tea. [1984]

Richard Thompson: [The Rafferty version] was really slick. Densely slick ... He was making records in the way he knows how ... [which] works well for him. [But] it made me feel really claustrophobic working with him. 'Cause he just likes to fill every possible space. [1993]

By the end of the sessions, Richard already knew he did not want to put his name to this record, even though he believed in the songs. An intractable issue was the great deal of time and money Rafferty had invested in the project. Thompson's manager, Jo Lustig, was also seeing dollar signs after six years of financial famine from his favourite duo.

Lustig had prematurely lined up a November 1980 tour to start spreading the word. Yet three radio broadcasts from this tour all suggest that the album could have been recorded live on-the-spot and still sound good, though a judicious selection of Linda's better live vocals would have been required.

By this time there was a finished sequence and mix from Rafferty and Murphy, who had convinced themselves that Richard would see reason in the end. They evidently did not know him well – unlike a certain person now hovering in the wings:

Joe Boyd: There was this contract which had been drawn up with Gerry and Hugh's production company, which Richard and Linda were [due] to sign. It was all drawn up, but it wasn't signed. A lot of records were made [then] without things being signed. It's not that shocking or unusual. You agree all the terms, and people are in the business and they have to deal with each other again over something else … [so] it's very, very rare that somebody's going to walk away, just because the contract isn't signed. But Jo Lustig had inserted in the contract a 25% [commission]. Over the course of the early stages of this process, going to hear them live and getting to know them, Gerry and Hugh are also starting a management company. They also learned to loath Jo Lustig in the course of the negotiations … So they were reluctant to sign [that part of the agreement]. They wanted to persuade Richard and Linda to leave Jo Lustig and come to their management company. They recognised, quite accurately, that the songs were great. They [also hoped to] manage them. But they couldn't, if they had to pay Jo Lustig 25%. It would defeat the purpose. If they stole them from Lustig, they'd still have to pay Lustig on this record. [So] there wouldn't be any money for them if they had a hit record. That is my understanding of why the contract was unsigned. The fact that they had gone ahead and spent money in studio, paid the musicians and everything, without having a signed contract was their choice – which made it morally a little easier for Richard to walk away. I think he needed to put [on] a last guitar solo, or there was some overdub that was still needed, and Richard basically said, 'I'm not doing anything more on this record. I don't want this record to come out. I'm not going to sign the contract. End of story.'

In fact, the impasse would drag on into 1981. Far from refusing to dub on one last solo or vocal overdub, Richard was trying to decide whether to bite his lip and okay the album Rafferty had produced. As of now, he had few other options. For a year or more his career had been on hold and it was high time he and Linda got back to releasing records and touring on the back of them.

But before he could definitively decide which road to travel, he found out his wife was pregnant for a third time. It meant there was little immediate prospect of touring the world. There was no imminent product and Linda's vocal problems were getting worse, as a soundboard of a 'Sour Grapes' trio show from February 1981 at Manchester's fabled Lesser Free Trade Hall demonstrates.[50] The dysphonia was becoming worse as the live work was drying up and the demands of motherhood were rearing up again.

———————

Richard, now anxious to get back on track, had one stop-gap option: to resume work as a session-musician. He had already taken his first tentative steps, embracing an off-kilter version of the modern dance the previous June, when he spent a number of challenging days in Regent's Park, not at the Open Air Theatre but at a little known local studio, making his most avant-garde (or avant-garage, if you prefer) music to date with a man whose stage name was once Crocus Behemoth.

David Thomas & The Pedestrians was an unholy amalgam of Pere Ubu's Jarryesque frontman, Young Marble Giant bassist Philip Moxham, Lounge Lizard drummer Anton Fier and folk-rocker Richard Thompson. It was a studio combo cooked up by Thomas – a long-time Thompson fan – and Rough Trade boss, Geoff Travis. When Richard was asked to do it, he told Thomas, 'I don't know what you want me to do, but I'm happy to do it.' The result was *The Sound Of The Sand* – and never was an album-title more apposite.

In fact, the local eccentrics just kept calling. A phone call from ex-Bonzo Vivian Stanshall resulted in Richard lending a hand on Stanshall's *Teddy Boys Don't Knit*, before he was asked to resurrect the *Full House* Fairport by a conciliatory Swarb, who was hoping to persuade the entire outfit to help him record a third solo album for Transatlantic. The experience proved (surprisingly) rewarding for all concerned:

Dave Swarbrick: We got on much better than I imagined. I had a lot of fear about it. Richard and I [had] never got on in the early days of Fairport ... We composed some bloody good songs together, but it was purely on the basis of 'you write that and I'll write this and [we'll] put it together'. But we never sat down together and had a real good chat. [1981]

[50] Though for most of the show Linda's singing retains all the precision of a radar station, there are a couple of moments, notably 'Lucky In Life', when her voice wanders painfully off-key.

The resultant album, *Smiddyburn*, was the best thing Swarb had put out in a decade, while the experience of the entire *Full House* five-piece working together – for fully half the album – made everyone appreciate just how special this combination remained.

However, the album – released in July 1981 – was, as Simon says, 'never gonna be anything other than a recording project for [Swarb]. It was never going to be a way forward. John Wood was the moving force behind it – which is one of the reasons it sounds so good. [Yet] Richard's input is significant. He very much liked the idea of playing with Swarb [again].' Indeed, Swarb later recalled that when John Wood was listening back to the album in the studio, he turned to the fiddler and said, 'Blimey, nothing's changed, has it!'

Where Swarb and Wood missed a trick – and Transatlantic missed out on a few thousand sales – was in not making *Smiddyburn* a full-blown *Full House* project and/or more of a collection of *songs*. Of the four *Full House*-style workouts on the final record, three were instrumental medleys. The only song was a show-stopping performance of Sandy's 'It Suits Me Well' given the kind of arrangement it had long deserved.

There was more than enough material for a full *Full House* reunion recorded at the same sessions. Instead, leftovers made with this line-up would fill out Swarb's fourth Transatlantic album, *Flittin'*, released in 1983. Included was one cut, the seven-minute 'Nathaniel Gow's Lament', that was perhaps the most ambitious traditional cut-up this legendary line-up ever recorded. It was as if Swarb, after years of trying to cast Fairport in his own image, now refused to trade on the association – and felt no one else should, either.

And yet, *Smiddyburn* was not the only album the *Full House* Fairport recorded that year, or the only time the five of them made a play for a wider audience. Granada TV devoted an entire half-hour programme to the *Full House* line-up, presented by that Lower Crumpsall cowboy Mike Harding, broadcast in October.

This *Celebration* opened with a frantic 'Dirty Linen', featured a most welcome 'Poor Will And The Jolly Hangman', and ended with a truncated 'Sloth'. Two of the tracks recorded for *Smiddyburn* were also debuted, 'Sir Charles Coote' and 'The Young Black Cow', along with two Richard and Linda songs, 'Bright Lights' and the still-unreleased 'Wall Of Death', both sung by a very pregnant Linda.

Though Linda's advancing pregnancy curtailed any further concert appearances – even precluding that year's Fairport reunion – it did not stop her from recording another TV special, this one no cameo. And it was for BBC One. Lustig had somehow secured the duo a spot on BBC's new all-music series, *A Little Night Music*, for another half-hour showcase.

Recorded a fortnight before the scheduled annual Fairport shindig, the skilfully filmed show offered few glimpses of how far gone Linda was, capturing her singing like a dream on 'I'm A Dreamer' and 'Dimming Of The Day' even as her dream turned into a nightmare.

If *A Little Night Music* was looking forward to the eventual release of *Shoot Out The Lights*, *Celebration* was looking back to the heyday of this brand of English folk-rock, something also captured on multitrack during a rare return to live performance for the not-so-famous five-piece during the second annual Fairport reunion, briefly relocated for 1981 to Broughton Castle.

Integrating the *Full House* line-up into a longer Fairport 'and family' set, the whole evening was recorded for a possible live album. Again the breadth of material almost belied any sense of nostalgia. Tackling everything from 'Mr Lacey' to 'Now Be Thankful', the occasionally augmented outfit even dared to tackle Swarb's 'Rosie' and Thompson's 'Woman Or A Man', while offering an olive branch to Judy Dyble, who joined them for 'Both Sides Now' and 'When Will I Be Loved', a song associated in Fairport fans' eyes with two angelic-voiced absentees.

If Sandy's ghost hung over the entire proceedings, Linda was at home awaiting the labour of Kamila, her second daughter. She had not felt well enough to even attend a solo gig her husband had arranged at a local folk club earlier the same month:

Linda Thompson: I got pregnant, and I was very sick … [so] Richard had to do a few things on his own and he did one folk club up in Hampstead … That was the night he met Nancy [Covey]. Nothing happened that night, but then at Cropredy [sic] … they started up something. And that continued throughout my pregnancy.

Sure enough, Nancy Covey, a booking agent for LA music club McCabes, had come over that summer with the specific intention of convincing Richard Thompson to come and play 'her' club. Only she knows whether she hoped to strike a more intimate note at their first brief encounter.

By the time they parted, after the Fairport reunion weekend, Thompson felt inspired to write directly about his predicament in a way that was as personal as anything he'd penned in the past half-decade. 'A Man In Need' was the song of a man who saw wife and kids as financial 'dependants', not nearest and dearest:

> I packed my rags, went down the hill,
> Left my dependants a-lying still,
> Just as the dawn was rising up, I was making good speed.
> I left a letter lying on the bed…

There would be no such 'Dear Linda' letter. These lovers were hiding at the dark end of the street. Their trysts would stay under wraps until after Richard had finally recorded a version of the 'Rafferty' album with which he was happy – featuring this angst-ridden song – and taken up Nancy's invitation to join her for some r&r in la-la-land.

[It was] so difficult, [working together]! It was ten years. It felt like twenty, because we were together so much. My eldest daughter said to me the other [day], 'You and Daddy are like peas in a pod. Every time you say to me I've just been to the Canaletto exhibition, he says the same thing.' We read the same books. Listen to the same music. But that was where it ended, because in day-to-day terms we're very different. Artistically, we love everything the same, but as people – very different.

—LINDA THOMPSON TO AUTHOR

I think we both were miserable and didn't quite know how to get it out. I think that's why the album is so good. We couldn't talk to each other, so we just did it on the record.

—LINDA THOMPSON, *ROLLING STONE*, 16TH NOVEMBER 1989

I had gotten caught in the trap of perfectionism. [Whereas] Shoot Out The Lights *… [is] the only kind of recordings I'm interested in doing now – not spending a lot of time at it, and getting it right as much as possible live.*

—RICHARD THOMPSON, 1983

I called up Richard and I said, 'Is it true? You're not going to finish the [Rafferty] record and you're not going to sign the contract?' He said, 'Yeah.' I said, 'Do you wanna make this record [with me]? We can go in and do it quickly. Here's my idea: we do it in three days and we take the money that we've saved and we put it into tour support. I book you a tour of America, because you've never been to America, except with Fairport. It's time.' And he said, 'That sounds good to me. Talk to Jo.' So I called Lustig and he was, of course, furious that this thing had fallen apart. He didn't like the idea of being with Hannibal [even before] I said, 'So here's what we're going to do. There's no advances here. We'll pay the musicians, pay your session fees. It all goes into tour support. I can get you a tour around America.' And he said, 'Absolutely not. When Richard and Linda go to America, the first show they do is Carnegie Hall. That's the way they're going to go to America, come in at the top.' I said, 'Okay, I won't do it. You go find somebody else to do the record.' And I hung up [and] called Richard. I told him about my conversation. He said, 'Let me talk to Jo.' I got a call back from Jo's assistant, saying, 'Okay, draw up the papers.' So we go into Sound Techniques and we did it in three days, except for Linda's vocals.

—JOE BOYD TO AUTHOR

In the biopic of Joe Boyd's eventful life it would surely go down this way: Gerry Rafferty would be left with an album – a rather good album – but no contract, while Jo Lustig would be left with a 25% share of thin air, after trusty ol' Joe rides to the rescue. In reality, Richard rode to the rescue, with Boyd's cherished independent record label already in trouble after Island pulled the plug on what was originally a joint enterprise:

Joe Boyd: Unit record sales had gone down – for the first time ever – [in] about '78 or '79. Record companies were dropping artists all over the place ... Blackwell and I agreed that a label which could handle the Taj Mahals or Richard Thompsons of this world was needed ... He had good memories of the relationship between Island and Witchseason, and thought we could do something similar in 1980 ... [But] by the time Hannibal's first records were ready for release, a number of things had happened for Island in America: [Steve Windwood's] Arc of a Diver, Marianne Faithful, U2 and Marley broke wide open, and Grace Jones had her first American dance-floor hit ... Island decided that they didn't want to renew Hannibal's deal at the end of the first year. I did the foolish thing and decided to keep the label going ... In a way the salvation of the label was my relationship with Richard.

Having spent a year living on borrowed time, relying on 'riders from the county' for work, Richard was as anxious as Joe to get the record out. The prospect of a US tour was also enticing for a man reaching for the parachute-chord on his rocky marriage. And he knew Boyd liked to work fast:

Richard Thompson: [Joe's] judgement is very good in the studio, knowing what to do at the time, knowing what to keep at the time, or when to stop. Which is very important, [because] otherwise you'll waste a lot of time and you'll lose a lot of momentum. [1984]

Were one searching for an exercise in contrasting working methods, Rafferty and Boyd's respective production techniques could hardly be bettered. This time, though, there was an elephant in the room in the shape of a heavily pregnant Linda, who by October 1981 was

on the verge of 'dropping' baby #3, something the producer thought
might warrant a little consideration:

Joe Boyd: I said, 'We do the record in four days.' ... The catch was,
it took more than four days to do Linda's vocals ... My impression [at
the time was that] it wasn't really a problem with Linda's voice, it was
a problem with her pregnancy. She was short of breath, because [she
was] eight [months pregnant]. And so she was nervous about cutting
vocals live. She did some guide vocals, but she said she wanted to do
them without Richard around. So in the end we cut the tracks in
three days and then it took me another [week] to finish the vocals,
because she couldn't work that long. We did a line at a time on some
of them, a verse at a time, whatever [it took]. [It seemed] Linda was
just feeling [that way because] she's pregnant, [so] hasn't got the range
for those songs ... [But she] was ... beginning to have that nervous
quaver in her voice.

Such a substantive obstacle would have changed the whole shape
of the album even if the issue really had been Linda's pregnancy.
Such was not the case. Her bouts of dysphonia, which her pregnancy
exacerbated, lay at the heart of the difficulties:

Linda Thompson: His performances are fine. It's my performances
that are awful because life was hard for me ... I'd just had this problem
and I didn't know what it was. It didn't get diagnosed till quite a long
time after I had it. I didn't know what it was and I couldn't figure it
out and it was very distressing. People kept saying, 'You're off mike.'
And I wasn't off mike. It was just coming out like a stutter. Which is
ironic because Richard has a bit of a stutter, but never when he sings.

Simon Nicol: The [second set of] sessions wasn't as much fun ...
[Linda's vocal problem] didn't have a name and a diagnosis; [so] she
didn't have a handle on it.

Pete Zorn: Everybody seemed tense when Linda was around, which
I thought was the norm ... I couldn't work out if it was between these
two, or the conditions [we were] working under.

Having reshaped the album in his head, Richard was also looking to cut some songs and add others. On a certain level, it was a question of practicalities. There simply wasn't the budget to tackle all the songs Richard had in his locker at the time of the Rafferty sessions, let alone those he had written in the last year. These included two Richard wanted on the album – not only 'A Man In Need' but also 'Did She Jump Or Was She Pushed?', a more cryptic piece which alluded to the abiding mystery surrounding Sandy's death, wrapped in a denouement suggesting Pavanne was up to her old tricks.

At least the latter was one song Richard and Joe could give Linda to sing; and it worked, perhaps because, as Linda says, ' My dysphonia doesn't kick in so much when the song is slow. Fast songs are hard for me [but] slow songs are much, *much* easier. I prefer slow songs.'

It served as a partial sop to the frequently sobbing lass, who had seen song after song taken away from her, or simply removed from the album sequence. Not that Linda herself wasn't party to this process. When it came to the compulsive 'Wall Of Death', what had been a solo Linda vocal on the Rafferty album became a duet on its doppelganger, a decision made entirely with her blessing: 'I just found it hard to sing. It's a tough song. I couldn't cope, so I said to Richard, you're gonna have to do it.'

Other changes in the album's order and selection inextricably took songs away from her, making it very much Richard's record. Such was the message from the first track, 'Don't Renege On Our Love', previously sung with unerring 'tonal breath control' by Linda; now hijacked by Richard. The switch made the opening lyric an ironic introduction to an album announcing a new independent spirit while covertly addressing the end of a marriage, 'Remember when we were hand in hand/ Remember we sealed it with a golden band/ Now your eyes don't meet mine...'

The real body blow, both to the album as a fully rounded portrait of a marriage on the rocks and to Linda's self-esteem, was the exclusion of three songs that in Raffertyland had all been solo Linda vocals – and A-list vocals at that – 'For Shame Of Doing Wrong', 'I'm A Dreamer' and, most tellingly of all, 'The Wrong Heartbeat'.

If there was a certain logic to the exclusion of the first two, 'The Wrong Heartbeat' had always shone its laser on the bright lights of sin. In fact, so pertinent was it that when Richard finally released the song on 1983's *Hand Of Kindness*, recognising it as far too good to leave in the reject locker till it withered and died, the *NME* reviewer decided it was written about the break-up of his marriage, which occurred nearly two years after its composition.

Its omission from *Shoot Out The Lights* in all its official incarnations remains mystifying, if only because – unlike the other songs absent from the Boyd version artist and producer dismissed from the outset – it *was* recorded in October 1981 with a Linda lead vocal, and a good one. It also featured on the original test-pressing of an album that is a few minutes short of the optimum length for a 1982 rock record.

As it proved, 'The Wrong Heartbeat' would be cut from the final eight-track sequence, leaving it light of Linda lead vocals, whether as deliberate policy or not. The album, even with the unexpectedly high costs vocal overdubs and mixing incurred, had come in at between $10,000 and $12,000, a bargain, the best Boyd ever had.

Boyd's approach to recording the guitar parts was night and day compared to Rafferty's, prompting Richard to later brag, 'Just about all the guitar playing [on *Shoot Out The Lights*] is live all the way through – I very rarely overdub on guitar ... If guitar bits get overdubbed, it's little bits of doubling or rhythm.'

Richard was delighted with the outcome, informing *Rolling Stone* in 1985, 'It was absolutely the right approach to wash out the taste of the seventies.' He presumably had in mind songs like 'Baker Street', a multi-layered sonic smorgasbord which sold ten times what the entire Richard and Linda catalogue has sold.

He probably hoped critics would never be able to debate whether, on a strictly commercial level, Rafferty's judgement was the sounder. The tapes did eventually leak, though, and for all the plaudits that have been deservedly showered on the 1982 album, and Rafferty's rather dated production values, his is probably the better audio artifact. It certainly has a greater breadth of material and far better vocal performances from Linda. But what really stuck in Richard's craw was that it didn't sound like a Richard Thompson record. And from now on those were the only kind of records he was planning to make.

A further assertion of artistic autonomy came at London's Barbican Hall on November 24th, 1981 – even if its significance was lost on the audience at the time. *Shoot Out The Lights* had only just gotten its final mix and Boyd had barely started putting together that promised US tour when Richard gave his first-ever 'Richard Thompson Band' performance. Though it was originally billed to Richard and Linda, his wife's condition meant an expectant hometown audience got to witness the shape of things to come.

Backed by just Pete Zorn, DM and John Kirkpatrick, a newly-energized Thompson opened the Barbican show – which sadly went unrecorded, a tape jamming on the most persistent of Thompson's seventies audio archivists – with two sledgehammer blows, 'A Man In Need' and 'Shoot Out The Lights', before taking to task a number of songs where he had previously deferred to Linda: 'Down Where The Drunkards Roll', 'Poor Ditching Boy', 'Wall Of Death' and, most tellingly, 'Did She Jump Or Was She Pushed?'

Also featured was a song demoed back in June 1980, whose subject-matter – explicated with its burden – seemed increasingly rhetorical, 'How many times do you have to fall before you end up walking?' In fact, most of the new songs seemed to address a state of affairs that was only now coming to a head; even if neither partner-in-crime nor their producer saw it Writ Large at the time:

Linda Thompson: People would say, years later, 'Oh, you know that song he wrote about you...,' or, 'That song he wrote about your first child. How awful.' And I'd go, 'Was it a fabulous song?' 'Yeah.' 'Well, what's awful about [it]? ... Art is art.' So I never cared ... I could be singing, 'I hate my wife and kids so much,' [just as long as] it was a great song ... I never would've said, 'Is that about me? Is that about her? Is that about them?' Never, never, never, never.

Richard Thompson: The theorists can theorize – and they may be right – but ... for myself, it was just the stuff I was writing, and it didn't bear any relationship to life as I could see it at the time. [1982]

Richard Thompson: The songs [on *Shoot Out The Lights*] are very relevant to that [break-up], but [they] were written two years ago. If it was true, then it was subconscious ... If you put them back to the person who was originally singing them, then it's even more true. It's [actually] kind of worrying. [1982]

Joe Boyd: It was almost as if Richard had spent [the past few] years writing songs for Linda to sing when he left her. [1982]

For the producer, who had himself jilted the poor lady a decade earlier, the penny didn't really drop even when it came time to do the album artwork and Linda was curiously reluctant to appear in the same shot as her husband:

Joe Boyd: It seemed like things were a little tense [at the sessions]. But I wasn't aware of any serious problems. We finished the record. Okay, we've got to have a cover. Linda, again, said, 'I'm not going to the photo session. I look bad. Here's a good picture of me.' And so they hang it on the wall and Richard sits there. In retrospect, you can see it as being hugely symbolic.

Of course, Thompson was a past master of writing in code. So perhaps it is not overly surprising that he took his time owning up. He did finally admit to his biographer, 'To actually bare your personal life in song [is something] I found very hard, so I would definitely draw veils over songs ... I don't want people to know this is really about me.'

It was a flaw he shared with the late, great Sandy, who only overcame it when it was too late to change her ill-fated trajectory. Thompson still felt there was time. But very, very soon his cover would be blown and there was very little he could do about it, save stay home with the new baby and an increasingly distraught wife, who could not bring herself to leave but subconsciously rather wished *he* would:

Linda Thompson: I can't speak for him, [but] I was just unhappy for a lot of years. I just thought, there's something that's not right in my life, it's just not working for me. And he obviously felt that, too. I felt I couldn't make a break because we had kids. I did leave a couple of times, but I always went back. So it was going to happen, you know. [He never left] until he left. I did, but went back. It just wasn't working ... [Most] break-ups are boiling [up] for a long time before they happen, you know, and .... there was [always] much more admiration and intellectual compatibility with me and Richard than there was mad love. [In the end] we both needed that in our lives, and so we had to go elsewhere.

For Richard, that protracted leave-taking started in earnest when he landed in LA in December 1981 ostensibly for a pair of shows at McCabe's, and a handful of shows further up the West Coast. Nancy Covey – who was waiting for him at LAX – recalled, 'When I set up a solo tour for him in order to get him to play McCabe's, we spent a lot of time together, at gigs and interviews. That's when we met each other properly and we spent a lot of time together.'

In fact, they were hardly apart for the ten days that Richard spent soaking up some California sun and connecting with a wellspring of West Coast fans of English folk-rock. Sadly, said legions were assuredly swimming against the eighties mainstream. Indeed, if he had hoped the great American unwashed might finally be ready to embrace his music, he was shocked to hear the kind of music coming out of the radio stations his hire car was tuned to:

Richard Thompson: Before I left England, I was despairing because English radio is so awful … And I got to America and I couldn't believe it. It's so abysmal … really conservative. It's like frightened music. Frightened to make anything that someone might object to, or might stick out too much. It's just elevator music as far as I'm concerned. I'd rather listen to elevator music, really. I think it serves a better environmental purpose than Journey, Styx, Foreigner, etc. [1982]

At least the music-scene in San Francisco – whose music once inspired him – was vibrant enough to generate healthy sales for two solo shows at the Great American Music Hall, and attuned enough to invite him to record a brief video performance for KCRW's cable TV set-up. During his time in the Bay Area, Richard came to a decision. He returned home to England, where he finally broke the news to a stunned wife, whose one retort in that unclear moment was, 'Can she sing?'

When Richard duly informed Linda he was returning to the States – this time to the East Coast – in early January, to further promote the imminent release of their record, and to play his first New York dates in a decade, there was no doubt in Linda's mind that Nancy would be joining him there.

But it was only when she spoke to her old beau Boyd, a week after the Bottom Line shows, that she learnt Richard and Nancy were now officially an item. The producer, who had met Nancy for the first time on the same summer visit as Richard, feared that the whole situation was getting out of hand at the exact point when he needed everyone focused on an album he, more than anyone, needed to succeed:

Joe Boyd: The previous summer, I'd been at a gig of Brass Monkey at The Roundhouse and I'd met this American woman who was over here looking at musicians to bring to McCabe's, named Nancy. And we had a nice chat. And so Richard says, 'I've been invited to go do a couple of nights at McCabe's in LA. They're going to pay my fare and stuff, but I'll just do acoustic. Is that okay?' He knew how much I was putting into the tour and I said, 'Yeah, that would be great. You can do some press … What are you doing in New York? Let's get hold of the Bottom Line.' [So] then he … came to the Bottom Line and I flew to New York, because I had other reasons to be in New York. I was at the Bottom Line gig and … that became Small Town Romance. We all went out to dinner. Nancy was there. She'd come to New York. And … three, four days later I got a phone call from Linda. She said, 'Joe have you seen my husband? Do you know where he is? He's kind of disappeared.' I said, 'No. Last time I saw him, we went out to dinner after the Bottom Line. I assumed he was on his way back to London.' By the time I got back to London … the whole thing had blown.

Suddenly the gerrymandered edifice Boyd had constructed to break the pair Stateside was in danger of toppling over just as initial reviews, after the album's mid–March release, praised it to the skies. Fortunately for his label's precarious finances, Linda was adamant – she was going to do the tour and her husband could go hang:

Joe Boyd: The tour had come together perfectly. Just everything I imagined … The record's rolling out and everything's coming together. Then I had a conversation with Jo Lustig about travel arrangements … and he said, 'Linda's not going on tour. She couldn't possibly. You know she and Richard have split up.' 'Yeah, of course I know. But has she said she's not going to go? Because she's singing on most of the record.' It would be like Sandy and *Liege & Lief* [all over again]. So once again, I hang up the phone ... and I phoned Linda. She said, 'Well, my view is I've lost my husband, I'll be fucked if I'm going to lose an American tour as well. But I'm not going to be the only girl on the tour. If you want to me to come on the tour, you've got to pay for me to have a friend come along.' So she brought this girl. She'd been a babysitter or something. I can't remember her name, even. She was much younger.

Linda Thompson: Richard said to me, 'You can't come. You can't come,' and the manager Jo Lustig said, 'You can't come. You've just had a baby.' And I said, 'I'm going.' ... I didn't even [have to] talk to Joe. But I did ask Joe to come along, because he was my friend, and he did, which was wonderful. But I was absolutely determined to go. Nobody wanted me to go, except Joe. Joe wanted me to go because it would help the record. Joe's intentions were pure. He said, 'You know, [if] you're not well enough, you shouldn't go.' He was very sweet.

Not everybody who signed up for the impending car crash remains convinced Joe acted entirely honorably on this occasion; let alone Richard, unexpectedly cast as a cad and bounder of the first water:

Simon Nicol: Zorn, Mattacks and I [had already] signed up for what we knew was going to be a difficult tour, because Kami had just been born. Joe had oblig[at]ed us to [tour]. Richard and Linda had agreed that this tour would go ahead to promote this album. Joe was very black and white about [some] things. His managerial skills were [a bit lacking here]. He just didn't see that it would be a problem if Linda was made to go on the road, having had a child six weeks previously, and was in a state of complete nervous collapse, to go and sing songs about love and heartbreak in this impossible [set of] condition[s]. We watched in horror as it came together ... I [already] knew the [full] picture.

The one and only North American Richard & Linda Thompson tour would run from May 11th to June 6th. It soon became the stuff of legends, nightly crossing into pure melodrama even as the music brimmed with emotion and Linda teetered on the brink of 'complete nervous collapse'.

Often required to play two sets a night – just to meet demand and make economic sense of the distances travelled and the costs incurred without major-label tour support – the group dynamic was often as dysfunctional as the Thompsons' collapsing marriage. As Simon says, 'We were all infected by Linda's hysteria, I suppose. And Mattacks and Zorn and myself clung together as a self-defending group. I just felt so sorry for *everybody*.'

It was particularly difficult for the poor bassist, who was the odd man out – being the one band member who had not shared a *Full House* back in the Angel days. He soon discovered that 'Jo [Lustig] had printed all the posters before he asked Dave [Pegg] if he was available … [So] at the end of every gig, somebody would always lurk up and say, "You're not Dave Pegg."'

To compound the confusion, the songs on the album had been evenly split between Zorn and Pegg for the simple reason that the latter was a busy man and was only available for two days. But for US audiences, the prospect of a near-reunion of the *Full House* line-up was a mouth-watering prospect. So no matter how adaptable Zorn was, or the variety of instruments to which he could turn his hand, he was only ever a pale substitute as far as diehard fans were concerned.

The attention of audience members, though, was soon diverted by a series of spectacular onstage bust-ups, most of which were instigated by a Linda who was finding the tour so much tougher than she had initially imagined:

Linda Thompson: It was torture for Simon [and the others]. Of course it was. Poor Simon. But believe you me, it was worse torture for me and Richard. I didn't care about how Simon felt – I'm sorry Simon, but I didn't – I was appalling.

Simon Nicol: One night in Detroit I broke five strings in one evening – seems a little extreme. [She was] kicking him during his solos … [One time] she disappeared from an airport in a car left running by the kerbside, and went for a ride … It was a life-enhancing experience, but it would have been a terrible thing if everyone had not survived. And there was no guarantee from one night to the next that this would be the case. It was that bad, that fraught. It was coast to coast, there was a lot of travel involved, and every gig you'd have to explain everything to the staff – not just the [sound] man … Richard didn't want to see Linda hurt any more than he had to, but the show had to go on. It was an impossible situation for everybody … and somehow we survived it all. I'm really proud of Linda, [just] for seeing it through.

Pete Zorn: Onstage, it was fantastic. Linda was fantastic … It was, with a few memorable exceptions, the only neutral area. [Yet] there were times when she kicked him in-between numbers, things like that. Richard would [have to] do a 'but seriously folks' kind of thing … There was a place on Rhode Island, a pit of a gig – the dressing room was under the dance floor – and the promoter had to pull Linda off Richard.

Richard Thompson: People were trying to be professional … I kinda hope that we played well and got through it, whatever else was going on. We shouldn't actually have done it. It was a stupid idea … I don't know how we got through it. We got to Santa Cruz [before] Linda bailed … She just didn't turn up for that one … I think we did well to get that far.

Linda Thompson: I was too annihilated to care about singing, so it was very free[ing] … After I hit Richard on the head with the Coca-Cola bottle [before an encore], it was fine … I felt fabulous! Hitting everybody. People'd say good morning to me and I'd say, 'Fuck off!' [1985]

Simon Nicol: She was in tears a lot of the time on the 1982 tour – partly because of the lyrics she was singing. [But] there is a similarity between the choking [back] of tears and dysphonia, which she has suffered from [ever] since.

The shows ran the full gamut of emotions from alphabet city. They also hit heights – and depths – rarely seen on your average rock tour, or indeed *Spinal Tap*. This was truly the tour from hell – if you were on it – and the tour from heaven above if you were a fan of the Richard and Linda records and/or early Fairport albums. However, for the poor nursemaid/travel companion who had been bribed to join the party, keep an eye on Linda and, as Simon bluntly says, 'try to steer her away from trouble,' it was a losing battle from their very first show in Philadelphia on May 11th.

When the band left New York, a week after Philly, and directly after four shows at New York's Bottom Line that featured some electrifying guitar-work from Thompson on 'Sloth', 'Borrowed Time' and 'For Shame Of Doing Wrong' and real high-wire performances from Linda on songs like 'Withered And Died','For Shame Of Doing Wrong', 'Strange Affair' and 'Dimming Of The Day', the prospect of the tour ever reaching San Francisco with the band intact and/or without Linda ending up in jail, seemed remote. Fortunately, good ol' Joe decided to show his face in New York:

Joe Boyd: I saw lots of the gigs. The New York, Bottom Line, I was there. I went to Chicago. I was in Toronto, and they were doing Detroit or Ann Arbor [next] and then Chicago, and she said to me, 'I can't do this. This is too weird. Too difficult.' I think they'd been [going] through Buffalo to come to Toronto, and she threw a bottle at him in the airport. [Finally,] she said, 'I can't deal with this.' And I said, 'Please, Linda. This tour is just going great. You've got to [keep going].' She said, 'Well, I need some time off. I'm not going to Detroit.' 'But you're going to do Chicago, right?' 'I'll do Chicago if you come. I need you to be there. I just need your support. It's really difficult for me.' And I said, 'Okay. I'll come to Chicago. Take a day off. Stay in Toronto.' I paid her hotel to stay and then changed her flight and arranged my flight. I went back to New York [and spent] two days [there]. I arranged my flight to land [in Chicago] at the same time as her flight landed from Toronto. So I meet her and her [companion] off the plane and we get in this taxi and we're going to the hotel … and she turns to me and she says, 'Great to see you, Joe. What are you doing here?' 'Linda, I'm here because you made me promise to come, [threatening that] you wouldn't play the gig if I didn't.' 'Did I?'

As far as Boyd was concerned, the Chicago concert was particularly important. He had lined up a live broadcast of the show on WXRT, so needed Linda to be on her best behaviour and in her finest voice. Save for crude two-track soundboards from the desk, this was the first opportunity to memorialise the US shows, and he was already thinking about a live album of the tour, a subject he now broached with the walking, talking Molotov cocktail:

Joe Boyd: I'm thinking, 'This is fucking incredible. I've never heard her sing like this. Whatever it is that's going on, I've got to get it down on tape.' I [had] talked to Linda in Toronto. I told her, 'You're singing so great, we're going to record it.' She said, 'For Christ's sake don't tell me when. I don't want to know. I'll just get nervous if you tell me. So don't tell me when you're going to record.' And so I didn't … I'd looked at the schedule and I started phoning for remote trucks, and the trucks in LA were horrendously expensive. And we're only doing one night at the Roxy. Then somebody turned me on to this really good truck in the Bay Area, [where] we had [booked] Santa Cruz and two nights [sic] at the Great American. So I said to myself, 'That's the play. It's the end of the tour. We've got three nights.'

Sticking largely to slow songs like 'Lonely Hearts', 'Dimming Of The Day' and 'Withered And Died' in Chicago allowed Linda to caress the verses, leaving it to Richard to cut loose when 'Hard Luck Stories', 'Shoot Out The Lights' and 'For Shame Of Doing Wrong' came around. It gave WXRT's Midwest listeners – otherwise out of luck with the schedule – a flavour of what they were missing.

At consecutive shows in Bloomington, Kansas City and Boulder, Colorado, the five-piece continued building up a head of steam. They were bound for LA and a West Coast rendezvous with Nancy, in Richard's case, and an almighty face-off with the LA music scene in Linda's case. Having become friends with a fair few female singers during her time in la-la-land in 1971, this lady on the brink was never going to pass up the opportunity to make the Roxy gig her own private therapy meeting:

Joe Boyd: Front row of the Roxy. Linda [Ronstadt], Carly [Simon], Maria [Muldaur], the whole gang is there. Nancy doesn't show, of course. [But] it's Nancy's turf. Linda's going to spray on Nancy's turf. And she was unbelievable. She was so good. I'm just sitting [there], the whole show. I couldn't really enjoy because I kept thinking to myself, 'Fuck! This is just the best.' And then afterwards I'm in the dressing room, [as is] Linda Ronstadt and she says, 'Linda you're coming with me. You're going to have a massage. We're going to have lunch with Jane Fonda. We're going to go see Jerry Brown.' [It's a] three-day break. [So] I said, 'Okay Linda, look out for her. Just make sure she gets to that plane ... to Santa Cruz in three days.' ... Suddenly, [though], there was this relaxation, all this pampering ... I think the companion went back. And so we go to LAX three days later – no Linda. I call and say, 'Where are you?' She says, 'Joe, I'm really sorry but I just can't do [it]. I can't make it right now. I just... I just can't.' ... I said, 'Linda, we're recording!' And she said, 'Oh, Joe, I'm so sorry. But I can't.' And so we recorded Santa Cruz without her.

Linda Thompson: I left Richard in Los Angeles 'cause he was gonna stay with his girlfriend ... I went to Linda Ronstadt's house. Al Stewart sent us a couple of bottles of champagne at the Roxy gig and I drank them and [then] Linda picked me up from the club in a limo and took me home ... After the [Santa Cruz] gig, I said to Richard, 'I'm sorry I didn't show up.' He said, 'Oh, nobody noticed' – only half joking ... [But] [Nancy] was there [in Santa Cruz]. You know, I didn't want to be there. That would've been too much.

Joe Boyd: After the [Roxy] show, [when] she went out with Linda Ronstadt ... it was like a watershed. It seemed to break the spell of touring with Richard, [and] all the intensities and weirdness involved in that ... She realises there's life after Richard, there's another world to inhabit, it's not the end of the world.

Thankfully, it was fast approaching the end of the tour. After Santa Cruz, there were just two shows to go – both at the Great American Music Hall, an early and a late show, for which Linda *did* show up. Here was Boyd's only chance to record Richard *and* Linda Thompson on the tour from hell, and an early and a late set meant they could cover almost the entire thirty-song repertoire.

According to the bereft producer, though, by the time Linda 'flies to San Francisco, it's like all the air's gone out. [After] those three days with Linda Ronstadt ... the intensity just went [way] down. There's some okay takes from the Great American, but it's nothing like what it was at the Roxy … We never got a [representative] recording of that tour as we should have done.'

I guess we will never know how good that unrecorded Roxy show was, but the shows either side of LA are extant, one from the soundboard, the other from good audience tapes. And on this substantive basis, Boyd allowed his memory of one show to convince him to turn a deaf ear to all the good things at the two 'duo' shows he did capture. In truth, the non-release of an official live album was a missed trick on his part.

Indeed, far from Boyd's recollection of 'some okay takes', the two San Francisco shows are full of powerful moments, even though it lacks the *edge* that there is on, say, the Bottom Line 'For Shame Of Doing Wrong', released on a bootleg CD from a fine Ed Haber soundboard. Likewise, the well-mixed WXRT broadcast has moments like the one when Linda finally gets to grips with Dylan's 'I'll Keep It With Mine', put there as a sop to fans of Sandy-era Fairport.[51]

A judicious two-CD set drawing on the early/late sets still begs to be released, if only to confirm that the 1982 US tour was not just a train wreck. It actually produced some of the greatest music the pair ever made, and served as one helluva swansong for the irreplaceable resident songbird. As it is, there was even still some drama to be had at the airport on the way home:

Simon Nicol: On the final trip back we flew from San Francisco to LA, then ninety minutes on the ground and off. And that's the only time in my life when a plane has been turned around. As we got back on the plane after the short lay over … the doors shut and the plane pushed back, and there was no sign of Linda. So before we got to the end of the runway, the captain said, 'We just have to return to the terminal to pick up some essential paperwork.' And they opened the door and she got back on. God knows what kind of an earthquake she'd created.

---

[51] The limited edition Rhino Handmade 2008 edition of *Shoot Out The Lights* with a 'bonus' live disc – fully half of which was taken from the non-Linda show in Santa Cruz – is a poor substitute. Just six songs on this unrepresentative CD – of the twenty-seven tracks available – derive from San Francisco and rather than using the impassioned 'Did She Jump Or Was She Pushed?' sung by Linda at the early Great American show, the release features Richard's unconvincing Santa Cruz rendition.

And that should have been that. But life is rarely so neat, and in one of the strangest codas in rock history, the last Richard and Linda Thompson show actually took place in Sheffield, at the South Yorkshire Folk Festival, six weeks after separate returns to Blighty. Presumably, this was another of Lustig's backfiring masterstrokes: setting up an FM broadcast of the show to promote the new album, an obligation both Richard and Linda felt powerless to pass up.

Linda remembers some people saying, 'I know you're splitting up, but you should go on working together.' It was not an option, largely because 'Richard wouldn't have entertained the idea'. As for their Sheffield soiree, Linda recalls, 'That was after we'd split up … It was an awful time. It was the same as the American tour.' Actually, it was far worse. Her pitch was not so much wayward as way off, and no one played with any real fire. This really was a bridge too far, one show too many. Linda had moved on, thanks to ol' dependable Joe:

Joe Boyd: We're both back in London after the tour. It's [the] World Cup. June. In Argentina[sic]. And I'm watching everything and occasionally talking to Linda on the phone, and she's really down. I invited her to one or two things and then I got invited to watch the final at somebody's house, on television. It was Ed Victor, the literary agent, and he was having a bunch of people over [for] lunch and [to] watch the final. So I called Linda. I said, 'Come on, Linda. Come with me. I'm going to Ed Victor's for lunch,' … 'No no. I don't want to go.' 'Oh come on Linda.' I persuaded her and we went, and Steve Kenis was there.

Linda had met the man who would pull her from the wreckage and help put her life – and career – back together again. In August, when she was still processing the split, she would make her last (unbilled) appearance at an annual Fairport reunion – one which Richard had elected to skip – offering backing vocals on whichever songs took her fancy, of which 'Sloth' was perhaps the most apposite and certainly the funniest. As a chaperoning Clare recalls, 'Linda was not in good shape. A lot of port. [But] she had this little badge made up, "Are you shaking, Nancy?"'

At least Linda's sense of humour had survived intact. And she was determined to enjoy being in the bosom of the Fairport family, the communing members of which had seen their fair share of tragedies and were still coming out swinging.

For Richard, the American tour had provided a different kind of epiphany. His new girlfriend had been right. He had found an audience which had been there all along, one appreciative of the work he and Linda had produced in the decade when they had stayed put in their safe European home. He also now knew he could make it on his own, if necessary on his acoustic own. Indeed, while the annual festivities were going on in Cropredy and the fortified wine was flowing, he was back at McCabe's, singing 'Ain't She A Pretty One?'

The following month, he was back in New York City playing four sets at the recently reopened Gerde's Folk City, the legendary locale where Dylan played his first two New York residencies, at the second of which he was spotted by a *New York Times* critic. The rest, as they say, was history.

Thompson also wowed New York critics with shows that covered every base from a distinguished fifteen-year career – from 'Genesis Hall' to 'Don't Renege On Our Love'. He even made a pitstop at *Henry The Human Fly* for 'The Old Changing Way' and 'Nobody's Wedding' and the Albion Country Band-era for 'Time To Ring Some Changes' and a one-off rendition of 'Rainbow Over The Hill'.

He then found the time to slot in a broad span of personal musical references from Hank Williams ('You're Gonna Change Or I'm Gonna Leave' and 'Honky Tonk Blues') to George Formby ('Why Don't Women Like Men Like Me'); reserving a special place for Scottish tradition, exemplified by 'Loch Lomond', 'Maggie Cameron' and 'The Flowers Of The Forest', a song he last heard at Putney Vale Cemetery.

And there were a couple of brand-new songs, of which 'How I Wanted To' seemed at the time – and still does – to be as close to a *mea culpa* to Linda in song as he would ever pen. It served to prove that he hadn't lost his great songwriting gift: the one which produced many a plaintive tune with a hint of tradition, set to lyrics designed to grab the listener by the short 'n' curlies from line one:

When we parted just like friends
We never tied loose ends
I could never say the words that would make amends
Oh, how I wanted to …

Coda:
One Last Bow

Fairport were never a successful band. But their influence as a group and as individuals has been enormous. There are only a couple of degrees of separation between them and most major figures in rock music.

—JOHN PEEL, OP. CIT. *FAIRPORT ON FAIRPORT*

By 1983, Fairport reunions were becoming institutionalized on a now-annual basis. And for the first time in many years, the fourth Cropredy reunion succeeded in bringing the three co-founders together again, Ashley joining a returning Richard and the ubiquitous Simon for a leisurely stroll through their *Heyday* canon, opening with 'Come All Ye' and encoring with 'Meet On The Ledge'.

But Ashley no longer felt part of the club. He had his own (largely dance-oriented) electric folk music to make. He would not return again until 1992. So although Ian Matthews finally joined the festivities in 1986, it would be 2000 before Ashley, Richard and Ian would share a Cropredy stage.

The now-departed Swarbrick was an altogether more regular fixture, as was Thompson – memorably reuniting the *Full House* line-up for an impressive set at the 1984 festival, partially broadcast on the BBC, and featuring a stunning 'John The Gun'. But the fiddler now had Whippersnapper and the guitarist his own band/s, each with audiences to call their own, in Thompson's case on both sides of the pond.

Indeed, Thompson was the only Fairportee with any future on a major label. After two more albums on Hannibal (the live album *Small Town Romance* and *Hand Of Kindness*), Bill Levenson signed him to Polygram in 1984 and after two strong albums, the gifted songwriter made the jump to Capitol for six well-marketed albums, before finally losing that business-class berth in 1996 after the catastrophically ill-judged *You? Me? Us?*

Remarkably, his ex-wife almost repeated Richard's trick, securing record deals with Warners and Sony in turn, though the latter never actually released her second solo album. But none of these records, or those by a solo Richard, could be called folk-rock by the most elastic stretch.

Even if the original spirit the founding trio conjured up had long dissipated, there were still great songs to come from Thompson's pen – 'Killing Jar', 'Beeswing' and 'Persuasion', to name but three – and at least one more great album from Mr Hutchings (1986's criminally overlooked *By Gloucester Docks I Sat Down And Wept*, which he actually advertised as 'the album you wish Richard Thompson [still] had the nerve – and inspiration – to record').

Of that original trio, only Simon kept one foot firmly in the folk-rock camp, joining a reformed Fairport in 1985 with DM and Peggy, a move that incensed Swarb, who refused to play any of the 'new' Fairport material at that year's Cropredy, determined to prove it does not all come 'round again.

Perhaps the real story of the last three-and-a-half decades has been a slowly dawning awareness among both folk and rock fraternities of just how great a contribution the Fairport family made to both forms.

Because when it came to that *historical* Fairport Convention, the whole invariably amounted to more than the sum of the parts. If those parts were never machine-finished well enough to fit together without a little sand and glue, no matter. Yes, bits were always falling off and being replaced but the machine kept on running. Actually, what everyone thought was a single working unit was really a whole way of working, uniquely English.

Archival releases galore – *Live At The BBC* boxed-sets, et al – have stoked the Fairportesque flame whenever it has seemed in danger of dying down. Now readily available – on Spotify and/or CD – are (almost) all of those early BBC Fairport sessions, early Steeleye radio 'in concerts', Fairport live at the Troubadour (both in 1970 and 1974), *Hark! The Village Wait, No Roses*, a live sample of the legendary 1975 Richard and Linda tour and Sandy Denny's sublime mid-seventies demos. The list goes on. As do the Universal repackagings.[52]

[52] Take a bow, Andrew Batt and Sue Armstrong. Frustratingly, and not a little shamefully, too many of the releases they perpetrated have featured inappropriate bonus tracks, lousy sleeve-notes and typically bad Universal packaging, while the contents have been imperfectly mixed and/or poorly sequenced by mere novices at the folk-rock well. An overpriced 2017 seven-CD retrospective of the 'real' Fairport from Universal managed to tick every one of these boxes. *Come All Ye* couldn't even get the band's lifespan right, suggesting it ran from 1968 to 1978.

Through it all, and despite Universal, those original five albums retain their lustre, ever capable of reigniting passion even in an era when Island's entire folk-rock oeuvre is constantly being repackaged to the sound of a pond being dredged.

The players themselves duly dispersed and developed their craft elsewhere, knowing that they could always come home. Simon and Sandy did, albeit only for a while. Other leading lights preferred to just show up for annual reunions. That bond, though, has never been broken.

With too much talent for one band to contain, Fairport's brand of folk-rock never was something a single outfit could, or should, nail down. Its leading lights have enjoyed being a little mercurial. In fact, as moving musical targets go, Ashley, Richard and Simon have led charmed lives ever since that July 1966 day when they made a plan which would change the face of English music forever. Now be thankful.

NOTES

My primary sources for this volume are my own interviews with the following, conducted either for my in-print, still-to-be-superseded biography of Sandy Denny, *No More Sad Refrains*, back in 2000, or for this weightier tome:

Bambi Ballard, Joe Boyd (2000 *and* 2016), Philippa Clare (2000 *and* 2016), Gerry Conway, Karl Dallas (RIP), Jerry Donahue, Ashley Hutchings (2000 *and* 2016), Gina Glazer, Colin Irwin, Richard Lewis, Iain Matthews, Simon Nicol, Dave Pegg, Andy Roberts, Sandy Roberton, Bruce Rowland (RIP), Dave Sandison (RIP), Dave Swarbrick (RIP), Linda Thompson (2000 *and* 2016), Richard Thompson, Pete Townshend, Miranda Ward and Richard Williams.

I have also drawn on transcripts of the full interviews Patrick Humphries conducted with band members for his 1982 history of Fairport, for which I again extend my warm thanks to Patrick.

Others who have trawled their archives and offered their thoughts on my behalf include Ed Haber, Bill Allison and Scott Curran; while Richard Lewis was kind enough to trawl his photo archives one last time, as were Philippa Clare and Sandy Roberton, who also generously loaned me his extensive cuttings files for Steeleye Span and Plainsong.

John Penhallow sent me his recollections of Fairport's first official gig in May 1967; Kingsley Abbott gave me permission to quote from his *FairportFolio* monograph; Jim Irvin – many moons ago – sent me a transcript of his interview with John Wood for his important *Mojo* feature on Sandy Denny; and Colin Davies was as helpful as could be.

Indeed, thanks to the various now-defunct Fairport and Thompson zines that kept the flame alive in the pre-digital era: Colin Davies's own Thompson newsletter *Hokey Pokey*, Ian Maun's *The Ledge* and, from the other side of the pond, *Dirty Linen*.

Finally, it would certainly be churlish, not to say ungracious, of me not to acknowledge all those who have come before. This is especially true as on occasion herein I have resorted to quotes from their published interviews, where mine have come up short (or where I simply have preferred theirs). As such, a nod of thanks to the following:

Kingsley Abbott: *FairportFolio: Personal Recollections of Fairport Convention from the 1967-69 Era* (pp, 1997).
Brian Hinton & Geoff Wall: *Ashley Hutchings: The Guv'nor & The Rise of Folk-Rock* (Helter Skelter Publishing, 2001); *Ashley Hutchings: Always Chasing Rainbows – The Authorised Biography Vol. 2 1974-92* (e-book, 2007).
Mick Houghton: *I've Always Kept A Unicorn: The Biography* [sic] *of Sandy Denny* (Faber, 2015).
Patrick Humphries: *Meet On The Ledge: A History of Fairport Convention* (Eel Pie, 1982).
Martyn Kenney: *Unscrapbooking: Another history of Fairport Convention* (pp, 1988).
Nigel Schofield: *Fairport By Fairport* (Rocket 88, 2013).
Pam Winters: *No Thought of Leaving* (unpublished ms. of her Sandy Denny biography, 2000).

Below are additional printed sources, largely from contemporary interviews or reviews, on a chapter by chapter basis, as well as recommended official releases, with the relevant in-print edition given where they have been expanded and/or remastered for CD reissue. All CDs are by Fairport Convention unless otherwise noted:

Chapter 1:

Selected discography: 'Washington At Valley Forge' by The Ethnic Shuffle Band, on *The Guv'nor Vol. 1* – Ashley Hutchings (HTD, 1994).

Quotes with individuals are derived from the following sources:
Judy Dyble: *Melody Maker* 8/8/70.
Richard Thompson: *Disc* 22/8/70; *NME* 8/3/75; *Dark Star* 12/78; *Guitar Player* 6/85.

Chapter 2:

Selected discography: *Fairport Convention* (Universal, 2003 w/ bonus tracks); *Live At The BBC* 4 CDs (Universal, 2007).

Quotes with individuals are derived from the following sources:
Joe Boyd: *Hokey Pokey* #10.
Jerry Donahue: *Hokey Pokey* #2a.
Judy Dyble: *Melody Maker* 8/8/70.
Ian Matthews: *ZigZag* #64; *Hokey Pokey* #5.
Richard Thompson: *Beat Instrumental* 11/68; *Disc* 22/8/70; *Liquorice* #1; *Omaha Rainbow* 12/82; *Guitar World* 2/89; *Q* 12/88.
Also quoted are articles from *Hornsey Journal* 11/8/67, *Melody Maker* 6/8/67 and *Melody Maker* 24/5/69.

Chapter 3:

Selected discography: *What We Did On Our Holidays* (Universal, 2003 w/ bonus tracks); *Heyday – The BBC Sessions 1968-69* (Universal, 2002 w/ bonus tracks); *Live At The BBC* 4 CDs (Universal, 2007).

Quotes with individuals are derived from the following sources:
Sandy Denny: *Melody Maker* 23/9/67; *Melody Maker* 27/7/68; *Disc* 8/2/69; *Disc* 12/9/70; i/view w/ Patrick Humphries 1977 [*Hokey Pokey* 4/88].
Jackson Frank: *Dirty Linen* 1995.
Trevor Lucas: *RAM* 25/1/89.

Richard Thompson: *Beat Instrumental* 11/68; *Q* 12/88; intro to Pam Winters' *No Thought of Leaving*.
Ian Matthews: *ZigZag* #64.
Also quoted are articles from *Hornsey Journal* 21/6/68, *ZigZag* #1, *Beat Instrumental* 7/68, *Melody Maker* 7/2/70.

Chapter 4:

Selected discography: *Unhalfbricking* (Universal, 2003 w/ bonus tracks); *Heyday – The BBC Sessions 1968-69* (Universal, 2002 w/ bonus tracks); *Live At The BBC* 4 CDs (Universal, 2007).

Quotes with individuals are derived from the following sources:
Sandy Denny: *Disc* 8/2/69; *Rolling Stone* 6/9/69; *Disc* 10/71.
Ian Matthews: *ZigZag* #64; *Melody Maker* 31/1/70; *Music Now* 14/2/70.
Simon Nicol: *Top Pops* 7/69; *ZigZag* 7/70.
Richard Thompson: *Beat Instrumental* 11/68; *Disc* 22/8/70; *Rolling Stone* 8/11/69.

Chapter 5:

Selected discography: *Liege & Lief* (Universal, 2002 w/ bonus tracks); *Heyday – The BBC Sessions 1968-69* (Universal, 2002 w/ bonus tracks).

Quotes with individuals are derived from the following sources:
Martin Carthy: *Record Mirror* 5/12/70; *Melody Maker* 6/3/71.
Sandy Denny: *NME* 16/8/69; *Music Now* 14/2/70; i/view w/ Patrick Humphries 1977 [*Hokey Pokey* 4/88].
Ashley Hutchings: *Sounds* 3/4/71.
Trevor Lucas: *RAM* 25/1/89.
Simon Nicol: *Beat Instrumental* 8/69; *Disc* 13/9/69.
Dave Swarbrick: *Melody Maker* 8/69; *Hokey Pokey* #18.
Richard Thompson: *Rolling Stone* 8/11/69; *Omaha Rainbow* 12/82; *Rolling Stone* 9/5/83.
Also quoted is John Mendelsohn's

review of *Liege & Lief*, *Rolling Stone* 11/6/70.

Chapter 6:
Selected discography: *Full House* (Universal, 2001 w/ bonus tracks); *Live At The LA Troubadour* (Island, 1976 – vinyl only); *House Full: Live At The LA Troubadour* (Universal, 2007 w/ bonus tracks); *Live At The BBC* 4 CDs (Universal, 2007).

Quotes with the following individuals are derived from the following sources:
Dave Mattacks: *Melody Maker* 12/10/75.
Simon Nicol: Club Folk 3-4/70; *Melody Maker* 14/7/70; *Melody Maker* 27/2/71.
Dave Swarbrick: *Music Now* 6/70; *Melody Maker* 24/10/70; *Hokey Pokey* #18.
Richard Thompson: *Club Folk* 3-4/70; *Top Pops* 18/7/70; *NME* 22/6/72; *NME* 15/6/74; *ZigZag* 5/77; *Dark Star* 12/78; *Q* 12/88.
Also quoted are articles from Ed Ward in *Rolling Stone* 12/11/70 and letters from Steve Lake (*Melody Maker* 25/7/70) and David Johnstone (*Melody Maker* 5/12/70).

Chapter 7:
Selected discography: *Morning Way* – Trader Horne (Earth Records, 2015 w/ bonus tracks); *Hark! The Village Wait* – Steeleye Span (Castle, 2008); *Matthews' Southern Comfort + Second Spring* (BGO, 2008); *Later That Same Year* (BGO, 2008 w/ bonus tracks); *Fotheringay* (Universal, 2004 w/ bonus tracks); *Nothing More: The Collected Fotheringay* 3 CDs + DVD (Universal, 2015).

Quotes with the following individuals are derived from the following sources:
Joe Boyd: *Hokey Pokey* #28.
Gerry Conway: *Hokey Pokey* #24.
Sandy Denny: *NME* 15/1/72; SD 17/1/70; *Beat Instrumental* 1970; *Music Now* 14/2/70; *Melody Maker* 20/6/70; *Sounds* 8/9/73; *Top Pops* 18/7/70; *Disc*

12/9/70; *Melody Maker* 15/5/71; *Melody Maker* 12/70; *Melody Maker* 19/9/70; *Sounds* 24/10/70; *Rolling Stone* 21/6/73.
Jerry Donahue: *Hokey Pokey* #2a.
Pat Donaldson: *Hokey Pokey* #17.
Judy Dyble: *Melody Maker* 8/8/70; *Record Collector* 9/2007.
Ashley Hutchings: *Melody Maker* 30/10/71; *Sounds* 20/12/69; *Melody Maker* 25/4/70; *Sounds* 3/4/71.
Ian Matthews: *ZigZag* #65; *Melody Maker* 15/5/71; *Melody Maker* 31/1/70; *Music Now* 14/2/70; *Disc* 17/1/70; *Melody Maker* 17/6/72; *Hokey Pokey* #5.
Sandy Roberton: *Beat Instrumental* 7/71; *Flashback* #3.
Richard Thompson: *NME* 22/6/72.
Also quoted are articles from Karl Dallas (*Saturday Times Review* 18/4/70), Jerry Gilbert (*Sounds* 20/12/69), Karl Dallas (*Melody Maker* 6/3/71) and Bob Pegg (*Club Folk* 3-4/70).

Chapter 8:
Selected discography: *North Star Grassman And The Ravens* – Sandy Denny (Universal, 2011 – deluxe 2-CD ed.); *If You Saw Thro' My Eyes + Tigers Will Survive* – Ian Matthews (Vertigo, 1993); *Orphans & Outcasts: A Collection of Demos* – Iain Matthews (Dirty Linen, 1991).

Quotes with the following individuals are derived from the following sources:
Sandy Denny: *Sounds* 16/1/71; *Melody Maker* 15/5/71; *Melody Maker* 19/6/71; *Sounds* 3/7/71; *Disc* 10/71; *Sounds* 1/72; *NME* 15/1/72; *NME* 15/4/72; *Sounds* 4/72; *Sounds* 8/9/73.
Ian Matthews: *Melody Maker* 16/1/71; *ZigZag* #65; *Melody Maker* 1/1/72; *Melody Maker* 17/6/72; *Sounds* 21/10/72; *Hokey Pokey* #5.
Also quoted is Robin Denselow's QEH review in *The Guardian* 10/9/71.

Chapter 9:
Selected discography: *Angel Delight*

(Universal, 2004 w/ bonus tracks); Babbacombe Lee (Universal, 2004 w/ bonus tracks); Please To See The King – Steeleye Span (Sanctuary, 2006 w/ bonus tracks); Ten Man Mop – Steeleye Span (Sanctuary, 2006 w/ bonus tracks); No Roses – Shirley Collins & The Albion Country Band (Transatlantic, 2008).

Quotes with the following individuals are derived from the following sources: Martin Carthy: Melody Maker 3/10/70. Shirley Collins: Melody Maker 6/11/71. Tim Hart: Music Now 7/11/70. Ashley Hutchings: Record Mirror 5/12/70; Sounds 3/4/71; Melody Maker 27/11/71; Disc 18/12/71; Sounds 6/12/75. Dave Pegg: Melody Maker 12/6/71; Melody Maker 30/6/73. Sandy Roberton: Flashback #3. Dave Swarbrick: ZigZag 3/72. Also quoted are articles from Karl Dallas Melody Maker 25/7/70, the Shields Gazette 22/3/71, Melody Maker 21/8/71, Ink 21/1/72, Disc 20/11/71 and Melody Maker 22/1/72.

Chapter 10:

Selected discography: Morris On (Fledg'ling, 2010); The Bunch Rock On (Talking Elephant, 2013 w/ bonus tracks); Henry The Human Fly – Richard Thompson (Fledg'ling, 2004); The Life and Music of Richard Thompson 5 CDs (Free Reed, 2006); I Want To See The Bright Lights Tonight – Richard & Linda Thompson (Universal, 2004 w/ bonus tracks); Bright Phoebus – The Watersons (Domino, 2017 w/ bonus tracks); Battle Of The Field – The Albion Band (BGO, 1999).

Quotes with the following individuals are derived from the following sources: Gerry Conway: Hokey Pokey #24. Ashley Hutchings: Melody Maker 20/7/74. Trevor Lucas: Melody Maker 29/4/72.

Simon Nicol: Uncut #208. Linda Thompson: Rolling Stone 9/5/85. Richard Thompson: Melody Maker 27/5/72; NME 22/6/72; NME 15/6/74; Melody Maker 15/6/74; NME 8/3/75; Melody Maker 7/10/78; Liquorice #1; Hokey Pokey #8; Uncut #208; Omaha Raimbow 12/82; Q 12/88.

Also quoted are articles from Disc 20/11/71, Andrew Means's review of Henry The Human Fly in Melody Maker 15/7/72, Ken Barnes's review of Henry in a 1972 Fusion, Melody Maker 27/5/72 and the A&M (US) press release for The Bunch Rock On.

Chapter 11:

Selected discography: Hokey Pokey – Richard & Linda Thompson (Universal, 2004 w/ bonus tracks); Live At The BBC 3 CDs + DVD – Richard & Linda Thompson (Universal, 2011).

Quotes with the following individuals are derived from the following sources: Ashley Hutchings: Melody Maker 20/7/74; letter to Folk Review 8/74. Linda Thompson: Rolling Stone 9/5/85. Richard Thompson: NME 15/6/74; Melody Maker 15/6/74; NME 8/3/75; Melody Maker 3/5/75; Melody Maker 15/11/75; Melody Maker 7/10/78; Dark Star 12/78; Q 12/88; Liquorice #1; Street Life #3; Omaha Rainbow 12/82. Richard Williams: Uncut #208. Also quoted are articles from Jerry Gilbert on Sour Grapes (Sounds 4/5/74) and Bob Woffinden (NME 15/6/74).

Chapter 12:

Selected discography: Journeys From Gospel Oak – Ian Matthews (Talking Elephant, 2018 w/ bonus tracks); Plainsong By Plainsong 2-CD (Abraxas, 2005 – includes In Search of Amelia Earhart); Plainsong On Air (Strange Fruit, 1997); Sandy – Sandy Denny (Universal, 2012 deluxe 2-CD ed.);

Like An Old Fashioned Waltz – Sandy Denny (Universal, 2012 deluxe 2-CD ed.); *Live At The BBC* 3 CDs + DVD – Sandy Denny (Universal, 2007); *Rosie* (Universal, 2004); *Nine* (Universal, 2005); *Live Convention* (Universal, 2005); *Live At The BBC* 4 CDs – Fairport Convention (Universal, 2007).

Quotes with the following individuals are derived from the following sources: Sandy Denny: *Melody Maker* 15/4/72; *Sounds* 23/9/72; *Disc* 7/10/72; *Sounds* 31/3/73; Village Voice 4/73; *Sounds* 8/9/73; *Melody Maker* 15/9/73; i/view w/ Patrick Humphries 1977 [*Hokey Pokey* 4/88].
Jerry Donahue: *Liquorice* #3; *Hokey Pokey* #2a.
Trevor Lucas: *Melody Maker* 29/4/72; *NME* 7/7/73.
Ian Matthews: *Melody Maker* 1/1/72; *Melody Maker* 17/6/72; *Sounds* 21/10/72; *ZigZag* #65; *Hokey Pokey* #5.
Dave Pegg: *Melody Maker* 30/6/73; *NME* 28/9/74.
Dave Swarbrick: *Melody Maker* 6/10/73.
Also quoted are articles from Karl Dallas *Melody Maker* 6/5/72, Stephen Holden in *Rolling Stone* 21/12/72 and Sandy Denny's 1973 Japanese Tour programme.

Chapter 13:
Selected discography: *Rising For The Moon* – Fairport Convention (Universal, 2013 deluxe 2-CD ed.); *Pour Down Like Silver* – Richard & Linda Thompson (Universal, 2004 w/ bonus tracks); *Live At The BBC* 3 CDs + DVD – Richard & Linda Thompson (Universal, 2011); *In Concert November 1975* – Richard & Linda Thompson (Universal, 2007); *(guitar, vocal)* – Richard Thompson (Hannibal, 1991).

Quotes with the following individuals are derived from the following sources: Sandy Denny: *Sounds* 8/9/73; *Melody Maker* 3/74; *NME* 20/4/74; *Go-Set* 29/6/74; *Sounds* 21/6/75; i/view w/ Patrick Humphries 1977 [*Hokey Pokey* 4/88].
Jerry Donahue: *Liquorice* #3; *Hokey Pokey* #2a.
Trevor Lucas: *Disc* 12/7/75.
Dave Mattacks: *Melody Maker* 12/10/75.
Dave Pegg: *NME* 28/9/74.
Dave Swarbrick: *Beetle* 2/75.
Richard Thompson: *NME* 8/3/75; *Melody Maker* 3/5/75; *Street Life* #3; *Liquorice* #1; *Melody Maker* 15/11/75; *Dark Star* 12/78.
Also quoted is Colin Irwin's June 1975 review of *Rising For The Moon* in *Melody Maker*.

Chapter 14:
Selected discography: *Son Of Morris On* – Ashley Hutchings (Talking Elephant, 2008; *The Prospect Before Us* – The Albion Band (BGO, 2009 w/ bonus tracks); *Gottle O'Geer* (Universal, 2008 w/ bonus track); *Rendezvous* – Sandy Denny (Universal, 2012 deluxe 2-CD ed.); *(guitar, vocal)* – Richard Thompson (Hannibal, 1993; *Doom & Gloom From The Tomb* – Richard Thompson (fan club cassette, nd).

Quotes with the following individuals are derived from the following sources:
Joe Boyd: *Hokey Pokey* #14.
Sandy Denny: i/view w/ Patrick Humphries 1977 [*Hokey Pokey* 4/88]; i/view w/ Karl Dallas in *Folk News* 1977.
Ashley Hutchings: *Street Life* #17; *Sutton Advertiser* 12/76.
Linda Thompson: *Rolling Stone* 9/5/85.
Richard Thompson: *Street Life* #3; *NME* 23/4/77; *Dark Star* 5/77; *Melody Maker* 7/10/78; *Rolling Stone* 5/4/79; *NME* 2/6/79.
Also quoted are articles from *NME* 3/7/76 and *Melody Maker* 7/1/78, as well as Richard Thompson's tribute to Sandy Denny in the US fanzine, *Flypaper*.

Chapter 15:

Selected discography: *The Bonny Bunch of Roses* (Commercial Marketing, 2007); *Gold Dust: Live at the Royalty* – Sandy Denny (Universal, 1998); *Julie Covington … Plus* – Julie Covington (Collector's Edition, 2009 w/ bonus tracks); *Rise Up Like The Sun* – The Albion Band (EMI, 1992 w/ bonus tracks).

Quotes with the following individuals are derived from the following sources:
Joe Boyd: *Hokey Pokey* #14.
Ashley Hutchings: *Yorkshire Post* 3/78.
Linda Thompson: *Rolling Stone* 9/5/85.
Richard Thompson: *Melody Maker* 7/10/78; *Dark Star* 12/78; *NME* 2/6/79.
Also quoted are articles from Angus McKinnon in *NME* 3/78 and Nick Ralphs *Dark Star* 5/78.

Chapter 16:

Selected discography: *Tippler's Tale* (Commercial Marketing, 2007); *Farewell, Farewell* (Total, 1994); *Julie Covington … Plus* – Julie Covington (Collector's Edition, 2009 w/ bonus tracks); *First Light* – Richard & Linda Thompson (Hannibal, 1992); *Sunnyvista* – Richard & Linda Thompson (Hannibal, 1992 w/ bonus track).

Quotes with the following individuals are derived from the following sources:
Dave Swarbrick: *Melody Maker* 6/81; *Hokey Pokey* #18.
Richard Thompson: *Rolling Stone* 5/4/79; *Melody Maker* 7/10/78; *NME* 2/6/79.
Also quoted are articles from Karl Dallas in *Melody Maker* 8/79 and a news item in *Melody Maker* 2/5/81.

Chapter 17:

Selected discography: *Before Joe Could Pull The Trigger* (nd, bootleg CD of the original 'Rafferty' version of *Shoot Out The Lights*) – Richard & Linda Thompson; *Live At The BBC* 3 CDs + DVD – Richard & Linda Thompson (Universal, 2011); *Monster* – David Thomas (Cooking Vinyl, 2002 – includes *The Sound of the Sand*); *The Transatlantic Recordings 1976-83* – Dave Swarbrick (Cherry Tree, 2016 – includes *Smiddyburn* and *Flittin'*).

Quotes with the following individuals are derived from the following sources:
Joe Boyd: *Hokey Pokey* #14.
Linda Thompson: *Melody Maker* 8/11/80.
Richard Thompson: *Swing 51* #8; *Tapers Quarterly* #3.

Chapter 18:

Selected discography: *Shoot Out The Lights* – Richard & Linda Thompson (Rhino Handmade, 2010 deluxe 2-CD ed.); *Live At The BBC* 3 CDs + DVD – Richard & Linda Thompson (Universal, 2011); *Small Town Romance* – Richard Thompson (Hannibal, 2002).

Quotes with the following individuals are derived from the following sources:
Joe Boyd: *Hokey Pokey* #14.
Linda Thompson: *Rolling Stone* 16/11/89.
Richard Thompson: *Creem* 9/82; *Swing 51* #8; *Rolling Stone* 16/11/82; *Omaha Rainbow* 12/82; *Rolling Stone* 9/5/85; *Tapers Quarterly* #3.

For more on this book, please visit
www.fairportbook.wordpress.com
www.route-online.com